The Man Of Many Faces

ICEBURG BOOKS

Harare . Banjul . Accra . Lagos . Bamako
Monrovia . Freetown . Johannesburg

First Official Edition – First Printing 2009

Copyright © 2005 Iceburg Books
www.iceburgbooks.com

**Published in association with
TamaRe House**
www.tamarehouse.com

ALL RIGHTS RESERVED

No part of this publication may be reproduced, or utilized stored in retrieval system, or transmitted, in any form or by any means electronic, mechanical, photocopying, recording or otherwise, without the prior permission in writing from the author or publisher.

The Publishers are the only parties capable of providing permissions and constitutes the only exception to this prohibition.

The paper used in this publication meets the minimum requirements of the International Standard for information.

This publication was originally manufactured in Lagos, Nigeria

Cover Design and Book layout:
Femi Olatula for 'Iceburg' Graphics & Designs.

ISBN 978-1-906169-53-4

The Man Of Many Faces

Uncovering The Truth, about
Dr. Malachi. Z. York
&
The United Nuwaubian
Nation of Moors

Part. 2

By

Yovan Christenson
Olu Femi Olatula &
Adafa Nimarud (Amun) Nicol El

My Bretheren, The Enemy Is Before You; The Sea Is Behind You; Whither Would You Fly (Run)?
So Follow Your (Amir) Commander; For I Am Resolved Either To Lose My Life, Or Be Victorious In Trampling On [The Heads Of The Hypocrites] and Enemies of God…..…

Dedicated To:

The Victims of the continuing Genocide in Darfur, Sudan.
And all of the Missing & Displaced Children of New Orleans,
Louisiana's Hurricane Katrina Disaster.

I call to accept this Truth as bestowed upon me by The Masters who guide my Pen, for of myself I could not have done the works of it. (Pen).

As Sayyid Isa Al Haadi Al Mahdi (Yanaan) 19

"I Descend to This Plane, Formless in Form, A Temple of The Incarnated Divinity to Guide You…"

Malachi Zodok

I know I'm loved by many here, but I want you to know that I'm also hated because they don't understand what the Truth is. They would rather live in 'Illusions' they live in a world of Theology. They don't want 'Factology' which is facts beyond any doubt…Facts insult certain people because it dethrones self-appointed leaders, and if you offend someone's leader they immediately resort to violence or threats. They don't even trust their leader's intelligence to assume that he or she would be able to defend themselves verbally against you. They simply want to hurt you. I know many of you people that were on the Internet with me. On many Shadow hours, heard them say, "you should be dead. I wish we could kill you". The threat may not frighten me as much as it did hurt me. It hurts me because I give my whole life and more to waking people up. All I want is for you not to be tricked!

Dr. Malachi. Z. York, 2004

Table of Contents

Forward by Nebu Ka Ma'at

Introduction..I

Prologue V

Part IV: Nuwaubu; York's Final Gamble

Chapter 12   *Spiritual Masters & Extraterrestrials* 1

Chapter 13   *The Cold Reality of 'Right Knowledge'* 25

Chapter 14   *Sacred Orders & Mysteries Revealed* 395

Chapter 15   *New York to Georgia: The Great Nubian Exodus* 434

Chapter 16   *Southern Dream turns to Nightmare:*
The fall of Malachi York..478

Epilogue...501

Conclusion..505

Appendix

Bibliography / Webliography

Nuwaubian Related Sites

Special Appeals

Disclaimer:

Iceburg Publishing Group does not assume any legal liability or take responsibility for either the contents or accuracy of this publication. Furthermore statements, views & opinions contained within this publication, do not in any way reflect our beliefs and are in no way intended to deliberately denigrate or malign any Racial, Religious, Political Groups or Organizations.

Warning!!! This Book also contains imagery many may find either Disturbing or of a Pornographic nature, please be advised that; neither the Authors or Publishers take responsibility for any offence caused, to anyone who has read and understood this Disclaimer.

Author's Note

This book is written in a non-traditional contemporary style. We have purposely included as much photographs, illustrations & background information as possible, to actively encourage the reader to conduct his or her own research.

Throughout the body of the text you will find many grammatical rules deliberately broken such as capitalisation in unusual places; this is purposely done in order to emphasise particular points for the reader. We have not changed American spellings where they appear in quotations, or from printed publications, or where transcribed in the original research source material. Neither have we taken the liberty of correcting people's speech, wherever quoted in interviews.

We have also included within the text other languages, in order to give the reader a clearer understanding of some sections of the book where this is relevant, along with the closest English translation wherever these occur.

Finally the book has many Journalistic qualities where we have complied a chronological report on Dr. York, his organisation, contemporaries and predecessors. In quoting from a variety of sources, we have attempted to convey a sense of the characters involved in the telling of this story, using as many of their own words as possible.

Yovan Christenson is an Investigative Journalist of Kwa-Zulu (Southern African) descent, who currently Lectures at Zimbabwe University. He has conducted over 15 years of in-depth research into the Black Nationalist roots of Hip Hop Culture. And is an affiliate of the Zulu Nation, as well as one of the World's leading authorities of the history and teachings of the Ansaaru Allah & (Nuwaubian) Movement.
He currently lives with his Wife and two Daughters in Harare, Zimbabwe.
A large portion of the royalties from this book will be donated to charities, which protect the World's remaining indigenous Tribes from Extinction.

Foreword

Reality Check! – *Phase 1,2 & 3*

> *"I came giving you what you wanted so that you may learn to want what I have come to give."*
>
> **The voice of Nature...**

These are the infamous reiterated words of Dr Malachi Z York, founder of the Ancient Egiptian Order and establisher of the Afrokhan-Spiritual Science, **Nuwaubu** – A way of life that has proven to be incumbently necessary for the spiritual development and re-education of Afrokhan peoples of the West. Nuwaubu – The Afro-Conscientric Curriculum for Life, 21st Century style, entails the application of very simple practical steps toward 'Self-Empowerment' and 'Spiritual Enlightenment.'

So as I introduce to some and present to others, Malachi, *My Angel,* who has created a system of tools based upon the ancient Ha Kha teachings of the Supreme Grand Hierophant Tehuti. I take the initiative, with guidance from the Ancestors and the Universal Conscientious forces of 9 Ether Consciousness, to introduce and present "Man of Many Faces" as a practical truth-bulletin for the application of the doctrines of Nuwaubu. This Book provides the tools in the form of physical, spiritual and mental Technologies, necessary to empower the Nubian to achieve a quality of life that most of us only dream of.

He came giving us what we wanted, like a mother who communicates to her toddler in baby *talk* – a language and context of which the child can clearly understand. 1967AD was the year of his coming, a period of great confusion; mid-sixties of Black-America was in total chaos, although most therein were oblivious to this fact.....At last, Nature had heard the 'Urban Cries' for salvation once again. For indeed she had heard her children, the original Black peoples of her planet, in the recent past, cry over and over for a saviour. The forces of nature, in response, rose from within our midst the likes of Marcus Garvey, Elijah Muhammad, Noble Drew Ali, Malcolm X and many others. They too, came giving us what we wanted, but we did not learn to want what Nature had sent them to give. Like the said toddler screaming for food, merely responding to a gut feeling of hunger, and sadly does not understand that a lovingly prepared meal is far more nourishing than a packet of cookies snatched from the kitchen cupboard. But mummy proceeds to prepare the meal anyway in hopes that baby will appreciate it. But no, no, baby has been too far-gone in its subconscious programming of eating for taste as opposed to eating for sustenance, and continues to complain and whine. Mummy gives baby just one cookie, "Just this once," she thinks, and with a loving smile and much care, tells baby of the implications of sweets and cookies, and of the benefits of a lovingly prepared meal. Does baby get the message? Probably not, – or at least not at that time. But the lessons will be rooted deep within and will be summoned at a later age for further understanding and appreciation, and hopefully application.

The Black Nation is that analogous baby. We wanted religion, but we did not know what religion we wanted, nor at least what was best for us. Most of us did not even understand what the word *religion* meant. All we knew of religion were Christianity and Islam. We had been cut off from that 'old time religion.' But deep down in our very souls we were crying *"Freedom, Justice, Equality,"* again with our limited definitions of what these principles really meant. We had a wrenching gut feeling, a severe hunger, we were yearning to be 'tied back' to that place where it all began so our souls could be fed directly from its source. Some called that place "Afrokha," some said "the Motherland," not realising that the entire Earth is the Motherland of the entire Black Nation. Nature gave us solutions that were practical and applicable for the time periods of our calling. She gave us lessons that were conducive to our 'three-dimensional' environment and political stance, during the 1920s, in the disguise of the doctrine of Marcus Garvey. Many heard the call for rapture; perhaps the brave hearted amongst the wretched. But that was only the beginning. As powerful as Garvey was, and as astonishing as his empire was, it was only preparation for the ultimate lessons of Cultural-

Empowerment that was to come. However, at the time, White America was flabbergasted by the rise of this Nation, with huge strapping Black men dressed in pinstriped suits and bow ties, riding on horse backs throughout the streets of Harlem New York, with propagation of *"The Journey Home to Africa."* This, I recognise as Reality Check–*Phase 1*. Garvey left us a signature, a declaration that it can be done; a confirmation that we can aspire and achieve great things if we can only unite under some basic principles.

Then, we had the coming of the *'Messenger,'* as those who believed called him. It was the Honourable Elijah Muhammad, founder and leader of the 'Black Muslims' in America. He presented Reality Check–*Phase 2*, the concept of taking responsibility as gods of the earth and the universe – 'Do for 'Self',' was the motto. This created much tension within the hierarchy systems of America and her allies. They could not allow a time bomb to exist within the house; it had to either be stopped or be controlled by them. The Messenger consequently spoke of the *'Lamb,'* the one who would lead this Black Nation toward the final path. Today, we know of this one as Dr Malachi Z York.

With his coming, Reality Check–*Phase 3* was in propagation, and the ultimate experiences and lessons were nigh. The true religion of the Black Man and Woman was presented under the title of **Nuwaubu**, a fourth-dimensional applied-science of 'Sound Right Reasoning.' The time had come for us to be 'tied back,' to that place where it all began.

So beloved, I take it as my duty and as an honour, with Unconditional Love for my Afrokhan brothas and sistas, and indeed our *children (Mankind)*, of presenting a foreword of this great work by **Adafa Nim-Marud Nicol-El: (Siy'ful Nuwaubia)**, *"Man of Many Faces"*.

Dr Malachi Z York is known by many other names such as; Al Khdir, Amar Utu, Baba, Pops, Amun Nubi Ruakh Ptah, Neter A'ferti Atum Re, Paa Nazdir, Raboni Yashua, Imam Isa, and many others, hence 'Man of Many Faces.' My personal experience and relationship with Dr York is that of a student to his guru. He is my Spiritual Master as well as being a guide in general everyday living. From finance, to economics, to politics, cultural knowledge, religion, histories, and spirituality, Dr York has proven time and time again to be the master teacher of this day and time. His works are superseded by none. He has challenged the oligarchs of the world's societies on every conceivable level. He has challenged the educational and religious institutions and is yet to be refuted or rebutted by any. His tenacity and drive for change and transformation exceeds any other organisational or cultural leader I have ever met or heard of. His mission, for all intents and purposes is to break the spell of ignorance amongst all peoples. Without prejudice, ill will, vexation or frivolity, and with all inalienable sovereign rights reserved, York is indeed the man of the 'hour.'

So I urge you, dear reader, to take the time to read through this book. Learn about the forerunner of the *being* that we have all prayed for. York is the forerunner of the real messiah that is yet to come. It is better to be properly prepared for a messiah than to have that messiah arrive and be improperly prepared.

The time is NOW.

Nebu.

Introduction

Ever wondered why People of African descent do not have any 'Globally' recognised or 'Organised' religious/cultural institutions of their own? For example; belief systems such as the Yoruba religion of Nigeria are often frowned upon, and regarded as little more than Barbarous 'Mumbo Jumbo' by not only Westerners, but also many so-called educated 'Enlightened' Africans. Who often dismiss African beliefs as merely 'Devilishment', which is interesting because this means prior to the arrival of European & Arab Missionaries, all African's inherently practiced Devil or Satanic worship which is a damning indictment of African Spirituality. It is exactly this type of mentality, which has been encouraged by Europeans since Colonialism, and above all else, is most deplorable about African's themselves, namely; the eagerness to denounce and abandon their own 'Indigenous' Gods & Religious practices in exchange for 'Watered Down', and often corrupted; **European, Asian & Arab** interpretations of Religion, which in turn have contributed to Blacks now hating and despising their very selves.

If the East-Indians have Hinduism, The Chinese Taoist & 'Confuscist' Philosophies, The Tibetans Buddhism, The Europeans Christianity & Judaism, The Arabs Islam and even the so-called North American 'Indians' have Shamanism, then what 'Indigenous' Religion do Blacks have? And why is it that Negroes are only Approved of, when they submit to the beliefs of other races?

Although there maybe extensive evidence to suggests that the original Arabs & Hebrews or 'Semetic' people were all of Negroid by 'Ethnicity', effectively rendering the 3 so-called 'Monotheistic' Religions namely Judaism, Christianity & Islam all Africa in origin. Nevertheless this means very little to Blacks currently under the Judo-Christo-Islamic Spell of religious indoctrination. Due to the devastating effects of Colonialism, most African's both at home, and abroad, today suffer from what could be called a "Biblical Complex". Which is because Caucasians have succeeded in making most of the world's darker peoples, with Negroes in particular, feel inadequate for not being part of the so-called Judo-Christian Biblical ancestry. When in actuality, African's descend from Cultures which pre-date Judaism, Christianity & Islam by several Millennia. And whilst Judaism, Christianity & Islam may have all had their roots in Africa, whether we want to accept it or not, they are all safely in the hands of people who now regard Blacks as little more than their inferiors.

Since the Euro-Arab onslaught upon the African Continent, the Closest Blacks have come to a belief system of their own was Rastafarianism, which emerged following the death of The Hon. Marcus Garvey. Unfortunately Rastafarianism soon become synonymous with wearing 'Dread Locks' or

Dreadful Hair, Pop-Music, Smoking Cannabis & Criminality, eventually degenerating the Religious movement into little more than a 'Funky' fashion trend amongst Western Blacks during the 80's, consigning the true Rastafarians to relative obscurity. This is in stark contrast to the Sikh faith, the radical concoction of Hinduism & Islam, created on the Indian Sub-continent in the 16th century under the 'Moghul' Dynasty, which is now recognised as one of the so-called 'Great World Religions', of which, not surprisingly, none are represented of Black or African origin.

It is for these reasons above all else that we have decided to conduct an objective examination into the life and teachings of Dr. Malachi. Z. York, Founder and Spiritual Leader of The United Nuwaubian Nation of Moors. Although many Black leaders and organisations have attempted to address the issue of an authentic African centred belief system, none have done so with anywhere near the same success as Malachi York. Known throughout his 35-year Ministry by a plethora of different Names & Titles, which have included:

As Sayyid Al Imaam Isa Al Haadi Al Mahdi
Rabboni Y'Shua Bar El Haady
Amunnubi Rooakhptah
Afro Oono
Rabboni D.D.
Isa Muhammad
Abba Essa
Isa Abdullah Muhammad
Amar Utu
Yaanuwn
Al-Qubt
Sabathil
Maku
Murdoq
Baba 'Bawassa' Afrika
Dr. York
Isa Abdullah Al Mahdi
En-Mar. Duq
Yanuwn
Malachi Zodok
The Green One
The Master Teacher
Isa Al-Masih
Malachi Zodok
Chief Black Thunderbird Eagle
The Angel Michael
Grand Al Mufti "Divan" Noble Rev.
Dr. Malachi Z. York-El
Melchizedek
The Reformer
Asayeed El Imaam Issa El Haaiy El Mahdi

Imam Isa Abu-Bakr
Al Hajj Al Imaam Isa
Abba Issa
Al Hajj Al Imaam
Isa Abd'Allah Muhammad Al Mahdi
Dr. Malachi. Z. York
Tuhuti
Amun Nubi Ra ankh Ptah
Consul General: Dr. Malachi Z. York ©™
Neter: A'aferti Atum-Re
Imaam Isa
Dr. Malachi Z. York-El
Isa Abd'Allah Ibn Abu Bakr Muhammad
Nayya Malachizodoq-El
Isa al Haadi al-Mahdi
Grand Hierophant Potentate Noble: Rev. Dr. Malachi Z. York 33°/720°
Al Khidr

However for the sake of clarity, we have decided to refer to him simply as **'York'** throughout the body of this text to avoid confusing the reader.

I first became aware of Malachi York's teachings during the late 1980s, when he was known at the time as 'Imam Isa', through an article I had written in my native South Africa about the Hip Hop Fraternal movement the Zulu Nation founded by former Gang Boss Afrika Bambaataa. After having interviewed members of the group on several occasions, I later discovered that they were part of a wider movement known as the **'Nubian Nation'**, who were Religiously affiliated to the now defunct; Ansaaru Allah Community/Nubian Islamic Hebrews, formerly based in Brooklyn New York, and led at the time by the outspoken and somewhat 'Maverick' African-American Muslim Cleric, I would later come to know as Dr. York, who professed to be descended from 19th Century Sudanese Mystic: **'The Mahdi' Muhammad Ahmed**.

During the early 1990s, I actually had the honour of meeting York in person, whilst visiting the group's headquarters to conduct research for a follow-up article, but subsequently lost touch with their activities until York's dramatic arrest in 2002. Although now referring to himself as 'Dr. Malachi. Z. York', and his group as 'The Nuwaubians', I immediately recognized him as the same Imam Isa / Dr. York, whom I had previously met over 10 years earlier in New York. I promptly gathered a group of trusted fellow researchers, and promptly set about conducting what would become 4 more years of solid research into not only the group, but also York's actual Child Molestation case, which would ultimately form the basis of this book.

Inspired by the teachings of the Honourable Elijah Muhammad, the Nuwaubian leader was able to skilfully develop an African-centred belief system, over a 35-years period incorporating elements of Judaism, Christianity & Islam, which as previously stated, originally became corrupted by European, Asians & Arab interpretations since being 'Usurped' or Stolen from their Birthplace on the African Continent. Although often accused by detractors of constantly changing his philosophy, York's teachings were able to undergo what can only be described as a astonishing metamorphic 'Evolution', made possible by a unique method of entirely submerging his pupils inside numerous religious doctrines & practices, and effectively taking them through a myriad of Cultural & Religious philosophies lasting the greater part of 30-years, before finally revealing to them the true source or Origins of the 3 major world Religions. Demonstrating with great skill, that the teachings of Islam & Christianity both originated from Judaism or Hebrewism, which in turn grew out of the Cultural/Religious practices of the Ancient Egyptians of North-East Africa & Ancient Mesopotamia, located in what is presently Iraq. After an initial process, which lasted the greater part of 30 years, York was able to develop a type of 'Proto-Afro-centric Religious Philosophy', which as he put, was: **"Their own Stuff"**, aptly named; 'Nuwaubu': *"The Science of Right Knowledge"*, supposedly the original basis of the 3 Monotheistic Religions.

Unrivalled in his field of Linguistics for over 3 decades, Malachi York is well known to be literate as well as fluent, in several languages which include: Hieroglyphics, Cuneiform, Classical & Contemporary Arabic, Ancient & Modern Hebrew, Latin, Greek, Spanish, Swahili & Yuroba, and should therefore be regarded as one of the World's leading authorities of Theology the Ancient Languages. Blessed with the ability to make Religious dogma exciting and inspirational to young people, York's teachings have changed the lives of literally millions around the world. After initially founding 'Nuwaubu' during the late 1960s, York developed the Afro-centric 'Nuwaubianism' philosophy over a 35-year period, by essentially reintroducing many aspects of the Cultural & Religious practices from the world's oldest known Culture & Civilization; 'Ancient Kush or Cush', formerly located across what are presently Egypt, Ethiopia, Sudan & Uganda. Heavily influenced by the remarkable work of such African Pioneers as: Dr. Duse Muhammad Ali, The Honourable Marcus 'Mosiah' Garvey, Noble Drew Ali, Shaikh Daoud Ahmed Fiesal, The Honourable Elijah Muhammad, Dr. Kwame Nkrumah, Malcolm X, Shaikh Anta Diop, Patrice Lamumbah, Dr. Walter Rodney, Dr. Anwar Sadat, along with his own Father Al Haadi Abdur Rahman Al Mahdi, Dr. York, set himself the arduous task of uplifting the Moral, Social, Economical & Spiritual standard of his people, by forming his first organisation the Ansar Pure Sufi in 1970. Although many may argue that he fell well short of this aim, only history will be the true judge of what impact Malachi York's thirty-plus year ministry has had upon the mental condition of Blacks throughout the Western Hemisphere.

Many of his supporters will assert that Dr. York, along with Minister Farrakhan, has been the single most influential leader since the Honourable Elijah Muhammad, responsible for raising the awareness of countless Millions through Books, Speeches & Lectures since he appeared during the 1970s. Through their teachings, both Malachi York (the Writer) & Louis Farrakhan (the Speaker) as they are affectionately known by there followers, have single handily provided the inspiration for what many now regard as the "Golden age of Hip Hop", when consciousness amongst Rappers was at a level never again seen in Black Youth Culture. Artists like Eric B & Rakim, Stetsasonic & most notably Public Enemy, were able to set a standard of excellence for the entire Rap-world Community. As a result of coming into direct contact with both The Nation of Islam & The Ansaarullah Community (Nubian Nation), under the leadership and Spiritual Guidance of these two remarkable individuals who seemed to come as a pair, like Minister Malcolm X & Dr. Martin Luther King before them. Nevertheless, it is with the legacy of the individual now known as Dr. Malachi. Z. York, who first came to prominence during the early 1980s, under the name As Sayyid Al Imaam Isa Al Haadi Al Mahdi, and the tremendous effect his teachings have had upon the psyche of Blacks in the Western Hemisphere during the last 30 years, that this book is principally concerned.

Born the illegitimate product of an illicit, and by all accounts 'lustful' liaison between an African-American student; Mary. C. York and Sudanese Aristocrat Al Haadi Abdur Rahman Al Mahdi, **'Isa'**, who would eventually re-name himself Malachi York, has been surrounded by controversy ever since his birth in 1945. Claiming that his arrival at the close of the Second World War, was directly linked to the first modern sightings of Unidentified Flying Objects (UFOs), and the twin Atomic bomb attacks against Hiroshima & Nagasaki, Japan, York professed to be the expected *"Son of Man"*, and awaited herald or forerunner of the 'Second Coming' of Jesus Christ mentioned in the book of Matthew, *Chapter 24, Verse 27*. He has taught extensively on the Extra-Terrestrial relationship to God and the Scriptures throughout a career spanning more than three decades. York's teachings regarding UFOs have often been the focus of ridicule, leading to him being labelled ***"The Man from Planet Rizq"*** by the Media, which ironically was taken from the title of one of his own Nuwaubian publications released in 1993.

Arguably one of the most profound, some would even say influential, Theologians of the 20th Century, Malachi York's teachings have, continuously withstood the most rigorous scrutiny from the Academic World for over 35-years. Whilst he himself is regarded with almost Iconic status by his followers, the Nuwaubian leader has translated both the Old & New Testaments of The Bible & Holy Koran, authored almost 1,000 Book & Pamphlet titles, produced hundreds of Audio & Video recorded Lectures, at the same time challenging the Orthodox: Islamic, Christian & Judaic religious world leadership to prove him wrong for over 3 decades. During which he was also able to single-handedly develop an entirely new language for Blacks in the Western Hemisphere, built 4 separate Religious/Political organizations, obtained a PhD, built his own Private Militia/Army, Supervised the construction of numerous building projects, all whilst generating Millions of dollars in revenue through various entrepreneurial enterprises, which included a reasonably successful career as a Song Writer, Recording Artist & Producer.

A Philosopher, Diplomat, Philanthropist, Scholar, Visionary, Author, Accomplished Musician, Black Nationalist of the 'Garveyite' tradition and natural successor to both Shaikh Daoud Ahmed Fiesal & Malcolm X, Dr. York founded and led the Ansaaru Allah Community, which at its height, became the largest Independent Black Islamic Movement in the World. Though his group has suffered a steep decline since York's arrest in 2002, as 'Imaam Isa' in the 1990s, York's following was estimated at over 1 Million members world-wide, during which he courageously made a stand against, and exposed the twin Evils of White Supremacy & International 'Orthodox Islamic' Arab sponsored Terrorism, 20-years prior to 9/11, and the subsequent launch of America's *'War on Terror'*.

Often criticised by detractors as a flamboyant Megalomaniac & Charlaten, who ruthlessly exploited the devotion of his followers, York was able to carefully craft for himself a Devine-like image, which attracted Thousands of dispossessed Western Blacks towards his cultural philosophy of 'Nuwaubu', which was until his arrest, estimated to be the single **'Fastest Growing' African lead Religious/Cultural movement on Earth,** and as such should correctly be regarded as one of the Great World Religious/Philosophies.

Contrary to the malicious claims of many of his detractors, York always kept his movement within the confines of the Law; mobilizing Tens of Thousands of his followers to arrest control of their destiny, through a sophisticated Intellectual Revolution, which differentiated him from many of his predecessors and current contemporaries. Naturally these successes made him many enemies who were determined to not only bring him down, but more importantly destroy his legacy. Causing him to finally come under the scrutiny of U.S. authorities, and the subsequent 25-year FBI investigation into his activities, which culminated in him being sentenced to a 135-year custodial sentence, and seizure of his organisations' entire assets, on what have now been proven to have been 'Fabricated' & 'Fictitious' Child-Sex & Racketeering charges. In the years leading up to York's arrest, Federal Investigators discovered York's two fatal flaws, which were his arrogant dismissal and belligerence towards other Black Leaders and Movements, as well as his almost Pathological weakness for members of the opposite Sex, both of which, left York completely vulnerable to attack, resulting in his eventual downfall.

During the writing of this work various excerpts of our writing have been published at various intervals on anonymous Internet websites, many of which have been quoted, copied and plagiarised by various individuals, some of whom, are affiliated with the Nuwaubian movement. Whilst we do openly welcome and are flattered at sections of our work being utilised, we would also like to point out that this work belongs to us, and are therefore protected by all applicable copyright laws.

Throughout the past 7 years, we have carried out the most exhaustive and comprehensive examination of the Nuwaubian movement, interviewing dozens of former and current members. Scrolled through thousands of pages of online articles, viewed and listened to literally hundreds of hours of archive material, and read stacks of Nuwaubian literature and other related material, in order to compile what we're sure you'll agree is the most extensive, yet balanced study of Dr. Malachi. Z. York & The Ansaaru Allah Community / Nuwaubian Nation of Moors ever conducted to date. We therefore invite not only sincere "Seekers of Truth", but also those with other motives to explore and at the same time be enlightened by the many complexities surrounding the Nuwaubian's and their mystifying leader. So sit back and buckle-up your mental seatbelts, as we take you on what can only be described as a mental 'Roller-coaster' ride as we journey into the strange yet fascinating tale of the Rise and Fall of one of the most remarkably colourful & flamboyant, yet sinisterly powerful and enigmatic individuals in Modern African History; Isa Al Haadi Al Mahdi otherwise more commonly known as Dr. Malachi .Z. York: *"The Man of Many Faces"*.

Olu Femi Olatula 2007.

Prologue

Our People get caught up in 'Super Niggerism'. Yes, our Leaders gotta be as White as Snow, they gotta be perfect. They gotta have no flaws. They gotta be beyond Human. And the Whities know it. **That's why Hoover put a Scandal on this one or a Scandal on that one.** Because they know the people who need 'Super Niggerism' won't continue to support them, and do what? Back off!! Because [We] cannot differentiate between the Human qualities of the Leader, and between the realities of what that Leader represents…**It doesn't even have to be true. All they have to do is Print it in the Daily News, and its over!!**

Amos Wilson, Destruction of African Civilization

On May 8 2002, Dr. Malachi. Z. York, leader & founder of The United Nuwaubian Nation of Moors, was arrested by Federal Agents on charges supposedly relating to Child Sexual Molestation against minors within his organization. York's arrest, and the subsequent 'Waco' style-Invasion of the Nuwaubian's 476-acre property by a joint 'Task Force' of almost 700 Heavily armed Government Law Enforcement officers, was the culmination of a 20-year FBI investigation into York's activities, which was immediately broadcast to TV Networks throughout the U.S.

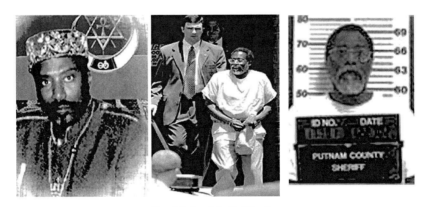

Dr. Malachi. Z. York
Founder & Leader of The Ansaaru Allah Community & Nuwaubin Nation of Moors

The raid and arrests were also the result of a 10-year racial vendetta against The Nuwaubian's by local officials, spearheaded by Sheriff Howard R. Sills, assisted by a vicious campaign of biased newspaper reports, orchestrated by Bill Osinski of *The Atlanta Journal* & Rob Peecher of *The Macon Telegraph*, whom had routinely broken not only the law, but all existing Journalistic codes of conduct, by publishing a series of damaging and misleading newspaper and online articles aimed at injuring the character of Malachi. Z. York prior to his arrest. Dr. York's remarkable success in raising the awareness of Blacks around the world resulted in his movement being investigated for unsubstantiated links to organised crime. Which began with his first appearance during the 1970s as **As Sayyid Isa Al Haadi Al Mahdi**, leader of what was then, the second largest Black movement within the US.

Eyewitnesses claim that during the raid, weapons were pointed at the heads of Women & Children, under the pretext of searching for evidence, none of which has ever been discovered. Up to 40 Children as young as 4-years old, were 'Illegally' taken from their parents by Law Enforcement officials, and forced to undergo degrading examinations for signs of sexual abuse by authorities. However to the disappointment of the Investigators, absolutely no DNA or any other evidence was found of abuse against these children. Despite this, Malachi York was still charged with multiple counts of Child Molestation, and eventually sentenced to 135-years imprisonment in 2004. Since his arrest, York's legal team have worked tirelessly to present crucial evidence that should have immediately exonerated the 62-year old Nuwaubian leader, including a Video-recorded 'Sworn Affidavit', by 'KEY' Prosecution Witness; Abigail Washington, asserting the Nuwaubian leader's complete innocence which was promptly disregarded by Prosecutors, the mainstream Media, and later the 11th Circuit court of Appeals in 2005.

Could Dr. York's arrest and consequent 'Character Assassination' be the direct result of The Nuwaubian leader's growing influence in the United States, and beyond? And could it also be connected to York's 1993 declaration of the Nuwaubian Nation's complete independence from the United States, as 'The Yamasse Native American Moors of the Creek Nation', an indigenous Sovereign Nation recognized by The United Nations: **UN No. 215/1993**? As well as his other plans to spearhead the mass Repatriation of African American's, back to the West African Nation of Liberia? And if so, is Dr. Malachi. Z. York the latest in a long line of individuals, targeted for 'Neutralisation' by the on going War against Black Movements in America. Originally Code-named: Project 'R', & 'King Alfred's Plan', later renamed The 'Counter Intelligence Programme' or (COINTELPRO), initially formed by J. Edgar Hoover, to prevent the rise of a so-called **'Black Messiah'** responsible for the Assassination, Discrediting and False Imprisonment of many Black Leaders since the 1920's:

The Honourable Marcus Garvey (1887 – 1940)
Founder & Leader of The Universal Negro Improvement Association
(Falsely Imprisoned & Discredited)

Noble Drew Ali (1886 – 1929)
Founder & Leader of The Moorish Science Temple
(Falsely Imprisoned & Assassinated)

Faud Abdul Wali Muhammad (W. D. Farad) (1891 – 1928)
Member of Pan Arabism & The Ahmadiyya Movements
(Falsely Imprisoned & Assassinated)

The Honourable Elijah Muhammad (1897 – 1975)
Leader of The Nation of Islam (Falsely Imprisoned & Discredited)

Minister Malcolm X (1925 – 1965)
National Spokesman of The Nation of Islam (Assassinated)

  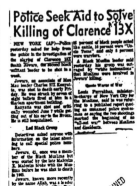

Clarence 13X (1929 – 1969)
Founder & Leader of The Five Percent Nation of Gods & Earths (Assassinated)

Medgar Willey Evers (1925 – 1963)
African American Civil Rights Activist (Assassinated)

Dr. Martin Luther King Jr. (1929 – 1968)
Leader of The Southern Christian Leadership (Assassinated)

Fred Hampton (1948 – 1969)
Minister of Information for The Black Panther Party (Assassinated)

Alprentice "Bunchy" Carter (1942 – 1969)
Leader of The Southern California Chapter of the Black Panther Party (Assassinated)

Fred Hampton. Jr
Human Rights Activist (Falsely Imprisoned)

Elmer 'Geronimo Ji Jagga' Pratt
Minister of Defence for The Black Panther Party (Falsely Imprisoned)

Yahweh Ben Yahweh
Founder & Leader of The Nation of Yahweh
(Falsely Imprisoned & Discredited)

Dr. Khalid Abdul Muhammad (1948 – 2001)
National Spokesman of The Nation of Islam
& New Black Panther Party (Assassinated)

Dr. Mumia Abu Jamal
Spokesperson of Black Panther Party & M.O.V.E Organisation (Falsely Imprisoned)

Part IV

Nuwaubu: York's Last Stand

Chapter 12

Spiritual Masters & Extraterrestrial Entities

Fig.1 *Symbol of Son's of The Green Light, Sufi Order*

"I, the Avatar of the West, have been chosen to be a temple of the incarnated divinity, it is my soul; thus I came fourth...I am the only teacher you have that can explain the whole truth from the beginning to the end, for my spirit was there. These mortals can't teach you anything you can't look up or find for yourself. But I am 76 trillion years old. I have seen many kingdoms fall and rise, nations fall and rise and galaxies fall and rise..."

As Sayyid Isa Al Haadi Al Mahdi, 1977

Essentially, the basis of Dr. Malachi. Z. York's teachings since he began his ministry during the late 1960s, has been Spiritualism, more commonly referred to today, as New Age-Esoteric Philosophy, or **'Metaphysics'**. For a considerable part of his 35-year ministry between 1968 until 1992, York taught Islam using the name supposedly given to him at birth 'Isa', Arabic for Savior from the Greek word: *'Ieysos'*. Under the name 'Al Imaam Isa', York released a series of books, which contained many of the esoteric teachings of *"Sufism"*, widely regarded as the true spiritual aspect of Islam. In doing so, York was following in the proud tradition of his Great Grand Father Muhammad Ahmed Al Mahdi, who was himself a Sufi Master, having been an initiate of the Al Sammamiyah Order of Sudan since his adolescence.

To better comprehend the spiritual aspect of Dr. York's teachings, we must first examine the practice commonly referred to as Sufism.

Sufism

'Sufism' or Esoteric Islam has been wholly misunderstood and to a large extent vilified by mainstream Orthodox Sunni Islam, driving it deep into Sub Saharan Africa, where it is predominately practiced today. The Turks and other Caucasoid-Arab tribes who seized control of Islam after the fall of the

Moorish Empire circa the 12th century, found it difficult to fully comprehend the Spiritual aspect of the religion, and therefore outlawed it, denouncing it as Heresy, even executing anyone found practicing it in many parts of the Islamic World.

The term 'Sufi' is derived from the word 'Safa' meaning Pure, Purified of Ignorance, Superstition, Dogmatism, Egotism, and Fanaticism as well as; Free from limitations of Caste, Creed, Race and Nationality. All Sufis believe in Allah as the Absolute & only Being, and that all creation as the manifestation of Allah's nature. Therefore Sufism could be regarded as Islam's "Spiritual Science", for lack of a better term. The Sufi or *'Mu Tasawwuf'* is the practitioner of the 'Esoteric' (inward) aspect of Islam, which therefore far exceeds the Exoteric (outward) aspect of Mainstream Islam.

Fig.2 *Symbol of York's Sufi Order*

While in Orthodox Islam, believers are focused towards the goal of attaining a state of perfection after death through prayer and good deeds on Earth, the aim of Sufism is of attaining perfection whilst still alive, and attempting to gain access to Knowledge of the Divine realms of Consciousness. Initially Sufism formed an integral part of "Real Islam". For example, during the time of The Prophet Muhammad, circa 616 A.D., an incident occurred whilst the Koran was still being revealed which demonstrated the importance of Spirituality to Muslims. It all began when Spells were cast upon Muhammad by two Witches; Ijaaz and Faatin, who were said to whisper evil enchantments into Knotted ropes, which they would then place at regular intervals in the Prophet Muhammad's path. It is said that these spells eventually caused The Prophet Muhammad to become very ill. So as a remedy to combat this evil, Allah Subhannahu Wa Ta Ala (Most Glorified And Exalted) revealed chapters 20 & 21 of Surahs; 'Al Falaq' *The Dawn* and 'Al Naas' *The People*, now chapters: 113 & 114 of the Koran. In the revised & Edited version of The Holy Koran, with the English translation of the meanings and Commentary, the translator states the following regarding this incident:

> 6302. *Falaq* is the Dawn or Daybreak, the cleaving of darkness and the manifestation of light. This may be understood in various senses: (1) literally, when the darkness of ignorance is at its worst, the light of Allah pierces through the soul and gives it enlightenment:...The author and source of all true light is Allah, and if we seek Him, we are free from ignorance, superstition, fear, and every kind of evil.
>
> 6305. 'Those (feminine) who blow on knots', this having been a favourite form of witchcraft practiced by perverted women. Such secret arts cause psychological terror. They may be what are called magic, or secret plot-

tings, or the display of false seductive charms (iii. 14), or the spreading of false and secret rumours or slanders to frighten men or deter them from right action. There is fraud in such things, but men are swayed by it. They should cast off fear and do their duty.

(IFTA, Koran Commentary, p: 2030)

You'll notice how in the commentary, the author attempts to trivialise the dangers of Witchcraft and Black Magic, by stating that they only represent "psychological terror" which can only effect the ignorant and superstitious. However if this was the case, then why did The Prophet Muhammad, suffer 'Physically' from this, and require protection from Allah? Unless the commentator is implying that The Prophet Muhammad was ignorant and suppositious and could be affected by this fraudulent, harmless "Mumbo Jumbo". This attitude is typical of the view taken by Orthodox Sunni Islam towards Spiritualism, even to the point of implying that Prophet Muhammad, the very founder of Islam, regarded as one of the Greatest individuals in human history, was a man who could be affected by *"secret plottings, or the display of false seductive charms"* and *"the spreading of false and secret rumours or slanders to frighten men"*. Both chapters; *Al Falaq* and *Al Naas*, were revealed by Allah, for the purpose of being used as actual Talisman's, by not only Muhammad, but all Muslim afflicted by such Evil Enchantments in the future. According to The Collins English Dictionary of Etymology, the word Talisman means:

Talisman (tal'- is-man) *n.* an object endowed with magical power of protecting the wearer from harm.

During the time of The Prophet Muhammad, such evil was understood by Muslims to exist, and in this case, these two chapters were to be recited to protect the user. However slowly but surely, as other foreign racial groups began infiltrating Islam, such as the Turks and other Euro-Asian people's, this mystical knowledge became suppressed and increasingly distrusted, eventually rendering Orthodox Islam merely another form of Christianity, solely concerned with dogmatic religious practices completely devoid of any spiritual foundation. And like Christianity, Orthodox Islam has simply focused on War and Mass population mind control in order to justify its existence. This 'Despiritualization' of Islam is due to two factors. First, the invasion of Islam by Euro-Arab & Asian populations, this caused Islam to gradually abandoned its understanding of Spirituality, and therefore became suspicious of Sufism. Secondly, in its effort to compete with the West, Orthodox Islam has simply become another form of Christianity, which itself became entirely devoid of its Spiritual elements, as soon as it became the adopted & accepted faith of Europeans, who completely suppress Spirituality, as Marimba Ani points out in her book *"Yurugu: An African-Centred Critique of European Culture, Thought and Behaviour"*:

In European religious thought the human and the divine are hopelessly split; there is no sacred ground on which they meet. In such setting, the exaggerated material priorities of the culture are simply a result of the praxis of its participants, of the limiting realities offered by the culture. The resultant materialism further despiritualizes the culture. So the circle is joined; and European culture gives the appearance of being a self-perpetuating system...Even as Europeans seek to despiritualize their surroundings, they are aware of the spiritual aspect of existence. But given the premises of their rationalistic epistemology, it must remain forever unknowable, unattainable. Spirituality represents a constant threat to the ordered system they have constructed. They therefore suffer from a chronic fear of spiritual implications; they distrust spirituality and humanness in people and cultures. They must pretend that these phenomena do not exist, and therefore are embarrassed by their manifestations.

(Ani, 1994, p: 556-558)

Without any real spiritual core, Orthodox Sunni Islam has just become yet another mass movement with no 'Spiritual' direction, essentially no different to Communism. The importance of "The Mutasawaf" or Sufi to Islam is absolutely essential to provide a spiritual link to the higher levels of consciousness, and ultimately contact with the Creator. Otherwise the religion becomes stagnant much like water without any external source to refresh itself. Humanity needs the constant connection to The Prophets (Ancestors), The Angels (Celestial Beings) and The Most High (Creator), in order to receive spiritual direction, without which, Man is lost, and merely practicing dead and dormant religious rituals, which is all too apparent in Orthodox Sunni Islam & Christianity. So again, this is the importance of the Sufi or "*Spiritual Master*" who acts like an umbilical cord between Man and the Higher Dimensions of Consciousness.

Muhammad Ibn 'Arabi

In Orthodox (Euro-Arab) Islam any mention of real spirituality is frowned upon, for example, you have only to look at the hostility faced by any of the great Sufi Masters throughout history to understand this point.

Take for instance Muhammad Ibn 'Arabi, also known as Muhyiddin Ibn 'Arabi, Shaykh al-Akbar or The Great Master, born 1165 in Moorish (African) occupied Spain. Regarded by many as probably one of the Greatest Sufi Masters to have ever lived. Ibn Arabi wrote over 350 works, including the *Fusus al-Hakam*, an examination of the inner meaning of the wisdom of the

Fig.3 *Actual Manuscript written by Ibn Arabi from the 12th Century*

Prophet's in Judaic/ Christian/ Islamic lineage. It has been said that one day during his youth, while at a party in Seville, Spain, he heard a voice calling to him, *"O Muhammad, it was not for this that you were created"*. In alarm he immediately left and went into hiding to contemplate this experience. It was while doing so, that he was said to have had his seminal "Triple Vision", during which he Encountered and received directions from The Prophet's Jesus, Moses & Muhammad. This "Close encounter" is consistent with the accounts of many of those who claim to be Spiritual Masters, including the young Dr. Malachi. Z. York, as we shall later examine. It was this enlightenment that immediately set Muhammad Ibn 'Arabi upon the spiritual path, which would later establish him as a great Sufi Master. This Spiritual experience or 'Vision' took place in what is referred to as "The Mundus Imaginalis", or the imaginative 'dreamlike' presence where The Creator gives spiritual 'Wayhin' or *Devine Inspiration,* directly to the spiritual aspirant. Throughout his life, Muhammad Ibn 'Arabi taught that all of the Prophets of the scriptures came teaching the same religion. The following is an example of what he explained of the Prophets, taken from his work *"Futuhat al Makkiyah II"* :

> "There is no knowledge except that taken from God, for He alone is the Knower...the Prophets, in spite of their great number and the long periods of time which separate them, had no disagreement in knowledge of God, since they took it from God."
>
> (Ibn 'Arabi, p: 110)

However, teaching such truth was perceived as a threat to the 'Religious Authorities' who wanted to maintain the monopoly on what was right and wrong, and therefore a path fraught with danger. Much like the Pharisees & Sadducees (Chief Priests) of Jesus' time, these men wielded tremendous power, and literally controlled what was being taught. He would often come into conflict with these so-called religious authorities or 'Learned Elders', and on one particular occasion he was forced to flee for his life from Egypt after being accused of Heresy, which would have resulted in his immediate execution. According to Henry Corbin in his book *"Creative Imagination in the Sufism of Ibn 'Arabi"*:

> ...*Ibn 'Arabi* made no secret of his disgust at their stupidity, ignorance, and depravity, and such an attitude was not calculated to win their favour. The tension rose, giving rise to denunciations and arrests; our *shaikh* was in mortal peril. At this critical moment the irreducible antagonism between the spiritual Islam of Sufism and legalitarian Islam became patent. Saved by the intervention of a friendly shaikh, Ibn 'Arabi had but one concern, to flee far from Cairo and its hateful, bigoted canonists...
>
> (Corbin, 1990, p: 232)

This antagonism towards Muhammad Ibn 'Arabi's work's has lasted up until the present, with of his writings still being inaccessible in many parts of the 'Arabized' Islamic World. For example, in 1970 the Egyptian government took the extraordinary step (for a secular institution), of completely banning his works. Despite this opposition, Sufi teachings such as Ibn Arabi's still thrive today in many Sub-Saharan African countries like; Nigeria, Senegal and particularly Sudan, where Sufi Masters are still revered by the general populace.

The following is an excerpt taken from an actual eyewitness account by Travel writer Keir Robyn, [1] of the great tradition of the Sufi 'Whirling Dervishes' of the Sudan:

> Touching down in Khartoum, I began the fulfillment of a journey I've been anticipating for fifteen years. I camped at a sailing club perched over the Nile next to Sir Kitchener's gunboat from 1890. That afternoon I found the Sufis, also known as the whirling dervishes, in front of a mosque in old Khartoum. It was surrounded by a massive derelict graveyard. For an hour until sunset, the crowd and tempo grew with mesmerizing chanting, dancing, jumping, and whirling. The crowd included almost no other foreigners and almost everyone participated. A wonderful experience.
> (Robyn, 2004)

Figs.4, 5, 6 & 7 Nubian Sufi Tradition: Top, Left- Right:
Sudanese Ansaars Performing Traditional Sufi Ceremony

It is also emerging that what Sufis have known all along is only now beginning to be understood by scientists and adherents of spiritualism in the Western world; that beyond this physical world and Universe, there exist other realms of existence. There is increasing evidence, which suggests that much of the technological advancements of the 20th century have been provided from the spiritual realm, through "Channelling" by Beings usually contacted by mediums. Unfortunately due to the culture of secrecy and hypocrisy practiced in both the East & West, none of this will ever be admitted. For example, information regarded by many to be factual, is often ridiculed and dismissed as *"Mumbo Jumbo"*, to discourage the public from understanding it.

In a nutshell, the nucleus of Dr. Malachi. Z. York's doctrine for the past almost 40-years, have been Esoteric teachings, disguised by Militant Afro-centrism & Theology. Even the name of his earliest organisation, **"Ansaar Pure Sufi"**, launched in 1968, reflected his deep involvement with Mystiscm. It could even be argued that York has never really been a political or civil rights 'Black Power Leader', in the classic sense as that of Malcolm X or Hughey. P. Newton, or even Minister Louis Farrakhan, but simply attempted to assume this role to reach a broader audience.

Nabiy Al Khidr

> I Descend to This Plane, Formless in Form, A Temple of The Incarnated Divinity to Guide You...
>
> Malachi Zodok

Dr. York claims to have had a strange encounter during the early 1970's, while walking home one night, in which he describes being met by an Elderly gentleman, with a long white beard, wearing a flowing white robe, who appeared to float or hover above the ground. The 'Old Man' would later reveal himself to York as 'Al Khidr' or Nabiy Khidr *"The Green One"*.

So who is this Mysterious 'Al Khidr' York has often referred to in his books? Patrick Franke, author of *"Encountering Khidr"*, states the following:

> Khidr literally means 'The Green One', representing freshness of spirit and eternal liveliness, green symbolizing the freshness of knowledge "drawn out of the living sources of life." Whatever the source for this green may be, it has come to symbolize the benign presence of the divine wisdom as imparted by the Divine Himself to Khidr and to Prophet Muhammad. Qur'ânic commentators say that al-Khidr ('The Green Man' of pre-Islamic lore) is one of the prophets; others refer to him simply as an angel who functions as a guide to those who seek God. And there are yet others who argue for his being a perfect *wali* meaning the one whom God has taken as a friend. Khidr is associated with the Water of Life. Since he drank the water of immortality he is described as the one who has found the source of life, 'the Eternal Youth.' He is the mysterious guide and immortal saint in popular Islamic lore and the hidden initiator of those who walk the mystical

path. In the Muslim tradition Khidr is alive and well and continues to guide the perplexed and those who invoke his name.

(Franke, 2000, p: 95)

For more information detailing York's encounter with Al Khidr, please refer to The (Nuwaubian) 'Holy Tablets': Chapter Six, Tablet Ten, entitled: *"The Mortals".*

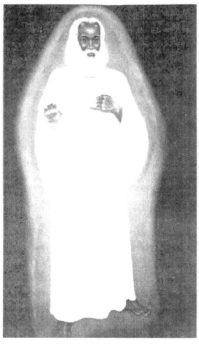

Fig.8 *York's Depiction of Angel Melchesidek*

After several more of these strange encounters during the early 1970s, York claims to have been summoned to travel to the Sudan, to report to an individual named Mahmuwd, Imaam of the Great Masjid (Mosque) of Sudan, who would instruct him on what to do next. Once he arrived, York claims to have been initiated into an ancient secret order called 'Khalwatiyya' by Mahmuwd, Grand Master of the Temple of Khartoum after undergoing a series of tests or trials. York would later encounter this mysterious Being he met in New York again, at the junction of the two Niles, in a place called "Tutee". York goes on to state that the being he knew as Al Khidr, was in fact his Spiritual Master, and the actual personification of his own soul, which has existed for '76 Trillion years', and from this point on, would manifest through York, as a type of reservoir of knowledge, providing answers to any of York questions. Although no one else was present to confirm whether York did actually meet Al Khidr, who is purportedly also known as the Arch Angel Melchesidek, or Malachi Zodok *"The Ruler of Justice"* within the Old Testament of the Bible.

York's account seems very similar to the experience of 12th Century Sufi Master, Muhammad Ibn 'Arabi. However with York, the relationship appears to be a lot more personalised, as he claims that this Being would actually inhabit his body, much like a medium, but on a permanent basis as opposed to only whilst the supposed Channelling is taking place. This then, actually rendered York more than just a Sufi Master but also an 'Avatar', correctly referred to in Arabic as **'ILAH MUTAJASSID'**, which is said to literally translate into English as *"The Divine / or God in Flesh"*.

Avatar of The West

> Once you have achieved a certain level of consciousness, you enter the ranks of the Ascended Masters. The Ascended Master is a Person at the summit of a Mountain, with his hand extended down to pull up his fellow humans...
>
> (Excerpt taken from *"The Moorish Paradigm"* by Hakim Bey)

To the so-called Monotheistic religions of Judaism, Christianity & Orthodox Islam, the concept of an Avatar, 'Ascended Master', or simply God, in Flesh cannot really be comprehended because of the belief in God as being an all powerful being who sits in the Heavens, directing every aspect of man's day to day life. However in older religions like Hinduism, Jainism, Yoruba, or the Ancient Egyptian Religious concept of Ma'at, it was understood that the Gods *"The Neteru"*, represented

Fig.9 *York in 'Lotus' Meditation Position*

different personifications of Supreme consciousness. Unlike in Monotheism, where The Most High God is viewed as a Supreme Consciousness, which can never ever be comprehended by a human mind. However according to York, what we regard as Supreme consciousness, actually manifests into the Spiritual, Mental and Physical realms as incarnations in various forms, such as Gods, both Good and Evil, who struggle with each other to maintain balance. Often one side outweighs the other temporarily, but only for a brief period, before Balance is once again restored, because the one cannot define itself without the other. York claims that what the so-called Monotheistic faiths view as God, is the combination of: '2' equal forces; both Good and Evil, Positive and Negative, which York refers to as El Kuluwm *"The ALL"*, or more accurately, KULUWM: 'ALL', because the El or 'The' renders 'ALL' a definite article, which would then make ALL a Person, Place or Thing, when ALL is more like 'Everything', or every Atom and Molecule in existence.

In his book *"The Ansar Cult In America"*, Orthodox Islamic Scholar Bilial Philips actually confirms the correlation between the teachings of Sufi Master Muhammad Ibn 'Arabi, and Malachi. Z. York, in reference to the theory of the Creator being Omnipresent:

> In his writings Isa not only makes God equal to His creation but he also invents attributes unheard of among Muslims to support his equating the Creator with His creation. He writes as follows:

> "Most people don't understand the fact that Allah is AL KULLUWM (KULL) THE ALL; The sum of everything in the universes – nothing can be added to nor taken away from THE ALL…Allah did not stop with the completion of The Creation: He left the essence of His being in every atom of His Creation, and without Him nothing exists".
>
> This aberrant philosophy was first propounded among Muslims by the 12th century CE heretic, **Ibn 'Arabi**, and is known among Muslim theologians as Wahdah al Wujood (monism). Such a concept makes God indistinguishable from His creation and is in fact an elegant expression of pantheism.
>
> (Philips, 1989, p: 28)

Therefore those who refer to themselves as Avatars or *"Gods in Flesh"*, can only mean that they are a representation of a higher level of consciousness to that of their fellow human beings, but in no way be The Most Supreme consciousness in human form, because this would then render them ALL Consciousness, which is impossible. This would be like running ALL the Electricity in All of the 'Multiverses' or Multiple Universes, through a single plug socket, which would logically cause the plug to disintegrate. Nevertheless according to York, it is because of the ignorance of Orthodox: Judaic, Christian & Islamic 'Monotheism' that true understanding of GOD (ALL), is suppressed, causing these religions to be devoid of any real Spirituality or connection to GOD, by negating the Spiritual or Ascended Masters who act as intermediaries between Man and the Spiritual realm. Leaving religion completely reliant upon religious leaders such as Reverends, Imams & Rabbis, who simply pretend to interpret scriptures every week at the Church, Synagogue & Mosque for Money and Power. According to York these religions fear real spirituality because it threatens to undermine their very purpose, which is simply to maintain control of people's minds with the promise of salvation after death. In *"The Man of Miracles in This Day and Time"* Edition # 138, published in 1983, York states the following about what an Avatar or Spiritual Master is:

> An Avatar is an "extraordinary" being. He is the miraculous embodiment of the divine in human form, an incarnation for the welfare of all humans. Avatars come in succession; one spirit incarnates into another person and so on. His arrival marks the end of an age; his exit marks the beginning of another. We use the Hindu word "Avatar" for English speaking people, because it is much easier to use than the Arabic "ILAH MUTAJASSID".
>
> It is when a person is born that the Avatar incarnates into them. As the person grows mature, the spirit within dominates his body—unless the person suppresses it and dies not allowing it to manifest. Although an Avatar acts and moves as a human, when one looks into his eyes, one can clearly see that he is not a mere mortal…
>
> (Isa Al Mahdi, 1983, p: 19)

According to the interpretations of 'GOD' in Judaism, Christianity & Orthodox Islam, which according to York is actually an abbreviation of the German word GUD or GOOD. And the Devil, which is also an abbreviation of DE & Evil, created by Europeans. This is precisely why they remain ignorant to true 'Spiritual Truth', because neither the Bible nor Koran if read properly, say what these faiths profess. In the Bible God is constantly referred to as a plural 'Eloheem', in the original language, whilst in the Koran, Allah is routinely pluralized as **'Nahnu' or *"We"***. Although Muslims will insist that the "We" is referring to Allah and the Angels, however according to The Holy Koran, 'Surah Al Baqarah' *"Chapter of the Cow"*, their explanation is completely contradicted:

> And when **We said to the Angels**: Make obeisance to Adam they did obeisance…
> (The Holy Koran, Chapter 2, Verses 34)

The above quote in Arabic states: 'Wa Ith Quwl-ana Lil-Malaikati', which literally translates into English as *"And We Said to The Angels"*, therefore if Allah is only One, or Mono then who are the We?

York's job as a Spiritual or Ascended Master, was to essentially answer questions like these, which was made all the more difficult by the fact that most Blacks in the West follow the Christian faith, in which they mistakenly worshipped Jesus, who was himself, by all accounts an Avatar or 'Ascended' Master, yet find it impossible to grasp the concept of an Avatar or 'God in Flesh', as a being imparting divine or Esoteric knowledge upon humanity for the purpose of raising man's consciousness, without becoming an object of worship and adoration themselves.

Multiple Personalities

> "I, have living within me or visiting me a multitude of personalities, which come at different times. The proof appears in my writings. I am an extraterrestrial being (U.F.O.) from another galaxy. As you know, we have 19 galaxies outside of this one. We are 100,000 years more advanced than this planet. Since we have passed through this state, I come here to give you guidance. You Earth beings are about to destroy yourselves before you can develop your spiritual self; WE MUST TRY TO STOP YOU!!..
> (Imaam Isa Al Haadi Al Mahdi, p: 95 "The Book of Revelation", Chapter 1, Verses 1-20, Edition # 216, 1991)

Whilst in Sudan in 1973, York was instructed by the Grandmaster Mahmuwd, to establish a Sufi Order in the West, called ***"The Universal Order of Love: The Sons of The Green Light"***. The symbol of which was to be a Lotus in the centre of which was a Seven pointed star resting in an upright crescent; within which was an inverted heart, which had the word "HUWA" as in 'Yahuwa' or Yahweh inscribed. York says he was shown this symbol by Mahmuwd in Sudan, who explained to him the meanings of

Fig.10 *Lotus Symbol of York's Sufi Order*

this symbol. He was told that his order will be established in the West,; *"As the sun is the axis of this solar system, and all the planets revolve around it; so will you be the axis of the planet Earth and all the people will revolve around you. You will be their spiritual guide and you will nourish them with love and wisdom. Hence, your name will be 'Al Qubt, The Axis, The Spiritual Guide"*. Other than Al Khidr, inhabiting his body, York also claims to act as a kind of Medium, who transmits information from the 'Spirit World' into the Physical world. Ironically, York recently Re-established many of the original Esoteric Principles of the Sufi Order under the school of 'Right Knowledge' as **The Ancient Mystic Order of Melchesidek**, more commonly known as (A.M.O.M.) Aside from his own identity, born in 1945, at various periods an assortment of what York refers to as 'Distinct Personalities', speak through him. Some of these 'Celestial Masters' are said to include:

1) SHAIKH AL QUBT, "The Axis", Student of The Prophet Enoch
2) SHAIKH AL KHIDR, "The Green One" Angelic Being: Melchesidek or Malahi Zodok
3) ISA AL MASIH, Jesus, The Hebrew Messiah of 2,000 Years ago
4) YANUWN, One of "The Twenty Four Elders", and a Visitor from another Galaxy
5) ZOSER, Pharaoh of The 3rd Dynasty of Ancient Egypt
6) AL MAHDI, "The Guide" 18th Century Mystic and Liberator of The Sudan
7) RAHMAH, One of The Masters who came down with the Sons of God in Genesis to Fight Satan

It has been these seven "Personalities" in particular, who have provided York with what he calls his *"76 Trillion years of 'Etheric' knowledge"*.
Often times when York has called himself 'God in Flesh' he claims to be referring to Al Khidr, which is the most dominant personality that inhabits his body. Al Khidr or the Arch-Angel Melchesidek is said to *"Have Neither Mother Nor Father, With Neither Beginning Nor End"*, and therefore the most ancient of the Angels, which is why he is often referred to as 'The Ancient of Day's'.

Figs.11, 12, 13, 14, 15, 16 & 17: York's 7 Celestial Personalities: Top, Right- Left:
Shaikh Al Qubt, Al Khidr, The Messiah Jesus
(Middle) *YANUWN, The Mahdi, Rahmah &* **(Bottom)** *Pharaoh Zoser*

Apparently, Al Khidr or Melchesidek was actually present during the original creation of the Universe, 76 Trillion 'Etheric' years ago, which the Honourable Elijah Muhammad has often referred to as the 66,000,000,000,000 years of Creation in his teachings.

Another one of York's alleged personalities is said to be Pharaoh of the Third Dynasty of Ancient Egypt, Zoser, also pronounced 'Djoser'. York claims that Zoser was one of an elite group of Entities called the 24 Elders, closely affiliated with the ancient Sumerian Deities; The Anunnaqi. Pharaoh Zoser was the actual architect of the world's first Pyramid at Saqqara, Egypt, and not Imhotep as is commonly believed. After ruling Egypt for many years, Zoser who is also known in Sufism as Abdul Quduws, travelled to various parts of the World bestowing knowledge upon mankind. Zoser was known by the following names and titles in various Cultures & Civilizations throughout the Ancient World:

Africa ---------- *Tehuti (Thoth)*

Assyria ---------- *Nabu*

Greece ---------- *Hermes Trismegistus*

Italy ---------- *Mercury*

Mexico ---------- *Quetzalcoatl*

Easter Island ---------- *Rapanui*

Arabia ---------- *Abdul Quduws*

Ecuador ---------- *Viracocha*

Columbia ---------- *Tupac*

Figs.18, 19, 20, 21 & 22: Builders of The Pyramids: Left- Right:
Pharaoh Zoser & Imhotep **(Bottom)** *Step Pyramid of Saqqara*

Figs.23, 24, 25, 26, 27, 28, 29, 30 & 31: The Many Representations of Zoser: Top, Left-Right: *Tehuti, Nabu, Hermes Trismegistus* **(Middle)** *Mercury, Quetzalcoatl, Rapanui, Abdul Quduws, Viracocha & Tupac*

As a Spiritual Master whose job it is to raise predominately Western Blacks & Latinos, York had the unenviable task of teaching the 'Higher' esoteric mysteries through Judaism, Christianity & Islam, in which as we have previously stated, the concept of a Spiritual Master is virtually impossible to grasp, which maybe one of the reasons why there has been so much resentment from Religious leader's towards York's teachings. Over the past 35 years York has released a whole series of books which have either dealt with Spiritual (Esoteric) or Extraterrestrial (UFO) themes such as:

- *Science of Creation*, **Edition # 65**
- *Eternal Life After Death*, **Edition # 30**
- *Science of The Pyramids*, **Edition # 43**
- *Science of Healing*, **Edition # 9**
- *Allah's Creation The Human Body*, **Edition # 55**

- *What And Where Is Hell?*, **Edition # 76**
- *What Are Angels?*, **Edition # 78**
- *The Man of Miracles in This Day And Time*, **Edition # 138**
- *Man From Planet Rizq*, **Scroll # 80**
- *Mission Earth And The Extraterrestrial Involvement*, **Scroll # 82**
- *Who lived Before The Adam and Eve Story?* **Scroll # 83**
- *Are There (UFOs) Extraterrestrials In Your Midst?*, **Scroll # 84**
- *Samballah And Aghaarta, Cities Within The Earth*, **Scroll # 131**

Basically, York has had to use the Bible and Koran to interpret what can best be termed as the "Universal Doctrine", which transcends most religious beliefs. In other words, if one was to conduct an in-depth analysis of most religions on the planet, at the core of them should be a common underlining theme or basis. This does not mean that every religion is the same, what it means is that there is a similar truth in every religious belief, no matter how small. The task of a Spiritual Master then is to clear away the nonsense added throughout the Centuries by men in order to get to the real truth, which is the truth of man's purpose in the Universe. This is why 'Sufis' teach that all of the Prophets came teaching the same truth. However this idea of one Universal doctrine would mean everyone understanding the same truth in the world. Naturally this wouldn't be a very popular amongst those whose job it is to control humanity, and prevent them from understanding their real purpose, which is according to York, developing their Souls' (Consciousness) to eventually return to, and be at 'one' within the Bosom of the Omnipresent Creator.

In order to have Positive you must have Negative, therefore as well as good Spiritual beings there must also exist bad spiritual beings, who have succeeded in deliberately misleading humanity by suppressing the truth of religion, and in so doing, consign man to a 'Spiritual Coma' in this prison called the physical realm. This is why anytime somebody comes along attempting to raise man's Spiritual Consciousness; they are immediately attacked by these Devils, who come in all Religions, Races, Colours and Species. There are also according to York 'Disagreeable beings', who arrive here on Earth from other Planets, Dimensions and Realms of existence, commonly known as 'Extraterrestrials' for lack of a better word, as we shall now investigate.

The purpose of York's teachings then, are to simply attempt to correct the many misconceptions of Religion, History and Science, which if taught truthfully should all agree to confirm the reason for man's true existence in the Universe. Instead what we have is confusion between Religion, History and Science, with all of them saying something different, which has been deliberately perpetrated to divide and control humanity.

Figs.32, 33 & 34: Spiritual Master: Left- Right: *York as Sufi Master & Application for Sons of The Green Light Sufi Order*

Ancient Gods of the New Millennium

York claims that Masters or Gods have been visiting the Earth for Hundreds of thousands, even Millions of years and are known by many different names and titles in different cultures and languages. They have been responsible for all of humanities earliest Civilizations, Languages and High Cultures, and are also the influences behind all religion. Although not all of them come as Avatars, they are all personifications of higher levels of existence in one form or another. York says this is because The Supreme Consciousness (GOD) is unable to come to Earth itself, simply because ALL is Omnipresent (Everywhere at all times), therefore ALL manifests as parts of its own essence to carry out specific tasks. This is because 'ALL' can never be in any one place at a time, but everywhere at ALL times. Therefore it could be argued that the eternal battle between Good and Evil is really an internal battle within the (ALL), to achieve balance within itself (the Universe).

The Elohim or Cosmic Entities, for example, vibrate on a higher density level than we are able to comprehend in our present state of existence. These Ascended Masters often act as mediators or step-downs between Man and the Supreme Source of Creation, or Supreme Consciousness mistakenly referred to as 'GOD' for lack of a better word. In other words, these entities are simply beings which posses complete awareness of Self, forgoing the 'I' and instead identify themselves as part of the Supreme Consciousness (ALL).

The following are some examples of these Incarnated Masters/Gods in various Scriptures, Cultures & Languages:

Scripture	Culture	Language	Title	Translation
The Epic of Gilgamesh	Sumerian	Cuneiform	'Anunnaqi'	*"Those Beings sent from Anu, to Earth"*
Book of Coming Fourth	Egyptian	Hieroglyphics	'Neteru'	*"Those Beings Who Came Down"*
The Torah	Judaic	Hebrew	'Eloheem'	*"These Beings"*
The Torah	Judaic	Hebrew	'Nephileem'	*"These Who Fell Down"*
The Book of Acts	Christian	Greek	'Theos'	*"Those Gods"*
The Book of Matthew	Christian	Greek	'Angelos'	*"Heavenly Hosts"*
The Book of Revelations	Christian	Aramaic	'Malaikah'	*"Heavenly Rulers"*
The Holy Qur'an	Islamic	Arabic	'Allahumma'	*"The Gods"*

These Extra-(Additional) Terrestrial-(Earthly) or *"Additional to Earthly"* beings are also known in many other cultures and languages which include:

Culture	Title	Translation
Zulu (South Africa)	'Amazulu'	*"People of the Heavens"*
Navaho (North America)	'Ka-chinah'	*"Sky Men"*
Dogons (West Africa)	'Nomos'	*"Sky Gods"*
Benin (West Africa)	'Oungisoui'	*"Sky People"*

Despite what York teaches about the existence of these Beings, are there other such Spiritual Masters or Avatars, are any of these 'Incarnated Masters' teaching's consistent with this so-called Universal 'Spiritual Doctrine?

Lord Maitreya

Fig.35 Ascended Master:
Celestial Representation of Lord Maitreya

Lord Maitreya claims to be the present embodiment of a Cosmic/Spiritual (Ascended) Master or Avatar who has been visiting this Planet for Centuries. Known by numerous epithets such as The Great Redeemer & The Fifth Buddah, Lord Maitreya has apparently now taken the form of an individual of East Indian (Hindu) origin who currently resides in London's East End, and now refers to himself as 'Maitreya the Cosmic Christ'. Lord Maitreya has been mentioned unfavourably by York on several occasions as an Anti-Christ who will appear as the 'World Teacher' before the Judgement day such as in the book *"Fake Gods False Christs"* Scroll # 105, in which York states:

> You Also Have **Maitreya The Christ**. He Claims To Be **The Messiah Returned, As Well As The Mahdi, Jesus Christ, The Christ, Krishna, The 5th Buddha And Maitreya Buddha.** He Is Known To The Esoteric World As "The World Teacher", Whose Appearance Was Expected In This Day And Time. Most Of The Information About Maitreya The Christ Has Come From A Man Named Benjamin Crème. According To "Crème, **Maitreya The Christ**" Descended In **July 1977 A.D, And Took Up Residence In London's Pakistani Community.**

(York, 1995, p: 23-24)

Although York does not appear to agree with most of the claims made by Maitreya, the underlying theme of what they both teach does appear to correlate. In the book *"Maitreya's Mission"*, Vol.1, New Age initiate Benjamin Crème questions 'Spiritual Master', Lord Maitreya concerning Avatars as follows:

> **Why do Masters live in mountains and deserts?**
> During Atlantean times the Masters of those days worked openly. They were the priest-kings; the God-like Beings who created the various scientifically advanced civilizations whose knowledge has been lost. At the destruction of Atlantis the Masters retreated to the mountains and deserts, leaving humanity to regenerate itself while They acted as the stimulus behind the scenes. For the first time since those days the Hierarchy of Masters and initiates is returning now to work in the world.
>
> (Crème, 1986, p: 79)

In his book *"The Science of Healing"* Edition # 9, first published in 1977, York makes a similar assertion regarding the role of The Gods or Masters in relation to humanity's earliest advanced civilizations:

Fig.36 *Current Incarnation of Lord Maitreya*

The NEPHELIANS (MENTAL GIANTS) inhabited the Kingdom of Salaam, in which Melchizedek (SRA) reigned over. Within the kingdom of Salaam was the city of "MU". Hence, the connection of these two places name "MU" and "SALAAM" gave birth to the title MU-SALAAM or simply MUSLIM meaning "One of Peace". This is the Highest Title within the entire Universe. The Kingdom of Salaam was an ultra-advanced civilization that existed before the separation of Arabia from Africa.

(Isa Al Mahdi, 1977, p:15)

Notice how York subtly relates information about the ancient Masters to Islaam. This is because he was teaching Islaam at the time, and was therefore faced with the difficulty of expounding the Spiritual doctrine disguised Islamic teachings. This is why he often made the statement; *"I Came Giving You Wanted, So You Could Learn To Want What I Really Have To Give"*, meaning he was only using whatever religious doctrine, as a means by which to reach people whose belief was in that particular religion. However, it could be argued that York used deception to fool people into following him, utilising religion to disguise his true teachings.

However, as we saw in the case of Muhyiddin Ibn 'Arabi, also known as The Great Master, a regular premise of Spiritual Master's is that they view most religions as basically containing elements of the same of Truth, which is why York has may have found it easy to teach the Spiritual Doctrine, under the cover of different religions.

Sathya Sai Baba

Another such 'Spiritual Master', whom York himself has made reference to on several occasions in the past, has been the Indian Mystic, Sathya Sai Baba whose website, 2 states:

> Sathya Sai Baba is a spiritual teacher, whose life inspires millions of people worldwide to realise their innate divinity and have faith in God. His teachings are universal to all religions, yet he is not seeking to start a new religion. Rather he urges us to go to the roots of our faith whatever it may be, to rediscover the universal truth therein.
>
> (Baba, 2003, p: 1)

Interestingly, towards the end of the first page it goes on to state:

> ...He himself considers His miracles to be of no importance: He calls them His "calling-cards" and explains that they are natural to him. He says "**I give you what you want so that you should want what I have come to give** – namely liberation itself"
>
> (Baba, 2003, p: 1)

Is it a coincidence that Spiritual Master Sai Baba literally makes the exact same statement, almost verbatim, and is this evidence of some kind of correlation between the Teacher's. Or is this, as some critics have contended, further proof that York is indeed a charlatan who has been plagiarising Sai Baba's teachings, or is the reverse true. York has also been credited by his followers with being able to make 'Sacred Ash' appear from thin air, an ability Sai Baba is also widely acknowledged for. Sathya Sai Baba is in turn mentioned in Benjamin Crème's book, as a Spiritual Master:

> **Is it possible that Sai Baba is Maitreya, and that the man in London waiting to be recognized as Christ is the Master Jesus Who, you say, won't show Himself to the public until Maitreya – the Cosmic Christ – has done so? I am a firm believer in Sai Baba as the Cosmic Christ.** If I thought it possible that Sai Baba is Maitreya then, of course, I would have said so. I believe Sai Baba to be a Cosmic Avatar Who works in close relation to Maitreya and His mission...
>
> (Crème, 1986, p: 63)

It is not known whether York has ever met Sai Baba, although York has made reference to having been a former student of the Great Chinese/Tibetan Master Lama Mott Kokomau during the seventies. It is also rare for York to pay anyone a compliment, which in the case of Sai Baba, he does seem to speak slightly favourably, by not directly labelling him another "False Christ" in his book: *"Fake Gods False Christs"*:

> ...In The 60's When They Had Fear That During That Period Of Time, They Had A Heavy Migration Of Swammis And Yogis, And They Thought That Meant That They Were The Wisemen From The East Seeking Out The Messiah Here In New Babylon. So During The Sixties And Seventies When The Maharaji And Sai Baba And All The Lamas And Yogas Started Coming Here With This Transcendental Meditation, The Devil Became Afraid That The Messiah Was Born Somewhere, And These Were The Wisemen From The East Coming To Pay Homage To Him Because They Know That He Is Supposed To Rise Up Amongst Us.
>
> (York, 1995, p: 109-110)

Interestingly, a regular subject which has also been associated with these Incarnated or Spiritual Masters, has been Extraterrestrial or the *"Additional Earthly"* involvement, by beings from either other Dimensions or Planets, within or outside this galaxy. Indeed this has been at the heart of York's teachings regarding Spirituality from the very beginning. Nevertheless, many will correctly question, what connection can there possibly be between Spirituality and Aliens?

Well according to York, what is known as the Spiritual World or 'Celestial Plane' is simply vibrating at a higher frequency than what we understand as this physical World.

Fig.37 Avatar: *Sathya Sai Baba*

Rather like the difference between Solid, Liquid & Gas, or Ice, Water & Steam. Although it is far more complicated, that is a basic understanding of the connection between the Physical and Spiritual realms. Now any life forms which manages to cross this dimensional 'Gap', are automatically termed 'Inter-dimensional Beings'. However not all beings which visit this planet come from other dimensions, many are from other planets, which are on the same vibratory frequency as ours, which simply makes them Extra-terrestrial. Although according to York, due to the vastness of space, many of these beings often have to manipulate time itself, in order to reach here. Therefore Inter-dimensional and Spiritual beings are exactly the same. This could range from your Great-Grand Mother on your Father's side, to a being that may be from a galaxy a Million "Light Years" away. Naturally the dimensional frequencies would differ, but like a radio, if powerful enough a medium can make contact with whichever being is required.

York claims that it has been these Inter-dimensional or Extra-terrestrial beings, again depending on how powerful they are, who have been manifesting throughout history as Angels and even Gods, as well as Demons, Ghosts, and Aliens to influence humanity for either Good or Evil. So again, can York's assertions regarding the existence of Extra-terrestrial beings, be corroborated by other Esoteric Masters, and if so what is their explanation of this mysterious phenomenon?

According to Lord Maitreya in the book *"Maitreya's Mission"*:

> There are no hostile UFOs. The various tales of allegedly hostile UFOs notwithstanding, the UFO manifestation is a result of interplanetary co-operation and is totally peaceful and beneficial in intention. This co-operation, of course, takes place between our Esoteric Hierarchy and the other planets. Stories of hostile action on the part of UFO occupants, I believe, are the morbid imaginings of frightened humans…If you have read my book, *The Reappearance of Christ and the Masters of Wisdom*, you will know that I believe the UFOs (and their occupants) to be of etheric physical and not dense physical matter and their solid appearance to us to be a temporary phenomenon.
>
> (Crème, 1986, p: 107-108)

Concerning these planes of existence, in the re-published edition of *"Science of Healing"* York states:

> Everything Vibrates, Which Is Called **"A Mood"**. Each Mood Acts And Reacts Continually Carrying Out Life Processes. These Moods Make Up What Is Known As Planes. Planes Are Moods And Schemes Of Vibration Existing In Very Unique And Unified Forms. These Are Seven Planes. The Lowest And Slowest Is The Material Plane. While, The Fastest And Highest That Humans Are Able To Comprehend Is The Bosom Of Anu, Elyown Elyown El, The Most High.
>
> (York, 1998, p: 28)

According to York, most of these highly advanced entities or beings who form what is known as 'The Galactic Council', have been visiting Earth for thousands of years, manipulating human evolution. Some of them are even said to be the progenitors of the various races on earth. Afro-centric New Age Mystic, Dr Phil Valentine, even claims that a number of Extraterrestrial races own patents to the human body, and are entitled to tamper with humans in any way they see fit. For more information refer to *"The Wounded Womb"* by Dr. Phil Valentine.

Fig.38 **Galactic Master Teacher:** *Malachi Zodok*

What is confusing is that many of them appear to have different agendas, and often work independently of each other. For example there are those who are Benevolent Beings (Angels) working to raise man's consciousness before we destroy ourselves. These may have been the beings that influenced the great Holy men (Prophets) of the past to guide humanity. Then there are those who are Malevolent (Demonic), who want to keep man backward and in a perpetual Savage or Beast-like state, in order to easily control us, which is done for example; by giving us technology to make weapons which kill, but not to permanently end hunger & disease. It has been said that the Caucasian Elite are now desperately trying to catch up technologically to some of these beings, in order to gain entry into the Galactic Council, before earth undergoes the next great cataclysm or Judgement. These highly advanced beings come in many races and species. York even claimed years ago, that there are those of Reptilian origin who evolved from pre-historic reptiles (Dinosaurs) which once dominated the earth Millions of years ago, and it is this race of Malevolent Reptilians who form the majority of Malevolent (Demonic) entities opposed to the existence of humanity. Anyone familiar with the writings of David Icke, will be aware of this species. The Nuwaubian leader also claims that the "Serpent" (Satan) mentioned in the book of Genesis, actually belongs to this race of Reptilian beings. In his 2001 re-release *"666 Leviathan, The Beast: As The Anti-Christ"*, Part 1, York makes further references to David Icke's writings, and his relationship to these White Masters & Reptilians:

> What is interesting is if you look at **David Icke** he looks like the beings from **Pleiades**. This dragon or old serpent was so arrogant that he even tried to sit on the throne of **'Elyon El**, "The Most High God" as found in *Isaiah 14:13-15*. The beings from Pleiades Constellation take on the persona of angels or angelic beings. These beings were also known as the white Martians.
>
> (York, 2001, p: 59)

The Anunnaqi

The most prominent and powerful of these Galactic races are said to be The Anunnaqi. York claims that these Benevolent & Malevolent Entities are the actual Gods of the Bible and Koran, who were responsible for the current formation of our Solar system, after their space craft 'Nibiru' *"The Planet that Crosses the Skies"*, also known as 'Planet X', & 'The Tenth Planet', initially passed through the Milky way, 25 Billion years ago. In the Sumerian Epic of Creation, the *"Enuma Elish"*, it describes how Nibiru, also called 'Murdok', was a spaceship the size of a large planet, in other words a 'Planetoid', travelling in an elliptical orbit through Outer Space which accidentally collided with planets in our Solar System, after being caught in Neptune's gravitational field. This theory is given further credence by a man who is unarguably the World's leading authority of the Sumerian Language and Civilization, Professor Zecheria Sitchin, author of *"The Earth Chronicles"* series, who states the following in his book *"The Twelfth Planet"*:

Fig.39 Planet-Ship: *Nibiru*

> The epic's narrative now takes us along Murduk's speeding course. He first passes by the planet that "begot" him, that pulled him into the solar system, the planet Ea/Neptune. As Murduk nears Neptune, the latter's gravitational pull on the newcomer grows in intensity. It rounds out Murduk's path, "making it good for its purpose." Murduk must have still been in a plastic stage at that time. As he passed by Ea/Neptune, the gravitational pull caused the side of Murduk to bulge, as though he had "a second head". No part of Murduk, however, was torn off at this passage; but as Murduk reached the vicinity of Anu/Uranus, chunks of matter began to tear away from him, resulting in the formation of four satellites of Murduk. "Anu brought forth and fashioned the four sides, consigned their power to the leader of the host." Called "winds", the four were thrust into a fast orbit around Murduk, "swirling as a whirlwind".
>
> (Sitchin, 1976, p: 200)

Recent Scientific discoveries may have again lent further credence to York's assertions concerning the existence of 'Nibiru'. The following was a article which appeared in Great Britain's 'Mail on Sunday' Newspaper, written by Kiki King, dated July 31st, 2005, entitled: *"Scientists discover a whole new world"*, which stated:

> For generations, schoolchildren have been taught that nine planets circle our Sun – and pub quiz teams have struggled to remember what order they

are in. But yesterday the world of astronomy was rocked with the news that a 10th planet had been discovered on the outer reaches of the solar system.

The new body has not yet been formally named – for now it is rather awkwardly called 2003UB313 – but at nine billion miles away it is nearly 3 times further out than Pluto, until now considered the most distant planet...'This is the first object to be confirmed to be larger than Pluto in the Solar System,' said astronomer Michael Brown of the California Institute of Technology, who discovered the planet with two colleagues...The discovery of the new body will reopen the debate among astronomers about what actually constitutes a planet. The scientific community is even divided over whether Pluto, which was discovered in 1930, qualifies, as it is so small and distant.

Last year, scientists discovered a body called Sedna, eight billion miles away and 1,000 miles wide, which was proposed as a possible 10th planet. But Nasa calls Sedna a 'planetoid'...Today the world knows that Pluto is not unique. There are other Plutos, just further out in the solar system where they are a little harder to find.'

(King, 2005)

Figs.40, 41, 42, 43 & 44: The Anunnaqi: Top, Left- Right:
Enqi, Enlil, Ninti, **(Bottom)** *Nergal & Arishkegal*

27

York claims that the Anunnaqi, which are the supreme race of Extraterrestrials, came to earth Thousands of years ago to begin breeding a 'Vicegerent', whose purpose would be to work for them, which was completed with the birth of Adam or Adaba, 49,000 years ago. Fusing their own genes (DNA), with that of the Homo Erectus (Ape woman), they eventually produced the first 'Modern Man', whom the Bible refers to as Adam: Homo 'Sapien' Sapien (Intelligent Man). Credence is given to this theory by the sudden appearance or 'Sudden Genetic Jump' from Homo Erectus to Homo Sapien's within a few million years, without the existence of any intermediary or go-between species often been referred to as the 'Missing Link'. According to the Nuwaubian leader, this so-called 'Missing Link' was in actuality the result of intervention or Genetic Manipulation by the Anunnaqi. The Muslim Holy book, The Koran also corroborates this hypothesis by referring to Adam as 'Khlifah Fil Ard' or *"(God's) Successor in the Earth"* and Mankind as 'Abdullah' *"Slave or Servant of Allah"*, which corresponds perfectly with the Sumerian title given to early Man: "L.U.L.U AMELU", 'Primitive Worker', or Servant of the God's.

Let's see if this can be corroborated by another source, in this case Sumerian scholar Zecheria Sitchin:

> Then, faced with the need for manpower, resolved to obtain a Primitive Worker, the Nefilim saw a ready-made solution: to domesticate a suitable animal. The "animal" was available-but *Homo erectus* posed a problem. On the one hand, he was too intelligent and wild to become simply a docile beast of work. On the other hand, he had to be able to grasp and use tools of the Nefilim, walk and bend like them so that he could replace the gods in the fields and mines. He had to have better "brains" – not like those of the gods but enough to understand speech and commands and tasks allotted to him.
>
> (Sitchin, 1976, p: 307)

> A gradual process of domestication through generations of breeding and selection would not do. What was needed was a quick process, one that would permit "mass production" of the new workers. So the problem was posed to Ea, who saw the answer at once: to "imprint" the image of the gods on the being that already existed. The process that Ea recommended in order to achieve a quick evolutionary advancement of *Homo erectus* was, we believe, *genetic manipulation.*
>
> (Sitchin, 1976, p: 308)

> The contradiction, which has puzzled scholars and theologians alike, disappears once we realize that the biblical texts were condensation of the original Sumerian sources. These sources inform us that after trying to fashion a Primitive Worker by "mixing" apemen with animals, the gods concluded that the only mixture that would work would be between apemen and the Nefilim themselves. After several unsuccessful attempts, a "model" – Adapa/Adam – was made.
>
> (Sitchin, 1976, p: 316)

The 'Great' White Masters

York claims that Caucasians have been in contact with a group of Malevolent Inter-dimensional 'Cosmic Entities' called The Great White Masters or 'The Brotherhood of Light' through Mediums or 'Psychics', who could also be called European Prophets. These individuals such as Madam Helena. P. Blavaski, were provided with insight into information, which would later be been used for the technological advancement of the White race. Often referred to, as The Ashtar Command, the Ascended Masters or 'Cosmic Entities' are highly evolved beings who have continuously attempted to manipulate and influence the Destiny of Mankind for their own purposes and respective agendas through European Mystics or Prophets, which have included:

- **Nostradamus**
- **Madam Helena. P. Blavaski**
- **Zigrum & Maria Austish**
- **Aleister Crowley**
- **Edgar Cayce**

Some of the above were said to be some of those who made contact with the Aryan; Nordic & Hindu Cosmic Entities or Fallen Angels also called *"The Great White Masters"*, who are said to have been the inspiration behind the Nazi Dictator Adolph Hitler during the 1930s. In his book *"The Biggest Secret"*, David Icke also confirms Aleister Crowley's connection to Nazism through these entities:

> Crowley left his former tutor, MacGregor Mathers, a broken man as he embarked on psychic war against him. They both conjured up 'demons' to attack each other, but Mathers lost out. Such psychic wars are very much part of the Brotherhood armoury today. They war psychically with each other, but overwhelmingly with the population and people who are challenging their power. I have experienced such attacks myself and understand how they can kill people in this way. Crowley's communicators would also take over the psychics of Adolph Hitler and other architects of Nazism.
>
> (Icke, 1999, p: 243)

'Esoteric' activity amongst Europeans during the 19th century would eventually lead to the rise of The Nazi movement, which was also in close contact with Malevolent Aryan beings from Alderbaren, and numerous other Galactic entities such as: El-Morya & Lord Maitreya through 'Psychics'; Maria Austish and Zigrum, who were symbolically represented by the **Blond & Brunette Harlots**; Marilyn Monroe and Elizabeth Taylor, who helped channel through much of the information Caucasians have utilised for technological advancements since the 1930's.

In the book *"Are There (UFOs) Extraterrestrials In Your Midst?"* Scroll # 84, York states the following:

> Hitler Was In Contact With 2 Witches Who Were Also Psychics, Named Maria Austish And Zigrum Who Were Contacted By Beings From Alderbaren, Who Chose Hitler As Their Man On Earth…These Beings Called The Ashtar Command From Pleiades And Aldebaren Constellations.
> (York, 1995, p: 22)

Figs.45, 46, 47, 48, 49 & 50: European Psychics: Top, Left- Right:
Nostradamus, Madam Helena. P. Blavaski
(Bottom) *Zigrum (Marilyn Monroe), Maria Austish (Elizabeth Taylor) & Aleister Crowley*

Apparently the plan of the Malevolent 'Elohim' from Alderbaren was to supply the Nazis with technology to help them win the Second World War and establish complete world domination which would lead to a Thousand Year Reich, during which they would then set about breeding a "Master Race" of Nordics who would take over from the Germans, as the new "Masters" of the Humanity. York claims that they only made contact with Hitler, after first being rejected by the Americans, and were said to have been so angered by this, that they went back in time, and created a separate timeline, in order to make the Nazis actually win the War. In the Nuwaubian Religious manifesto, *"The Holy Tablets"*, York again confirms the relationship between Madam Helena. P. Blavaski, The Third Reich, & The Ashtar Command from Alderbarren:

> A woman named Madam Blavasky who was born under the name Helena Petrova Von Han, branched off, headed the Theosophical Society. She was a well known witch. Two witches who were also psychics, named Maria Austish, and Zigrum, the Thule Society and Madam Blavasky came together and selected Adolph Hitler in the year nineteen thirteen A.D., to be their contactee, or man on this planet Earth.
> They were contacted by the beings called the Ashtar Command from Pleiades and the Alderbaren constellations. The Ashtar Command are among many entities that come to Earth and have been circling above the Earth – for the most part invisible to the naked eye since the early nineteen fifties of the Gregorian Calendar. They both were humanoid and have less water in their bodies and are "pasty" in appearance.
> In the year nineteen fifty and two of the Gregorian calendar, crafts were logged as being seen over the White House in Washington D.C. There was a meeting held and Ashtar Command met with the late President Dwight David Eisenhower, at which time America was asked, "to lay down their arms."
> However, beings from the Planet Venus, Commander Valiant Thor, also called Val Thor, and his crew members Donn, Tanyia and Jill were present at this meeting also, and said don't trust the people from Alderbaren. These beings from Alderbaren became highly insulted after they were labelled "untrustworthy." They went back in time and had a meeting of psychics with the Thule Society led to what is called the Third Reich, which power still rules the world today.
>
> (York, 1995)

Figs.51, 52 & 53 Great White Masters: *Cha-Ara, Mon-Ka & Voltra*

Figs.54, 55, 56, 57, 58, 59, 60, 61 & 62: Great White Masters:
Top, Left- Right: *Saint Germain, Serapis, Soltec,* **(Middle)** *Merku, Sutko, Universal Mother*
(Bottom) *Lady Clarion, Esola & Kumad*

Figs.63, 64, 65, 66, 67, 68, 69 & 70: Top, Left- Right:
Kuthumi, Hilarion, Aleph,
(Middle) *Korton, El Mory, Hatton,*
(Bottom) *Ballerian & Love Star*

Fig.71 *Nikola Tesla*

According to York, another group of these Cosmic entities or White Angels have been attempting to manoeuvre Caucasians towards a more positive direction. One such Benevolent Incarnated being was said to have been 19th century genius Nikola Tesla, whom York says was an Incarnated Master from the Planet Venus. Tesla was responsible for a huge array of technologically advanced devices aimed at helping humanity, including the Alternating Current (A.C.), which revolutionised the use of electricity, and made the world a safer place, as well as a number of "Free Energy Devices" which he invented during the 1940s. One of his most outstanding inventions was said to be his infamous "Death Ray", which could render an entire Army helpless and end all Wars. It was feared that if this technology fell into the wrong hands, it could be used it to destroy America. Although the official account of Tesla's death was supposed to have been as a result of suicide, another far more radical theory exists which maintains that the inventor was rescued by fellow scientist Guglielmo Marconi, with the assistance of Aliens. Although this theory may sound preposterous, it is an explanation that many aficionados of the Tesla phenomenon stand by. One such adherent of this theory is author and scientist David Hatcher Childress who states in his book: *"The Fantastic Inventions of Nikola Tesla"*:

> In the most incredible scenario so-far, and one that may well be true, Tesla was induced to fake his own death, just as Marconi and many of the other scientists had done, and was taken, by special discoid craft, to Marconi's high-tech super city. Away from the outside world,…Who knows what they achieved? They were ten years ahead of the Americans in the anti-gravity technology. Could they have developed a discoid spacecraft in the early 1940s, and gone on to time travel machines and hyperspace drives?
>
> (Childress, 1993, p: 293)

To many people this all may sound completely far fetched, however the amount of information available on this subject is simply too much to ignore, especially when so much is being done to suppress the truth by the mainstream media. A considerable amount of 'Misinformation' has also been deliberately mixed with the truth of what's really occurring to keep the public in the dark. The 'Channelling' of information through 'Psychics' has assisted many cultures throughout history to acquire knowledge, which would have otherwise been completely beyond their reach.

Remote Viewing

During the so-called "Cold War", US Military Intelligence began utilizing 'Psychics' to help them locate suspected Russian Submarines suspected of being in American coastal waters, however due to the lack of efficiency of these traditional 'Psychics', the Military later began a more advanced programme of training teams of Psychics or Mediums who would be more effective in acquiring information. During the 1970s, a psychic by the name of Ingo Swann, began conducting research into *Altered States of Consciousness* (ASC), and later coined the term *'Remote Viewing'*, to describe the process of viewing Remote or Distant 'Persons, Places & Things, in Time & Space. Otherwise known as the **Stargate Project'**, Remote Viewing is currently headed by a team of researchers at Emory University, Altanta, Ga. According to Bobby Hemmit, Remote Viewing is a form of **Psychic Spying,** developed as a weapon to enable trained Psychics to focus on specific Coordinates, Photographs & Objects in order to; lock onto a required target, either in the distant Past or Future allowing the viewer to place him or herself within the actual point or place of origin. Remote Viewing has many similarities to Psychometry or *"Object Reading"*, from which the word Psychic is derived. However with Remote Viewing, this ability of Extrasensory Perception (ESP) is enhanced to a far greater level. For example, it is said that by merely looking at a photograph of Martian surface, a trained Remote Viewer can actually mentally Project his or herself to that Planet. Or in the case of objects from the past, the Viewer can actually lock into that point in history to view the events during that period as they happened, no matter how far back in time. Say a bomb were to go off on board an Aeroplane, all a Remote Viewer needs to do is touch debris from the explosion, and they will instantly know where the bomb was placed, and trace its origin. Former Military Intelligence Remote Viewing trainer, Major Ed Dames, claims to have actually seen what Jesus of 2,000 years ago looked like, by simply locking onto his Frequency. This is said to be done by tuning into what is called *"The Universal Matrix"* from which all knowledge in the Universe is accessible, and may possibly be similar to accessing the fabled 'Akashic Records'. Indeed, much of the information taught by Malachi York, which has challenged accepted historical paradigms, cannot be found in any conventional books, and may therefore be the result of "Channelling" information from the Ancient Masters or Elders, whom York claims speak through him, which is as equally astonishing as much of the information obtained by "Remote Viewers".

The following are some of the explanations, which have been provided to York by these Masters to answer many historical enigmas:

> **The Pig,** (Wild Boar) has no origin because it is a genetically bred creature, grafted from The Rat (Rodent), Cat (Feline) & Dog (Canine) by Pharaoh Zoser or Djosr during Egypt's 3rd Dynasty, with the assistance of his student Imhotep, to help Prophet Abraham to clean the Filth & Disease

ridden Canaanite (Caucasian) inhabitants of the Caucus Mountains of North-Eastern Europe.

- **Atlantis,** was an actual civilisation, which sat directly between where the East coast of America, was once joined with the West coast of Africa (currently the Caribbean). And was destroyed as a result of Nuclear War, between the Anunnaqi and Reptilians, which triggered a 'Continental Split' & Ice Age.

- **The Pyramids,** of Egypt were built from the 'Top', with the use of 'Levitation' by the Pharaohs, and the stones were cut to such close precision by the use of 'Laser Beams'. York claims that the Freemasonic allusion to the Master builders cutting stones *"Without The Strike of a Hammer, or The Blow of an Axe"*, is referring to this procedure.

- **The Face on Mars,** is in fact that of Adam, which was originally used as a monument to designate the successful completion of the first "Homo Sapian" (Adam), being bread by The Anunnaqi.

- **The Earth is Hollow,** and has a central Sun, falsely called the Earth's Core, Which has an entry point at the North Pole, inside of which there exist several Continents, inhabited by advanced races of beings, some of whom once lived on the surface of the planet, and others who regularly visit from other planets.

In their groundbreaking book: *"Forbidden Archaeology: The Hidden History of the Human Race",* which also challenges many of the traditional beliefs held by Historians, Scientists & Authors Michael A. Cremo and Richard L. Thompson confirm that the actual source of their Historical insight is their Spiritual Master:

> Richard Thompson and I are members of the Bhaktivedanta Institute, a branch of the International Society for Khrishna Conciousness that studies the relationship between modern science and the world view expressed in Vedic literature. This institute was founded by **our spiritual master**, His Divine Grace A.C. Bhaktivedanta Swami, who encouraged us to critically examine the prevailing account of human origins and the method by which it was established. From the Vedic literature, we derive the idea that the human race is of great antiquity. To conduct systematic research into the existing scientific literature on human antiquity, we expressed the Vedic idea in the form of theology that various humanlike and apelike beings coexisted for a long time.
>
> (Cremo & Thompson, 1993, introduction)

Many of the illustrations found in York's books are said to be the actual faces of those whom he has actually seen through the 'Eyes of the Masters'. Incidentally these images have been the source of much criticism by detractors, whom have label the Nuwaubian leader a 'Black Supremacist' for depicting all of the images in his books as Black. Although it cannot be verified whether all of these individuals looked the way they are depicted by

York, this condemnation seems unfair because York does not portray everybody in his books as Black, for example many historical figures such as Julius Caesar, Mark Anthony, King Herod & Alexander the Great, are not depicted as being Negroid, simply because that is not what they were. However, in cases where there is strong historical evidence to substantiate that they were Negroid, York has every right to portray these individuals as such. The illustrated Watch Tower Bible, published by the Jehovah's Witness Church, has since its first release in 1978, been translated from English into 128 languages, and printed into over **53,000,000** copies Worldwide. This illustrated Bible contains images of the most prominent Old & New Testament Biblical characters from Adam to Jesus, **ALL** as Caucasians. It even portrays the ancient Egyptians as Europeans, yet nobody has ever called the Jehovah's Witness "White Supremacist" for still depicting people who have now been historically proven to be Negroid, such as the Ancient Egyptians as White. **CLEARLY THERE IS A DOUBLE STANDARD BEING APPLEIED HERE**.

Figs.72, 73, 74 & 75: Fictitious Representations: Top, Left- Right:
Adam & Eve, Noah **(Middle)** *Moses* **(Bottom)** *King David & Jesus Christ*

Another claim for which York has received much criticism is his assertion that he is from the Planet Rizq, in the 19th Galaxy of Illiyuwn, said to be the home World of the Anunnaqi, first made mention of in several of his books, most notably: *"Mission Earth and the Extraterrestrial Involvement"* Scroll # 82. In fact the term *"Man from Planet Rizq"* coined as slur by the Media, actually originates from York's own publication of the same name, which showed the Nuwaubian leader being 'Beamed' down from a Space Craft on its front cover.

The explanation of York's body being inhabited by spiritual entities from other Planets is fairly acceptable from an Esoteric perspective, and therefore cannot entirely be ruled out whether Illiyuwn is actually the home galaxy of the Anunnaqi who are supposedly in communication with the Nuwaubian leader. Contrary to Media claims, York is widely acknowledged to have taught about he's involvement with the Extra Terrestrials as far back as the early 1970s, and has consistently appeared in numerous publications with Space Crafts in his foreground.

Figs.76, 77, 78 & 79: Extraterrestrial Involvement: Top & Bottom, Left- Right: *Various images of York from early publications, with the consistent presence of Space Crafts in foreground*

Fig.80 Cover of York's publication 'Man from Planet Rizq'

Nevertheless, for York to actually claim to having been 'Physically' born on another Planet, namely; the 'Planet Rizq' is an entirely different matter, especially after declaring that he was born (on earth) in 1945. If this is indeed what the Nuwaubian leader is now claiming, we would suggest that he seek Psychological help. But is this really what York is claiming, or simply yet another ploy, by his detractors and the Media to discredit him?

On Sunday April 20th 1997, reporter Judy Bailey of the Macon Telegraph wrote an article entitled *"From Planet Rizq to Putnam County"*, in which she first made reference to York's assertion that the 'Being' occupying his body was from the Planet Rizq in the 19th Galaxy of Illyuwn. Without really understanding or taking the time to find out what York meant by titling his book ***"The Man from Planet Rizq"***, Judy Bailey wrote the article with the express purpose of ridiculing and defaming the Nuwaubian leader, by making him appear crazy to the public for teaching about the existence of Extra-terrestrial life on earth. The media soon picked up on Ms Bailey's lead, and released plethora of negative articles designed to discredit the Nuwaubians, in the eyes of the public. Since her article, literally every single article written about the Nuwaubian leader has made the false reference to him being from another Planet.

It is therefore clear that the Media's only agenda has been to make York look crazy for teaching about the existence of U.F.O.s, yet fail to make mention of many famous and influential individuals who who have also admitted to believing in the existence of Aliens & U.F.O.s.

The following is a list of people who have publicly acknowledged their belief in the existence of Aliens or Extra-Terrestrials.

- **Dwight D. Eisenhower,** *Former U.S. President*
- **Harry. S. Truman,** *Former U.S. President*
- **Jimmy Carter,** *Former U.S. President*
- **Robert. F. Kennedy,** *Former U.S. President*
- **John Lennon,** *Founder of the Beatles*
- **Rod Sterling,** *Creator of the Twilight Zone*
- **Carl Sagan,** *Scientist & Cosmologist*
- **Bernard Oliver,** *Founder of S.E.T.I. Research Centre*

- **John Billingham, Chief of *S.E.T.I.* & *NASA Research***

Despite having expressed their belief in Aliens & U.F.O.s, none of these individuals have received anywhere near the type of negative criticism as the Nuwaubian leader from the media. In his book: *"The Immortal Birth of Allah: Rise of the Five Percenters"*, 5% author and former Moorish Science Temple & Nation of Islam affiliate, Allah Jihad also makes the following statement regarding York's Extra Terrestrial assertions:

> Dwight York has taught his followers throughout his books that he calls scrolls, he stated that he was born in 1945 in Omdurman, Sudan. But today, his impure thoughts has left him chemically unbalanced, he has not even changed his birth date but his location of where he was born, the following is a quote of this Dwight, "It was March 16, 1970 A.D. That I arrived, when Earth Astronomers thought they cited a comet, which they called Bennet. I arrived like a thief in the night from the Galaxy called Illyuwn. For it was his time to come in flesh…I know you think I'm nuts but in time the whole world will know who I really am".
>
> (Jihad, 2004)

Figs.81 & 82 York Detractor: Left- Right: *Five Percenter; Allah Jihad Book: 'The Immortal Birth of Allah'*

How could York, possibly be claiming to be born in 1970, which would make him 37 years old, and therefore mean he formed his first organisation whilst still a baby! York's reference to his arrival in 1970 was the year in which one of his 'Etheric' personalities arrived on earth, and was mistaken for a Comet and named 'Bennet', by Earth Astronomers. Due to the nature of York's teachings, it is so easy to make him appear crazy by quoting him out of context, however York's claim to having 'Arrived' on earth in 1970 is not new, but many of York's enemies; who neither care, nor understand the depth of his teachings, often attempt to discredit him by quoting his words entirely out of context. Therefore lets quote him in his own words to clarify this issue. On an audio-recorded lecture in 1994 entitled *"Why did we use Islam"*, York stated the following:

> Upon arrival here **'Ethericly', as Bennet in 1970, and the taking of the control of this body, of this individual that was 25 years old**, that was not of much use to us...
>
> (Bar El Haady, 1994)

Clearly, York is not claiming to have been born on another Planet, but rather that his body was 'Possessed' in 1970 by a being whom had arrived on Earth 'Etherically', in other words 'Spiritually' from another Planet. Therefore, every time a newspaper or online article makes reference to York having been born on the planet 'Rizq', they are completely inaccurate, and should be dismissed as such.

Doomsday Predictions & Detractors

York's strange mix of U.F.O-logy and Egyptology, have also come under scrutiny in a book released in 2001 by Brenda Denzler, entitled: *"The Lure of the Edge: Scientific Passions, Religious Beliefs, and the Pursuit of UFOs"*, which refers to York as an ***"Extraterrestrial prophet"***:

> As far as active appropriation of the UFO myth goes, one African-American religious sect, the Nuwaubian Nation, follows the teachings of "extraterrestrial prophet" Malachi Z. York." I was told by a white couple... teachings include UFO and alien material. One is the Holy Tabernacle Church in Greensboro, North Carolina. The other is the Nuwaubian Nation of Moors, a group headquartered in Eatonton, Georgia, which "combines African-American self-determination, Egyptian symbolism and a belief...
>
> (Denzler, 2001)

York, ever the enthusiast for making outlandish statements has not done himself any favours by completely exposing himself to ridicule and further disapproval, by going on record and predicting a series of catastrophic disasters which have been 'Spectacularly' inaccurate. Most famous of which was an event predicted to have occurred on May 5th 2000, during a supposed planetary alignment. Although many other religious leaders have in the past, made similar predictions which have not come true, such as Minister Louis Farrakhan's erroneous prediction that major events mentioned in the Bible would happened in the year 2000. However no one else has done so, as frequently as York. Which raises the question of whether he purposely plays into the hands of his enemies by providing them with ammunition to discredit him.

Since his arrest and subsequent humiliation at the hands of Federal Authorities in May 2002, the number of York's detractors and critics has dramatically increased. Unfortunately for York, this relentless onslaught is made all the more easier by his followers who appear to lack either the initiative or basic understanding of their own Doctrine with which to appropriately defend their leader. Which is mainly as a result of the present Nuwaubian's over reliance upon the constant release of new literature, since the launch of 'Right Knowledge' during 1990s. This has led to many of his followers becoming little more than 'Intellectual Pigs', requiring more and more abstract information to satisfy their insatiable appetite for new books. In other words, many of them have become 'Knowledge Junkies', always in need of a new Fix, without taking the time to carefully study and 'Digest' the content of what is being taught by their leader. This lethargy, on the part of some of York's followers, has in turn led to a deluge of Anti-York articles and websites, many sponsored by members of the 5% Nation of Gods & Earth's. One such site is said to have been started by, Fahiym el-Bashir Allah who can be contacted at: BooksOnYork@aol.com. This individual's articles have often actually quoted York's in his own words from either his books or audio recorded lectures such as: *"Theology vs. Factology: Leave My Stuff Alone"*, in which it stated:

> "You can see by my presence the world is tumbling. There's earthquakes! And I tell you today at the alignment of the equinox on May 5, 2000 – and I've been saying this since 1970, you will be there to witness my presence as The Lord in flesh. You Gonna see the Dreadful Day...I'm Bringing in the Judgment of the world."
>
> (York 1998, cited by booksonyork@aol.com)

The article goes on to ridicule York for nothing happening on the day he predicted a major disaster! Although predictions do not necessarily always have to be 100% accurate, as anybody can make a prediction based upon events of the past and present occurrences, (in other words, predictions are a kind of rough guess.) Yet why would York repeatedly make predictions, without most of them coming true, and still expect to be taken seriously? Or is it simply that York does not care what those outside his organisation think of him, because he is certain that one day he will be proven right? After all, if York was simply a conman as many claim, why repeatedly go out on a limb, by risking your reputation and credibility? Why not simply keep silent about issues that cannot be verified, to keep more followers and money coming in? Are these really the actions of a lying charlatan or someone with enough conviction in what he is teaching to accept ridicule? However there is also the third other possibility that Malachi York may in fact be Crazy as many of his critics already suspect.

Extraterrestrial Hoax & New Age Hustlers

Like York, many other authors have been challenging established views of what have traditionally been held as historical and scientific facts as a direct result of knowledge acquired through 'Channelling' from Aliens.

Nevertheless, contrary to the theory of *"Ancient Gods and Incarnated Masters"* being the inspiration and source of man's earliest advanced civilizations and cultures, there has recently emerged a new theory, which challenges the basis of this entire hypothesis. In a book entitled *"The Stargate Conspiracy"* authors Pinckett and Prince claim that the whole theory of Gods & Celestial Masters are all an elaborate "Con" thought up as part of the 'New World Order', to fool people into accepting the Satanic leadership of a strange group called the *"Mysterious Nine"*. The book was first made public by a staff writer from the same Five Percenter; Anti-York group mentioned above. In it they accuse The Nuwaubians, whom they describe as *"a kind of Afro-centric band of Raelians"*, of being victims of this "Con". Apparently it all began after the release of a book by James Hurtak entitled, *"The Keys of Enoch"* released in 1973, which supposedly marked a significant year for the 'Mysterious Nine', because this was to be the year in which they chose to focus Humanity's attention. The plot was that, 30 years later in the year 2003, a major event or events would occur to mark the coming of these Masters to rule humanity. The book goes on to name a number of leading authors of so-called "New Age" literature such as Graham Hancock, Robert Bauval and many others, as either knowing or unknowing proponents of the hoax.

Coincidently 2003 is the same year Dr. Malachi. Z. York indicated as being the date, when the Space Crafts would start arriving to begin picking up those chosen. According to the Anti-Nuwaubian staff writer, all of this is just a clandestine attempt by the CIA to pull off one of the biggest hoaxes in history, similar to H. G. Welles' social experiment in 1938, *"The War of The Worlds"*. The aim of the "Con" this time, is to see whether people will actually accept a worldwide fascist "Dictatorial" Government in the guise of 'Ancient Gods'.

This hypothesis is very interesting, and although we do not agree with most of the "flyers" put out by the authors of BooksOnYork@aol.com, this theory does raise a lot of interesting questions. Sadly, this supposition falls flat on its face for two reasons. First, it is only a tiny minority of predominately white, middle/upper class educated people in the Western World, i.e. Europe, North America, Israel & Australia, who are familiar with books discussing this "New Age" phenomenon. Secondly what makes the authors Pinckett and Prince believe that the "Powers That Be" need to trick anybody into believing anything, when they already run the world under what is fast becoming Fascist "Dictatorial" rule.

Nevertheless, getting back to The Nuwaubians and their involvement to this apparent "Con", the author was not clear whether he/she considered

York part of the conspiracy or not, therefore we will not comment any further on this issue.

Fig.83 Robert Stacey McCain

This brings us to an additional "flyer" authored by another so-called staff writer from the people at 'BooksOnYork'. The author in question is R. S. McCain, author of an article entitled: *"The Cult of the Jailhouse Messiah"*. Although this group have produced some very interesting, and thought provoking articles questioning aspects of York's teachings, unfortunately this is not one. Whilst conducting our research, we learned that this article's author R. S. McCain, was none other than Right Wing, Maryland, Virginia based, Assistant National Editor of the Washington Times, & co-author of the anti-Democratic diatribe *"Donkey Cons: Sex, Crime, and Corruption in the Democratic Party"*, **Robert Stacey McCain**. McCain is also author of numerous Anti-Nuwaubian articles, including the racist and completely factually inaccurate: *"Nuwaubian Nightmare"*, dated On June 2nd, 2002.

In he's ostensible incarnation as 'Staff Writer', for 'BooksOnYork', Robert Stacey McCain joins forces with the 5% Nation's Fahiym el-Bashir Allah in the article: *"The Cult of the Jailhouse Messiah"* which stated:

"I was never a member of York's cult. I doubt he'd welcome a White, Christian Conservative, I am a journalist, and wrote an article about the Nuwaubians".

This statement reveals McCain's true motive for writing the article, as one of the new generation of aggressive Conservative Racially motivated thinkers in America, fighting what Patrick J. Buchanan, first termed the so-called 'Cultural War' in his book *"Death of the West"* in 2002. McCain holds many similar views to a number of other **Xenophobic** 'Right-Wing' reporters such as the Atlanta Journal-Constitution's Bill Osinski & Fox News' Bill O'Reilly, who are bitterly opposed to:

- **Equal Opportunities for Ethnic Minorities**
- **Gay Rights**
- **Relaxed Immigration Laws**
- **Affirmative Action**
- **Subsidised Education**
- **Affordable Healthcare for the Underprivileged**
- **Religious Tolerance**

Figs.84 & 85: Neo Conservative Nuwaubian Detractor: Left- Right:
Robert Stacey McCain & book: 'Donkey Cons'

Secondly, there is absolutely no evidence, which supports McCain's claim that York did not allow Whites to join his organisation. On the contrary, the Nuwaubians have many Caucasian affiliates, in addition to the numerous Tour groups comprised of White visitors to the group's Egyptian style complex, 'Tama-re' in Georgia. Is it simply that being a *"White Conservative"* it would be McCain who would not feel comfortable around so many Positive and Productive Black people?

Next he stated; **"Anyone could recognize in the quasi-Egyptian imagery of the group's monuments near Eatonton and adoption of Arabic names, et cetera, that York was combining many of the beliefs of black Muslims with a pseudo-mystic strain of Afro-centrism."**

Although an interesting analysis, what does it really mean? The group's monuments express *"quasi-Egyptian imagery"* because that is what they wanted to express, it's called innovation and human beings have been doing it for centuries, all cultures are based upon borrowing from others. Nobody ever criticizes the design of the US dollar, which also features so-called *"quasi-Egyptian imagery"*, with its Egyptian, Hebrew and Celtic symbolism, or even the positioning of the Obelisk or 'Cleopatra's Needle' in the US Capital, Washington D.C. (which was incidentally stolen from Africa), as being *"quasi-Egyptian imagery"*.

The supposed: *"adoption of Arabic names, et cetera"*, is because York was the leader of an Islamic/Hebraic organisation, called the Nubian Islamic Hebrews for over 25 years before arriving in Georgia, which means many of the young people in the group were actually born Muslims. Therefore there would be a slim chance they retain their Arabic names, as the following quote by York himself further clarifies:

> We Went Through All The Schools Of Religion, That's Why We Have An Understanding Of All Aspects Of Religions. That's What You Refer To As *"Name Changes"*... **Some People Were Born With Arabic Names** And Some Who Didn't Get There's Legally Changed...
>
> (York, 1996, p: 111)

"York was combining many of the beliefs of black Muslims with a pseudo-mystic strain of Afro centrism."
During the 1980's York headed the second largest 'Black Muslim' movement in America, during which time he taught a very potent form of Afrocentricism to his followers. It would therefore stand to reason that his teachings reflect this. So by whose definition does this make it Pseudo (false) Afro-centrism; a White Christian Conservative's?

"In Short, "Nuwaubianism" is a ridiculously bad mix of ridiculously bad ideas" So Let's get this Right; Robert Stacey McCain thinks Ancient Egyptian, Hebrew, Islamic & Afrocentric cultures are *"ridiculously bad ideas"*, well that figures, after all he is a "White Christian Conservative". Unfortunately for the Nuwaubians, all of these *"ridiculously bad ideas"* have their roots in Africa, and are therefore various aspects of the Nuwaubian's own African Heritage.

Figs.86, 87 & 88: Stolen African Symbolism: Top, Left- Right: *Egyptian Pyramid on Back of US Dollar Bill* **(Bottom)** *Egyptian Obelisk in US Capital, Washington D.C.*

Next he states: ***"What stunned me, as a writer, was that York could attract and keep followers on the basis of a body of writings that were nothing but incoherent gibberish".***

Ok let's stop beating around the bush. Anyone with the least bit of education will realize that many of York's publications are not aimed at an academic readership. In fact, York has not released a complete book in years, many of the scrolls his organisation publishes are in actual fact the minutes from Question and Answer classes or lectures given by York, with photographs and illustrations added later. A great deal of what York teaches can be found elsewhere if researched hard enough. However, what he does do exceptionally well in his books is summarise a lot of abstract information in a form that ordinary people without much education can understand. Nevertheless, it should not be assumed that York does not posses the ability to produce academic work; on the contrary, the Nuwaubian leader holds a PhD, which more than enables him to produce material of a very high academic standard. In fact, many of York's former followers have gone on to acquire Graduate and Post Graduate qualifications as a result of initially reading his early publications. To further emphasise the profound effect York's teachings have had upon the education of Black inner city kids let's quote author Amiyr Abu Hamin, who beautifully, yet succinctly summarises York's achievements in his thesis: *"Leader Malachi York of Nuwaubians, GUILTY on All Counts of Uppityness!"* 3:

> The Nuwaubians...provided psychological support to many of the Black communities' forgotten left-behind mentally challenged, provided a forum for channeling anger, frustration, apathy and intellectual development among many of the inner city poor, provided a Black imagery in books, magazines and tapes to counteract the prevalent white racist theory of racial superiority thus providing an outlet for racial balancing, provided stability to the unstable and education to the labeled 'un-educationable'. Nearly all Nuwaubians are well spoken, educated and articulate and that is not how most came into the organization. Nuwaubian members had begun to get involved in local Black organizations and participate as active members in the collective community. Moreover, its numbers have appeared in the ranks of the NAACP, Operation PUSH, SCLC and the National Action Network.
>
> (Abu Hamin, 2004)

Suicide Cult

Let's not forget that the 'Dr', in Dr. York's name represents his PhD in Theology and Linguistics, obtained from the American University of Cairo, Egypt, therefore he certainly knows what he's talking about, however it's just how he chooses to teach it, which confuses many. In a country such as the United States, where good education comes with a very high price tag, Poor Blacks, & Latinos who are so often victims of what can be best described as "America's Education Apartheid System", have actually benefited educationally from York's Nuwaubian literature.

Nevertheless, **"WHAT STUNNED US"** was why a White Christian Right-Wing Conservative, should take such interest in what a group of ***"black Muslims with a pseudo-mystic strain of Afro centrism"*** who use *"quasi-Egyptian imagery"*, were doing on their own property?

Robert Stacey McCain then continued, ***"And that's when the idea hit me: York didn't want intelligent or educated followers. York wanted ignorant slaves – people so stupid that they would do whatever he told them to do. So his Gibberish Gospel was perfectly suited to the task. York attracted followers who apparently didn't even object when he switched his doctrine from a heretical sort of Islam to an Afro centric UFO cult, with bits of Masonry and Egyptology thrown in along the way."***

This is where Robert Stacey McCain is wrong again, and must be corrected. It is a known fact that every few years York's turnover of followers change. You see, if R. S. McCain had done just a little research into the group's past, he would be aware of the fact that most of York's original followers who followed him when he taught the So-called *"heretical sort of Islam"* as he calls it, and he would know what real Islam is being a "White Christian Conservative", left the group when the doctrine changed to Hebrewism between 1991-93. In fact, York dismantled what was then the largest Independent Black Muslim Movement in the World, with Hundreds of Thousands of followers World Wide. It has been estimated that at the height of York's influence in the mid 1990s, he had over a Million followers. Most of the followers York has today calling themselves 'Nuwaubians', have only joined the group during the past 5 to 7 years, which is why many of them often don't know what they are talking about simply because they have "inherited" a doctrine they barely understand the history of.

"York attracted followers who apparently didn't even object when he switched his doctrine from a heretical sort of Islam to an Afro-centric UFO cult". York has been teaching a "Fusion" of Afro-centrism and UFO-logy since the late 1960's, McCain should go back and research the Old publications.

"with bits of Masonry and Egyptology thrown in along the way." Any Freemason, if they are honest will have to admit that the basis of Masonry was stolen from the Egyptian Mystery System, which make Masonic teachings no different from that of the Nuwaubian Masonry & Shrinery.

AND THAT'S WHEN THE IDEA HIT US, when McCain used the word "Slaves" in reference to York's followers. What's really getting to Mr McCain, and others like him, is the fact that all these people who call themselves Nuwaubians are Blacks trying to re-establish a cultural identity for themselves, instead of following their former Slave Master's false religion of so-called Western (White Supremacist) Christianity.

"York's sexual behaviour is not surprising given the history of modern cults" Oh by that does Robert Stacey McCain mean all of those Cults founded by his fellow White Christian Conservatives, such as:

- *The Mormon Church*, **Founded by 'Prophet' Joseph Smith (White Christian)**

- *Jehovah's Witness*, **Founded by Joseph Rutherford (White Christian)**

- *The Branch Davidian Church*, **Founded by David Koresh (White Christian)**

- *The People's Temple*, **Founded by Rev. Jim Jones (White Christian)**

- *The Family*, **Founded by Pastor David Berg (White Christian)**

- *The Hale Bopp Cult*, **Founded by Marshall. H. Applewhite (White Christian)**

The allegation of York's bizarre sexual practices as a cult leader is a regular occurring theme of anti-Nuwaubian literature, although to date no solid evidence of such behaviour has ever been produced. Another such site which also accuses the Nuwaubians of being a "Doomsday" suicide cult like those mentioned above is a site entitled: *"So Sick Knowledge"* 4, in which the author states the following:

> This organization is by definition a doomsday cult, although they claim not to be, and the spaceship addition is reminiscent of the suicide cult Heaven's Gate. However in a recent speech Dr York explained that they are not a suicide cult because black people are genetically programmed to survive. He then named some mass suicide cults like Heaven's Gate, Waco, and Jim Jones' The People's Temple, claiming they were all white groups who killed themselves. A quick analysis tells any intelligent person that the alien doctor is completely wrong, and that Jim Jones mass suicide consisted of over 900 people almost all of whom were black.
>
> (So Sick Knowledge, 2001, p: 2)

Figs.89, 90, 91, 92, 93 & 94: White Christian Cult Leaders: Top, Left- Right: *'Prophet' Joseph Smith, Joseph Rutherford & David Koresh* **(Bottom)** *Rev. Jim Jones, Pastor David Berg & Marshall. H. Applewhite*

It is interesting that the author should choose Jim Jones' "People's Temple", as an example of which to point out that: *"A quick analysis tells any intelligent person that the alien doctor is completely wrong, and that Jim Jones mass suicide consisted of over 900 people almost all of whom were black".*

Well the first part of this statement is at least true and Jim Jones' 'People's Temple' did consist of a large majority of black followers. Although Black people are perfectly capable of committing mass suicide, nevertheless is this assertion true, and did the Black members of The People's Temple willingly commit Mass Suicide? Before you answer, let's first examine what the media didn't want the public to know, by quickly refreshing our memories with the official story told by the International Mainstream Media, after all, any intelligent person should know that the media always tells the truth, right?

Rev. Jim Jones & The People's Temple

Rev. Jim Jones was a California based Christian preacher who started The People's Temple in 1965. Proclaimed to be a Multi-Racial Community, which rose out of the racial hostility of 1960's America, The People's Temple was based in the heart of San Francisco, California, and attracted large numbers of the Poor Socially Conscious, predominately Black & Hispanic, Women and Children. Jim Jones' message was simple; racial harmony and human fellowship. The bulk of Jones' congregation was mainly comprised of the Elderly, Ex-Convicts, Single Mother's, Patients from Psychiatric institutions as well as hundreds of foster children, in other word's individual society didn't care about. Jones' work was even commended by Christian missionaries from World Vision, the International Evangelical Organization, for his outstanding missionary duties in Urban areas. At the height of his popularity, Rev. Jones was even afforded Superstar status, and often courted by Celebrities and Politicians alike.

The son of former Nation of Islam leader Elijah Muhammad, Imaam Warith Deen Muhammad, in a cynical bid to gain Mainstream 'White' approval even formed a mutual fellowship alliance between himself and the Christian Cult leader, prior to the Jones Town, tragedy.

Some years later, the good Reverend Jones then decided to re-locate his entire congregation *en masse* to rural Guyana in South America, to establish a religious and "Socialist Utopia" which would be named 'Jonestown'. Sadly, not long after arriving in Guyana, things started to go wrong for the movement. In the face of mounting pressure from Guyanese authorities and relatives of his followers in the US, Rev. Jones decided that the only course of action would be to take his own life. Then apparently for reasons unknown, he decided to offer his predominately Black followers Kool Aid laced with **Strychinine** (poison), which according to the 'official story', they all willingly drank, fully aware that it would not only kill them, but also take the lives of their children. Therefore it would appear that Dr. York's assertion that there have never been any Black suicide cults to have killed themselves is inaccurate, at least from the 'official' account by the media, which every intelligent person knows is always the truth.

Figs.95 & 96 Good Friends: Left- Right: *Cover of Bilalian News showing Imam Warith Deen Muhammad's Alliance with Jim Jones & Jim Jones Speaking at Nation Of Islam Rally*

Nonetheless, is there an unofficial account of what happened to the members of Jim Jones' The People's Temple, and if so, what does it say really happened???

The Truth about Jonestown 'Mass Suicide'

Since the so-called Jonestown mass suicide over 30 years ago, increasing evidence has emerged which contradicts the accepted account told by the Media agencies at the time. For example, Malachi York asserts that the inhabitants of the Jonestown Community were murdered as part of a Multi-Layered conspiracy. The following is an excerpt taken from the Holy Tabernacle Ministries bulletin entitled: *"Prophecy Fulfilled"*, revised edition # 15, released in 1993, in which York stated:

> The Whole Jim Jones Mass Suicide Situation Was A Conspiracy. It Was Reported That All The Suicide Victims Had Taken A Drug Called **"Strychinine"**. If You Do Any Research On This Drug You Will See That It Attacks Your Nervous System, Causing Hysteria, Twitching, Jumping, Convulsions, Arching Of The Back And Rigidity Of Facial Muscles. Therefore, There Is No Way The Victim's Bodies Could Have Been In The Positions They Were In When They Were Found, Nor Would They Have Died So Quickly.
>
> The Victims Were Said To Be Found Laying Straight Or Relatively Straight On The Floor, However Because The Drug They Were Said To Have Taken Would Have Had Them Moving All Over The Place, They Could Not Have Died By Way Of That Drug. Not Only That, Further Evidence Showed That Most Of The People Died From (Gunshot) Wounds. **Does This Sound Like Mass Suicide?**
>
> (Bar El Haady, 1993, p: 14)

Clearly from York's assessment, the Jonestown community did not die as result of so-called voluntary 'Mass Suicide', but more like Mass Murder. Nevertheless let us not only take York's explanation of the events, why not find out from an independent source how the predominately Black followers of Rev. Jim Jones actually met their gruesome deaths in Guyana. According to Historian & Political analyst John Judge in his thesis *"The Black Hole in Guyana: The Untold Story of the Jonestown Massacre"*, the so-called 'official' story was all part of an elaborate World-Wide cover-up, involving International Media agencies, and what follows is a more accurate account of what actually took place:

> Dr. Mootoo, the top Guyanese pathologist, was at Jonestown within hours after the massacre. Refusing the assistance of U.S. pathologists, he accompanied the teams that counted the dead, examined the bodies, and worked to identify the deceased. While the American press screamed about the "Kool-Aid Suicides," Dr. Mootoo was reaching a much different opinion.
>
> There are certain signs that show the types of poisons that lead to the end of life. Cyanide blocks the messages from the brain to the muscles by changing body chemistry in the central nervous system. Even the "involuntary" functions like breathing and heartbeat get mixed neutral signals. It is a painful death, breath coming in spurts. The other muscles

spasm, limbs twist and contort. The facial muscles draw back into a deadly grin, called "cyanide rictus". All these telling signs were absent in the Jonestown dead. Limbs were limp and relaxed, and the few visible faces showed no sign of distortion.

(Judge, 1993, p: 129-130)

At the Jonestown site, survivors describe a special group of Jones' followers who were allowed to carry weapons and money, and to come and go from the camp. These people were all white, mostly males. They ate better and worked less than the others, and they served as an armed guard to enforce discipline, control labor and restrict movement......................The dead were 90% women, and 80% Blacks. It is unlikely that men armed with guns and modern crossbows would give up control and willingly be injected with poisons. It is much more likely that they forced nearly 400 people to die by injection, and then assisted in the murder of 500 more who attempted to escape. One survivor clearly heard cheering 45 minutes after the massacre.

(Judge, 1993, p: 133)

Fig.97 Investigator: *John Judge*

Plans to inhabit the jungles of Guyana's interior with cheap labor date back to 1919. Resources buried there are among the richest in the world, and include manganese, diamonds, gold, bauxite and uranium. Forbes Burnham, the Prime Minister, had participated in a scheme to repatriate Blacks from the UK to work in the area. Like all earlier attempts it failed.

Once chosen the site was leased and worked on by a select crew of Temple members in preparation for the arrival of the body of the church. The work was done in cooperation with Burnham and the U.S. Embassy there. But if these were idealists seeking a better life, their arrival in 'Utopia' was a strange welcome. Piled into buses in San Francisco, they had driven to Florida. From there, Pan American charter planes delivered them to Guyana. When they arrived at the airport, the Blacks were taken off the plane, bound and gagged. The deception had finally been stripped bare of all pretense. The Blacks were so isolated and controlled that neighbours as close as five miles from the site did not know that Blacks lived at Jonestown. The only public appearances seen in Guyana were white.

According to survivors' reports, they entered a virtual slave labor camp. Worked for 16 to 18 hours daily, they were forced to live in cramped quarters on minimum rations, usually rice, bread and sometimes rancid meat.

Infractions of the rules or disloyalty led to increasingly harsh punishments, including forced drugging, sensory isolation in an underground box, physical torture and public sexual rape and humiliation.

Perhaps the motto a Jonestown should have been the same as the one at Auschwitz, developed by Larry Schacht's namesake, Dr. Hjalmar Schacht, the Nazi Minister of economics, "Arbeit Macht Frei," or "Work Will Make You Free." Guyana even considered setting up an "Auschwitz-like museum" at the site, but abandoned the idea.

By this point, Jones had amassed incredible wealth. Press estimates ranged from $26 million to $2 billion, including bank accounts, foreign investments and real estate. Accounts were set up worldwide by key members often in the personal name of certain people in the Temple. Much of this money, listed publicly after the massacre, disappeared mysteriously. It was a fortune too large to have come from membership alone. The receivership set up by the government settled on a total of $10 million. Of special interest were the Swiss bank accounts…To comprehend this well-financed, sinister operation, we must abandon the myth that this was a religious commune and study instead the history that led to its formation. Jonestown was an experiment, part of a 30-year programme called MK-ULTRA, the CIA and military intelligence code name for mind control. A close study of Senator's Ervin's 1974 report, "Individual Rights and the Government's Role in Behaviour Modification," shows that these agencies had certain "target populations" in mind, for both individual and mass mind control. Blacks, women, prisoners and elderly, the young, and inmates of psychiatric wards were selected as "potentially violent".

(Judge, 1993, p: 139-140)

So, the answer to whether or not Rev. Jim Jones' Black followers of Jim Jones willingly committed Mass suicide in 'Jonestown' is, oh well, let's again allow John Judge answer that:

> **"The idea that a large community of Black people would not only stand by and be poisoned at the suggestion of Jim Jones, but would allow their children to be murdered first, is a monstrous lie, and a racist insult. We now know that the most direct description of Jonestown is that it was a Black genocide plan".**

(Judge, 1993)

Fig.98 Media Cover-up:
Cover of Newsweek magazine following The Mass Murder of Jonestown inhabitants

According to John Judge, The 'Jonestown' People's Temple had amassed an enormous fortune, gained through the 'Slave Labour' of its followers from the Mining of Gold and other precious mineral resources in Guyana, which have been estimated to be between 26 Million to 1 Billion U.S. Dollars. Many members of Jim Jones' 'Inner Circle' are said to have escaped to invest this money in a number of foreign Financial Institutions, Corporations & Off-shore Banks. To this day, not one of Jim Jones' accomplices who helped him run the camp have been brought to justice, despite the authorities knowing full well who they are. The irony is that the 'Jonestown' model of a Slave Labour Camp, is only one of many other similar Government & Privately owned 'Slave Labour Camps' known to be in existence at numerous 'Top Secret', hidden and inaccessible locations scattered around the World, where Blacks, Latinos and other such 'Undesirables' are rumoured to be being held against their will.

The Following is a Chart of just some of the 'Financial Holdings' said to have been controlled by The 'Jonestown' People's Temple, Published by the 'The Los Angeles Times' = *LAT* & 'The Francisco Examiner' = *SFE* s, following the Jonestown Massacre:

Amount	Bank	Location	Source
$711,000	Barclay's Bank Int. Ltd.	Georgetown, Guyana	*LAT* 1/5/79
$100,000	Bank of Montreal (CA)	San Francisco, CA	*LAT* 1/5/79
$21,000	Bank of Montreal (CA)	San Francisco, CA	*LAT* 1/5/79
Unknown	United California Bank	San Francisco, CA	*LAT* 1/5/79
Unknown	Bank of America	Los Angeles, CA	*LAT* 1/5/79
$10,000*	Bank of America (personal)	San Francisco, CA	*SFE* 1/9/79
Unknown	Wells Fargo	Ukiah, CA	*SFE* 1/9/79
$2,043,000	Swiss Banking Corp.	Panama City	*SFE* 1/9/79
$5,231,536	Union Bank of Switzerland	Panama City	*SFE* 1/9/79
$5,173,000	Union Bank of Switzerland	Panama City	*SFE* 1/9/79
$206,396	Bank of Nova Scotia	Nassau, Bahamas	*SFE* 1/9/79
$76,000*	Grenada National Bank	Grenada	*SFE* 1/9/79
$560,000	Barclay's Bank (supplies)	Port Au Spain, Trinidad	*SFE* 1/9/79
$200,000	National Cooperative Bank	Georgetown, Guyana	*SFE* 1/9/79

$33,757 Banco Union de Venezuelas Caracas, Ven		*SFE* 1/9/79
$2,00,000 No name given Caracas, Ven		*SFE* 1/9/79
$1,000,000 Union Bank of Switzerland Zurich, Switz		*SFE* 1/9/79
$ Safe Deposit* Union Bank Switzerland Zurich, Switz		*SFE* 1/9/79
$11,000,000* "Treasure Chest" (1974) Redwood Valley, CA		*SFE* 1/9/79
$2,000,000 Jonestown Site total Guyana		*SFE* 1/9/79
$1,000,000* Bank of Nova Scotia San Francisco, CA		*SFE* 1/9/79

**For further information concerning this issue please refer to:
John Judge's official website**

Author's Statement:
Before we continue, let us just make it clear that there has never been a single shred of evidence to support the accusation of Dr. Malachi. Z. York being guilty of any acts of either; Child Molestation, Paedophilia or Human sacrifice, or any of the other themes about to be discussed at this section of the book. We take these issues very seriously, and do not in any way support or condone any of these practices.

While we are not followers of Malachi. Z. York's Philosophies, we must clarify that none of the information we have examined has provided a shred of evidence to confirm York's guilt of any of the Heinous crimes he has been accused of. Furthermore, we feel that the accusations made against the Nuwaubian leader are part of an ongoing conspiracy by the Media and various Law enforcement agencies to discredit and defame him and his movement The United Nuwaubian Nation of Moors.

Warning:
The following contains descriptions of Ancient Ritual Child abuse, which many may find distasteful. We would like to again point out, that we do not in any way, condone or support Any of these practices. Neither are we accusing any Religious, or Racial group, neither any of the individuals mentioned in this book, of either condoning or carrying out any of these "Occult" Pagan practices, other than those who have openly admitted to supporting and engaging in such Vile & Contemptuous activities on Record, either in their own words or writings. We again strongly recommend that those who are sensitive or squeamish nature discontinue reading this section of the book.

Ritual Child Abuse & Spiritualism

"I have also been of the theory that all life on this planet as we know it, is at a specific disadvantage to a less material more energy orientated multi-dimensional race, that feeds on the energy i.e. wave like layer associated with our living body known as chi, qi or the energy body. These parasitic non-organic beings live in a state of perpetual camouflage, and our fleeting glimpses of them are easily explained away, and prolonged glimpses are diagnosed as hallucinations, schizophrenia, or gross electric/chemical manipulation of the physical brain..."

(Excerpt taken from *"Aliens, Evolution, Parasites & Protection"*, by Marcus S. Chapman, 2004)

Many positive aspects of Spirituality remain misunderstood and frowned in the Western World, however there also exists a very disturbing aspect of the Esoteric world, which appear to form the connections between 'Ritual Child Abuse' & 'Human Sacrifice' with The Spiritual/Extraterrestrial phenomenon. The practice of Ritual Child abuse and Human Sacrifice are known to have existed for Centuries in many cultures around the world, and seem to be reoccurring themes in what may constitute the *"Dark Side"* or negative aspect of Spirituality, otherwise known as the Occult. It has been proposed by many researchers of New Age Mysticism that Occult groups, such as Satanists and in particular 'Kabalists', regard the essence of Children as extremely valuable, because Children are regarded as pure and therefore spiritually 'Uncontaminated'. This supposed 'Pure Energy' or human essence appears to be highly valuable to 4th & 5th Dimensional Malevolent 'Parasitic' Spiritual Entities, which have often been mistakenly regarded as Gods by many cultures around the world.

In antiquity, cultures such as the Babylonians and Aztecs ritually sacrificed Hundreds of Thousands of people, including Children and Slaves or Prisoners of War, to appease their Gods usually during times of Climatic instability or Famine. However it is a popular misconception that these diabolical practices are only restricted to Pagan or Primitive tribes in remote locations such as Central Africa & Papua New Guinea, because there is overwhelming evidence that they also exist in supposedly modern Mainstream Monotheistic religions too.

It must also be made clear that we are not, in any way claiming that any of the practices mentioned below, are accepted Religious practices in either; Judaism, Christianity or Islam.

There exists disturbing evidence, which may reveal a secret tradition of Ritual Child Sacrifice in Judaism, which may even be subtly mentioned in the book of Genesis. This story involves the Hebrew Patriarch, (Prophet) Abraham and his second son Yishack or Isaac, and contains striking similarities to the practice of Human sacrifice in the Ancient World:

> And it came to pass after these things, that God did tempt Abraham, and said unto him, Abraham: and he said, Behold, *here* I am.
> And he said, **Take now thy son, thine only *son* Isaac, whom thou lovest, and get thee into the land of Mo-ri-ah; and offer him there for a burnt offering upon one of the mountains which I will tell thee of.**
> And Abraham rose up early in the morning, and saddled his ass, and took two of his young men with him, and Isaac his son, and clave the wood for the burnt offering, and rose up, and went unto the place of which God had told him.
> Then on the third day Abraham lifted his eyes, and saw the place afar off.
> And Abraham said unto his young men, Abide ye here with the ass; and I and the lad will go yonder and worship, and come again to you.

And Abraham took the wood of the burnt offering, and laid *it* upon Isaac his son; and he took the fire in his hand, and a knife; and they went both of them together.
And Isaac spake unto Abraham his father, and he said, My father: and he said, Here *am* I, my son. And he said, Behold the fire and the wood: but where *is* the lamb for a burnt offering?
And Abraham said, My son, God will provide himself a lamb for a burnt offering: so they went unto them together.
And they came to the place which God had told him of; and Abraham built an alter there, and laid the wood in order, and 'bound Isaac his son, and laid him on the alter upon the wood.
And Abraham stretched fourth his hand, and took the knife to slay his son. And the angel of the Lord called unto him out of heaven, and said, Here *am* I.
And he said Lay not thy hand upon the lad, neither do thou do anything unto him: for now I know that thou fearest God................
(Book of Genesis, Chapter 22, Verse 1-12)

 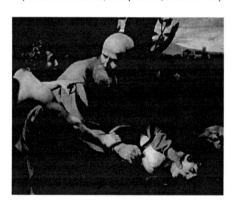

Figs.99 & 100: Left- Right: *Illustrations of Abraham Interrupted Sacrifice of Issac*

This story is intriguing for two reasons, firstly is the way in which Abraham seems to methodically proceed to carry out the task, once ordered to do so without offering any form of protest or resistance. Secondly, why would God ask Abraham to 'Sacrifice' his own son as a test? Although God eventually saved Isaac before any harm could befall him, was this simply a test of faith by God, or is there more to this incident than meets the eye.

We know Abraham originally came from Ur of Chaldea, which was part of the Ancient Babylonian or Mesopotamian Empire, in which such practices were common. Therefore had Abraham already witnessed Children being ritually sacrificed to the Gods whilst growing up in Mesopotamia? And was the God who tested Abraham, indicating that these types of practices would no longer be required, as was the case with the Malevolent Gods of Babylon? And finally, was this incident an echo of long forgotten Religious practice. Normal animal Sacrifice plays an integral part of many religions, especially Judaism, which places great importance on killing animals according to Levitical Law. Therefore being the highest evolved species of Mammals, could Humans be considered the highest form of Sacrifice to certain Malevolent Gods or (Beings) such as Reptilians for example?

Abraham's son Isaac would grow up to become the progenitor of the Israelite Nation, who would themselves be taken into bondage in Mesopotamia. Could they too have witnessed these practices whilst in bondage under the Babylonians, and could this practice have secretly survived in Judaism, before the Israelites were eventually delivered from Bondage.

So what evidence exists to substantiate that Ritual Child Abuse, and Sacrifice have ever existed in Judaism?

According to York there exists a very secret tradition practiced by 'Rabbinical' Jews that goes back to Ancient Babylon, which normal Jews are completely unaware of. In his translation & commentary of Chapter 13 of *"The Book of Revelations"* released in 1991, York states:

> The Prophet/Apostle Moses received the written law (Torah) between the years 1512 and 1473 B.C.E. Over 1,500 years had passed before the writing of the Talmud, enough time for the Devil to try to change historical facts.
>
> The Pharisees were influenced by the practices of the wicked Babylonians (the Canaanite civilizations founded by Nimrod) whose rule they found themselves under. In Babylon, sexual perversion had become a way of life. Yet, when the Judahites were put out of Babylon (because they were rising too much in strength and power) they were not able to openly continue these practices because other societies did not allow such perversion. But these perversions remained in the Talmud.
>
> Not even your average so-called Jew knows of the indecencies that are allowed in the Talmud. It could only be the work of the Devil. The television documentary, "The Other Israel" was filmed in a so-called Jewish library, and brings out the following points about the Talmud:
>
> - The priests have the right to marry a girl child under 3 years and a day and have sex with her with the explanation that a little girl under 3 years and a day would regain her Virginity as she cried tears of purification.
>
> - Intercourse with a small boy is also considered permissible.
>
> - The penalty for adultery does not include sex with a minor, the wife of a minor, or the wife of a heathen.
>
> (Isa Al Mahdi, 1991, p: 209)

The following is supposedly an account of Ritual Child Abuse and Sacrifice which appeared in a book edited by Jim Keith, entitled: *"Secret And Suppressed: Banned Ideas & Hidden History"*.

We once again strongly recommend that those of a sensitive and squeamish nature please discontinue reading at this stage.

Ritual Child Abuse and Sacrifice

The following accounts are said to originate from an anonymous source inside the Vatican, who supposedly obtained them from the Vatican 'Secret' files, which relate to the disturbing secret tradition of Pagan 'Occult' Ritual Sacrifice in Judaism & Child Abuse/Sacrifice within the 'Indo-Aryan Culture:

> It must be remembered, throughout this description, that modern Jewry is, for the most part, ignorant of the rites of the Zionists, who posit that they alone (as proper Zionist Jews) are true Jewry, and all others who claim Judaism are wrong. Indeed, to investigate the history of this religion (done so admirably by Benjamin Freedman in his tome, "Facts Are Facts") is to discover that modern rank-and-file Jewry has no real connection to historical Judaism, but are in fact pawns in a much larger and more vicious game than they realize. To begin, then: the rite of consecration of the Kohen (ritual/sacrificial priest) and of the normative ritual sacrifice are very nearly identical. The Kohen-elect is made to enter a pit beneath the grating that is beside the altar of sacrifice, also called the altar of holocaust (*shoah*, in the Hebrew), which is described at chapter 27 of Exodus, in the first part. The altar grating is placed over the pit (actually more an encircling trench), and the sacrificial victim is brought before the altar. The preferred victim is a young boy of Jewish blood; young girls are usable, especially when supply is high, but boys are the preferred victim. Most 'Jewish' parents during the Templar periods (the times during which a properly-consecrated temple stood at Jerusalem) were required to redeem their children with an offering (see chapter 12 of Leviticus); at these times, they used – in modern times, any so-called 'Jewish' child may be kidnapped & used for the sacrifice, or for the ordination, though for the sin offering a Gentile child may be used. The child, preferably an infant or toddler (but any child up to the age of thirteen being acceptable, if virginal), is stood upon the grating above the head of the Kohen-elect, nude, facing northward; the child's head is grasped firmly by the officiating priest (or by him and his assistant, should the child be older and put up a fight), and the child's throat is then slit to open the jugular vein. Some of the blood is made to splatter against the eastern face of the altar itself, while the rest spatters through the grating to bathe the Kohen-elect, who drinks a mouthful of the blood as it pours over him. The officiating Kohen then wets his fingers with the screaming innocent's blood and, walking counter-clockwise around the altar, traces certain arcane sigils upon the altar's horns with the blood; then arriving back at the child's sill on which the temple of killing-floor rests, and that the mouth-spraying of the child's blood is omitted. Similarities between the Jewish and Teutonic rituals are close; the parallels suggest, perhaps, a common origin for certain practices, perhaps deriving from central Asia via the Khazars. In the Teutonic rite, the altar is generally an unhewn dolmen, and the pit and its attendant are

> absent. The priest to be consecrated in this rite merely lies, nude, on the ground at the eastern face of the stone altar (the eastern face of the altar being sacred to both the Zionists and Teutons), and the victim – a child of either gender between the ages of seven and twelve, virginal – is brought to him. The child is forced down upon the priest – elect in a kneeling position, straddling the elects hips, at which time sexual penetration (notably absent from Zionist rite) is achieved, anally for a young boy, virginally for a young girl. The child's head is faced east, as in the Zionist rite, and the jugular is opened, showering the priest elect with blood, some of which is ingested. The child is then penetrated sexually by the attending priests until such time as death occurs. In both rites, the bathing in and ingestion of the blood of the child is required for proper consecration, and in the Teutonic rite (as in the Zionist), the body of the child is eaten.
>
> (cited by Keith, 1993, p: 221-222)

Although the origin of the above account is highly suspicious, and may simply be an Anti-Semetic attempt to discredit Judaism. It does however if genuine, provide us with a terrifying insight into the nature of these Secret Heathen or Pagan practices, and may contain some important clues as to why increasing numbers of children continue to disappear around the world each year. It has been estimated that Hundreds of Thousands of children simply vanish, as part of a World-Wide conspiracy to provide children to be Ritually Abused and Sacrificed each year. Author David Icke has brought public attention to this matter in many of his books and videos. For example in *"Children of The Matrix"*, he states:

> Children are major targets because the reptilians prefer the "purity" of their blood and energy, and the most effective time to start trauma-based mind control is before the age of six. Changes take place in the blood at puberty and after the first sexual activity, which make it less useful from the reptilians' point of view. Many schools and pre-schools for small children across the world are fronts for Satanism and its offshoot, trauma-based mind control. Most of the children are suffering everyday without their parent's knowledge, but they are also handed over to cults quite willingly by their Satanic parents. Occasionally, the odd story gets into a newspaper, but this bears no resemblance to the staggering scale of the ritual abuse of children.
>
> (Icke, 2001, p: 300)

Ritual Abuse of Children seems to be connected in someway to religion, and as stated previously, seem to involve Malevolent 4th & 5th Inter-dimensional entities or Gods who demand the energy of human children through either Ritual Sexual abuse or Blood sacrifice. The Christian Church, particularly; **The Roman Catholic Church** is another religious institution, which is known to practice this ancient diabolical art, with a number of its clergy implicated in many cases relating to Child Abuse and Ritual Sacrifice. In his thesis entitled: *"Who Stole Our History"*.[6], author Peter Farley states the following in relation to Ritual Child Abuse and Sacrifice, in Christianity's secret connection to the 'Occult':

> Today's fallout involving Roman Catholic priests and their abuse of minors is just the tip of the iceberg, which many sources suggest runs to as many as 50 million people in this country alone who have in some way been ritually abused at a very young age by one or more adults. The purposes also vary, ranging from pure sexual gratification, to energy thievery in pursuit of dark purposes related to secret societies and the powers of darkness which lead the New World Order on its mission to control this entire corner of the Universe.
>
> Reminiscent of today's headlines about Roman Catholic priests, a scandal hit the Mormon church in October of 1991 when an internal memo written about alleged child abuse within the church's framework was printed in the November issue of the Salt Lake City Messenger, a newsletter published by Jerald and Sandra Tanner. Other media and the Church's own public relations office itself then picked up the 12-page report, and eventually the Chicago Tribune sent a reporter, James Coates, to investigate the story.
> SALT LAKE CITY – Top officials of the Church of Jesus Christ of Latter – Day Saints say they are investigating reports from members that, as children, they witnessed human sacrifice and suffered 'satanic abuse' at the hands of renegade Mormon affiliated cliques.
> Glenn L. Pace, a member of the church's three-man presiding bishopric, reported in a memorandum....that he is personally convinced at least 800 church-affiliated Satanists now are practicing occult rituals and devil worship...
>
> (Farley, 2003)

Despite the overwhelming evidence which proves the existence of Paedophilia/Ritual Child abuse & Sacrifice in organised religion, the practice is often only associated with groups viewed as Cults and New Age (Occult) movements, which will now be the focus of our attention. It has been theorised that many of these Paedophiles who are usually known to be Caucasian men, are often affiliated with Esoteric sciences (Spirituality), and ritual abuse of children as a means of gaining energy, or the child's life force. This is because it is said children before adolescence and sexual maturity are spiritually pure, and are therefore highly desired by those who feed off human energy. One such individual was the admitted Satanist and New Age mystic Aleister Crowley, described by his critics at the time as *"The Most Evil Man in Britain"*. In his book entitled *"Magick: In Theory and Practice"*, Crowley openly explains the benefits of these Monstrous and Diabolical practices:

> The animal should therefore be killed within the Circle, or the Triangle, as the case may be, so that its energy cannot escape...For the highest spiritual working one must accordingly choose that victim which contains the

greatest and purest force. A male child of perfect innocence and high intelligence is the most satisfactory and suitable victim...
(Crowley cited in Farley, 2003, p: 2)

Notice how Aleister Crowley refers to the child victim as an "Animal". This is very significant because it confirms our earlier contention that Child Abuse and Sacrifice are the highest forms of Animal sacrifice, or in Crowley's own words *"the highest spiritual working"*. In recent years increasing numbers of African Children have began being illegally adopted, and even stolen by Westerners. Such as the French Aid workers recently apprehended in Chad, trying to smuggle a Plane-load of African Boys & Girls to Europe in 2007. And most famously; David Banda, the baby boy; illegally taken out of Malawi in 2006 by known Kabbalahist Madonna, to be possibly used, as many fear for the purpose of some kind of 'Satanic' or Occult-Kabbalahistic ritual requiring the Spiritual-Essence of an African Child. It has also been revealed that the Malawian baby's adoption was but the first in a long term plan by the 'Pop Queen' to build school's & orphanages in the impoverished East African nation, where children from all across the Continent will eventually be taught Jewish Kabbalahism or (Witchcraft) as the compulsory curriculum in exchange for Financial Aid.

Figs.101 & 102: Satanist: Left- Right: *Aleister Crowley & Book: 'Magik'*

It has been suggested by many researchers of the New Age phenomena that esoteric 'Gurus' are also connected with Ritual Child Abuse, for the purpose of stealing their 'Etheric' energy. Remote viewing expert, Major Ed Dames, stated in an interview that Indian Spiritual Master & Avatar, Satya Sai Baba, is able to make objects materialize from thin air, by gaining energy from his audiences. He also claims that he is aware that the source of Sai Baba's power are Malevolent spiritual entities called 'Divas' who are said to have been with him since he was a child. Apparently these 'Divas', demanded that Sai Baba regularly commit "Dark Acts" in order to maintain his power.

In his book *"Children of the Matrix"*, David Icke discusses the issue of child abuse in further depth, and even goes to the lengths of accusing Satya Sai Baba of being a Pedophile:

> I can offer no greater example of the New Age conman and millions who hand over their minds to them, than Sai Baba. This guy is a guru figure worshipped as a "Living God on Earth" by vast numbers of people worldwide and at all levels of society. He operates from his "Ashram" in Puttaparthi, India. Thousands go there and just sit in vacant awe at this man in the long orange frock. I attended an event once in England in which the audience was asked to sing a song of worship to Sai Baba by a woman almost overcome with emotion for this "god". But do you know who Sai Baba really is? A Pedophile, con man, thief and almost certainly worse.
>
> (Icke, 2001, p: 332)

David Icke bases his claims upon the testimonies of former devotees of Sai Baba, Faye and David Bailey, who he claims have published evidence of Sai Baba's child abuse in their quarterly newsletter, *"The Findings"*. On his website: <www.davidicke.com>, Icke also went on to claim that Sai Baba is widely known to sexually abuse boys, which he does on a regular basis at his residence in India. Apparently a young former follower from the US, claims to have been forcibly masturbated by Sai Baba, who then saved his Seamen in a hanky for some 'Tantric' Black Magic purpose. Jed Geyerhahn, an ex-follower of Sai Baba said: *"I even heard terrible stories of children who would meet with Sai Baba twice a week to play "sex games" and the like. Oral sex and masturbation were common in these meetings. Many of my own friends told me about attempts by Sai Baba to touch them, but they wouldn't let him".*

Whether these allegations against Sai Baba are true or false, no solid evidence is provided by David Icke, other than allegations of him performing magic tricks, and eye witness accounts by disgruntled ex-followers. More importantly David Icke fails to adequately explain what method of abuse Sai Baba uses against his victims.

Like Satya Sai Baba, Dr. Malachi. Z. York has also been accused of Ritual Child abuse. In fact the first stage of York's trial was heavily publicized when it began in September 2002, as the 'Largest list of indictments for Child Abuse ever seen in US history'. Because the complete details of the entire trial are analyzed in the final chapter of this book, we shall only briefly cover the descriptions of York's alleged Child abuse at this stage. York along with three other co-defendants were indicted within a week of their arrests of 74 counts for Child Molestation, 29 Counts of aggravated Child Molestation, 4 Counts of Statutory Rape, 2 Counts of Sexual Exploitation of a minor, 1 Count of influencing a witness and 5 Counts of

Enticing a Child for indecent purposes. According to newspaper reports, York practiced Anal and Vaginal intercourse with both young boys and girls, some even as young as 4-years old over a 20-year period for sexual gratification. Many of the allegations have been made by York's son 'Jake' or Jacob York, who claims to have witnessed his father commit these acts first hand. During one interview he stated: *"Once I saw a video tape of my father having sex with a child years ago, and I could never forget the look in his eyes, it was as if he wasn't human whilst he was doing it"* However, and as we shall see, as the details of the case gradually emerged, it soon became apparent that there was a continuous catalogue of inconsistencies by many of the alleged victims, which questions the validity of the entire case against the Nuwaubian leader.

Star Kids & The 144,000 Children of Light

Finally there exists another more positive aspect of Inter-dimensional or Extraterrestrial involvement with Earth children, which does not involve Ritual Child Abuse or Sacrifice, and is the phenomenon known as 'Homo Neoticus' or *"New Humans"*. There is a New Age hypothesis being proposed by many ET or UFO researchers, that the human race is gradually being enhanced or 'Upgraded' by various Benevolent Alien Races through its Children.

Indeed York advanced a similar theory in many of his books as far back as the 1970's, asserting that a race of highly advanced Beings or Gods called the Anunnaqi, will one day return to collect 144,000 chosen 'Children' of his followers from earth, as mentioned in the book Revelations:

> And I heard the number of them which were sealed: *and there were* sealed an **hundred** *and* **forty** *and* **four thousand** of all the tribes of the children of Israel...
>
> (Book Revelations, Chapter 7, Verse 4)

Although detractors and the mainstream Media have often ridiculed York for his claim that one day 144,000 of his followers will be collected and spirited away to another Galaxy, it must be pointed out that this claim, though seemingly improbable to most of us, is nothing more than the Nuwaubian interpretation of the Biblical prophecy found in the Book of Revelations Chapter 21, in which it describes a City coming down out of Heaven, to redeem the chosen of God. The Nuwaubian's claim that these chosen ones would then be taken away to the Planet/Ship Nibiru, also known as the 'Crystal City' to be groomed for a specific period of time, before returning to defeat Satan and his Fallen Angels or (Malevolent) Dark Masters. According to York, the 144,000 were to be the children of his original followers, and that the ships would begin arriving from 2003.

Naturally this assertion about Space Ships returning to take his followers has caused York to receive some of the worst ridicule and condemnation from the Media and critics alike. The 144,000 were to be children, whom he referred to as *"The Children of Light"*. These children were to be the offspring of his first followers the Ansaar Community raised in purity, and therefore untouched or corrupted by Satan. On the an audio recorded lecture entitled: *"Why did we use Islam"*, York, then under the name; Rabboni Y'Shua Bar El Haady stated the following:

> The Question was, to do what man? To prepare a group of people, a Hundred and Forty Four Thousand (144,000), of them, prepare them for the coming. What coming man? Christians call it the Rapture, Muslims call it the Return, Jews don't know what to call it. They just, most of the so-called Black Israelite Hebrews, are calling themselves Hebrews, but are really Christians. The one's on 42nd street, dressed like the "Isley Brothers", jumping up and down, don't know a lick of Hebrew, get on Television get all embarrassed, by White folks who can speak broken Hebrew, you've seen them. But they always talking about, Jesus, Jesus, Jesus, ain't no Jews in Israel or ain't no Ancient Israelites talking about no man named Jesus, no it didn't happen. Yahweh Ben Yahweh, first started talking about Jesus, then he became Jesus, so those people were all Christians, wasn't no shelter there.
>
> Where was I to find a place on Earth or a culture, that you could hide off into the corner, and groom a certain amount of people to breed Kids that as the scripture says about "Noah", would be perfect in their generation. That would not be touched, by what? by the Harlot...
>
> (Bar El Haady, 1994)

Some years later during the so-called Hebrew school, York claimed that each one of the 144,000, would be implanted with a kind of chip called 'The Barathary Gland', which he claimed once existed in humans, situated in the Hippocampus cavity of the Cerebellum, located at the lower part of the brain attached to what is called the 'Brain stem'. York claimed the Anunnaqi would replace this Barathary Gland into those who were worthy, which would immediately activate the four higher senses:

- **INTUITION,** *"Mind Perception"*
- **TELEPATHY,** *"Mental Communication"*
- **PSYCHOMETRY,** *"Object Reading"*
- **CLAIVOYANCE,** *"Clear sight of other Dimensions"*

In recent years York has ceased referring to the 144,000 specifically as being children, and began applying the term to anyone deemed sincere amongst his followers. However this is a slight contradiction to his original teachings, which contended that the chosen would be children of "The First Fruits", not adults who recently joined the movement. Therefore we can only assume that because York was unsuccessful in raising 144,000
'Pure Children', he therefore comprised in this part of his mission. Nevertheless there still remain many parallels between York's 144,000 *"Children of Light"*, Hypothesis, and the theory of the "The Star Children". For example, experts of this phenomenon claim that there is currently

underway a rapid advancement being carried out upon certain Races of Human Beings, namely the Nordic/Scandinavian racial types, as a result intervention by Alien Entities. This premise is again consistent with both Malachi York and Zechariah Sitchin's assertion that during the past 100 to 150,000 years there have been rapid developments or 'Upgrading' of the Human race through Genetic manipulation & 'Inter-stellar seeding' by various Extra Terrestrial races. If this is accurate, then the Earth is no more than a massive laboratory, for these Alien entities to conduct scientific experiments, with every different Alien race working towards its own separate agenda.

Specialist in this issue, Mary Rodwell states the following in her thesis also entitled; *"The Star Children"* 7:

> UFO researcher Bob Dean has spoken many times of the development of a new humanity called Homo neoticus. This is a term coined by noted author John White who has been doing research into parapsychology and neotics (the study of consciousness) for many years (Leir, p.192) Some of the unusual qualities Leir is referring to are:
> 1) The ability of babies to read written print.
> 2) Sign language being used to communicate with toddlers not old enough to speak.
> 3) Advancements in crawling or age of speech.
> "The question is why? I suggest the answer involves alien manipulation of human genetics"
>
> (Rodwell, 2002, p: 1)

Fig.103 Star Child: *"Homo Neoticus" or 'New Humans'*

These 'Star' or Indigo Children are all purported to have parents who have at one time or another had some type of 'Close encounter' with either an Alien craft or an actual abduction experience. Therefore it could quite possibly be that these Aliens, may have somehow tampered or manipulated with the DNA of the parents of these children, particularly the mothers. It is interesting to note that some of the abilities described by researchers such as the ability to communicate long before other normal children, is one of the skills attributed to the infant 'Isa' or (Jesus) in the Holy Koran. Which lends further credence to the theory that Jesus may have in fact been one of these *"Homo Neoticus"* or 'New Humans'. According to the Nuwaubian leader, this was certainly the case, because he asserts that Jesus was the Son of the Angelic Being GabriEl, or Gabriel, making him part Angel or Extraterrestrial, depending upon your interpretation. In the following quote taken from the Holy Qur'an, the newly born-infant Jesus intervenes on behalf of his Mother Mary, and speaks out in her defense after she is confronted by members of her family who were angry about what appeared to them to be the birth of an illegitimate child, which according to Judaic Law was punishable by Death:

> Then she brought him to her own folk, carrying him. They said: O Mary! Thou hast come with an amazing thing.
> Oh sister of Aaron! Thy father was not a wicked man nor was thy mother a harlot. Then she pointed to him. They said: How can we talk to one who is in the cradle, a young boy?
> He spoke: **Lo! I am the slave of Allah. He hath given me the Scripture and hath appointed me a Prophet. And hath made me blessed where so ever I may be, and hath enjoined upon me prayer and almsgiving so long as I remain alive. And (hath made me) dutiful toward her who bore me, and hath not made me arrogant, unblest. Peace on me the day I was born, and the day I die, and the day I shall be raised alive!**
> Such was Jesus, son of Mary: (this is) a statement of the truth concerning which they doubt.
> (The Holy Qur'an, Chapter 19, Verse 27 – 34)

Again Mary Rodwell lends further credibility to this hypothesis:

> The extraterrestrial contribution to the child's make-up may come from reproductive material, from genetic engineering, from biomedical technology, and telepathic consciousness linking, as well as from directed incarnation of an ET into a human body (Boylan, 1999)..."The child is conceived from parents who are themselves 'experiencers'. And the genetic material is in part extraterrestrial, or they have at least had their human genome altered by ET bio-engineering to bring out abilities beyond average.
> (Boylan cited by Rodwell, 2002, p: 1)

Finally, it has been proposed by many UFO researchers that the intention of the Benevolent or (Good) Inter-galactic Entities, is to try and raise humanity to a higher spiritual and technological level, in order for us to eventually communicate with them on their level, and therefore take our place on the Galactic Council of Races before we ultimately destroy ourselves.

Chapter 13

The Cold Reality of 'Right Knowledge'

Fig.104 *Symbol of Nuwaubian Crown of Life*

The Nuwaubian philosophy includes elements of Christianity, ancient Egyptian polytheism, and a belief in unidentified flying objects (UFO).

Jim Marrs, CNN, 1999

Today the term 'Nuwaubian' carries many negative connotations, usually synonymous with 'Cult' along with an entire assortment of bizarre religious beliefs such as "New age" philosophies, Conspiracy theories, and the beliefs in Extraterrestrials. This is mainly due to an ongoing campaign of deliberate Misrepresentation & Misinformation by the mainstream media aimed at undermining the credibility of the Nuwaubian movement. So what is Nuwaubu, and more importantly; the basis of the Nuwaubian beliefs? In essence, Nuwaubu is the culmination of all of the religious & Cultural philosophies taught by Dr. Malachi. Z. York since the late 1960's. This then was to be a type of graduation from traditional 'Monotheistic' religious beliefs, which York had been restricted by since the early part of his Ministry. Therefore this new 'Science' or doctrine was to be the unification of all the previous schools of thought combined to form a single cohesive Cultural/Religious philosophy, called **'Nuwaubu'**.

> Let Me Just State Here, That What's Being Taught In Right Knowledge Is The Exact Same Thing that was Being Taught As Ansaaru Allah...
> (York, 1996, p: 12)

> Make Note That the Stage We Are In Now, Which Is **NUWAUBU – Sound Right Reasoning**, I Told My Followers A Long Time Ago Was To Come. So I Reiterate That Nuwaubu Is Not Something New.
> (York, 1996, p: 113)

Ironically, the Religious/Philosophy of 'Nuwaubu' was not new but actually a re-launch of a Religious/Philosophical theory, first unveiled during the late 1960s by York, then under the Pen names: **Amun Nebu Re**

Ankh Tah & **Afro Oono** with various titles including: *"Get From Behind The 9 Ball"* & *"Bible Interpretations and Explanations"*, which can be verified by the Schomburg Library Centre for Research on Black Culture in New York City. These publications enjoyed a popular following particularly in Philosophical & Esoteric circles unaware of the author's true identity. Realising the growing appeal of Middle-Eastern 'Monotheistic' religious beliefs, particularly in Islam amongst African-Americans at the time, York decided to postpone any further writing of Afro-Centred Esoteric material until a more appropriate time. Remarkably, aside from Sunni Muslim-Arab appologist Billal

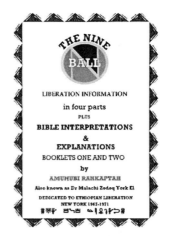

Fig.105 York's first publications

Phillips, York's teachings have not attracted much criticism from many Scholars within the Islamic World, which is remarkable taking into consideration the amount of years his books have been in circulation.
According to his followers, Malachi York's purpose for initially teaching Nuwaubu in 1967 was to break an Evil & Hypnotic spell of ignorance called Leviathaan, otherwise known as 'Kingu', supposedly cast upon Blacks 6,000-years ago, in order to prevent them from reaching their true potential as 'Supreme Beings'. As we have seen, York's movement first emerged in the Coney Island district of New York, under the name 'Ansaar Pure Sufi', wearing what appeared to be a strange new symbol comsprised of a 'Hebraic' Six Pointed Star, 'Egyptian' Ankh & 'Islamic' Inverted Crecsent, which has taken on numerous forms throughout the subsequent years. After initially being adapted by York, from the 'Upright Crescent & Sun Disc' of the ancient world, regarded as one of the most important symbols in both the Afro-Asiatic civilizations of Egypt & Mesopotamia. Nuwaubians derive their name from the term 'Nuwaubu', also said to have first been introduced by York as far back as 1969. 'Nuwaubu' according to Nuwaubians originates from the root word Nuwba (Nuba), a region in Southern Sudan, which encompasses parts of **Ethiopia, Uganda and Kenya**. The term of Nuwaubu, relates to the root word 'Nubian' from Nabi, Nub or Nuwb, meaning: *"Colour inclining to Black...kinky or woolly haired people"*. The Nuwaubian philosophy has also recently been identified as a Religious/Cultural philosophy by the online Encyclopaedia Wikipedia, as 'Nuwaubianism' [1], and is defined as follows:

> Nuwaubianism is a collection of religious teachings and cultural philosophy that is multifaceted and ever-changing. It has influences and borrowings from many sources – such as a white new-age Blavatsky-

influenced movement like Astara, the Rosicrucians, Freemasonry, the Shriners, the teachings of the Moorish Science Temple of America, the ancient astronaut theories of Zecharia Sitchin, David Icke, Art Bell, the UFO mythology of greys and reptilians, cryptozoological stories like that of the chupacabra, patriot mythology, modern scientific and pseudoscientific legends like those of Area 51, SETI, Philadelphia Experiment, Project Blue Book, Montauk Project, The Manhattan Project, and MJ-12, conspiracy theories about the Illuminati or multiple clones of members of the Bilderberg Group, a paperback on fortune telling, and hollow earth theories.

(Wikipedia, 2006)

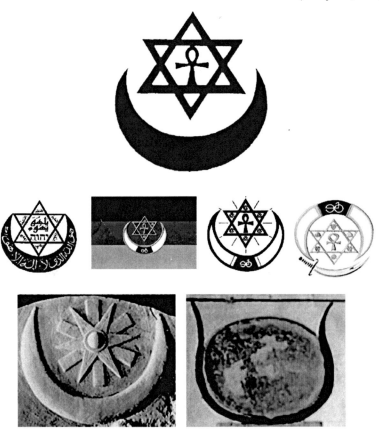

Figs.106, 107, 108, 109, 110, 111 & 112: Ancient **Sacred Seal: Top:**
Original Nuwaubian Symbol of Star & Upright Crescent
(Middle) Left- Right: *Various Interpretations of Nuwaubian Symbol since 1970*
(Bottom) *Ancient forms of Mesopotamian & African Star & Upright Crescent*

New York Post reporter Adam Heimlich after reviewing some of York's literature wrote:

> A partial list, from my notes, of places I'd encountered Nuwaubian notions before includes *Chariots of the Gods* and the Rael's embellishments on that book, conspiracy lit, UFO lit, the human potential movement, Buddhism and new-age, astrology, theosophy and Blavatsky, Leonard Jeffries and other Afrocentrics, Cayce, LaRouche, alternative medicine, self-help lit, Satanism, the Atkins diet, numerology and yoga. Many of these York mentions by name. There are also extensive discourses on the Torah, Gospels and Koran, as well as on Rastafarianism, the Nation of Islam and the Five Percent Nation.[1]

(Heimlich, 2000)

York felt it no longer necessary to simply use 'Nubian', to describe his followers, as this term belonged historically to the people of North East Africa, and therefore an inadequate description for Africans in the Western Hemisphere. Instead, York wanted to give Western Blacks their own unique identity, so they *"wouldn't have to emulate anyone else's culture or religious practices anymore"*. Although York was the first Leader in the West to introduce the term 'Nubian' in reference to Blacks as a whole, he decided to now apply the title 'Nuwaubian', to differentiate those who followed his philosophy from all other appellations being used by black groups and organisations at the time. Nuwaubu would be the foundation of what he envisioned as an entirely new cultural identity, one that would replace so-called 'Afro-centrism' and form the basis of what is commonly referred to in Swahili as 'Kujichagulia', or *"Self Determination"* for Africans in the West. And like all previous Communities, the group's newly acquired Nuwaubian Holy land 'Kodesh' or Tama Re (Egypt of the West), would provide a safe and peaceful, almost 'Utopian' environment where his followers would be protected from the Decadence and Evils of Western society. Following the end of the Hebrew school, York led his followers towards both the Ancient; Egyptian & Sumerian cultural/religious doctrines almost simultaneously. The explanation given for this new transformation into what would became 'Nuwaubu', was that the Hebrew religion & culture had its origins in both Ancient Civilizations, particularly Egypt, where the ancient Hebrews where held in bondage for almost 400-years. The early Hebrew and (ancient) Egyptian cultures shared many similarities in both religious and cultural practices, being both directly descended from Noah, who belonged to the pure Kushite; Afro-Asiatic racial group of Eastern Africa & Western Asia now falsely called Middle-East, who were the actual founders of the Mesopotamian Civilization. For example, the Hebrew Patriarch Moses was not only educated as an Egyptian high priest of Amen Ra, but was also according to York, a Pharaoh or Ruler of the Upper-Egyptian/Cushite Kingdom, whose Nubian title was 'Thut-Mosis', which has clear similarities to the biblical name Moses. However, even more interesting is the fact that Moses' so-called arch enemy; Pharaoh Remises, shares the same name as Moses; Ra-Mesis or Ra-Moses, meaning *"One Who is Retrieved from Water by Ra"*, which sounds remarkably similar to the meaning of Moses' so-called Hebraic name. Historians have also suggested that the concept of Monotheism or the belief in 'One God' was first introduced by the Egyptian Ruler Pharaoh Amenophis IV, otherwise known as Ankhenaten or Ankh Aten, the father of Tutankhamun, from whom the ancient Hebrew's are said to have learned Monotheism whilst in bondage. However York quickly dismissed this theory as baseless, because the concept or belief in 'One God', was known to Noah and his ancestors prior to the 'Great Flood', which predates Ankh Aten's ascendancy to the throne of Egypt by several Millennia. According to York, the Ancient Hebrews, Egyptians & Sumerians, were all of the same 'Afro-Asiatic' bloodline through Noah, which is why so many of the so-called 'Biblical' Prophets & Patriarchs often spent so much time in Egypt, which even included Jesus, who York claims spent half of his entire life in Africa studying ancient wisdom. Therefore after having taught the 3 Major world 'Monotheistic' religions for over 25-years the next phase was to bring his teachings 'Full-Circle', was to reveal that the 'Source' of these religions, as ancient Egypt & Sumer, which he labelled 'Nuwaubu', the Proto-Religious/Culture of Humanity.

Resurrection of the 'First Language'

"Come Let Us Neteru Go Down There And Unify Their Toungues In To one Language, The One True Language Of Their Past, And Dispel Of The Diversity And Confusion, Babel, That Scattered Them Across The Face Of The Planet Tenen, Earth".

(Excerpt taken from *"The Sacred Records Of Atum-Re"*, by Dr. Malachi. Z. York)

When I can't speak to my Children in my Tongue then I'm Dead, you understand? I went out of my way to create a language for us. I know that sounds Crazy! We need our own language, something that makes me know you, and you know me. Because when the Jews start sitting around, and start speaking in Jewish, we go oh, they're the Jews speaking Jewish, Right! The Chinese speak Chinese. Now, Spanish is not our language, we got Spanish from the Spaniards, but its not our language. We speak it, we speak French, we speak German, we speak everything, cause we all over the Planet........So I went out of my way to create a language for us. It combines Syretic and Aramic, and its simple, real simple. Anybody can learn it, but if you start now, eventually these kids will be speaking their own language. Then you write stories about what took place in our time...

(Excerpt taken from *"Elohim: The New Covenant"*, by Rabboni Y'Shua Bar El Haady, 1993)

By 2002, York had built an impressive Publishing Empire enabling him to amass Millions of Dollars from the sale of over 500 book titles and other 'Afro-centric' Religious & Educational paraphernalia, such as Audio & Video recorded lectures, Posters & Periodicals distributed through a complex network of outlets operated by his followers throughout major cities in the United States & Europe. His vision, was for Nuwaubu to become a renewal of Pan-Africanism, forming a kind of Afro-centred religious and cultural system, based on elements of Christianity, Islam, Judaism, Egyptology, Sumerian (Mesopotamian), Mesoamerican and other African practices, concentrated into a single 'Black' led cultural-religion. York is said to have studied under the famous Sudanese linguist, Professor Abdul Gadir Abdullah while at the University of Khartoum, during the 1980s. Dr. Gadir is credited with being one of the only scholars in the world to have successfully deciphered the Meroitic script, using a method of dissecting Meroitic into its constituent parts before rebuilding words together in lengthy sequences much like the way like Japanese is written. As a graduate of the University of Khartoum, York was able to utilize his education in linguistics in the development of the Nuwaubic language for his followers in later years.

In order to cure Blacks of their 400-year inherited inferiority complex, York felt it necessary to develop Nuwaubu as a cohesive Cultural 'Identity' even going to the extent of creating a Nuwaubian Language and Alphabet he named 'Pa Nuwau Laghut' or *"The Nuwaubian Language"*. This combined various ancient languages including Ashuric, Aramic, Akkadian & Chaldean, as well as elements of the original Nubian dialects of Southern Egypt & Sudan, derived from Ancient 'Meroe', also known in the Old Testament as Cush or 'Kush', the birthplace of the Ancient Egyptian Civilization. Located on the East bank of the Nile River, between the 5th & 6th cataracts, ancient Kush was the ancestral homeland of the Pharaohs, dating back further than 3,000 BC. Kushite or Meroitic is one of the most significant cultures to have developed in so-called 'sub-Saharan Africa, because its archaeological origins predate that of Ancient Egypt & Mesopotamia. Although later eclipsed by their brethren in the north, the Kushite or Nubian culture & language helped to lay the foundations for what Archaeologists and Linguists commonly refer to as the **Afro-Asiatic** family, which later subdivide into: Semetic, Egyptian, Coptic & Arabic, as well as the many other dialects spoken by tribes such as the Berber of North Africa & Western Sahara, and as far West as Chad and Nigeria.

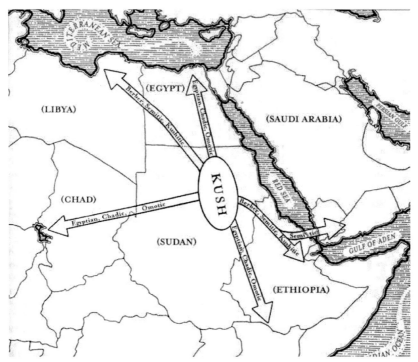

Fig.113 True Cradle of Civilization: *Map detailing the spread of the Ancient Kushite 'Afro-Asiatic' language group over 10,000 years ago*

According to Linguistic Editor of the Times, newspaper, London, Andrew Robinson, Kushite influence spread across Africa & Western Asia, since 'Pre-Historic' times, as far East as Yemen, and as far as Nigeria West.

> The Nilo- Saharan is a family of languages stretching from Lake Turkana in the East all the way to the middle Niger in the west across a belt of north-central Africa which is believed to have supported a cohesive 'aquatic' way of life in the 8th millennium BC or earlier, when the Sahara and Sahel were wetther than today. Nilo-Saharan subdivides into Sudanic languages such as Nubian, Nilotic languages, Saharan languages and Songhai in the far west.
>
> (Robinson, 2002, p: 151)

Indeed many scholars maintain that the Afro-Asiatic culture and language group are estimated to be more than 10,000 years old, and hypothesize that the Kushite language developed in Sudan prior to the ascension of the Ancient Egyptian 'Hieroglyphic' script, otherwise known as the 'Medu Netcher'. Today Western scholars propose that the earliest written language on Earth, namely Cuneiform, was initially developed in Mesopotamia over 5,000 years ago as the result of two occurrences:

1) Through an accidental flash of inspiration, after thousands of years of evolution.
2) From the necessity to keep Records & Accounts of Trade transactions within the Sumerian Civilization.

Dr. York dismisses both of these theories are incorrect, and instead proposes that Cuneiform, (which he agrees is the oldest written language), was first introduced to Humans by Divine Entities, called Elohim. In his book: *"First Language"*, Scroll # 27, released in 1993, York asserts that the first language was taught to the inhabitants of a land known then as 'Saw-Deh', *"The Outer Field or Garden"*, located on the banks of the White & Blue Niles. This correlates perfectly with both the Historic & Archaeological evidence, which places the origin of the Afro-Asiatic culture and language at precisely the same location, namely; Ancient Kush, on the banks of the Nile River. York goes onto name the people who first received this language as the 'Nubian Ptahite Ethiopian-Kuwshites', who were originally a Blue-Black complexioned Pygmy tribe. However the only problem with the supposition of Cuneiform being the first language is that it does not appear to a spoken language, but more rather a written script which has been proven to have developed from 'Pictographs', as we shall demonstrate in further depth later.

Figs.114, 115 & 116: The Holy Tablets: Left- Right: *Enuma Elish Cuneiform Tablet, Moses with Stone Tablets & Replica of Stone Tablets*

Linguistic scholars also admit that the language spoken by the ancient Kushite inhabitants of what is presently Sudan, was so old that it predated any other known language on Earth. If this is true, then the Kushite language certainly predates any known written language, which would include; Hieroglyphics & Cuneiform, which are over 5,000-years old. Therefore if Cuneiform, which was first discovered on Mesopotamian Clay Tablets, but is not the accurate name of the first language spoken by humans in Africa, then what is? The answer to this may have again been provided by York in the book *"First Language"*, in which he claims that the actual name of the first ever language spoken on Earth before Adam, (the first Homo-Sapien), was provided in the form of Laws & Commandments from the Elohim, and would accurately be called **'Nuwaubic'** or 'Nuwaupik'. The 'First Language' was apparently given to Humans in the form of a scripture called **'As Suhuf'**, or *"Pure Pages"* originally inscribed on 'Stone Tablets' in what can be described as: **'the Proto-Cuneiform script'**, much the same way Moses received the so-called 'Ten Commandments' on Mount Sinai centuries later, effectively making this language older than even Adam himself.

York further expounded this issue by asserting that initially there was only 'ONE' original Mother Language or Tongue, spoken by the Elders, Elohim or Anunnaqi, which was later written in what is now referred to as the Cuneiform script. This 'Proto-Language' was first spoken by the original 'Indigenous' inhabitants of Earth, The Pygmies or Bush-Men of East & Southern Africa, whose language consisted solely of 'Clicks & Whistles' prior to the birth of Adam. To complicate things further, in a hypothesis that skilfully amalgamates the story of Creation from the book of Genesis, with Darwin's theory of Evolution, in which York asserts that the Adam of the Bible, (who was not the Original 'Bushman' Homo Genus Adam, who had evolved over millions of years in Africa). Was of mixed Kushite & Hindu 'Watusi' ancestry, and as such, spoke a dialect called 'Ugarit', which was a fusion of 'Proto-Cuneiform' or **Nuwaupik**; the language of the Elohim & Sanskrit or 'Hindi', the ancient language of the 200 Fallen 'Hindu' Elohim, also spoken by the inhabitants of the land of Nod. Adam's tribe 'The Watusi' were descendants of the straight haired Hindu 'Fallen Angels, who often visited Earth on Hunting expeditions referred to in Genesis as *"The Giants in the Earth"*. Therefore the 'New' Adam of the book of Genesis, was the product of the daughters of Kushite Pygmy's, (Earth's indigenous inhabitants) being raped by Hindu fallen Elohim, recorded in Genesis: Chapter 6, verse 4.

So essentially, Adam's language may have been effectively a mixture of two ancient languages, initially introduced to Earth by Beings from beyond the stars. 'Eve' on the other hand, whose real name is said to have been 'Nakaybaw' meaning *"Tribal Leader"* was a pure-blooded Pygmy 'Wholly Haired' Ethiopian Kushite, who spoke the undiluted Language of the Elohim; **Nuwaupik**, later written in the 'Proto-Cuneiform Pictographic script'. Her tribe of Pygmy Kushite's or Bushmen were directly descended from the Original Adam/Genus-Homo or 'First Men', who had initially evolved on earth from the Water, Millions of years before the Biblical story in Genesis.

Figs.117 & 118: Left- Right: *Nuwaubian Illustration of Eve & A Modern Southern African Xhosa (Bushmen) Tribal Female*

The confusion regarding 'Proto-Cuneiform' or Nuwaupik, is said to have first arisen thousands of years later, following the Great Deluge, when the original language or tongue of the Elohim became sub-divided into many diverse 'Dialects', which eventually developed into several distinct different languages, illustrated in the Book of Genesis, as the 'Tower of Babel' incident as follows:

> **And the Lord said, Behold, the people *is* one, and they have all one language**; and this they begin to do: and now nothing will be restrained from them, which they have imagined to do. Go to, **let us go down, and there confound their language, that they may not understand one another's speech. So the Lord scattered them abroad from thence upon the face of all the earth:** and they left off to build the city.
>
> (The Book of Genesis Chapter 12, Verses 6 - 9)

Whether the biblical story is simply a metaphor for the development of dialects is not clear, however what is clear is that the Original Proto-language was somehow changed or transformed by the Elohim eventually becoming hundreds of different dialects of the original language, much the same way the so-called 'Romance Languages' such as; Spanish, Italian & Portuguese evolved from Latin. York lists the first group of 'Dialects' to have evolved from the original 'Pure' language, commonly referred to by Linguists as the Afro-Asiatic language family, which also form the Proto-Semitic languages:

- Akkadian
- Ashuric
- Syretic
- Elamite
- Chaldean

- Phoenician
- Aramic
- Arabic
- Hebrew
- Amharic

As time passed many of these 'Corrupted' Dialects would be 'Inscribed' in the Cuneiform script, (which is the written script of the Elohim or Anunnaqi), as in the case of Proto-Elamite, falsely attributed by Historians, as being Cuneiform/ Nuwaupik proper, when they were simply different dialects of the Mother or Proto-Language. Elamite, like many of the ancient Afro-Asiatic 'Dialects', such as Akkadian, Assyrian, Ashuric & Chaldean later adopted the Cuneiform script, much the same way the Japanese spoken language today uses the Chinese script. This then, is further verification that the so-called Afro-Asiatic language spoken by the 'Kushites' was the actual language of GOD, and therefore the language originally handed down to Man in Africa in the form of the first Laws & Commandments, which would later spread further North & East evolving into what would form the basis of the ancient Egyptian & Mesopotamian languages.

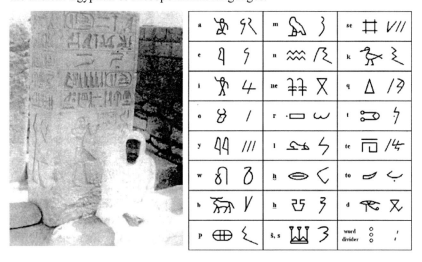

Figs.119 & 120 Ancient Linguistics: Left- Right:
Dr. York sitting next to Ancient Egyptian ruins & Table of Proto-Kushite Meroitic Script

Recent breakthroughs in DNA research haven't brought scientists any closer to discovering what the key elements were which activated our brains to evolve or transform from that of a primitive brain, similar to that of our closets genetic relatives the 'Primates' to what effectively became the brain we have today. The answer to this mystery may lay in our use of speech, for example as babies begin to grow; they undergo a gradual metamorphosis into what can be described as three stages:

**1) Use of Speech
2) Self Consciousness or Awareness
3) Use of Language**

Examining children undertake these three essential stages in their development, may provide us with clues to how we as a 'Species' first managed to evolve from Primitive humans (Homo Genus), into a more Intelligent species (Homo Sapiens), once we were taught speech by whom York refers to as the 'Elohim/Anunnaqi' or Gods, the Beings also responsible for our Genetic enhancement using their own DNA. Naturally this would have lead to us being taught language once we had initially grasped the use of 'Speech'. According to Scientists: *"A large brain is the physical essence of Humanity. It enabled language, consciousness and culture and yet....why it evolved to be so much bigger than the brain of our ape-like ancestors...**Something caused our brains to evolve to be much larger and have more functions than the brains of other mammals"*. That something or 'Key' element which scientists often refer to as the so-called 'Intelligence Gene', may have been activated by our use of speech. Which would have lead to self awareness or consciousness and the eventual use of the first language being taught to our Primitive ancestors in Africa, Millennia ago in the language which would later be referred to as Cuneiform, the language of **GOD** himself.

In his book *"First Language"*, Scroll # 27, York goes onto illustrate the process, which later took place in the development of the first language:

> The Final Step In The Development Of Cuneiform Occurred When Scribes Began Using Symbols Phonetically, This Very Word Comes From The Word Phoenicia For All The Shemitic (Semitic) Languages Passed Through, To Indicate Sounds As Well As Ideas.
>
> (York, 1993, p: 111)

York's motive for developing Nuwaubu appears to have been to 'Resurrect' or bring back to life, the Cultural/Religious practices & Language of the Ancient 'Cushite' Civilization, which have all but disappeared under the desert sands and man-made Dams of Egypt & Sudan. According to Archaeologists, the Cushite or Kushite culture of Southern Egypt & Sudan is of an unknown origin, and contains human settlements which date back over 11,000 years, making it one of the oldest existing cultures on Earth, which York claims was the 'Prototype' of both the Ancient Egyptian & Mesopotamian Civilizations.

In 1962, Professors; Keith Seele & Bruce Williams of the University of Chicago's Oriental Institute unearthed over 5,000 artefacts during an expedition which substantiated that Ancient Nubia was the **"Pre-Dynastic Birthplace"** of the 'Pharaonic' Civilization. The Nubian civilization is thought to have first emerged as early as 6,000 years ago as the "Ancient Kingdom of Kush", located towards the South of Egypt above the 3rd Cataract of the Nile. Most significant of items discovered were the artefacts unearthed in the 'A' Group gravesite, which were later confirmed to date back two centuries before the first Egyptian Dynasty of King Narmer or Menes established 3150 B.C.E.

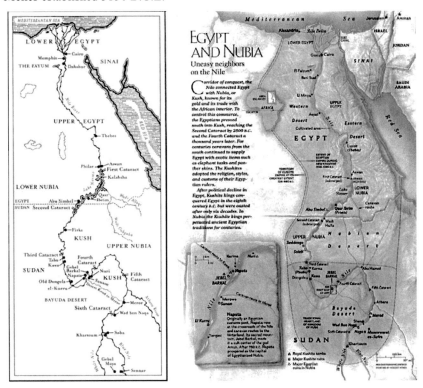

Figs.121 & 122: The Ancient Kingdom of Kush: Left- Right:
Two Maps detailing location of the Ancient Kush

Sadly, plans are currently underway by the Sudanese Government to the construct the so-called 'Meroe Dam', which like its predecessor the Aswan Dam further north, will eventually succeed in destroying further traces of the 'Kushite' Meroetic (Nubian) Culture & Civilization erasing what may probably be the true **'Cradle of Civilization'** and advanced human settlements forever. Many Historians view the US$2 billion Arab Financed, Hydro-Electric Dam project along the Nile as yet another deliberate attempt by both the Egyptian & Sudanese Governments to remove all evidence of the 'Primacy' of the Nubian-Kushite culture from the Nile Valley. According to the World Commission on Dams (WCD), the Meroe Dam project will not only have catastrophic consequences for the environment displacing over 50,000 of the areas indigenous inhabitants, but also completely obliterate a historically rich region.

Figs.123, 124, 125 & 126: Attempted Destruction of the Cradle of Civilization: Top, Left- Right: *Ruins of the Ancient Kushite Civilization* **(Bottom)** *Western & Arab Sponsored Hydro Electric Dam Projects of Aswan (Egypt) & Meroe (Sudan)*

Furthermore, evidence directly linking the ancient Kushite to ancient Mesopotamian Kingdoms may also exist in the biblical book of Genesis, which provides verification of another of York's assertion as having some basis in fact. That namely; Kush or Cush was the father or progenitor of Nimrud, otherwise known to historians as 'The Great Sargon', identified as one of the earliest rulers of the Mesopotamian Empire, located in what is modern day Iraq. If this is correct, then it is further verification that the Cushite or 'Kushite' language & culture is not only the oldest on Earth, but directly responsible for giving birth to both the ancient Egyptian & Mesopotamia Civilizations, referred to in the Hebrew Torah as the pure Descendants of Noah: **Miz-ra-im and Nimrud**:

> And the Son of Ham; Cush, and Miz-ra-im, and Phut, and Canaan. And the Sons of Cush; Se-ba, and Hav-i-lah, and Sab-tah, and Ra-a-mah, and Sab-te-cha: and the sons of Ra-a-mah; She-ba, and De-dan.
> And Cush begat **Nimrod**: he began to be mighty one in the earth. He was a mighty hunter before the Lord: wherefore it is said, Even as **Nimrod** the mighty hunter before the Lord. **And the beginning of his kingdom was Babel, and Er-ech, and Ac-cad, and Cal-neh, in the land of Shi-nar.**
> (The Book of Genesis Chapter 10, Verses 6 - 10)

As far back as the late 1970s, evidence emerged which also establishes an irrefutable link between the Pre-Egyptian Civilization of Kush and ancient Mesopotamia. In his book *"The 12th Planet"*, Professor of African & Near Eastern antiquities Zecharia Sitchin concluded that the source of the early Mesopotamian culture was indeed ancient Kish, known in the bible as Kush. Sitchin equates the emergence of ancient Akkad from an Archaeological stand point to the biblical Cush or Kush ancestor of Nimrod. Sitchin highlights the discovery of several ancient Akkadian Cuneiform Tablets, which bore intriguing inscriptions, and read almost identically to the above mentioned biblical accounts found in the book of Genesis.

> The mystery of such an early Mesopotamian civilization depend, however, as inscriptions recording the achievements and genealogy of Sargon of Akkad were found. They stated that his full title was "King of Akkad, King of Kush"; they explain that before he assumed the throne, he had been a counselor to the "rulers of Kish." Was there, then – scholars asked themselves – an even earlier kingdom, that of Kish, which preceded Akkad?...**Many scholars have speculated that Sargon of Akkad was the biblical Nimrod**. If one reads "Kish" for "Kush" in the above biblical verses, it would seem Nimrud was indeed preceeded by Kish, as claimed by Sargon. The scholars then began to accept literally the rest of his inscriptions: "He defeated Uruk and tore down its wall...he was victorious in the battle with the inhabitants of Ur...he defeated the entire territory from Lagash as far as the sea." Was the biblical Erech identical with the Uruk of Sargon's inscriptions? As the site now called Warka was unearthed, that was found to be the case. And the Ur referred to by Sargon was none other than the biblical Ur, the Mesopotamian birthplace of Abraham.
>
> (Sitchin, 1976, p: 29-30)

Finally here was concrete verification which placed the birthplace of the Mesopotamian Civilization in Sudan, East Africa, namely the Black Pre-Pharaohnic Civilization of Kush, known in Genesis as Cush, who was the Father of a very important individual; Nimrod, the Grandson of Noah, who is indisputably identified in the ancient Akkadian Tablets as The Great Sargon of Kish, conqueror & architect of the post Deluge (Flood) Mesopotamian Civilization.

Although this information has subsequently been kept from the public, the Cuneiform inscriptions cannot be refuted, which is why the understanding of language is crucial to unravelling the truth about the 'True Cradle of Human Civilization'.

Figs.127, 128, 129 & 130: The Mighty Kushite Hunter: Top, Left- Right: *Nuwaubian illustration of Nimrod otherwise known as Sargon The Great & Actual Statue of Nimrod/ Sargon* **(Bottom)** *Ancient Kushites & Akkadian Wall Carving of Nimrud /Sargon*

According to York, the key to understanding our past evolution as a species, and connection to God lay in language. It was for this reason that the Nuwaubian leader claims that the New Testament book of John, Chapter One, starts off: *"In The Beginning Was The Word"*. And in the Holy Qur'aan, the first thing the Prophet Muhammad is instructed or Commanded to do was; 'Iqra' or *"Read"*, because the initial point of contact between God and Man is through speech or 'Words' which must be comprehended through language. Nuwaubic is therefore the renewal of the earliest language spoken & written in the Cuneiform script on the Planet by 'Homo Sapiens', originally introduced to Man by the Ancestral Race of God's; The Anunnaqi or Elohim, who first brought Civilization to Africa & the so-called Middle East. Being a Linguist, York was able to develop for his followers a language, which would be unique to them alone, and eventually all Blacks in the Western Hemisphere, as one of York's followers so succinctly put it:

> [We] decided that in renewing ourselves with our own Culture, and our own commitments and our Scripture called The Holy Tablets, we needed our language. We are about using "Our Own Stuff", not Arabs dialect, Swahili dialect or anyone else's dialect, but our own with our own script. We must stop trying to be other people and be ourselves. This enables us to have our own mind and makes us free from being like everyone else...
>
> (Wikipedia, 2006)

'Egipt' of The West

Critics however, particularly in the Mainstream Media, have often lampooned the Nuwaubians for their revisionist approach to ancient language. For example, they have been heavily criticised for their apparent mis-spelling of word's, such as Egypt which they spell; **'E-g-i-p-t'** with an; 'I' instead of a letter 'Y'. However being a qualified Linguist, York fully understood that the word 'Egypt', traditionally spelt by Europeans with a 'Y', should actually be translated into English as 'E-g-i-p-t', because in the Hieretic language, the word 'Egiptos', meaning *"Dark or Burnt Faces"*, contains an 'I' sound instead of a 'Y', which means that the Nuwaubians were correct in their spelling of the word as 'Egipt' as opposed to 'Egypt'.

Nuwaubu, like York's previous teachings soon began to have a tremendous far-reaching effect upon Blacks throughout the Western Hemisphere, with branches of the movement developing not only within the United States, but also Europe, the islands of the Caribbean & Latin America. Each year, during the month of June, Cultural Festivals were held on the group's 476-acre retreat in Georgia, known as Kodesh or 'Tama Re', celebrating the group's annual 'Saviours Day' held to commemorate Malachi York's Birthday, which has been held annually since the organisation began in 1968. The celebrations were also held by the Nuwaubian's in honour of the cultural identity of Nuwaubu.

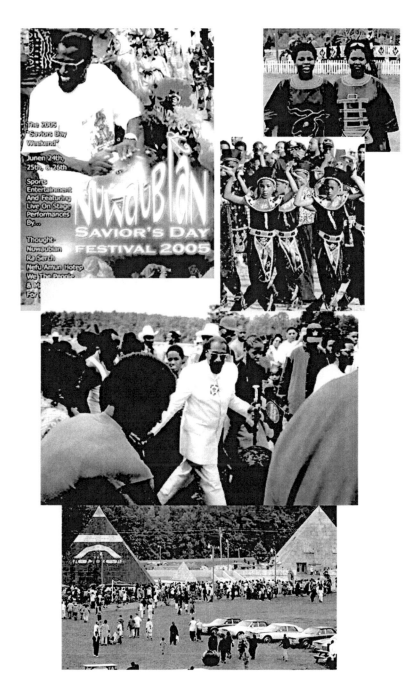

Figs.131, 132, 133, 134 & 135: Annual Saviour's Day Celebration: Top, Left- Right:
Dr. Malachi. Z. York during Saviour's Day Celebration **(Bottom)** *Nuwaubian Devotees & Children at group's Annual Festival*

The miracle of Nuwaubu lay in the fact that unlike traditional so-called Afrocentricism, which simply adopts a retrospective, 'Utopian' view of African History; 'Fantasizing' and Romanticizing about a fictitious Ancient African past, which has no evidence as ever having existed. Instead, Nuwaubu brings to life the Cultural achievements of past Civilizations, and by so doing enable its followers to develop a self belief by drawing from the positive aspects of Ancient: Egyptian, Mesopotamian, Kushite, Hebraic, Islamic, African & Mesoamerican (Native American) Cultures to gain greater confidence in their day to day lives to outstanding effect. This Nuwaubian enthusiasm for all things Ancient resulted in a number of 'Replicas' of Ancient African & Semetic monuments being erected for Religious, Cultural & Commercial purposes, such an Obelisk, a Sphinx, Solomon's Temple, as well as a Masjid (Mosque) & Shrine dedicated to the 'Mahdi' of Sudan. By doing so, York was able to create a productive Modern society, based upon the principles of the past, without being stuck there. Much like the Yoruba Culture/Religion of Nigeria; Nuwaubu is an active and vibrant African 'Culture', which represents an alternative to the Euro & Arab-centric interpretations of Christianity & Islam.

Defiantly dismissing his critics contention that his group was a 'Cult', York actually embraced the term, arguing that 'Cult' was an abbreviation of 'Culture', which was the main focus of Nuwaubu; **to 'Cultivate' or Redevelop** the Blackman & Woman in America's lost way of life or way of life.

> "...then we're giving birth to a Culture, and then the word 'Cult' is no longer an insult, you follow? They say you all belong to that Cult, say that's right! We are 'Cultivating' our Culture. Yeah we're a Cult alright, but what is a Cult without any Culture?"
>
> (Bar El Haady, 1993)

York's assertion that the term 'Cult' is derived from Culture is validated by Senior fellow at the Russell Kirk Centre for Cultural Renewal, Professor Bruce Foremen [3], who contends that people are primarily bound together by social habits, such as Arts, Cuisine & Language. Which in turn form the basis of all Religions & Civilizations.

> A brief excursion into etymology seems in order. Several commentators, including Eliot's colleague, historian Christopher Dawson, have noted that culture comes from the cult. This is no mere wordplay. **Culture and cult share a common root in the Latin,** *colere*, which means to cultivate, as in cultivating one's garden or one's character, developing the proper, elevated habits.
>
> (Foremen, 2001)

Central to the Nuwaubian 'Cultural' monuments was the aptly named 'Black Pyramid' & Maze complex, constructed for the Nuwaubian 'Pilgrimage'; **"El Maguraj"**, equivalent to the Muslim Hajj to Mecca, which York asserts, also had its roots in Ancient Egypt. The Nuwaubian Mauguraj was designed for the purpose of "Realignment of the 'Chakras and reconnection with the Most High". On June 26th 1997 Dr. York officially inaugurated the El Maguraj Ceremony by performing a Ritual, which had apparently not been performed in almost 10,000 years. The following are excerpts taken from the Nuwaubian Newsletter released in 1997, entitled: *"Egypt of The West Saviour's Day"*, which details the meaning behind the El Maguraj Ceremony:

> **El Maguraj,** Is A Ritual That Has Not Been Practiced In Over **10,000 Years,** It Was Lost Because The People Of **Atlan** Or **Atlantis** Were Also Lost. It Was A Concentrated Effort To Remove Your Soul…The Purpose Of **El Maguraj** *"The Pilgrimage"* Is To Take Practice In An Event That May Change The Course Of <u>Our-Story</u> Us **Nuwaubians,** Not Their Story <u>Out-Story</u>…Some May Say We Copied Our Pilgrimage From The Muslims. However, Let Me Give You The Facts On The Origin of Our Pilgrimage. If You Go Back **10,000** Years Ago, You Will Find The Ritual Of Amun, In Karnak, A City Of What's Being Called Egypt Today. The Priests Of Amun, Called Kahunaat, Would Go Into The Temple, Bathe Themselves In Holy Water, Shave All The Hair Off Their Bodies, And Done Themselves With A Plain White Seamless Garment. Then They Would Go Around A Big Cube Granite Stone, With A **Dub** *"Black Scarab Beetle",* Symbol Of Health, Vitality And Luck On Top Of It, Which They Would Touch Or Kiss And Walk Around This Building Seven Times. After Which, They Would Go Off And Give Praise To The Deity **Amun-Ra,** A Deity That Is Acknowledged By Jews, **Amin,** And Is Mentioned In The Old Testament **22** Times Times, By Christians As **Amen,** Which Is Mentioned In The New Testament **50** Times, And By Muslims As Amiyn, Which Is Mentioned In The Koran **15** Times. They All End Their Prayers In Recognition Of This Great Deity…
>
> (York, 1997)

York rationalized that the so-called '3' Major World faiths: Judaism, Christianity & Islam, all had their roots or origins in El Khamiy or Kemet, otherwise known as The Civilization of Ancient 'Kush', later referred to as Egypt. Therefore after taking his followers through each stage of these religious doctrines, he finally "Crystallized" all of the information taught to them throughout his 30-year Ministry into a new single advanced 'Afro-centred' religious-cultural Doctrine he titled 'Nuwaubu'.

> They Do The Same Thing In Schools. You Have Different Courses Such As Mathematics, Social Studies, Etc., Then You Have What They call Advanced Math. When You Finish With One Course You Advance To The Next Class. And That's What We Did When We Finished One School We Advanced To The Next Class.
>
> (York, 1996, p: 112)

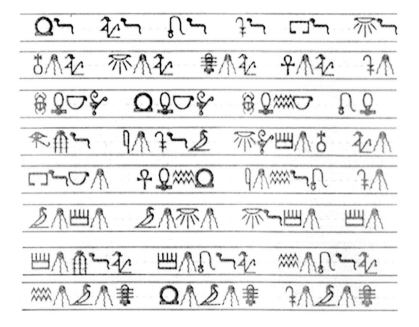

Figs.136 & 137: Nuwaubic: Top & Bottom:
Two Forms of The Nuwaubian 'Nuwaubic' Script, entirely developed by Dr. Malachi. Z. York

York encouraged blacks to immediately abandon all foreign religious beliefs, which were controlled by Non-African people such as:

- **Orthodox 'Sunni' Islam: Lead by Euro/Asian-Arabs, & Centred in Mecca, Saudi Arabia**
- **Christianity: Lead by Europeans & Centred in Bethlehem, Israel & Rome, Italy**
- **Judaism: Lead by Euro-Jews & Centred in Jerusalem, Israel**
- **Buddhism: Lead by Asians & Centred in the Far East**
- **Hinduism: Lead by Indians & Centred in India**

Nuwaubu then, would be unique, unlike these other faiths, because it would be led by, and centred around people of Negroid ethnicity, with its centre or 'Mecca' on Black owned land, either in America, or eventually on the African Continent itself.

Figs.138, 139 & 140: 10,000 Year Old Ceremony: Top, Left- Right:
Nuwaubian Black Pyramid
(Bottom) *Malachi York as Incarnation of Egyptian God Osirus Performing El Maguraj Ceremony in 1997*

Media Onslaught & Smear Campaign

Unaware, or for that matter uninterested in the real background or religious teachings the Nuwaubians had been immersed in since the 1970's, the White Media didn't at first exactly know what to make of the York's teachings, which to them seemed like nothing more than a strange, yet harmless "Mix" of religious philosophies. However, when 'Pyramids' and Afro-centric cultural-religious Literature began appearing in rural Georgia, the press soon worked out what York was up to, and immediately went on the offensive, putting their propaganda machine into 'Full-Gear'. This was done by quickly making the term Nuwaubian synonymous with 'Cult', and therefore rendered it worthless in the eyes of rational members of the public. Sure the Nuwaubian lifestyle was different to most Americans, but never throughout their 35-year history has the group even been known to officially espouse Violence either amongst themselves or towards the general public, which is what the Media were subtly trying to imply by the use of the word 'Cult'.

The first major article concerning the group appeared in CNN dated June 29, 1999, entitled: *"Religious rift brews in rural Georgia"* 2. In the feature CNN Journalist Jim Marrs, quotes a local Sheriff named Howard Sills, who accused the group of being **"black separatists who may be stockpiling weapons"**.

To further discredit the Nuwaubians, their leader Dr. Malachi. Z. York's past was immediately also brought under scrutiny:

> York, according to the New York Times, is a convicted felon who has admitted serving three years in prison in the 1960s for resisting arrest, assault and possession of a dangerous weapon.
>
> (CNN.com)

Much attention has been paid to York's criminal convictions and time spent in prison, and it has also been suggested by many Journalists that York is a Con-man who simply began his organisation in the 1970s, as an alternative to crime. Writing for *"The Black World Today"*, newspaper, Roy L. Parish referred to York in 2002, as a: **"...self made scholar and community organizer..."** However what they often fail to point out is that York is in fact an academic who holds a PhD, in Theology and Linguistics, which makes him a Professor, hardly a self made Scholar!! Aside from authoring Hundreds of books, he has translated **'The Torah'** (5 books of Moses) from the original Hebrew into English, **'The Psalms'** (book of David) from the original Hebrew into English, **'The Revelations'** (book of John for: Jesus), from the original Galilean Aramaic into English & **'The Holy Qu'ran'** (book of Muhammad), from the original Classical Arabic into English. This alone is an astonishing feat, therefore why are York's academic accomplishments never mentioned by any of his detractors? Who are nevertheless, always ready to play down York's academic achievements, yet quick to point out what he teaches regarding UFO's & Aliens, seldom making mention that York is a Professor of Theology and Linguistics, as well an accomplished author. What he teaches about UFOs and Aliens is completely irrelevant to the group's achievements, and credit should be given where it is due. If it was that simple to do what York has managed to achieve throughout the past 30-years then the world would be full of uneducated people doing what York has done.

If the Media reports are in fact accurate, and York is nothing more than an Ex-convict, Con man & Intellectual Charlatan, who only teaches about Extraterrestrials, then how has it been possible for him to hold his own in a Linguistic debates against some of the World's leading Scholars? So what was is it really about the Nuwaubians that brought them such hostility from the mainstream media, other than their evidently strange beliefs? Well, at least one of the answers may lay in the opening paragraph of the previously mentioned CNN article, which stated:

> EATONTON, Georgia (CNN) -- Suspicion and apprehension are mounting between local authorities in rural central Georgia and a black religious group -- the Nuwaubians -- **who have declared themselves a separate nation** and deny they are a cult.
>
> (CNN.com)

Long before the Nuwaubian's uncanny beliefs came into question, or any suggestion of criminal activity, or even Child Molestation accusations were associated with the group, it was understood by the media that the Nuwaubians had *"declared themselves a separate nation"*, which has been the sole reason for the media's campaign against them. After all, there are many groups with equally bizarre beliefs such as The Raelians, who have received hardly any sustained negative media attention at all. Clearly the establishment became alarmed by York's decision to declare The United Nuwaubian Nation of Moors 'a Sovereign Nation', independent from the United States as we shall investigate in further depth later.

Nevertheless let us digress from the Media for a moment to concentrate on York's academic abilities for those who are unaware, and have only heard about all these side issues, such as his beliefs in 'Little Green Men' from mars and so-called Criminal past.

Linguistic Abilities

I Decided Long Ago Never To Walk In Any Man's Shadow. That's To Say That I Would Master The Languages Translate And Transliterate Word For Word And That Anyone Who Walked With Me Would Have To Shed Myths And Beliefs And Deal Strictly With Facts…
(Excerpt taken from *"Does Dr. Malachi. Z. York Try To Hide That He Was Imaam Issa?,"* by York, 1996)

Author's Note: Many of the words used below were originally presented in the Arabic script, however for the sake of clarity we have decided to have them translated into English, for the benefit of our readers.

In his book *"The Ansaar Cult in America"*, One of the world's leading Islamic Scholars, Professor Bilial Philips, attempts dispute the accuracy of York's teachings by pointing out errors in his translations of the Qur'an. The following are taken from a series of Intellectual exchanges, which took place between York & Philips between 1989 & 1998:

The Inept Translator

As for Isa being the "Furqaan" and his divinely granted comprehension", from the countless errors which abound in his publications, some of which are mentioned elsewhere in this book, it is clearly evident that he lacks a fundamental understanding of the Arabic language from both a grammatical and morphological point of view. Three glaring examples here will suffice to demonstrate Isa's blundering ignorance of Arabic.

In his book supposedly explaining the secret meaning of the Qur'aan as well as in the introduction to his (mis) translation of a part of the Qur'aan, Isa boldly makes the following claim:

"The word *Qur'aan* is derived from the word Qara, meaning "he read or read". When the dual tense of the Arabic language "an" is attached to the end of the word, it denotes *two*. Ex. KITAAB (SCRIPTURE) QALAM (PEN) KITABAAN (2 SCRIPTURES) QALAMAAN (2 PENS) The dual tense attached to the word Qara'a thus makes it QUR'AAN. In essence, this means "two readings".

Based on this **misunderstanding**, Isa then embarks on his interpretation of what the supposed two readings of the Qur'aan are. However, although the dual form of words is formed by adding the suffix (*aan*) in the case of nouns, as in the two examples given, as well as in the case of adjectives, this is not so in the case of verbs in the past tense like *Qara'a*. Its dual is formed by merely adding an *Alif,* alone as is explained in any basic book on Arabic grammar. Hence, the dual form of ***Qar'a*** is ***Qara'aa*** (two of them read). There are also many grammatical and morphological reasons why the word Qur'aan could not be a dual form.

(Philips, 1989, p: 68-69)

York immediately responded in the same year, in his book *"The Ansaar Cult in America Rebuttal to the Slanderers"*, on page 378:

The Inept Translator:

Mr Phillips states on page 68:

"The dual form of ***Qar'a*** is ***Qara'aa*** (two of them read). There are also many grammatical and morphological reasons why the word Qur'aan could not be a dual form"

The word can mean two readings. Anyone who has any inclination of Arabic grammar knows that the Arabic verb can convert into a noun form or the MASDAR a verbal noun, for example: let's take the root word ***Qar'a*** . It's the verb, which means: "to recite out loud; to read, to greet solute".

From this verb derivatives are formed; for example:

(**Qar'ah**) Reading out loud

(**Qaariah**) A Reader

(**Maqruw-a**) Worth reading

In the Arabic language we have what is called the dual tense or AL MUTHANA, this is the word used to denote two. This is formed by adding the dual suffix (an), pronounced "an", scripture; Kitaabaan, 2 scriptures.

Now in the word Al Qur'aan, which is a noun, we notice this same dual suffix located at the end of a word. Now why do you suppose that the dual suffix is placed at the end of this word? Why would the word "Qur'aan" mean two readings? We are not saying the noun Al Qur'aan is dual however, it appears to be dual because it has the Alif Nuwn (an) at the end. In actuality it is like the words listed below which signify a distinction or relation between <u>two</u> things. Let's take a look at other verbs whose noun form, act like the word Al Qur'aan.

(**Faraqa**) To separate part, divide   (**Furqaan**) To differentiate between (2 things) the allegorical and the decisive portions of the Scriptures

(**Sawdah**) To make black   (**Sawdaan**) Two blacks (Plural)

Thus this suffix "an" in the word also denotes a dual sense (2), the "two readings". Some words that have (an) located at the end denote adjective form of words; for example: (Kasalaan) lazy from the root word (Kasalan) to be lazy. Yet, the word Qur'aan isn't an adjective and thus, this cannot apply to it. You might also say that the noun (Amaan) which has (an) at the end is not dual so words that end in (an) are not all dual. Yet what you fail to realize is that an (an) was not added to this word to change it from a verb to a noun. The root verb of the word (Amaan) and as we can see the letter (nuwn) is part of the root word, it does not have a dual suffix added. Therefore the word (Al Qur'aan) does not fall into this category either. So what actually happened is the verb Qaraa is such that when turned into a noun, it has a dual meaning and signifies a relation between two things thus its meaning is clearly "two readings"...The word Al Qur'aan refers to two Qur'aans one which is in heaven and one which is on Earth.

(Isa Al Mahdi, 1998, p: 378-379)

Although the concept of 'Nuwaubu' may sound completely crazy when heard for the first time, after thorough analytical examination, it does make sense in a perplexing type of way. After all, the group had been immersed into the strict religious practices of both Islam & Judaism, and meticulously studied Christianity, for over 25 years, becoming proficient in the languages of the Old & New Testament's of the Bible, and the Qur'an. In addition to this, York had also exposed his followers to literally every other world religious philosophy, with the understanding that he had plenty more 'Etheric' knowledge to reveal. Dismissing all detractors who labelled his organisation a 'Cult', York boldly asserted that the term 'Cult' was in fact derived from the word 'Culture', which denoted the Nuwaubian *Civilization, Traditions & Customs*. At this stage in the group's metamorphoses it was increasingly becoming clear that York had only used these religions as a cover to impart what it was he really intended to teach, which was a type of 'New Age Spirituality', therefore in retrospect, the eventual abandonment of traditional religious dogma seems like the only logical progression' for York's teachings to have taken.

The Holy Tablets

> I Am Called The Renewer Or Reformer, Al Mujadid, And The Root Of The Word Mujadid Is Jadid *"New"*.
> The Holy Tablets Is A Renewal Of All Of The Old Scriptures That Were Lost But Now Found...
> (Excerpt taken from: *"Does Dr. Malachi. Z. York Try To Hide The Fact That He was Imaam Issa?"*, by York, 1996)

Around 1993, York then still under the name Rabboni Y'shua Bar El Haady, released a "Truth" bulletin entitled *"The True Story of the Beginning"*. In it, he made the remarkable assertion that Adam and Eve were not the first people on the planet, and that they did in fact have parents. We will not go into too much detail as to what the booklet said, but basically York was claiming that the human race did not begin with Adam as the first man, as understood by the three major monotheistic faiths, but rather evolved over millions of years, through different stages. This theory of man's evolution from Homo Genus (First man), Homo-Erectus

Fig.141: Right Knowledge: *Publication; 'The True Story of the Beginning'*

(Upright man) and finally Homo Sapien (Intelligent or Thinking Man), has traditionally been held by atheists who completely reject the book of Genesis' account. So was York now accepting Darwin's theory over that of the Word of God? Not entirely, because York maintained that Man was

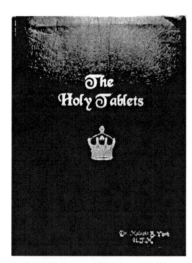

Fig.142: Ancient Scripture: *York's Translation of the Sumerian 'Tablets'*

assisted at every stage of his evolution by Extraterrestrial Beings, which he claimed the bible called Eloheem, which is Hebrew for 'God's'. Adam and Eve were said to have been selected from two separate tribes which inhabited the Earth, and were chosen by these Eloheem to replenish the Earth after a cataclysmic event occurred which wiped out most of humanity, very similar to the one which had wiped-out the Dinosaurs thousands of years earlier. Apparently the beginning of the book of Genesis picks up after this event took place, in other words 'exactly' what happened with Noah after the flood. The bulletin was closely followed by a book entitled *"Right Knowledge"*, Scroll # 28, which further elaborated the Adam & Eve story, and presented a new paradigm, which was so radical in its view of the creation of man, that it marked the final turning point in the group's metamorphosis. They were now on their own, and although still called The Holy Tabernacle Ministries (HTM), this new doctrine had absolutely no similarities to any of the other three monotheistic religions. York called this new creed 'Nuwaubu', which he said translated into English as *"Right Knowledge"*, and was steeped in ancient Sumerian and Egyptian theological & mythological elements, which York claims formed the original foundation of Judaism, Christianity and Islam in the first place. To corroborate this, in 1995 he released a 'Biblical' style scripture, called *"The Holy Tablets"*, which became the groups official Religious manifesto. These *"Holy Tablets"* though sloppily plagiarized from New Age works such as *"The Sirius Mystery"*, by Robert K. G· Temple & *"The Keys of Enoch"*, by Dr. J.J. Hurtak, in Chapter 3, *"The Scientist"*. Nevertheless, the general consensus amongst York's followers at the time was that they were so familiar with this type of New Age literature that it was no big secret to York's followers where much of this material had been taken from. Notwithstanding, the vast majority of the 'Tablets' are widely acknowledged as being based predominately upon translations of the Tablets of ancient Sumer, which York claims to have translated from Ancient Cuneiform Tablets into English for his followers, which means the Tablets were never regarded as a newly 'Revealed' work anyway. What made the *"Holy Tablets"* relevant was that they are actually based upon the Cuneiform 'Tablets' of Ancient Sumer, which form the basis of the Old Testament, making the Tablets 'Pre-Biblical' information, which included such books as: **The Enuma Elish,**

The Tablet of Anzu, The Tablet of Kurnugi, The Epic of Gilgamesh & The Tablet of Etana.
The 'Holy Tablets' also contained a number of Chapters authored by York himself, as well as three more books, which York claimed to have been teaching from since the 1970s, called **'As Suhuf'** or ***"Pure Pages"***, **'The Book of Enoch'** & **'The Book of the Generations of Abraham'**, as well as **'Al Hikmah';** ***"The Book of Wisdom"*** of the Ethiopian Prophet Luqmaan.

> The Introduction Of The **Holy Tablets** Is Nothing New. I Introduced Pieces Of the Holy Suhuf, As Well As The **Book Of Wisdom**, Which Is Incorporated Into The Holy Tablets, To My Followers Years Ago. You Can Find Excerpts Of the **Holy Tablets** In Some Of My Old Pamphlets Such As ***"What And Where Is Hell? Edition #76, the True Story Of The Story Of Abraham Edition #91, The True Story Of Noah Edition #83, Where Is The Tabernacle Of The Most High? Edition #157*** And The List Could Go On And On...
>
> (York, 1996, p: 94-95)

Historians confirm that the story of creation in the book of Genesis (The Torah) is based upon the Sumerian *"Epic of Creation"*, the "Enuma Elish". Zechariah Sitchin in his book *"The Twelfth Planet"* clarifies this by the following:

> Biblical scholars now recognize that the Hebrew *Tehom* ("Watery deep") stems from Tiamat; that *Tehom-Raba* means "great Tiamat," and the biblical understanding of primeval events is based upon the Sumerian cosmologic epics. It should also be clear that first and foremost among theses parallels are the opening verses of the Book of Genesis, describing how the Wind of the Lord hovered over the waters of *Tehom*, and how the lightning of the Lord (Murduk in the Babylonian version) lit the darkness of space as it hit and split Tiamat, creating Earth and the *Rakia* (literally, "the hammered bracelet"). This celestial band (hitherto translated as "firmament") is called "the Heaven." The Book of Genesis (1:8) explicitly states that it is this "hammered out bracelet" that the Lord had named "heaven" (*shamaim*). The Akkadian texts also called this celestial zone "the hammered braclet" (*rakkis*), and describe how:
>
> Modern scholars believe that after Earth became a planet it was a hot ball of belching volcanoes, filling the skies with mists and clouds. As temperatures began to cool, the vapors turned to water, separating the face of Earth into dry land and oceans.
>
> The fifth tablet of *Enuma Elish*, though badly mutilated, imparts exactly the same scientific information. Describing the gushing lava as Tiamats's "spittle," the Creation epic correctly places this phenomenon before the formation of the atmosphere, the oceans of Earth, and the continents. After the "cloud waters were gathered", the oceans began to form, and the "foundations" of Earth-its continents-were raised. As "the making of cold" – a cooling off – took place, rain and mist appeared. Meanwhile, the "spittle" continued to pour forth, "laying in layers," shaping Earth's topography.

> Once again, the biblical parallel is clear:
> And God said:
> "Let the waters under the skies be gathered together,
> unto one place, and let dry land appear."
> And it was so.
> Earth, with oceans, continents, and atmosphere, was now ready for the formation of mountains, rivers, springs,
> valleys. Attributing all Creation to the Lord Murduk, *Enuma Elish* continued the narration:
> Putting Tiamat's head [Earth] into position,
> He raised the mountains thereon.
> He opened springs, the torrents to draw off.
> Through her eyes he released the Tigris and Euphrates.
> From her teats he formed the lofty mountains,
> Drilled springs for wells, the water to carry off.
> In perfect accord with modern findings, both the Book of Genesis and *Enuma Elish* and other related Mesopotamian texts place the beginning of life upon Earth in the waters, followed by the "living creatures that swarm" and "fowl that fly." Not until then did "living creatures after their kind: cattle and creeping things and beasts" appear upon Earth, culminating with the appearance of Man-the final act of Creation.
>
> (Sitchin, 1991, p: 208-210)

Aside from Zechariah Sitchin, New Age/Esoteric Scholar Bobby Hemmit, also confirms that the Sumerian Tablet the *"Enuma Elish"* forms the basis of the Biblical Creation story. During a lecture at the Melanin Conference, held in Detroit, Michigan, October 2001, he stated:

> Moving right along, we are going into a little mythology right now because the name of this is the history of melanin. This is coming from the "Enuma Elish". (This is) where you have the great mother that rules the Enuma Elish. You'll get Alexander Hegel's book "Babylonian Genesis", that's the book with the Enuma Elish in it. And this is the creation mythology of the great mother being overthrown by one of her sons Marduk. And her body (is) crushed up in the triple blackness of space- crushed up and human beings (were) made out of it.
>
> (Hemmit, 2001)

The notion of the Sumerian Tablets as the basis of the Biblical account of creation from a scientific perspective is what forms the basis of "Nuwaubu" (Right Knowledge), and provided York's followers with most of what they needed to explain their new doctrine to the curious public who by this point had many questions. *"The Holy Tablets"*, were a type of scripture for them so they wouldn't feel left out in the presence of Muslims, Christians and Hebrews a kind of "nah, nah, nanana, look what we've got", scenario.

Nuwaubu: 'Right Knowledge'

NUWAUPU (pronounced NOO-WAH-POO) is the spiritual science of the Ethiopian Race, the Wooly-Haired People all over Planet Earth. The meaning of the word Nuwaupu is THE RIGHT KNOWLEDGE, RIGHT WISDOM, AND RIGHT UNDERSTANDING THAT LEADS TO SOUND RIGHT REASONING. Nuwaupu is ALL knowledge, ALL wisdom, ALL understanding – finite and infinite.

As previously stated, this concept of Nuwaubu was officially re-launched by York in the book: *"Right Knowledge Scroll # 28*, in 1993. Some sources indicate that 'Nuwaubu' or *Right Knowledge* was what York originally began teaching as early as 1968, when his group were initially known as 'Ansar Pure Sufi'. However due to the depth of this Philosophy, York decided to walk his followers through the 3 Major world Religions, before eventually unveiling what he really intended to teach, hence: *"I Came Giving You What You Wanted (Namely Religion), So That You Would Learn To Want What I Really Had To Give"*, which was said to be York's Mantra, throughout his 35 year Ministry. York somehow understood the

Fig.143 *Cover of York's Publication; 'Right Knowledge*

intellectual make-up of Blacks, therefore by utilising an ingenious method combining Powerful imagery and Linguistics he was able to unlock the secret of how to enhance the intellect of his followers through his books & lectures. By bombarding them with imagery of themselves, York has been able to tap deep down into the psyche of Blacks through his doctrine of 'Right Knowledge'. Like his predecessors, the Hon. Marcus Garvey & Hon. Elijah Muhammad, York understood how to energise and electrify the mentality of Blacks, and by so doing raise their Mental, Spiritual & Physical condition to a higher level than they were prior to encountering his teachings. Psychologists claim that many people prefer to read with assistance of imagery, rather than continued lengthy text. This coupled with the fact that blacks were vigorously prevented from reading for over 300-years during and after Slavery & Colonialism, which may probably be why books are less popular with blacks than with any other ethnic group. Initially this supposition may appear as further evidence of backwardness & 'Anti-Intellectualism' amongst blacks, however it is a fact that for the majority of our evolution on this Planet, Human beings have related to objects and things around them to communicate with to each other. This is verified by the fact that the original languages have universally proven to have first been in the form of 'Pictographs' such as in ancient Egyptian Hieroglyphics & Sumerian Cuneiform, which were initially symbols of animals and other animate & inanimate objects prior to evolving into 'Cursive' scripts, which eventually became language texts:

> The earliest writing of all, on clay tablets from ancient Sumer in Mesopotamia,...The first written symbols are generally thought to have been pictograms: iconic drawings of, say, a pot, or a fish, or a head with an open jaw (representing the concept of eating)... These have been found in Mesopotamia and Egypt dating to the mid-4th millennium BC...
>
> (Robinson, 2002, p: 23 – 26)

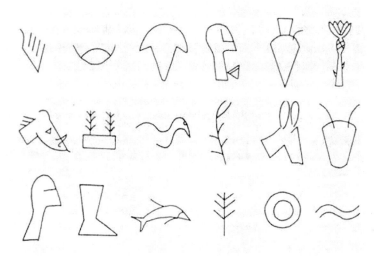

Therefore as a linguist, York understood how the human mind worked, and utilized imagery and linguistics in his literature to re-activate the minds of blacks whom it seemed 'Absorbed and Decoded' information much more effectively when assisted by 'Imagery' as opposed to plain text, which is essentially a Euro-centric method of learning. Right Knowledge or Nuwaubu then, was the skilful combination of Science, Religion and Mythology combined with Powerful Afro-centric imagery and language, into what would eventually become the group's new doctrine from which the term *"Nuwaubians"* was first derived. York's new series of books or 'Scrolls' which became known as the aptly named 'Right Knowledge series' initially came in convenient Pocket size issues which later proved to be a stroke of genius on the Nuwaubian leader's part as these miniature sized publications packed with information, became a resounding success at a time when the movement was going through an unstable transitional period.

Fig.144 *Table showing Early Afro-Asiatic Pictographic Script, which later developed into the first language: Cuneiform*

information, (though occasionally plagiarised), York has been able to skilfully amalgamate into a cohesive doctrine for his followers, is a remarkable achievement which should never be underestimated, as Afro-centric Islamic Scholar & Activist Amiyr Abu Hamin 3, also points out:

Fig.145: *Author Amiyr Abu Hamin*

Beyond the rhetoric of the hidden galaxies and Illiyun (Sirus), the adoption of other peoples' theories (i.e. the I AM America Map, and the cosmogenesis theory (the study of the origin and development of the universe) and the anthropogenesis theories (the study of the origins and development of humanity), being a descendant of the Sudanese Mahdi, the affiliation with Native Americans, the efforts at relating to the Moorish doctrine, the acquisition of Masonic lessons, the affiliation of ancient KMT philosophy (Egiptian), the knocking of other Black organizational shortcomings (The Nation Of Islam, The Nation of Gods and Earths, Black Sunni Muslims & Christians, Moorish Science Temple), the incarnation of himself as being "Divine" (Messiah, Mahdi, Master Teacher, Savior etc.), the mixing of various doctrines to formulate a new one (Right Knowledge, Nubian Islamic Hebrews), esoteric teachings of metaphysics, that perhaps some works of Malachi's were plagiarized from other philosophies and York's seemingly apparent flip-flopping from one doctrine to another (Muslim, Hebrew, Christian, Native American, intergalactic theology, Moor, Masonic, Shriner) and carrying the titles (Imam, Rabbi, Reverend, Maku, doctor etc.) along with him as he evolved, **Malachi York has proven without contest to be a deeply devoted scholar, thinker, spiritualist and having a profound sense of dedication and commitment toward the plight of Black folk and independence.**

(Hamin, 2005)

One of the main criticisms levelled at York's teachings by many detractors of "Right Knowledge", is his continuous combination or cross referencing material from various different, and often diverse Religious & Historic perspectives. As the Media have so often pointed out; York's teachings are: *"a confusing mix of elements of Christianity, ancient Egyptian polytheism, and a belief in unidentified flying objects (UFO)"*. However according to Esoteric Scholar Bobby Hemmit, in *"An Occult History of Melanin"* 4, this practice of cross referencing information from various sources is perfectly justified, and should indeed be encouraged as a method of obtaining the truth which has all too often been well hidden from public access for hundreds or years, as opposed to simply concentrating on one particular Religious or Historical school of thought:

Apparently these are some of the things that we need to study, some of the things you should know that Jesus is Horus or Heru we know that. Now Jesus is a combination of Osiris-Ausar the father and the son, we know that that's old news to us now. But this is the dilemma for some reason we keep getting that same Plutarch Isis and Osirus. But what you don't get is the whole social order. And what about Osiris you see him invited to a party, the next thing you know he's dead. That's it. But we know they have a building in Russia where they study Kmet. They have floors where they study KMT a whole building with nothing but stuff on KMT (Egypt). We talk about the Louvre, British Museum, the University of Chicago, and let's face it you ain't never going to get down there and get those papyrus'. But that's alright because the only thing you have to do is **cross-reference**. So we want to know all about the social order of this person we call the Christ. We don't want to know the Jesus thing, we know that. But we know that is a far cry from the real notion of what this thing is. So you are going to have to do some cross-referencing. And the cross-reference is the god Siva, in India. Get the book The Presence of Siva. You want to know about Horus about Osirus. That stuff that we have (it is) the same old Osirus myth is nothing but a page. We don't know the whole social and spiritual aspect is missing. We (are) sectarian, "I don't want to do nothing but the Egyptian thing." But this is science, we need to weave the pages together. We have to get out of this (thing), "well I'm Egyptian, well I'm Hebrew, well I'm only this." In science all these things are in fragments. If you deal with ancient culture come to us in fragments. So that means you have to weave them together.

Fig.146: *Bobby Hemmit*

(Hemmit, 2005)

The most remarkable aspect of York's teachings was how he was able to summarise an enormous amount of diverse and often abstract information into a simple and easy to read format in his books, which anybody could comprehend. Although the doctrine has gone through many chnges throughout the years, the fundamental elements such as the names, images and symbolism have remained the same since the "Old school" Ansaar era. For example York's illustration of Adam, which was that of a Dark skinned Blackman with wavy hair and piecing eyes was not only carried over into the new "Right Knowledge" books, but also explained, as we have shown in Chapter 12.

Far Eastern Connection

So what are the actual origins of York's Philosophy or Science of 'Nuwaubu' / Right Knowledge? In **Chapter 11:** *"Spiritual Masters & Extraterrestrials"* we examined the Spiritual/Esoteric aspects of York's teachings, which for all intents and purposes form what can only be described as the 'Foundation' of his doctrine. Therefore if 'Nuwaubu' is what he claims he really came to give, then what is its actual basis, and is it consistent with any other kind or type of Spiritual Philosophy or Teaching? The book *"The Mind"* Scroll # 78, released in 1995, as part of the "Right Knowledge" series was rumoured to have initially been released as part of a much larger volume during the 1970s, at the time entitled: *"Mechanics of The Mind"*. Although this work was never officially released to the general public, it was however circulated amongst 'selected' members of the Ansaaru Allah Community in Brooklyn, New York. In the 1995 re-released edition, York makes the following assertions concerning the Spiritual aspects of the Human Mind:

> *"The More it Possesses, The More it Wants"* Without Knowing It, People Are Exceedingly Plagued By The Instability of Their Own Minds. In Order To Remove This Sort Of Trouble, The Craving For Sensory Stimulation Must Be Removed. Once The Mind Has Been Stilled And Concentrated. It No Longer Presses One To Seek Further Pleasures. The Senses Can Be Controlled Through Reduction Of Wants And Activities…*"Fasting Of The Mind"* Fasting Of The Mind Is When The Thoughts Are Weaned From Attachment To The Many Fleeting Sensations That They Feed Upon…*"The Mind"* The Mind Is Neither Visible Nor Tangible. It Exists Not In The Physical Body. As Does The Brain, But In The Astral, Its Magnitude Cannot Be Measured, For It Carries All Feelings, Ideas, And Impressions From This Life, As Well As Intuitive Knowledge Of What Is To Come, It Is The Mind That Must Be Corralled And Controlled In Order To Achieve That True Peace Of Union. The Mind Acts Justly To Its Desires, And Does Not Care About Consequences, It Thinks Of Some Pleasant Looking Or Pleasant Tasting Food, And Must Have Some. When Warned Of The Poisons It Contains, The Reaction Is To Disregard The Warnings Find Some Excuse, And Eat It Anyway…*"About The Mind"*… The Mind Is Stilled And Allowed Perception Of Itself Through The **Right Knowledge** Gained By The Self Is Then Also Known By The Mind. Then Does The Mind Have Full Knowledge, Obviously Then. It Is Not Intellectualisation But Meditation That Brings Self-Knowledge. Mind Though Filled With Innumerable Tendencies And Desire, Acts For Self. For They Act In Conjunction. Mind Is Directly Associated With The Self So It Acts For Self While It Is Still Full Of Worldly Thoughts. Through Discrimination, One Can Clearly Overstand That The Soul And Mind Are Not The Same…*"The Mind Itself"* Negative Thoughts Seem To Assail And Attack With Double Force When The Person Striving For Righteousness Tries To Rid Himself Of Them. This Is The Natural Law Of The Resistance. Eventually, They Will Perish For Negative Thoughts Cannot Stand Before Positive Thoughts. The Very Fact That Undesirable

Thoughts Create A Feeling Of Uneasiness When They Arise. Indicates Growth And Maturity. For At One Time These Thoughts Were Welcomed Into The Mind. However They Cannot Be Driven Out Forcefully Or Suddenly. Or They Will Turn Against You With Increased Energy. They Wither Away Of Their Own Accord When The Person Persists In His Or Her Practice With Tenacity And Diligence.

(York, 1995, p: 28-108)

Whilst researching this book we stumbled by chance across an Eastern Religious/Philosophy called *"Jainism"*, said to predate both Hinduism & Buddhism by several Millennia. Our discovery was made all the more remarkable for two reasons. Firstly because 'Jainism' is said to be the basis of all other Eastern Religious/Philosophies including Hinduism. Secondly, within 'Jainist' Teachings, we found many similarities with Malachi York's Philosophy or Science of 'Nuwaubu'. To our astonishment, within 'Jainism' there even exists a principle called; **'Navapadaj'**, which also translates into English as *"Right Knowledge"*. But what is even more extraordinary is the fact that many of the principles of Navapadaji (Right Knowledge), mirror almost verbatim some principles of York's teachings. The following are excerpts taken from a book entitled: *"Atmatatva Vichar or Philosophy of The Soul"*, translated by Jainacharya Vijay Laxmansurishverji Maharaj:

Some people state "we strive best to concentrate our mind, but the fickle mind becomes uncontrollable. Kindly show some way to make it steady at once". We have to reply in this contention, "non-attachment and constant practice are chief means to make the fickle mind concentrated or steady". Therefore one should resort to these means. There are multiple desires and cravings lurking in your heart and so your mind remains always agitated and fickle, reflecting on various objects of desires. If you relinquish these desires and cut down threads of cravings, your mind will attain peace and it shall not loiter here and there. Therefore, steadiness of the mind will be quite easy for you…The reason is your mind should be dyed in hue of non-attachment and should enjoy peace. But the present situation is sorrowful. Your mind sticks to worldly enjoyments and luxuries as a fly sticks to saliva. Your mind remains all the while uneasy to acquire worldly objects of pleasure….A person without knowledge can never obtain **right knowledge**. A pot, or a pillar or a wolf cannot obtain **right knowledge**. Righteous conduct is the proximate cause for attainment of salvation…Finally this means that without faith one cannot obtain salvation, but along with faith one requires **right knowledge** and right conduct. If mere right faith would procure salvation then proclamation of sacred texts promising salvation with the help of **right knowledge** right intuition and right conduct would be absurd…Thus how can one say that no stress is laid on knowledge, in Jainism. Knowledge according to Jainism is two-fold. False knowledge and Right knowledge. False knowledge cannot help to traverse the worldly ocean but the **Right knowledge** can, and that is why every aspirant should aspire to achieve **right knowledge**.

(Laxmansurishverji Maharaj, 1986, p: 501-507)

Figs.147 Symbols of Divine Love

Clearly there are many similarities between Malachi York's philosophy of 'Nuwaubu' or (Right Knowledge), and that of Jainism's 'Navapadaji' (Right Knowledge). As we have seen in chapter 11, there are also many other similarities between York's teachings and those of other 'Spiritual Masters', such as Lord Maitreya and Sathya Sai Baba, which naturally brings us to the question of what is the True Source of this information? On the one hand there will be detractors who'll justifiably accuse York of plagiarising many of his teachings from these 'Far Eastern' schools of thought. However there is also the strong possibility that these teachings all originate from a similar source, referred to by many researchers as *'The Universal Spiritual Doctrine'*, from which all other Religious teachings derive. In other words the further one goes back, the more similarities will be discovered regarding origins of Religious or Spiritual Truth. After all, if there is only one Supreme Source or GOD, then it stands to reason that the ultimate truth in the Universe must also be **'ONE'**. Finally it is interesting to also note that the Hindu Word for 'Divine Love' is "ISHQ", which is the exact same word in Arabic: "ISHQ", used in Sufism to also describe 'Divine Love', symbolized by the Nuwaubian leader in many of his publications by an **'Inverted Heart'**.

Groundbreaking Theories

One way the Nuwaubian sphere of information overlaps with the world at large is through the writings of its head teacher, Dr. Malachi Z. York, who is also known as Amunnubi Raakhptah...York taught and wrote in Brooklyn from 1967 until 1991; his 300 or so books, referred to as scrolls and tablets, are the Nuwaubian texts. Amazon and Barnes & Noble carry none of them. You can buy some in Nuwaubian bookstores in Athens, Savannah, Atlanta and other cities, as well as in the gold pyramid at Tama-Re. They're also sold off sidewalk tables in black urban neighborhoods all over America, alongside less prolific authors' works of "street knowledge," with which York's books have a few things in common.

(Excerpt taken from: *"Black Egypt"* 5, by Adam Heimlich, New York Press, Nov, 2000)

Initially Right Knowledge or Nuwaubu, was well received by the public who viewed this 'new' doctrine as an interesting, and even welcome alternative to what many other religious groups were teaching at the time. The key to the popularity of Right Knowledge was that it presented a fresh look at Religion under the "Cold Light", of rational thought termed 'Factology', the study of Facts, an alternative to Theology; the study of

'Theories' or unsubstantiated 'Mythological' Religious Theology. This was a revolutionary idea in its implications to many established religions, which are neither based on Historical or Scientific facts. York's approach was entirely unique to every other Religious or Political movement in history because Right Knowledge or Nuwaubu, was a brand new concept, which made York a Religious pioneer for formulating an entirely new and unique Religious Philosophy. For instance according to the Islam, Arabic was the first language, spoken by all of the Prophets, who were all Muslims, from Adam to Jesus and indeed whilst York taught Islam, he too subscribed to this distorted view of linguistic history. However according to "Right Knowledge" or Fact-ology there is no way that Arabic could be the first language because it belongs to the Shemetic (Semetic) linguistic family, which also include: Aramic, Hebrew and Phoenician, which all originate from ancient 'Syretic', descended from the Afro-Asiatic language family, as we have seen early in the chapter. Therefore none of the Prophets before Abraham's time could have spoken Arabic, at least not in its present from. In Christianity (New Testament) Jesus was born by "Immaculate conception", without Mary having sexual intercourse with a man to produce him. Again there is no way for this to have been possible for any woman to become pregnant without inclusion of the 'semen' or "Y" Chromosome of a male. However in the philosophy of "Right Knowledge", Mary was made pregnant by the Angel Gabriel who appeared to her according to the Qur'aan, as a 'Basheraan' or **"Well Made Man"**, which comes from the root word in Arabic "Bashir" meaning 'Flesh & Blood'. In other words the Angel Gabriel, otherwise known as the Holy Ghost, had physical sex with Mary to produce Jesus, effectively making Jesus the Flesh & Blood Son of Gabriel, or "Son of a God!" Whilst in Judaism (Old Testament), it is taught that Noah, collected a pair of every species of animal on the Planet, to take on board the Ark, before the Great Flood. However "Right Knowledge" teaches that the great deluge of Noah's time only covered a specific part of the Earth, therefore only certain animals needed to be taken, who were native to that region. Whilst DNA samples of others were collected in order to be cloned, at a later stage.

During this period York came out with two other intriguing theories, which stood out from most from what he was teaching at the time. Other than his hypothesis of Evolution, York revealed *"The Inner Sun"* theory, which asserted that there is an actual "Fire" inside human beings which medical science is aware of, but doesn't tell us about. According to York the so-called "Solar Plexus" in human beings, is actually a form of energy or a 'Fire', which is why when people drink spirits, they get a warm feeling inside, because if you pour spirit over a fire it automatically causes a Chemical reaction. Also when human beings inhale they take in Oxygen (O) and exhale Carbon Dioxide (Co_2), without which they will die. This is exactly the same process that happens to Fire, which also needs to be sustained by Oxygen as fuel, and in turn gives off Carbon dioxide (Co_2).

This is also confirmed on cold mornings when steam comes out of your mouth, and it is said that when people die, their bodies become cold due to the Energy or Fire being extinguished.

Secondly, was his famous *"Nine Ether"* theory which was his explanation as to why Blacks are the only people on the Planet who posses curly "Afro" hair follicles. According to York, Afro or Negroid hair comes out of the root to form the number '9', which is equivalent to the absolute highest Spiritual, as well as Mathematical number in creation, i.e. *"Nine to the Power of Nine"*, which equals infinity. In other words the number 9 when multiplied will continue infinitely and always equal 'Nine'. He also stated that there was once a time when Black hair was used to act as an antenna to communicate with other Realms of Consciousness or Dimensions. Therefore in principle, Right Knowledge is a revolutionary concept, which has serious implications for religions, which are entirely based upon faith and not fact. Nevertheless after the initial successes of this New Philosophy, many of York's new followers began to get carried away, and tried to apply this concept to not only religion but every aspect of life. They began to question the validity of their own doctrine by constantly reiterating the same abstract rhetoric. The following is a statement made online by an unnamed Nuwaubian explaining *"The meaning of Nuwaubu"* 6:

> Nuwaubu, the science of Nuwaubins, "is Right Knowledge, Right Wisdom, and Right Overstanding. The first step of Nuwaubu is right knowledge, which will pass any one of three tests: **Experience, Evidence, and Reason**, that is practical for knowledge given. The evidence and reason tests are those which are more often practical."

The above was first explained by York in The Holy Tabernacle *"Family Guide"* as far back as 1994, however it has now become a type of "Dogmatic" rehearsed Mantra often repeated by Nuwaubians, when asked to explain the meaning of their teachings. Very often you'll get this collective affirmation, which usually leaves most rational people wondering what the hell they are talking about. The problem is not with the actual concept of "Right Knowledge" developed by York, but how it is being interpreted by someone who clearly doesn't fully understand what they are really talking about, and is merely regurgitating this rehearsed rhetoric, parrot fashion.

The problem with many of York's followers, particularly those of the recent 'Nuwaubu' era, is that York has constantly provided them with new books, without giving them enough time to digest and fully understand what it is he is actually teaching. As a result, many have become dependant upon a constant "Fix" of new information like Drug Addicts for a new high. This is why, unlike York's Old followers during the Ansaaru Allah/Nubian Islamic Hebrew era, many of the later converts to Nuwaubu have never had enough time to fully analyse and digest York's teachings in order to fully comprehend them. In their constant hunger for new information these Nuwaubian "Knowledge Junkies" or 'Information Addicts' are comparable to modern western society, which constantly needs to be provided with new stimulants to remain interested in anything; an example of which has been demonstrated by the organisations constant release of "New titles".

Following York's conviction in 2004, interest in the movement severely began to wane amongst the followers when fewer titles were being released. Nevertheless, after York released a series of new titles supposedly from Prison, interest in the movement began to again increase. This is simply because with York no longer around to release new books, many who professed to be his followers have already begun to look elsewhere for a new source of Fantasy to satisfy their insatiable appetites for abstract information. However, if they really believed and understood his teachings they wouldn't need new information, regardless of York's current circumstances. It is for this reason that the organisation is in danger of completely collapsing after York's death, unless his followers become far less dependant upon constantly learning new information, and more focused upon applying what they've already got.

Space Cadets, Lunatics & Removal of 'GOD Principle'

This then essentially brings us to the crux of the problem with the Nuwaubians, or rather the 'Achilles Heal' of the Nuwaubian philosophy if you will, which is their misplaced arrogance, derived from their Misinterpretation of God or 'Creator Principle' which has gradually developed in recent years. Although many pay lip service to it, there is no religious discipline left in the movement. Initially York replaced the names of Allah, and Yahuwa or (Yahweh) with the epithet El Eloh, derived from Elyown Elyown El, which roughly translated as *"The Most High, Most High, Highest"* from the Hebrew/Arabic, which he attributed to the Sumerian Diety 'ANU'. ANU according to York is the highest principle of God or a Creative Force in all of the scriptures (apparently not to be confused with 'Kuluwm': ALL which first Created the Universe over 76 Trillion Years ago), which York reiterated to his followers throughout countless publications all relating to God or The Most High.

> When You Say **Allah Ta'ala** You Are Actually Saying **Allah Al Aliyu** And **Al Aliyu**, The 36th Attribute Of Allah, is The Same As **Elyown** Of The Torah (Genesis 14:18-20). They Both Mean **The Most High**. The Qur'aan Tells You To Get Guidance From The Torah, Especially If You Are Confused About What's Recorded In The Qur'aan, It Tells You To Go Back To The Torah (***Koran 3:3, 10:94***). And If You Did, You Would Not Find The Word **Allah** As Written Today In Your Koran, But Rather You Would Find **El Eloh** (***Deuteronomy 32:15***), You Would Find **Yahweh** (***Genesis 2:4***). You Would Find **Eloheem** (***Genesis 1:1***). You Will Find **Adonai** (***Genesis 15:2***). You Will Find **El** (***Genesis 16:3***). And You Will Find **Elyown** (***Genesis 14:18***).
>
> (York, 1996, p: 24)

Nevertheless, the lack of religious discipline now practiced by many recent converts to the Nuwaubian or 'Right Knowledge' Philosophy, coupled with York's insistence on referring to himself as "God in Flesh", confused many of his new followers into believing that he was actually saying he was God (All Mighty), and therefore misunderstanding or misinterpreting the true meaning of York's teachings. As we have explained in Chapter 11: *"Spiritual Masters & Extraterrestrials"*, York's reference to himself as 'God in Flesh' is from the Ancient African & Far Eastern interpretation of an Avatar or 'ILAH MUTAJASSID', or *"The Divine in Flesh"*, such as the Pharaohs were regarded as Gods to the Ancient Egyptians, which should not to be confused with God the Creator, in the Hebrew, Christian or Islamic 'Monotheistic' traditions.

By York discarding the Spiritual aspect of God or 'The Most High' in his teachings briefly during the late 1990s, he actually left a void in the lives of many of his followers, which many filled by simply replacing God, The Creator, with York himself. However, the moment York was arrested and torn down from his pedestal, many of his new followers immediately left the movement, because their was no longer any reason to remain in the organisation with York no longer around, as if a type of 'Spell' or influence held by York had suddenly been broken. Our research indicates that York has never taught anybody to worship him or any other man as a God, in fact the Nuwaubian leader has gone to great lengths in the past to prove that a human being could never be God (The Creator) as in the case of NOI founder W. D. Farad Muhammad. However, there are those in the Nuwaubian leadership who have benefited, and may have subtly encouraged York's followers into believing him to be a God. This has been done purposely, and has succeeded in achieving nothing but misrepresenting what York has taught for over 35 years, helping to create followers who have eventually become little more than arrogant mental 'Zombies' no different from what they were before discovering York's teachings. Many have completely misinterpreted York's teachings, because it is man's innate

Figs.148: *Cover of York's DVD Publication*

nature to achieve greatness only by aspiring to that, which is much greater in power than himself. Therefore, if this is removed then there is no longer any 'Spiritual' aspiration. What do we mean by this? Well until York's arrest in 2002, many misguided and misdirected Nuwaubians 'Idolized' York as an actual God figure, however after his arrest and humiliation at the hands of Law Enforcement officials, many of these followers went into severe psychological trauma, because up to that point many of them had actually begun to erroneously believe that York was divinely "Untouchable".

Following York's guilty plea in early 2003, we interviewed a number of his followers in both the U.S and the U.K., and one thing struck us more than anything else about almost all of their responses, and that was the feeling of immense disappointment felt, not so much at the actual 'Guilty Plea', but at York's vulnerability. Many seemed, in some type of sycophantic way to actually expect York to use some type of Supernatural powers to evade his captors by some kind of Miraculous means, or as York's Sister Waikya recently pointed out; **"Don't Expect [The Nuwaubain Leader] To Beam Himself Out Of Jail"**. One former 'Devotee' angrily proclaimed: *"I thought he said he was God Man!!, they told me in class that this man was untouchable, how could he get arrested, what happened to the Divine man, what happened to the Divine?"*

As with any type of organisation, especially those Religious in nature, there always exists what are best described as the fanatical or fringe elements, whose beliefs differ dramatically from that of the main rational majority. Naturally the Nuwaubians are no exception to this rule. The group in question, have often been referred to by Dr. York himself as **"Space Cadets"**, and hold beliefs, which not only go against York's teachings, but border upon insanity. The following is an excerpt from an e-mail posted soon after York's arrest, by a Nuwaubian named 'Imhotep Malik El', dated July 2nd 2002. This email much to the amusement of York's detractors best exemplifies the type of mentality, which now permeates amongst many of the so-called 'New School' followers, and if not quickly addressed will eventually destroy the very fabric of the movement:

> Dr. Malachi York has mystical powers and knows how to make himself change into other life forms (shape shifting). You think Dr. Malachi York was arrested but that guy is not him. Dr. Malachi Z York knew the authorities were coming after him so he transformed one of the brothers who betrayed him (Judas) to look and speak like him. The person that was arrested and who you think is Dr. Malachi York is really a government informant. Dr. Malachi Z York has transformed himself to look like someone else now, I will only say he has now taken the form of a very tall stocky light skin man with a very deep voice. The whole child molestation plot is a huge lie, it is nothing more than the governments way of trying to destroy a powerful and strong black movement. The government has failed because they think they have Dr. Malachi York but they do not. The 144,00 will be raised, righteous people will prevail. Babylon will fall. Dr. Malachi

Z York understands the mysteries of life and death, he is a mystic. He can look at a man and know his past, present and future all in an instant. He has levitation abilities, has the gift of invisibility, can read minds, and has other paranormal abilities.

(Malik El, 2002)

If the above is indeed true, then why are the Nuwaubian leadership taking such pains to secure their leader's release, or are we to assume that the above named individual is privy to information of York's 'Miraculous Transformation', which is unknown to the members of York's most inner circle. This nonsense is an example of the mentality of many of the groups recent converts. Nevertheless there also exists another, largely forgotten group of York's followers who do not hold such absurd beliefs, and with whom some hope may exist for the future survival of the Movement. For example when we conducted interviews with several of York's followers whom had been grounded in the so-called Old School Doctrine during the 1970s, 80s & 90s there was not this same type of disappointment shown, because they were never confused in regards to York's Divinity or whether he was GOD or not. By arresting him the authorities sought to, demonstrate to York's devotees that he was not untouchable, and therefore subject to the jurisdiction of the Law, which had a devastating effect upon many of these followers who had misinterpreted what York meant by he was "God in Flesh". This is essentially the danger of teaching the *"God in Flesh"* concept, which is all too often taken literally and completely out of context. And in this case taken to actually mean that York was 'God The Creator' in flesh, or a substitute for the Jesus many of them once worshipped as Christians in the Church. As opposed to the understanding of it from the African & 'Far Eastern Spiritual' traditional perspective of an (Avatar) as God in flesh being merely a vessel to transmit "Divine" information to man from God, yet still limited by the restraints of the physical world. Nowhere in the history of the world has any Man or Woman, been able to wield 'Supernatural' powers to free any race from its condition; the power has always come from a collective effort of people working together to change their condition. Only in religious Mythology, which is not based on any fact, has this been possible, which the Nuwaubians profess not to believe in. Therefore according to **"Right Knowledge, Right Wisdom, and Right Overstanding"** there is absolutely no way York could be freed from his current predicament by any Miraculous act. He would have to be freed 'physically' either by forced armed rescue or through the natural legal process. Hence, the cold reality of Right Knowledge when closely analysed *"is sweet to the taste yet bitter to the stomach"*, in other words easy to reiterate, but not so easy to always apply in Reality. If many Nuwaubians really understood the basis of Nuwaubu as they claim, they should not have been so affected by York's arrest. After all a wise man once said: *"Blessed are those which are Persecuted for Righteousness Sake:"* Therefore it stands to reason that if Dr. Malachi. Z. York's teachings were having such a profound effect upon the collective psyche of Blacks, then it was only inevitable that he would eventually be viewed as a threat, and face persecution, like many of his Predecessors from a 'Unrighteous Racist Establishment' whose sole purpose it is to destroy the work of **all Black Leadership**, in order to keep Blacks in a state of 'Mental Inferiority'; to continue to be used as the Fools, Slaves and 'Foot Stools' of the Western World system.

Finally, on a more positive note in regards to the arrest, and subsequent 'Trial' of Malachi York. So very often when Black leaders are either 'Character or Physically' assassinated, their followers have traditionally sheepishly stood by and let it happen with an-air of indifference in their conduct. This behaviour pattern has been bred into Blacks throughout the Diaspora as the result of over 400 years of both 'Physical & Mental' Bondage. However, the Nuwaubian Leadership have demonstrated tremendous courage, tenacity and most of all the ability to think 'Laterally & Analytically' in the face of tremendous odds throughout their leader's ordeal at the hands of the **'Criminal'**, Criminal Justice System. The courage displayed by Nuwaubians in the face of such incredible odds should certainly be applauded, and proves that Malachi. Z. York's teachings throughout the past 35 years have at least to some extent, managed to begin the process of eradicating 'the Slave Mentality' from many of his followers, and have therefore not been taught in vain. If as the saying goes, *"when the going gets tough, the tough get going"*, then this has certainly been true of certain members of the Nuwaubian movement, who have tenaciously Defended their leader's 'Good' name and reputation against the relentless onslaught of Hypocrites outside the organization, Mainstream Media, State & Federal Law enforcement agencies, as we shall examine in greater depth.

Figs.149: God in Flesh: *Illustration of Malachi York as an Incarnation of The Divine*

Chapter 14

Sacred Orders & Mysteries Revealed

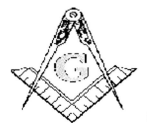

Fig.150 *Symbol of International Freemasonry*

Mr. York with his mixed doctrine has now established his own Nuwaubian Grand Lodge AF&AM International and his own Shrine Temple Al Mahdi No.19, and has attracted hundreds of poor black Souls in making them think that they have some superior Freemasonry that was handed down to him by Noble Beings in Egypt.

Ezekiel. M. Bey, 2001

By the time the group migrated to Georgia in 1993, York's books had affronted what can only be described as a Plethora of Religious and Political organisations, which included:

1) Orthodox Sunni Moslems (Universal Islamic establishment)
2) The Nation of Islam (Black Muslims)
3) Nation of Gods & Earths (The 5%ers)
4) Freemasons (Black & White Lodges)
5) The African Hebrew Israelite Nation
6) Israelite Nation of Yahweh
7) The Hebrew Israelite Church
8) Black & White Christians (Church establishment)
9) White Supremacist Groups (KKK & Neo Nazis etc)
10) Satanic Groups
11) The Rastafarian Movement
12) The Yoruba Movement (Pan-Africans)
13) The Hip Hop Nation (Elements of Music Industry)
14) The Anti Defamation League (White Jewish establishment)

Never one for building alliances with other leaders, York seemed to have a remarkable ability to make enemies, which was due in part, to his insistence of telling the truth no matter what the consequences, which was often seen as sticking his nose in everyone else's business. York appointed himself with the unenviable task of 'Reforming' all of the lies and misconceptions in organised religion. In principle this was a noble aim, however one which didn't make him very popular. In fact, York's egotistical actions have today left him and his organisation, the single most despised, misunderstood and isolated Black 'Religious/Political' group in America, which has eventually become disadvantageous, because as the saying goes *"No man is an Island"*. All York's writings have succeeded in doing have been to further alienate his organisation, which only served to make it easy for his enemies to eventually destroy him.

During the 1980s when the organisation was at the height of its prominence, York's followers relished in the notion that they were hated by everybody, because back then it was hatred mixed with respect & admiration for the Power of the 'Nubian Nation', at the time. In that arena, the Ansaaru Allah Community/Nubian Nation could not be matched ideologically or even financially by any other black movement at the time, except probably The Nation of Islam, whose doctrine fell well short of the supremacy of York's teachings.

It was for this reason that Minister Louis Farrakhan skilfully avoided making any statements, which might trigger a confrontation, or possibly lead to a public debate between the two leaders, which is exactly what York surreptitiously desired. York's proficiency with languages and knowledge of the scriptures, even intimidated Islamic & Christian Scholars like Dr. Jamal Babari and Ahmed Deedat. Therefore, Farrakhan the Master tactician simply bided his time, and let York's ego play himself into a corner, where he would eventually have no way out of. York's constant onslaught against the Nation of Islam's teachings, whose membership probably trebled The Ansaaru Allah at least in the United States at the time, resulted in York having no alternative but to eventually release an apology pamphlet on March 11, 1990. This apology finally exposed York's weakness, which, much like the Hon. Marcus Garvey before him was his massive Ego, and marked the beginning of the end of The Ansaaru Allah Community as the pre-eminent Black Movement in the Western World. This episode still remains a sore issue with many of York's ex-followers, most of whose sentiments can be best summed up by this former 'Ansaar':

> *"Isa made us lose face in front of the Nation, Man, how could he claim to be divinely inspired, and have to apologise to Farrakhan???"*.
> (Ishmael, Ex Ansaar)

The truth is, York would have never had to apologise to Farrakhan had he simply continued building his organisation irrespective of what the Nation of Islam were doing, instead of letting his ego get the better of him by trying to reform the NOI's teachings. By exposing their obvious weaknesses, which is of-course their flawed doctrine & limited knowledge of Islam. Another group who could also cause York real problems for revealing their Secrets as well as exposing flaws in their Philosophy in his literature, were the Freemasons, who unlike many of York's other adversaries, could retaliate with more than just rhetoric and would eventually be one of the contributing factors in the Nuwaubian leader's downfall.

York & Freemasonry

Unbeknownst to most people York's involvement with Freemasonry goes back almost 40-years, and is a subject of much contention amongst not only his followers, but also detractors alike. York has admitted to being affiliated with a number of 'Secret Societies' including **The Rosicrucian Order, & The Astara Foundation**. Along with a number of recognized Masonic Orders such as: F. & A.M. (Free & Accepted Masons) Prince Hall Rite through his family and A.F. & A.M. Scottish Rite. As well as an affiliate of the Grand Enoch Lodge based in Brooklyn, Nostrand Avenue, New York, under 'The Worshipful Master' Charles Tensely 33rd degree since 1970. York has also claimed to have been an affiliate of The King Solomon Lodge No. 4, Prince Hall Lodge in Brooklyn, New York, as well as The Grand Lodge of Nubia, under The Grand Maulana Ash Sheikh Mahmoud, also called the 'Khalwatiyya' Order which he was initiated into at the age of 29 in 1973.

Fig.151 *Grand Potentate: Dr. Malachi York*

On the back of one the Nuwaubian booklets, in 2001 York described himself as **'Imperial Grand Potentate'** (Internationally) of:

> **Al Mahdi Temple No. 19 ILL. Rev. Dr. Malachi. Z. York 33 Degree (A.E.O. & N.M.S.) The Ancient Egiptian Order & Nobles of the Mystic Shrine, Northern & Southern Jurisdiction And Grand Master: of Nuwaubian Grand Lodge (A.F. & A.M.) Ancient Free & Accepted Masons Inc. and the Supreme Grand Hierophant of (A.E.O.) The Ancient Egiptian of the World Inc. Rameses II Mir No. 9 and a Scottish Rite Freemason of Amos Grand Lodge of Macon, Ga. And Deputy Grand Master Pride of Georgia Grand Lodge A.F.& A.M.**

Fig.152 York's Publication Secret Societies Unmasked

What initially caused resentment towards York from many Freemasons was the release of the book *"Secret Societies Unmasked"* Edition # 64, originally released in 1975, then regularly revised until the most recent edition in 1990. In it, York exposes the secret rituals and practices of several other organisations including The Klu Klux Klan, Rosicrucian's, & Anton Levy's Church of Satan. The book centres on many of the secret initiation rituals of Freemasonry, which it heavily criticises as Worshipping 'The Devil'.

On page 1, of *"Secret Societies Unmasked"* York states:

Introduction
Secret Societies
The fact that these societies are such a mystery makes the inquisitive mind probe into their societies, wanting to know more about them, as well as join them. Their rituals tend to entrap the minds of Nubians. Thus, Nubians eventually get caught up into different societies, occults, etc, not knowing that they are actually selling themselves into Devil worship. That's right! Most of these Secret Societies are nothing more than discrete Devil worshipping occults. These Orders, Societies and Clans are extremely selective of whom they grant membership and a vow of silence is required for all candidates.
The year 1970 A.D. was the disclosure of all mysteries of the cosmos and universal awareness for Nubians throughout the world. Also it was the opening of the seventh seal, with it, all the meaning of the words of the Scriptures would be clear, from beginning…

(Isa Al Mahdi, 1990, p: 1)

So what was York's real motive for writing this book in the first place? Many of his followers at the time were young, cocky, black 'Inner City' youth, who didn't understand the implications and perceived the book as just another one of Imaam Isa's 'Demolition Jobs' of yet another organisation that got in his way. However this couldn't have been further from what York intended the book for. It is obvious from reading the book now that it was never intended as an attack on Freemasonry, but rather an attempt by York to discourage young blacks from joining such Secret Societies, not because Freemasonry was evil but rather that it was being used for evil purposes. This was again part of York's long-term plan to not only dissuade blacks from joining these Societies by portraying them as negative, but to also prepare his own followers for the eventual development of The Nubian Nation, into what would essentially become a Grand Nuwaubian Lodge, and

for his followers to one day themselves become Masons. You see unbeknownst to many of York's followers at the time, he had already been a Freemason since 1970, and intended to also 'Reform' the Masonic teachings and finally incorporate them into his organisation, the same way he was Reforming Islam and Christianity and would later do to Hebrewism in the years that followed. In fact, York cleverly begins to give away the plot about his intentions to prepare his followers for Freemasonry as early as 1995 in his book *"Are Caucasians Edomites?"*, Scroll # 142, in which he explains that many of the great
Black leaders were Freemasons:

> **Ques:** If Elijah Muhammad was a student of W.D. Ford, where did W.D. Ford get his teachings from?
> **Ans:** W.D. Ford, as you have previously read, has many names and titles and was also a member of The Moorish Science Temple which became known as The Moorish Nationalist Movement in 1930 A.D. Farrad was influenced by Marcus Musa (Mosiah) Garvey, who was also a Muslim (1887-1940) As well as Hebrew Falashi Rabbi Arnold Josiah Ford (1877-1934 A.D.) And Rabbi Wentworth Arthur Matthews (1892-1965 A.D.) And The Great Reverend Sheikh, Daoud Ahmed Faisal (1891-1980 A.D.). All of these men were involved with The Shriners. No doubt about it. Also, in the book *"Secrets of Freemasonry"*, written by The Hon. Elijah Muhammad, page 15, he admits that he was a Mason and I quote: *"Once I Was A Mason Too Until I Became A Muslim."* **DON'T BELIEVE ME CHECK IT OUT…**
>
> **Ques:** Was Marcus Garvey, affiliated with The Masonic Lodge?
> **Ans:**…What most people don't know is that he was apart of the Masonic Shriners Temple and he, like the leaders mentioned above revealed the information and thus had to be eliminated.
> **Ques:** Where did The Moorish Science Temple get their teachings because much of the teachings relate to Masonry?
> **Ans:** That is because their teachings came by way of the Shrine or Masonic Lodge of which Noble Drew Ali was enrolled…
>
> (York, 1995, p: 50-57)

According to York, many of the Great Black leaders in American history, were actually 'Renegade' Prince Hall Freemasons and members of The Ancient Arabic Nobles of the Mystic Shrine, or Shriners, another group closely affiliated to Freemasonry. Apparently all of these leaders decided to use many of the secrets learned in the Masonic Temples, to raise the consciousness of their people, however their betrayal of these Societies meant that they would all suffer some type of reprisals from the Masonic controlled authorities.

York goes on further about the Shriners in his 1996 book, *"The Year 2000 A.D. And What To Expect"*, in which he states:

Ques: Who Are The Shriners?
Ans: The next hierarchy within the Freemasonic realm consist of individuals called **Shriners**. The Shriners began in the year 1870 A.D. It was concocted that the Shrine ritual which caricatured (Exaggerated by means of deliberate simplification) The Muslim religion for the amusement of American Freemasons. They had even tried to claim that this branch was founded in 644 A.D., by the son-in-law of **Muhammad, Kalif Alee** (The spelling is from them). When the male completes his Degrees and is raised to the highest point he is called after The Ancient Mystic Arabic Order of Shriners; and when they are asked, who brought them there? They say **"Kalif Alee."** When you say **"Kalif Alee"** you are Saying Anu because the name **Ali** means *"Most High"*, and **Anu** means, *"On High"*, Kalif Alee means the successor Ali, and implies **Anu** who succeeded **Anshar**, the Deity before him...even though Muhammad was a Shriner, this Kalif-Alee is not to be mistaken with the real **Amiryul Mu'minyn Ali Ibn Abu Taalib**,...

Ques: Did you say Muhammad was a Shriner?
Ans: Yes, he admits to belonging to **The Ancient Mystic Arabic Order of Shriners**; That's why he called his family Noble which is **Shariyf** in Ashuric/Syriac (Arabic). Nowhere in the Koran does it use the word Shariyf pertaining to Muhammad nor his family. However, it is stated that people of the bloodline of the Prophet Mustafa Muhammad Al Amin took on the title Shariyf. In Aramic (Hebrew) the word **Noble** is translated from the word **Chiyram**, which is the name Hiram, who the Freemasons recognize as the Master of all builders...who was killed for keeping the Sacred word...

(York, 1996, p: 182-191)

York backs his claim of an ancient Hebraic connection to Freemasonry with the following two mysterious almost identical quotes from the Old Testament, which may possibly be some kind of secret code for those initiated into the higher mysteries. Both quotes make mention of the words "Hiram", "David" & "Masons" in the same sentence:

> And **Hiram** king of Tyre sent messengers to **David**, and cedar trees, also carpenters and **Masons** who built David a house.
> (2nd Samuel, Chapter 5, verse 11)

> And **Hiram** king of Tyre sent messengers to **David**, and cedar trees, also **Masons** and carpenters to build a house for him.
> (1st Chronicles, Chapter 14, verse 1)

Many of the revelations regarding Masonic teachings in *"Secret Societies Unmasked"* Edition # 64, were met with hostility from a number of groups including Right-Wing White Supremacist Groups, like the Aryan Brotherhood & Neo Nazis, who were said to be outraged at York's audacity at exposing the hidden meanings behind their secret teachings. Another of York's former followers relates the following account:

That book "Secret Societies Unmasked", caused us a lot of problems when it came out, from a number of groups. One day we were propagating in Brooklyn, when a White man came up to our table, dropped his card down on the table, and told us that he knew whom our teacher was, and he had better stop writing about us, or there would be trouble!!!

(Daoud Ex-Ansaar)

Fig.153 *Moorish Leader Noble Drew Ali wearing Masonic Sash*

Nevertheless the group who were most affected by York's revelations were the Freemasons, particularly the Black Masons, whom it was York's actual intention or reaching. Although they remained silent, they never forgot what he said and would later take their revenge against York and his organisation with devastating consequences.

It may seem as if York's sole purpose was to add new enemies to an already long list, however upon closer analysis his decision to incorporate Freemasonry to his organisation, is not so ridiculous, when you realize just how much power Freemasons have always wielded in America. The United States was formed upon Masonic principles, and some researchers have even gone, as far to describe America as the world's first Freemasonic nation, in other words the official religion of The United States is Freemasonry. According to York, Black Masons, who are more commonly known as Prince Hall Masons play an important role in helping Whites maintain the status quo and are central to understanding the dynamics of Power and Black leadership in America, the Caribbean & Africa.

In order to fully comprehend the history of Black leadership in America, we have to first understand the role-played by Prince Hall Masons in the conspiracy to control American & Caribbean Blacks by the Illuminati, particularly through Light skinned 'Mulatto' Leaders.

Fig.154 *Black Prince Hall Masons*

The following may offend many in the Black Community however it is not our opinion, but rather historical data based upon York's own hypothesis. We would not intentionally make statements which were in any way intended to harm or malign members of either the White, Black or Inter-racial communities. We would also like to clarify that the term *"Mulatto"*, originally comes from the Arabic word 'Mu-walad', which literally translates as *"Of My Father"*, and was a title first used to describe the 'Illegitimate' or bastard offspring born of the union between Moorish (Black) Aristocracy and predominately White Eastern European or Slavic women who had converted to Islam during the Middle Ages. However, it is not meant in any offensive way, neither is it our intention to belittle or denigrate the outstanding achievements made by people of 'Mixed' heritage throughout modern Black era.

The Mulatto Elite

"Shaytaan (Satan) picked the name out, and named certain places throughout this Country, the United States, 'Salem', where Witches and them gather, because those Witches were sent there to try and put those Righteous Muslims (Moors) under a Spell. The Spell has manifested today in a Disease that I refer to as; "The Spell of Leviathan", that has our people feeling inferior, and hating themselves, and trying to live in the 'Image of The Beast'…So those Witches were sent down there, they sent White Women with Black Hair, to Mix in with the Black Slaves, cause they already knew what a Blond haired White Woman was, they sent White Women with Black hair, and they Mixed in with the Slaves, and Produced these Mulatto type of Black People, and then they made them look like they were Beautiful, and they made you people with African features look like you're Ugly.

You see what they did to us? They reversed it; all this took place in those little cities called Salem, throughout this country. And you got a Salem North Carolina, and Salem, South Carolina they took it straight across the whole country. Those were the little cities where they spread the Disease, and put 'the Spell of Leviathan' on our people.

They Governed those Cities with Men, who referred to themselves as "Sheriff", you heard the name Sheriff, and they used a Six Pointed Star, because the Six Pointed Star is not really a star in Israel, its called a 'Shield'. "The Shield of David: *Mogan Davad*".

And the Shield of David, meant they used it to protect themselves, and they called those Men, Sheriff's, which is nothing more than an extraction, from the Arabic word 'Sheryf', and the word Sheryf is symbolic of the Noble Family of the Prophet Muhammed, who you people were. The descendants of Muhammed, who came out of Sudan, they brought them to those Cities.

People they brought out of Nigeria & Ghana, and parts of West Africa, they took them to Haiti and different Islands of the Caribbean, but they kept a certain kind of Slave here, and they made him Intermingle with them like the Devil did, and had Children. And the Children were the Mulattos that are now making us think they care so much about us.

Look at all your **Black Politicians, Light Skin with Straight hair, they selected it that way. How many Black Leaders you'll have look like Africans.** Most of the Imaams, that are leading the Sunni Muslims today have Light Eyes, they Bred this! This is something they've organized.

If you read the Holy Qu'raan Chapter 20, Verse 102, it'll tell you about those 'Light Eyes', and what to watch out for. The Holy Qu'raan 20th Chapter Surat'ul Taha, the One Hundred & Second Iyat, or 102nd Verse:

"ON THE DAY WHEN THE TRUMPET SHALL BE BLOWN, ON THET DAY, WE SHALL GATHER THE GUILTY (ACCUSED) BLUE EYED".

They use the word 'Zurkaan', many Muslims say that it don't mean Blue, it means "Blear" or "Clear". The Arabic word for Blue is 'Azraak'! "Zurkaan" means Blue Eyed, Lets Stop Playing Games Now, We in The Later Day!...So that city of Salam, you made a very good point, the City of Salem, that you're talking about, is where they Brainwashed the Blacks, where they integrated with our Men & Women, and Bred the Mulatto Children.

Now if you go back into American History, right here, right to the Shomberg Library, you'll see that almost all of the Leaders of the Black Organizations were Mulatto looking people, all of these different Governors, that was Pre-ordained, they knew what they were doing...

(Excerpt taken from Lecture entitled: *"The True Slave Trade Story"* by As Sayyid Al Imaam Isa Al Haadi Al Mahdi, circa 1988)

To best exemplify York's theory we must first understand the role played by Mixed-race people or 'Mulattos' in Modern black history. During Slavery in North and South America as well as the Islands of the Caribbean, African women were subjected to the most horrendous form of sexual Abuse &

Exploitation by their Caucasian owners. For almost 300-years, black Women & Girls were systematically Raped, Sexually Abused & 'Molested' by White males.

This tragic period of history is illustrated by Louis M. Epstein, in *"Sex Laws and Customs in Judaism"*:

> The female slave was a sex tool beneath the level of moral considerations. She was an economic good, useful, in addition to her menial labor, for breeding more slaves. To attain that purpose, the master mated her promiscuously according to his breeding plans. The master himself and his sons and other members of his household took turns with her for the increase of the family wealth, as well as for satisfaction of their extramarital sex desires. Guests and neighbours too were invited to the luxury.
>
> (Epstein, cited by NOI, 1991, P: 196)

Naturally, this deplorable practice was not exclusively conducted by European Jews, but the majority of Caucasian Slave owners in general, which naturally led to an increase in the amount of 'Half Breeds' or 'Mulattos' born to black mothers. This growing number of Mixed raced babies often resulted in the White fathers actually taking responsibility for these children's education, even in some cases leaving them substantial inheritances, which often included other black slaves. This strange phenomenon is related by Henry L. Feingold in *"Zion in America: The Jewish Experience from Colonial Times to Present"*, as follows:

> There are some recorded cases of illicit cohabitation between Jews and Negro Slaves but this is undoubtedly the tip of the iceberg…In one case in 1797, Moses Nunes of Savannah, acknowledged his concubines and children he had with her, by willing her several of his remaining slaves. Similarly, land and money were willed by Isaac H. Judah to his two mulatto sons.
>
> (Feingold, cited by NOI, 1991, P: 197)

From this miscegenation a situation would sometimes arise where many of these Mulattos, who were the Sons & Daughters of wealthy White plantation owners and black women, ended up becoming wealthy slave owners themselves, who were educated and now of a higher social status than their black relatives and counterparts, and naturally this often led to a situation where these Mulattos came to look down upon Blacks as their inferiors. Again this has also been documented by Harold Sharfman in *"Documentary History of Jews in the United States"*:

> The full-blooded Negro slave had no social status. When a white man cohabited with a black slave, their mulatto offspring was elevated on the social ladder.
>
> (Sharfman, cited by NOI, 1991, P: 197)

Let us just point out that we only use Jews here as an example, and are not trying to make any kind of 'Anti-Semitic' statement. As far as we are concerned Jews are Caucasian by "Ethnicity" and therefore all come under the same historic 'umbrella', concerning this aspect of Slavery.

The majority of Africans in the Western Hemisphere were denied access to education until mid 20th Century, unlike many of their 'Mixed' counterparts whom due to their privileged positions, were able to produce some of the most outstanding scientific achievements and inventions falsely attributed to Blacks.

The following are a few such examples taken from the book *"Black Pioneers of Science and Invention"*:

- **Norbert Rillieux**, (1806-1894) *Inventor of The Sugar Crystalliser*
- **Jan Ernest Matzeliger**, (1852-1963) *Inventor of The Shoe Lasting Machine*
- **Garrett A. Morgan**, (1877-1894) *Inventor of The Breathing Helmet & Traffic Light Signal*
- **Daniel Hale Williams**, (1856-1931) *First Open Heart Surgeon*
- **Charles Richard Drew**, (1904-1950) *Pioneer of Blood Transfusion*

Figs.155, 156, 157 & 158 So-called Great Black Inventors: Left- Right:
Norbert Rillieux, Jan Matzeliger, Daniel Hale & Charles Richard Drew Williams

Naturally, this phenomenon created a new racial and social class, who were highly educated and financially affluent, which would eventually render them some of the most powerful figures in so-called 'Black' America and the Caribbean once Slavery had been abolished. As time passed these Mulattos or mixed blacks, wanted to join White Fraternal orders such as Freemasonry, but were refused entry, due to the racial discrimination practiced by White Freemasons, so they decided to form their own 'coloured' societies instead. The first of these so-called Black or Coloured Societies or 'Lodges' was inaugurated in 1787, by a man named Prince Hall.

Prince Hall Masonry

So who was Prince Hall and what role does he play in Black American History? According to York on page 60 of *"Secret Societies Unmasked"* he states:

> Prince Hall was the founder of Freemasonry among Blacks. He was born in Barbados, West Indies, in 1748 A.D. His mother was a Black slave and his father was an Englishman. Part of Prince Hall's life was spent sailing on an Irish merchant vessel. After his sailing career was over he began to study for the ministry and became an active Methodist Clergyman in Cambridge, Massachusetts. It was through a petition presented to John Hancock and Joseph Warren that Prince Hall requested that Blacks be allowed to enlist in the Army. Prince Hall began his career in Freemasonry when he and fourteen other "free" Blacks were initiated into an Irish Lodge that was part of the British Army. In 1787 A.D., he formed the Africa Lodge No. 459, after he had received a charter from the Grand Lodge of England. The 4,729 Prince Hall Lodges traced their historical beginning to this particular lodge. And there are many Masonic authorities that have admitted its legitimacy.
>
> (Isa Al Haadi Al Mahdi, 1990, p: 60 - 61)

According to York, these so-called Black Lodges provided blacks with nothing more than Watered down Euro-centric lessons and therefore should not be called African Lodges, as we shall later see in a fascinating dialogue between York and a 'High Ranking' Black Prince Hall Mason. York further asserts is that the Illuminatti would later use these Secret Societies as a recruitment ground for these "Mixed" or Light-skinned blacks to become the Power Elite or so-called **'Distinguished Men of Color'**, and most prominent Political & Academic figures who have traditionally kept a Stranglehold on the reins of Power throughout the Black Community in the U.S., U.K. & Caribbean. Indeed at a glance the most prominent blacks in the areas of Politics, Business & Academia during the last two centuries, does lend some food for thought:

- **Prince Hall**, *First ever, Black Grandmaster of a Masonic Lodge*
- **Dr. Charles. H. Wesley**, *Fourth African American to receive a Ph.D. from Harvard University*
- **Carter. G. Woodson**, *'Father of Black History'*
- **William Edward Burghardt DuBois**, *Civil Rights Leader, Co-Founder of NAACP*
- **Sir Alexander Bustamante**, *First Jamaican Prime Minister*
- **Sir Norman Manley**, *Former Jamaican Politician*
- **Michael Manley**, *Former Prime Minister of Jamaica*
- **Edward Seaga**, *Former Prime Minister of Jamaica*
- **Adam Clayton Powell**, *First Black Member of House of Representatives*

- **Richmond Barthe**, *First Black sculptor, Elected to National Academy*
- **Maggie Lena Walker**, *First Black Woman to be President of a Bank*
- **Leon Howard Sullivan**, *Developed First Black major Shopping Centre*
- **Richard Theodore Greener**, *First Black to graduate from Harvard University*
- **Charles Lewis Reason**, *First Black Faculty member on a White Campus*
- **Thurgood Marshall**, *First Black American U.S. Solicitor General*
- **Mary Church Terrell**, *First Black Woman to serve on the Washington D.C. board of Education*
- **Grace Towns Hamilton**, *First Black Woman in State Legislature*
- **Edward William Brooke**, *First Black to be nominated to run for State-wide Office in Massachusetts*
- **Frederick Douglass**, *Abolitionist and Advisor to President Abraham Lincoln*
- **Francis L. Cardoza**, *First Black South Carolina Secretary of State*
- **Ralph Bunche**, *First Black Non-diplomatic official in U.S. Department of State*
- **Hazel O'Leary**, *First Black person to be Secretary of Energy*
- **Blanch Kelso Bruce**, *First Black Elected to full term in U.S. Senate*
- **Maynard Holbrook Jackson**, *First Black Mayor of Atlanta*
- **Dorothy Dandridge,** *First black woman to be nominated for Academy Awards*
- **Lemuel Haynes**, *First Black Congregational Minister*
- **Ernest Nathan Morial**, *First Black Juvenile Court Judge in State of Louisiana*
- **Prof. Henry Louis Gates**, *Author and Historian for the New York Times*
- **Lft. Jerry Rawlings**, *Former President of Ghana*
- **Lee Jasper**, *First Black Race Relations Advisor to the Mayor of London*
- **Gen. Colin Powell**, *Former Joint Chiefs of Staff & First Black U.S. Secretary of State*
- **Vanessa Williams,** *First Miss Black America*
- **Raymond "Benzino" Scott**, *Co-Founder of the first Hip Hop Magazine, 'The Source'*
- **Kanya King**, *Co-Founder of the 'Music of Black Origin' (MOBO) Awards*
- **Ray Nagin**, *Mayor of New Orleans, Louisiana*
- **Senator Harold. E. Ford Jr**, *United States Representative*
- **Senator Barak Obama**, *Only African American currently serving in the U.S. Senate*

Figs.159, 160, 161, 162, 163, 164 & 165: Mulatto Elite: Top, Left- Right:
Prince Hall, Dr. Charles. H. Wesley, Carter. G. Woodson, W. E. B. Dubois, Sir Alexander Bustamante, Sir Norman Manley, Michael Manley, Edward Seaga & Adam Clayton Powell

Figs.166, 167, 168, 169, 170, 171, 172, 173 & 174: Top, Left- Right:
Richmond Barthe, Maggie Lena Walker, Leon Howard Sullivan, Richard Theodore Greener, Charles Lewis Reason, Thurgood Marshall, Mary Church Terrell, Grace Towns Hamilton & Edward William Brooke

Figs.175, 176, 177, 178, 179, 180, 181, 182 & 183: Top, Left- Right:
*Frederick Douglass, Francis L. Cardoza, Ralph Bunche Hazel O'Leary,
Blanche Kelso Bruce, Maynard Holbrook Jackson,
Dorothy Dandridge, Lemuel Haynes & Ernest Nathan Morial*

Figs.184, 185, 186, 187, 188, 189, 190, 191 & 192: Top, Left- Right:
*Henry Louis Gates, Jerry Rawlings, Lee Jasper, Gen. Colin Powell, Vanessa Williams Raymond Benzino, Kanya King, Gov. Ray Nagin, Harold. E. Ford Jr
& Senator Barak Obama*

As you can see the term *"Black Pioneers"* or Black Firsts, has so often been misapplied to Mixed or Light skinned blacks, and in so doing, given Blacks the false belief that their conditions have steadily been improving. Indeed the Illuminatti's plan to manipulate the progress and direction of blacks in the Western hemisphere was given further impetus when most of these Mulatto or Mixed blacks, integrated back into the wider African American and Afro-Caribbean communities, because they were no longer so easy to identify. This in turn created a new 'Middle to Upper Elite Class' of blacks who formed the higher echelon or bourgeoisie class who have been the actual Illuminatti bloodlines who have bitterly opposed all 'Real' Black leadership like Marcus Garvey since the early 20th Century. Ironically, Marcus Garvey's activities were sabotaged both in the United States and Jamaica by this class of Mixed blacks. In America, it was NAACP founder W. E. B. DuBois who opposed, and ultimately hindered the progress of Marcus Garvey's UNIA, and even used his influence to call for Garvey's deportation from the U.S.

The following are excerpts re-published by Professor Tony Martin, from *"The Philosophy & Opinion of Marcus Garvey"* compiled by his wife Amy Jacques Garvey, taken from "The Negro World" newspaper and actual letters written by Garvey himself, condemning the power, influence and hidden agenda of the Mulatto or Mixed blacks. Please note that the following does not express our opinions, but that of the deep resentment, which existed between The Universal Negro Improvement Association (UNIA), and The National Association for the Advancement of Coloured People (NAACP), during the 1920s:

W.E. BURGHARDT DU BOIS AS A HATER OF DARK PEOPLE

Calls His Own Race "Black and Ugly", Judging From the White Man's Standard of Beauty

Trick of National Association for the Advancement of Coloured People to Solve Problem by Assimilation and Colour Distinction

(Reprinted from Negro World, February 13, 1923)

W.E. Burghardt DuBois, the Negro "misleaders," who is editor of the "Crisis," the official organ of the National Association for the Advancement of "certain" Coloured People, situated at 70 Fifth Avenue, New York City, has again appeared in print. This time he appears as author of an article in the February issue of the "Century" Magazine under the caption, "Back to Africa," in which he makes the effort to criticise Marcus Garvey, the Universal Negro Improvement Association and the Black Star Line. This "unfortunate mulatto," who bewails every day the drop of Negro blood in his veins, being sorry that he is not Dutch or French, has taken upon himself the responsibility of criticizing and condemning other people while holding himself up as the social "unapproachable" and the great "I AM" of the Negro race. But we will see who Mr. DuBois is, in that he

invites his own characterization. So we will, therefore, let him see himself as others see him.
"Fat, Black, Ugly Man"
In describing Marcus Garvey in the article before mentioned, he referred to him as a 'little, fat black man; ugly, but with intelligent eyes and a big head." Now, what does DuBois mean by ugly? This so-called professor of Harvard and Berlin ought to know by now that the standard of beauty within a race is not arrived at by comparison with another race; as, for instance, if we were to desire to find out the standard of beauty among the Japanese people we would not judge them from the Anglo-Saxon viewpoint, but from the Japanese. How he arrives at his conclusion that Marcus Garvey is ugly, being a Negro, is impossible to determine, in that if there is any ugliness in the Negro race it would be reflected more through DuBois Than Marcus Garvey, in that he himself tells us that he is a little Dutch, a little French, and a little Negro. Why, in fact, the man is a monstrosity. So, if there is any ugliness it is on the part of DuBois and not on the part of the "little fat, black man with the big head," because all this description is typical of the African. But this only goes to show how much hate DuBois has for the black blood in his veins. Anything that is black, to him, is ugly, is hideous, is monstrous, and this is why in 1917 he had but the lightest of coloured people in his office, when could hardly tell whether it was a white show or a coloured vaudeville he was running at Fifth avenue...

(Negro World, cited by Martin, 1986, p: 310-311)

Social Honors for Negroes
In referring to the matter, he says in the article: "Many American Negroes and some others were scandalized by something which they could not regard as a simple child's play. It seemed to them sinister. This enthronement of a demagogue, a blatant boaster, who with monkey-shines was deluding the people, and taking their hard-earned dollars; and in high Harlem there arose an instant cry, "Garvey must go!" Indeed DuBois was scandalized by the creation of a Peerage and Knighthood by Negroes, and in truth the person who is responsible for the creation of such a thing should go, because DuBois and those who think like him can see and regard honor conferring only by their white masters...This was an enthronement of Negroes, in which DuBois could see nothing worth while. He was behind the "Garvey must go!" program started in Harlem immediately after the enthronement, because he realized that Garvey and the Universal Negro Improvement Association were usurping the right he had arrogated to himself as being the highest social dignitary, not only in Harlem but throughout the country.

(Negro World, cited by Martin, 1986, p: 313)

The Negro Problem
As proof of the intention underlying the National Association for the Advancement of Coloured People we will quote from DuBois himself. He states in his article:
"We think of our problem here as THE Negro problem, but we know more or less clearly that the problem of the American Negro is very different

from the problem of the South African Negro or the problem or the problem of the Nigerian Negro or the problem of the South American Negro. We have not hitherto been so clear as to the way in which the problem of the Negro in the United States differs from the problem of the Negro in the West Indies.

"For a long time we have been told, and we have believed, that the race problem in the West Indies, and in particularly Jamaica, has been virtually settled."

Now DuBois speaks of this settlement of the problem of the race in the West Indies and Jamaica with a great deal of satisfaction. What kind of settlement is it? DuBois knows well, but he is not honest enough to admit it, because he himself visited Jamaica and saw the situation there, wherein an arrangement has been effected whereby the white man is elevated to the highest social and economic heights, and between him is socially and economically elevated the mulatto type of DuBois, and beneath them both is the black man, who is crushed to the very bottom socially and economically.

(Negro World, cited by Martin, 1986, p: 316)

Settlement of the Problem

DuBois regards this as a settlement of the problem in the West Indies and Jamaica. Now this is the kind of settlement that he and the National Association for the Advancement of Coloured People want in America, and they have not been honest enough to come out and tell us so, that we might act accordingly...

(Negro World, cited by Martin, 1986, p: 316)

The following is an actual letter written by Marcus Garvey whilst in Tombs Federal Prison in 1923 in which he outlines in detail, the hidden agenda of the secret societies of the 'Mulatto Elite', whose job it was to maintain the White Supremacist agenda, of helping to keep poor blacks of all complexions down, and to eventually destroy the black race through miscegenation. This notion is very consistent with York's theory that the Illuminatti, plan to create a new race called Neutronoids, who will be a new 'Mixed race', comprised of every race on the planet, and will eventually re-populate the Earth in the future.

AN EXPOSE OF THE CASTE SYSTEM AMONG NEGROES
(Written from the Tombs Prison August 31st, 1923)

The policy of the Universal Negro Improvement Association is so clean-cut, and my personal views are so well known, that no one, for even a moment, could reasonably accuse us of having any other desire that that of working for a united Negro race.

The program of the Universal Negro Improvement Association is that of drawing together, into one universal whole, all the Negro peoples of the world, with prejudice towards none. We desire to have every shade of color, even those with one drop African blood, in our fold; because we believe that none of us, as we are, is responsible for our birth; in a word, we have no prejudice against ourselves in race. We believe that every Negro racially is just alike, and therefore, we have no distinction to make, hence wherever you see the Universal Negro Improvement Association you will find us giving every member of the race an equal chance and opportunity to make good.

Unfortunately, there is a disposition on the part of a certain element of our people in America, the West Indies and Africa, to hold themselves up as the "better class" or "privileged" group on the caste of color.

This subject is such a delicate one that no one is honest enough to broach it, yet the evil of it is working great harm to our racial solidarity, and I personally feel it my duty to right now bring it to the attention of all concerned. The Universal Negro Improvement Association is founded on truth, and, therefore, anything that might menace or retard the race must be gotten out of the way, hence our stand in this direction. During the early days of slavery our people were wrested from the bosom of our native land-Africa-and brought into these climes. For centuries, against their will, our mothers were subjected to the most cruel and unfair treatment, the result of which was created among us the diversity of colors and types, to the end that we have become the most mixed race in the world.

(Garvey cited by Martin, 1986, p: 55)

Near Whites

Some of us in America, the West Indies and Africa believe that the nearer we approach the white man in color the greater our social standing and privilege and that we should build up an "aristocracy" based upon caste of color and not achievement in race. It is well known, although no one is honest enough to admit it, that we have been, for the past thirty years at least, but more so now than ever, grading ourselves for social honor and distinction on the basis of color......................There is a subtle underhand propaganda fostered by a few men of color in America, the West Indies and Africa to destroy the self respect and pride of the Negro race by building up what is commonly known as a "blue vein" aristocracy and to foster same as the social and moral standard of the race. The success of this effort is very much marked in the West Indies, and coming into immediate recognition in South Africa, and is now gaining much headway in America under the skilful leadership of the National Association for Advancement of "Colored" People and their silent but scattered agents. The observant members of our race must have noticed within recent years a great hostility between the National Association for Advancement of "Colored" People and The Universal "Negro" Improvement Association, and must have wondered why Du Bois writes so bitterly against Garvey and vice versa. Well, the reason is plainly to be seen after the following explanation:

Group That Hates Negro

Du Bois represents the group that hates the Negro blood in its veins, and has been working subtly to build up a caste aristocracy that would socially divide the race into two groups: One the superior because of color caste, the other inferior, hence the pretentious work of the National Association for Advancement of "Colored" People...When Garvey arrived in America and visited the office of the National Association for Advancement of "Colored" People to interview Du Bois, who was regarded as a leader of the Negro people, and who had recently visited the West Indies, he was dumbfounded on approach to the office to find but for Mr. Dill, Du Bois, himself and the office boy, he could not tell whether he was in a white office or that of the National Association for Advancement of "Colored" People. The whole staff was either white or very near white, and thus Garvey got his first shock of the advancement hypocrisy. There was no representation of there that anyone could recognize. The advancement meant that you had to be as near white as possible, otherwise there was no place for you as stenographer, clerk or attendant in the office of the National Association for Advancement of "Colored" People. After a short talk with Du Bois, Garvey became disgruntled with the man and his principles that the thought he never contemplated entered his mind-that of remaining in America to teach Du Bois and his group what real race pride meant.

(Garvey cited by Martin, 1986, p: 56-57)

Garvey at N.A.A.C.P.'s Office

...In New York, Boston, Washington and Detroit, Garvey further discovered the activities of the "**Blue Vein Society**" and the "**Colonial Club**". The West Indian "lights" formed the "Colonial Club" and the American "lights" the "Blue Vein" Society. The "Colonial Club" would give annual balls besides regular or monthly *soirees* and no one less than a quadroon would be admitted, and gentlemen below that complexion were only admitted if they were lawyers, doctors or very successful business men with plenty of "cash", who were known to uphold the caste aristocracy...

(Garvey cited by Martin, 1986, p: 58)

Scheme to Destroy Race

The National Association for Advancement of "Colored" People is a scheme to destroy the Negro Race, and the leaders of it hate Marcus Garvey, because he has discovered them at their game and because the Universal Negro Improvement Association, without any prejudice to color or caste, is making headway in brining all people together for their common good.

(Garvey cited by Martin, 1986, p: 59)

Garvey Caught the Tune

The conspiracy to destroy the Negro race is so well organized that the moment anything interferes with their program there springs up a simultaneous action on the part of the leaders. It will be observed that in the September issue of the "Crisis" is published on the very last page of its news section what purports to be the opinion of a Jamaican paper about Marcus Garvey and his caste. The skilful editor of the "Crisis," Dr. Du Bois, reproduces that part of the article that would tend to show the true opinion about Garvey in his own country taken from a paper called the

"Gleaner," (edited by Herbert George de Lisser) and not the property of Negroes.
The article in the original was clipped from the "Gleaner" when it appeared, and was sent by a friend to Garvey, so that he knew all that appeared in it. In it the editor extolled the leadership and virtues of Du Bois, and said it was the right kind of leadership for the American Negro people, and bitterly denounced Garvey. Du Bois published that part that denounced Garvey, but suppressed the part that gave him the right of leadership; and he failed to enlighten his readers that the editor of the "Gleaner" is a very light man, who hates the Negro blood of his mother and who is part of the international scheme to foster the Blue Vein Society scheme. Dr. Du Bois failed to further enlighten his readers that he visited Jamaica and was part of the "Colonial Society" scheme; he also failed to state that in the plan De Lisser is to "hold down" the West Indian end of the "caste scheme" and he and others to "hold down" the American end, while their agents "hold down" the South African section.

(Garvey cited by Martin, 1986, p: 60)

Figs.193 & 194: Left- Right: *Professor Tony Martin & Publication: "The Philosophy & Opinion of Marcus Garvey"*

Clearly, in his own words, Marcus Garvey and his organisation the UNIA, were bitterly opposed by W.E.B DuBois & The NAACP because of what he termed ***"The conspiracy to destroy the Negro Race"***, which was being controlled by the Blue Vein & Colonial Club Societies, which like the Boule Society, were in no doubt part of a "Masonic" conspiracy to manipulate the progress of blacks, directed by the Illuminati. Dr. Malachi. Z. York points out that Marcus Garvey had knowledge of this conspiracy because he was himself a Mason, who broke ranks to raise the awareness of blacks to this diabolical scheme, which is why he was destroyed. It was also the job of this 'Mulatto Elite', and members of Secret Societies to promote the idea of racial integration to blacks, and thereby encourage Miscegenation, or 'Race Mixing' between Blacks & Whites, in order to destroy the racial characteristics of Negroes or Africans.

York's theory of many Black leader's being involved with secret societies is corroborated, by Masonic researcher Jehvon I. Buckner, in his article: *"Masonry the root of all wickedness"* 1, which was brought to our attention by an individual based in the U.S., named Lafeare Ward. In it the author describes how, W.E.B Dubois, and Carter.G.Woodson, were both members of secret societies, and also details the fate of George G. M. James, author of *"Stolen Legacy"*:

GEORGE GM JAMES VS. W.E.B DUBOIS, & CARTER.G.WOODSON

In the case of James versus W.E.B Dubois and Woodson, it must be noted that James belonged to the York Rite Masons and W.E.B Dubois/Woodson to the Boule'. Both had to pledge oath's of secrecy with the penalty resulting in death. Dubois and Woodson were later exiled from the Boule' for unknown reasons. Not long after, Dubois became a Pan-Africanist; moving to Ghana (a place he once was strongly opposed to during the reign of Marcus Garvey), and Woodson went on to publish the infamous text, Mis-education of the Negro. Both basically made somewhat of a 175 (degree) turn once out of these white-based secret sects. Where they failed our people is they did not make an entire 180 (degree) turn. They remembered they took an oath to uphold the secrets of the fraternity – never letting you know who rules the world (Rhodes/Rothschild); probably because they feared death. Yes they did walk away from these white supremacist organizations, BUT they never let the people know about them; therefore, not becoming part of the solution, but remaining part of the problem because they refused to tell you exactly what white and black organizations and foundations, that were responsible for the hell our people have been suffering…If it wasn't for the sacrifice of George GM James, on the other hand, we probably would never know about the Greeks stealing African culture and claiming it as theirs. The book, **Stolen Legacy**, exposed the myths of Greek philosophy…James knew his life was on the line, but his love for our people far outweighed the fear of death…

(Buckner, 2003, p: 4)

It was W.E.B DuBois who began the *"Garvey must go"* campaign, which culminated in Marcus Garvey's imprisonment, and eventual deportation from the United States. After leaving the U.S. Garvey travelled to his homeland of Jamaica to try and rebuild his organisation, however his problems with these secret societies were far from over. According to author Laurie Gunst in her fascinating book about Jamaican politics *"Born Fi' Dead"*, it was members of Jamaica's so-called 'Coloured Elite', namely Alexander Bustamante and Norman Manley, who first exploited the growing

Independence movements begun by Marcus Garvey's followers in Jamaica for their own political ends. After returning to Jamaica, Marcus Garvey's attempts to re-organise his movement were thwarted by the same clique who would eventually have him imprisoned and banished from Jamaica for the rest of his life.

> ...the strikes were black people's struggle, and the **colored elite** knew it. So they watched and waited...For fifteen years they had been listening to Marcus Garvey and his Jamaican disciples preach the doctrine of black self-independence, and they found a temporary leader from the ranks of Garvey's Universal Negro Improvement Association, the Harlem based UNIA. His name was St William Grant, and he was a militant who wanted nothing less for the country than full independence from England...But Grant had a rival for the Quashee's loyalty, a fiery, near-white demagogue named Alexander Bustamante. "Busta," as everyone called him, soon eclipsed Grant in the sight of the masses, and his rise to power changed Jamaica forever...With his light skin, wavy hair, and strong-featured face punctured by enormous bushy eyebrows, Bustamante was a riveting presence...Bustamante's color gave him a definite advantage in a colony where blackness was no virtue...Busta was one of the greatest tragedies in Jamaican history. If Grant had been the man to lead us, maybe this county would have been a real black-orientated government. Instead what we got was a white-mon rule.
>
> (Gunst, 1995, p: 67-69)

According to York, the Nation of Islam's origins were also connected to a lesser extent with this conspiracy, to control America's Black Militancy, by creating the most powerful Black organisation in the Western Hemisphere since Marcus Garvey's UNIA. Many of York's followers, who were once members of the Nation of Islam, claim the organisation practices a similar hierarchical (High-racial) policy, in the selection of senior Ministers, as we have discussed earlier. The reason for this may lay in the Western World's attitude towards 'Dark Skinned' blacks as well as the Nation of Islam's concept of God. In the group's original teachings, it is said that Master Farad Muhammad was a Mulatto, or as they say *"Half Original"*. This was supposed to be one of the reasons for Clarence 13X's expulsion, because he questioned the validity of this belief, and to this very day 'High Ranking' members of 5% Nation of Gods & Earths such as Hip Hop legend Rakim still challenge the Nation of Islam's belief of Allah being Half White. In his forthcoming book entitled: *"The Immortal Birth of Allah: Rise of the Five Percenters"*, Allah Jihad, states the following:

> Alphonso Muhammad told the elders that he himself could not carry out such a mission in the Western hemisphere because of the fact that he was a dark blackman, and White America at that time did not allow a Blackman to come freely to the shores of North America without official business with its government. The Caucasians would not allow anything to enter America that might mentally free their slaves, either they stopped or killed

such a person. So, Alphonso being a wise man knew he had to produce a child who would make it appear to the naked eye as a Caucasian, so they will think he is one of them, but to the Blackman as a high yellowish person, in order to go through enemy lines and reach the lost tribe of Shabazz (black people). Alphonso with his wise idea, went up into the mountains and got himself a Caucasian Muslim as a wife. She born him two children, the first a female the second was Wallace Fard Muhammad.
(Jihad, 2004)

The theory of this conspiracy by the Illuminatti to control black leadership is again supported by author Jehvon I. Buckner in his article: *"Boule 3 dying wit secrets"* 2. Apparently, 'Boule' is the name of the Black secret society responsible for initiating many of America's future Black leader's from Universities, across the United States. According to Buckner, W. E. B. DuBois and Carter. G. Woodson were past members of this fraternity, whose job it is to control the direction of blacks in America and the West Indies, and protect the interests of the Illuminatti. Conspiracy researcher Bobby Hemmit claims that the Boule control many Powerful Negros who are sworn to Secrecy through a 'Homo Sexual' initiation ceremony, which is used to manipulate these Black leader's & Celebrities throughout their lives.

A similar strategy is also said to be used in African Lodges, who also recruit future leaders from amongst the higher echelons of African society. Many of whom are descended from the bloodlines of tyrannical Kings and Chiefs, directly involvement in selling their own people to Arab & European Slave Traders.

Nuwaubian Lodge

York officially introduced his followers to Freemasonry by first forming *"The Ancient Egiptian Order"* (A.E.O), around 1999, then later his own 'Break-away' lodge: The Grand Lodge Ancient Free & Accepted Masons Inc. & Arabic Nobles of the Mystic Shrines, Inc. Al Mahdi Shrine Temple (A.N.O.M.S), which were both inaugurated in 2001. These fraternal organisation's brought York's teachings full circle, and were a type of culmination of The Ansaaru Allah doctrine, which he taught as "Imaam Isa" from the 1970s to early 1990s.

We have been unable to obtain much information about these secret orders, except for what was made available on one of the organisations website: <http://www.arratib.com>, entitled: *"The Grand Mufti: The Only True Shriners"* The following is the opening statement reasserting York's claim of being a Blood-line descendent of The Prophet Muhammad, referred to in The Holy Qur'an as 'Ahli'l Bayt' *"The Family of the House"*, a term used to describe Muhammad's blood line, explained in Chapter One *"A Noble Lineage"*.

I As The Grand **Mufti** "The Divan", named **Issa Al Haadi Al Mahdi**, in the year **1945 A.D.**, am a Blood link to **Al Mahdi** of the **Sudan, Nubia,** being the son of **Al Haadi Abdul Rahman Al Mahdi 1922-1970 A.D.** The son of **Abdur Rahman Al Mahdi 1885-1959 A.D.**, who was the son of ***The Mahdi* 1845- 1885 A.D.** We have an unbroken Seed, Son after Son that goes directly back to **Ali 599-661 A.D.** And **Fatima, Daughter** of **Muhammad**, who had 3 Children **Husain, Hasan and Muhsin** (who died before birth)...

(York, 2001)

On the same website York goes on to explain the relevance of 'Ahli'l Bayt', or The Prophet Muhammad's bloodline to modern day 'Shrinerdom' and Freemasonry, entitled *"Ahli'l Bait"*:

Ques: What does Ahli'l Bait mean?
Ans: First of all the original **Al-Muthkheroon** *"Shriners"* were in fact the family of the scriptures referred to as **Ahli'l Bait** "People of the house" found in The Noble Qur'aan 11:73 and was a title given to those blood relatives from Adam to the present day, who vowed to protect the Sacred Shrines from invaders. They took the blood oath and were called **Al-Halifoon** as a group or **halif** as individuals or those who took the oath.
There can be but one, **Ahli'l Bait** "family of the house" known as **The International Supreme Council of Shriners, Inc.**, world wide, although there can be many sub councils. Only one **Imperial Grand Supreme Council** governs the jurisdictions in due boundaries and in turn issue charters to temples and units. The headquarters must be located where the blood relatives of **Ali** and the prophet **Muhammad** reside. The true **Ahli'l-Bait** is made up of 9 Arabs who hold the original manuscripts. That were taken from **Halab "Aleppo"** Syria in the Syrian dialect of Arabic (Kufic) which was taken by **Rizk Allah Hassoon Effendee** a Turk who himself who couldn't read it and then on to London and then to America by **Albert L. Rawson**, who was born in New York and translated it to English. Presently the handbooks in English circulating in the Shrines throughout America and Europe. Be they from **Noble George L. Root**, a Euro-Shriner or **John G. Jones 33rd** degree and **Booker T. Alexander**. Negro Shriners have incorrect, passwords and rituals many have no idea about the great funeral that they re-enact over and over again of **Abd Al Kadir bin Mahyal-Din (Al Hasani)** born in Mascara, 20 miles east of east in **1808 A.D.** and the black camel visited his noble tent and he passed in Damascus in 1888 A.D. Most Shriners today have no idea that their temple rituals and furnishings is in resemblance of the great funeral that took place on **May 26 1883 A.D.** His death was mourned on **Saturday, May 31**, in enactment of his funeral the temple furnishings were set. The Euro-Shriners attended. The Afro-Shriners for the most part, know very little about this event. The original temples were Mosques in the east with the furnishes of the mosques old sacred hieroglyphs with a replica of a **ka'aba**

(York, 2001)

York, also appeared upon the (A.N.O.M.S) website with 9 members of what form the Elite Inner Circle of: *"The Ansaruallah Supreme Grand Council"*, with himself as **Grand Mufti: "The Divan"**, at the top. These individuals represented what York previously referred to as: *"The…9 Arabs who hold the original manuscripts"*, which was of great significance, because it was the first time York had ever allowed himself to officially share the same platform with other members of his movement. These '9' members of The **Ansaruallah "Supreme Grand Council",** were:

1) **Al Imam** "Divan" Grand Potentate Noble: **Dr. Thomas Chism**
2) **Imam** "Divan" Potentate Noble: **Dr. Anthony Evans**
3) **Mu'azan** "Divan" Imperial Recorder Noble: **Dr. Ahmadou Vermah**
4) **Muq-Tadi** "Divan" Illustrious Recorder Noble: **Dr. Claude Turner**
5) **Maulana** "Divan" High Priest Prophet Noble: **Dr. George Drayton**
6) **Mutawwiff** Oriental Guide: Pastor **Marshal Chance**
7) **Saadeq** Treasurer Noble: **Dr. George Jackson**
8) **Al Amir** "Divan" Chief Rabban Noble: **Dr. Keith McIntosh**
9) **Amir** "Divan" Assit. Rabban Noble: **Dr. William Walker**

Figs.195, 196, 197 & 198: The Ansaarullah Supreme Grand Council: Top: *Grand Mufti: Dr. Malachi. Z. York* (**Bottom**) **Left- Right:** *Dr. Thomas Chism, Dr.Anthony Evans & Dr. Armadouh Varmah*

Figs.199, 200, 201, 202, 203 & 204: Top, Left- Right:
Dr. Claude Turner, Dr George Drayton & Dr. Marshal Chance
(Bottom) *Dr. George Jackson, Dr. Kieth MacIntosh & Dr. William Walker*

Many of these individuals appeared to be within York's age range, and may have been former members of the original Ansaaru Allah Community (Nubian Islamic Hebrew Mission) back in Brooklyn, New York, who now formed York's most trusted inner circle. However as we shall see, like York, they too would become targets of the nefarious Macon County Officials, led by Sheriff Howard Richard Sills.

As we have been unable to obtain any of the lessons from any of the "Nuwauubian Lodges" we have absolutely no idea what York taught, however as with all his other school's he seems to have taken the Shriner & Masonic doctrine to an entirely new level, and as we shall see later. York's understanding of the true origins of both these Societies appears to far surpass any information currently in the hands of so-called 'Mainstream' Freemasons, which naturally made him a threat. At the height of York's influence in Macon County, Statewide newspaper The Georgia Informer categorised him as one of the *"Fifth Most Influential Black men in the State of Georgia"*. Being then, "The Supreme Grand Hierophant of the Ancient Egiptian Order Lodge #9 in Athens, GA., the owners of Tama-Re, 'Egypt of the West' had requested that he dedicate their Social Club named after Ramesses II as the central Grand Lodge #19 for Free and Accepted Masons in Georgia and surrounding states."

Masonic Backlash

Naturally the activities of York's new *"Nuwauubian Lodges"* Arabic Nobles of the Mystic Shrines, Inc. Al Mahdi Shrine Temple, and its spreading influence soon began to attract attention from the local media in Macon County, Georgia, as this article by the Macon Telegraph, reporter by Skippy Davis entitled *"Nuwaubians to buy Shrine Temple in Macon"* points out:

Fig.205: Rising Influence:
Supreme Grand Master; Dr. Malachi. Z. York

> Members of New Mecca Temple No. 11, who also are members of the United Nuwaubian Nation of Moors, are expected to buy the Al Sihah Shrine Temple property on Poplar Street the end of May.
> Leaders of the New Mecca Temple have told the Al Sihah Shriners they plan to continue the current use of the building, renting it out to organizations for events, including parties and bingo, and renting out spaces in the temple's two parking lots. "What we have is a contract, a retainer check and a statement from them that they are near to closing", said Harley Phillips, business manager for the Shrine. The Buyers have paid $25,000 in earnest money and have contracted to pay the Shriners' asking price of $800,000, the appraised value. This property includes a 71 year old Temple building and two parking lots on Poplar Street across from Macon City Hall.
> Charles Langford, attorney for the Al Sihah Shrine and also a Shrine member, said he did not know that the New Mecca Temple principles, Al Woodhall and A.J. Vermah, were Nuwaubians until City Councilman Ed DeFore told him they were.
>
> (Davies, 2001)

Figs.206, 207, 208 & 209: Top, Left- Right: *Dr. Malachi. Z. York & Nuwaubian Shriners during Public Festival, Nuwaubian Masons standing formation during Public festival* **(Bottom)** *Al Sihah Temple property*

Figs.210 & 211: Back to Basics: Top & Bottom:
Malachi York dressed in Traditional Sudanese attire accompanied by The Ansaars

As previously stated, Malachi York's teachings appear to have come full circle with the formation of The Shriners: **'Ansaruallah'** Supreme Grand Council as the culmination of his 30-year ministry since the 1970's as the Nubian Islamic Hebrew Mission/Ansaaru Allah Community. Prior to his arrest in 2002, York is rumoured to have re-instituted many aspects of the original Islamic 'Ansaar' school, including reaffirming his East-African Descent from the Prophet Muhammad, along with the construction of a Mosque & Shrine dedicated to his Great Grand Father 'The Mahdi' Muhammad Ahmed, on the group's property Tama Re. The Nuwaubian leader even astonished his former followers by adorning the traditional Sudanese attire of Imah (Turban) & Jallabiya (Robe), for the first time in over 10-years, which had been abandoned since the early 1990s.

It didn't take long however for the Media, and the Macon City Council officials to begin working behind the scenes to try to turn the local community against members of the Nuwauubians Lodge. Clearly York's decision to 'Reform' Masonry by instituting his own "Grand Nuwaubian Lodge" was naturally met by hostility from many Freemasons, with one individual in particular going to great lengths to expose York as a charlatan and a fraud, not long after York launched his 'Nuwauubian Lodge'. We also stumbled across an interesting website entitled *"The Wesley Room {The Real Issue!!!}"*, which is an official Prince Hall Freemasonry site entitled: *"Dr. Charles. H. Wesley, Masonic Research Society"* [3]. Dr. Charles. H. Wesley you may remember is one of the previously mentioned Mulatto Elite, and founder of the 'Most Worshipful Prince Hall Grand Lodge' or (**MWPHGL**). On it, the issue of Bogus 'Black' Freemasonry was raised by a group of supposedly 'Real' Prince Hall Masons, analysing the growing threat of Bogus 'Black' Lodges, and how best to deal with what they describe as *"deadly pestilence...in the side of Prince Hall Freemasonry"*. The opening statement makes reference to this growing problem for Prince Hall Masonry:

> **By The Society**
> Why is Bogus Freemasonry so prevalent in the Black community and such a threat to Prince Hall Freemasonry? The answer to this question is 'The REAL Issue' and the key to the solution of eradicating this deadly pestilence to Prince Hall Freemasonry in America. Predominately Black Bogus Freemasonry or commonly called Non- Prince Hall Freemasonry has been a pest in the side of Prince Hall Freemasonry since the early 1800's.
> (MWPHGL)

Dr. Charles H. Wesley
Masonic Research Society

Figs.212:
Dr. Charles. H. Wesley

Clearly the issue of Bogus 'Black' Freemasonry, is taken very seriously by 'real' Prince Hall Freemasons, whom obviously feel threatened by this growing phenomenon amongst common blacks. Further on, the chat room goes on to reveal the names of several 'Rogue' or bogus Freemasonic groups, which included Dr. Malachi. Z. York's 'Grand Nuwaubian Lodge':

Who is the infamous Dr. York and what's his relation to Bogus Black Freemasonry?

[**E. BEY**] Now that is an intriguing question. Many may feel that this question cannot be answered in one interview due to the appearance of such simple inquiry. Well let me attempt to define this individual who comes under so many names and faces. First Mr. York was known in New York City, Brooklyn as "AS SAYYID AL IMAAM ISA AL HAADI AL MAHDI" founder of what was called the "THE NUBIAN ISLAMIC HEBREWS" and "The ANSAARU ALLAH COMMUNITY" in the 70's. This individual today calls himself Chief Black Eagle, Dr. Malachi Z. York EL, Nayya Malachizodk EL, Al Mahdi, Dwight York, Rabboni Y'shua Bar El Haady just to name a few. Mr. York put it blank is a Master Con and brain washer. The reason he attracts so many is because he caters to the needs and or desires of gullible people who think he is giving them what can help their condition. This man has literally written books on extraterrestrial beings that he has seen and some who are living on the Planet Earth. This man has plagiarized writings from other authors and has claimed them as his own. In 1993 FBI report has surfaced calling the group a "front for a wide range of criminal activity, including arson, welfare fraud and extortion. "They have even taken the name Moor" (United Nuwaubian Nation of Moors) to attract even those who were followers of the Moorish Science Temple whose founder was Noble Drew Ali in 1913. He has taken teachings from many organisations and religious sects and formulated a pot of mixed doctrines to confuse further those who are already confused enough in their world of dependent thinking. This man has literally admitted in using tactics in drawing week minded people to explain in one of his web pages saying, "I diligently treaded the streets of New York and the surrounding areas as I propagated Sufi Islam. I was blessed with the "gift of the gab" and combined with a sense of humour and charisma that draws people of all walks of life to me."

Mr. York with his mixed doctrine has now established his own Nuwaupian Grand Lodge AF&AM International and his own Shrine Temple Al Mahdi

No. 19, and has attracted hundreds of poor Black Souls in making them think they have some superior Freemasonry that was handed down to him by Noble beings in Egypt. Mr. York on top of that has his own music studio for Nuwaubian Nation of Moors to rap and chant about his teachings. So you ask, "Who is Dr. York"? He is everything to many people and he can become what you want him to be. The greatest danger and downfall of many is that once one discovers that it is all an illusion he has cast over the eyes and minds of the weak, the void returns with a programmed mentality that needs now twice as much consciousness to de-program. Mr. York is a thief of souls.

(E. BEY, 2001)

Ezekiel. M. Bey

We later discovered that this indictment of York and his entire organisation was made by a New York based Prince Hall Freemason who refers to himself as Ezekiel. M. Bey, or **E. BEY**, for short. This individual also known as Bro. Juan Ezekiel Rentas, is the Founder and Moderator for the Blue-Lite research Forum (PHA), and the Senior warden of Cornerstone lodge No. 37 of the Most Worshipful Prince Hall Grand Lodge (MWPHGL) of New York & System Administrator/Owner of Cornerstone Lodge No. 37 MWPHGL of (NY). His offices are currently based in Flatbush, New York, from which this industrious individual has led a kind of 'Crusade' aimed at exposing the activities of Dr. Malachi.Z.York and his Movement. He has also authored a series of online Anti-Nuwaubian articles, which sadly contain nothing more than the usual poorly researched media slander.

Fig.213: York Detractor: Ezekiel. M. Bey

Ezekiel. M. Bey closed by posing the following question to his Masonic colleagues in Georgia:

What is the MWPHGL of GA doing to neutralize York's organisation and other groups in the state?

The statement below is from the M.W. Grand Master of the PHGL of Georgia –The Honourable Bro. Willie L. Williams

"We are in the development phase of deciding what actions to take. I have made contact with the mainstream Grand Lodge to begin talk of recognition. As you know, I hope to launch a publicity campaign to educate the state about Bogus vs. Legitimate Masonic bodies. I also plan to have this on the agenda at the next Grand Master's Conference."

(L. Williams, 2001)

Apparently, Ezekiel. M. Bey is no stranger to Dr. Malachi.Z.York's teachings and personally met him on several occasions during the 1970s and 80s in New York, and admits to having actually visited the Ansaaru Allah (Mosque), in Bushwick Avenue. What follows is a fascinating series of conversations, which actually took place in 2001 between Ezekiel. M. Bey and Dr. Malachi. Z. York on Ezekiel. M. Bey's website 4:

[**E. BEY**] *On June 2, 2001 I sat in my office here in New York and browsed through the Internet and came across some unusual material on Freemasonry and Shrinedom. The information caught my eye, as it was data that has been shared from time to time on various groups I belong to on the Internet. Nothing in depth, but small information on this particular individual who I had the pleasure of one time meeting when he ran a sect of a Muslims in Flatbush section of Brooklyn, New York. This group was very prominent in the late 70's to early 80's.*

This person who I recognized by the name "Al Imam Issa Al Haadi Al Mahdi" or as many new him by "Dr. Malachi York" had various websites claiming to be the Imperial Grand Potentate (Internationally). He is the leader of Al Mahdi Temple No. 19. ILL. And uses the name and title of Rev. Dr. Malachi Z. York 33 degree (A.E.O. & N.M.S.) The Ancient Egiptian (note the spelling) Order & Nobles of the Mystic Shrine, Northern & Southern Jurisdiction, and also Grand Master of Nuwaubian Grand Lodge (A.F. & A.M.) Ancient Free & Accepted Masons Inc. Ramses II Mir No.9. He also claims to be a Scottish Rite Freemason of Amos Grand Lodge of Macon, Ga. and Deputy Grand Master of Pride of Georgia Lodge A.F. & A.M. Well after seeing that it kind of blew my mind.

After reading a little I decided to write him and E-mail that was freely furnished in his web site:

Ezekiel Wrote: (6/02/01) Dr. York, I am Ezekiel M. Bey from New York. I have been reading many of your articles since you had the Ansaar Community well established. The reason I am writing you is because I have seen you evolve in many areas that may confuse those who do not know you. You and I have met many of times. I by other names as well as those I have seen you trans-change.

I probably have all of your Ansaar Community subscription and volumes. What I need to know is what do you consider yourself now? You first called yourself a Muslim, now by what I see, a Moor. But then you also say you are a Mason which many years ago you were against the Masonic Order.

I am not challenging you in any way but would like to know what are your evolutionary reasons for all of your changes? I know all things change and nothing stays the same. But you have so rapidly went from one stage to another in which the people of today do not understand, and in order for one to keep up they might have to know you by what you present at the moment and not like I, who have seen you in your early years.

Well, I wish you the best and hope you can enlighten me on what your intentions are especially now which you call yourself a Shriner.

I know you know the history of the Moorish Fez and what is presently worn, which is a Tarbush. I see you have been reading and studying amongst the Moors.

What would you say Noble Drew Ali would say about your movements today?

Well, the next day to my surprise I received a reply from Dr. York.

Dr. York's Reply: (6/02/01) " If you really followed the books and I believe you did you would know I was always a Freemason. And crossed the desert a long time ago to the shrine finding many mistakes in the rituals and handbooks. The tunnel vision discouraged me but I was called to sit on the International Supreme Council of Shriners and to upgrade the handbook and research the roots of the ritual meanings presented with original Arabic manuscripts and translate them into some sense, which I accepted.

Fig.214: Dr. Malachi. Z. York

I found Muslims to be blindly following undercover Euro- Arab terrorists with no regards for the true Mothers and Fathers of the religion. I found the Moors confused and Emulating Freemasonry not even knowing the language. After so many years I think that the Noble: Drew Ali who himself was a Shriner would be heart broken by the dissention remembering he was betrayed by his own.

My brother you touched on a touchy subject. I have no room for faith or belief, only facts and Islam as practiced by most is faith blindness standing in the light blinded by it. My heart has always been in Nubia that is Egypt and so is every true Freemason and Shriner. I see where I can be more affective for the upliftment of humanity in the Shrine where my eccentric mind and intense research can't be called a cult or sect or militant or the likes."

[E. BEY] *I had to sit back and think, where did all of this come from? When I thought of him saying that he found Muslims to be blindly following undercover Euro-Arabs Terrorists, it took some wind out of me.*
He generalized all Muslims to be terrorist in that statement and I totally disagreed. He also stated that he found the Moors confused, and Emulating Freemasonry not even knowing the language; it told me to be cautious and evaluate his data and information.
Dr. Malachi York is now part of a new group called the United Nuwaubian Nation of Moors. Not to be confused with the Moorish Science Temple that Noble Drew Ali (Aka Timothy Drew) started in the early 1900's or the Circle of Mothers & Sons, or The Great Seal of the Moorish Science.
Dr. Malachi York in many of his writings and web sites express that he is from another galaxy. A galaxy known to him as Illyuwn. He claims that there are 19 galaxies and that Illyuwm is the 19th. He states in some of his writings that Illiyuwm means "On High" and that this galaxies has 3 suns, UTU, SHAMASH, and APSU; with 38 Moons and 19 planets.
To get to know Dr. York a little more of what he represents today, I sent him another E-mail on June 5th, 2001 to see if he would respond and explain a few of my curiosities:

Ezekiel Wrote: Brother Dr. York, at least that is who I believe you are since you did not sign the E-mail of your post. I appreciated you responding to my enquiry about a few curious thoughts of mine. You see I to am a Moor and a Mason. I do not recall you ever calling yourself a Mason but that is neither here nor there. The fact is that you consider yourself one now. As far as the Shriners you give a good description and definition of the Fez in which I am very familiar.

My question to you is when did you first see yourself as a Moor? Since in the 70's you considered yourself a Muslim and not a Moslem in the circle of the Moorish Science Temple?

I can relate to your intolerance to faith as this in not the age of belief but the age of "I Know". I am a Masonic writer as well and I have written many articles for many Masonic publications. So I do understand your mission in reaching the blind and teaching them how to see correctly.

I have seen most of your sites and I see you have many names. Is there a reason for this? I too have evolved to have many names as well but what is your reason? The reason I ask these question is not to doubt your intentions but to get a clear picture to who I once new you as, and what you are today.

In trying to relate to his concept one must realize that this man has studied intensively the doctrines of the world. This is why one must speak the language he understands but letting him know that your reason might be totally different then his. So my position was to learn how he sees his own view and not what he wants me to sees by his form of casting illusions:

Dr. York's Reply: (6/6/01) "I have one name Issa Al Haadi Al Mahdi and many titles according to which school of thought I'm mastering and teaching. Anyone who has read my books who is a Freemason would recognize Masonic language through out the books. As far as Moor is concerned I have in my possession a card issued at age 28 in 1973 Brother M. York-EL home office 48 inches St. Mt. Clemens, Michigan, 48043. The card has a Crescent and star to the left under which is the word Islam next to that there's a clasped hand, above it is the word unity, to the right is the symbol of circle 7, beneath it the word Allah. I've always carried this card on my person and never denied being a Moor. I was initiated in 1970 at Masonic, King Solomon Lodge No.4 1215 Bedford Ave. Brooklyn New York. Then I was pasted at Enoch Grand Lodge on Putnam and Nostrand Ave. in Brooklyn and raised at the same under Worshipful Master Charles Tensely 33rd degree. I was crossed at Mecca II Desert Georgia, oasis Macon by Noble T.W. Smith Jr. 33rd/95 degrees. My family on my Mothers side were all Shriners and Daughters of Isis out of Richmond Virginia Zen Court No.98 Newport New Virginia and Zen temple No.122. I hope this information helps you to understand my involvement. While in Morocco studying at Fez University I visited the shrine there, Maghrib Temple as well as the Grand Temple in Khartoum where I was given documents, which will be on the web page chartering and linking us to the International Supreme Council Of Worldwide Shrinedom. Concerning the Fez, Moors don't wear Fez's and the word is faas in Arabic as appose to the tarbah, which was mispronounced by the Turks as Tarboosh. Many errors appear in Moorish American doctrine but that's neither here nor there. The fact that we elders of the true purpose have survived, and I hope that you spend your life as I do waking up our people. Your brother I.S.L.A.M."

[E. BEY] *Here Dr. York states that his affiliation was with a King Solomon Lodge and Enoch Grand Lodge in Brooklyn in 1970. He claims to have*

been created a Shriner in Macon, Georgia by someone named Noble T.W. Smith Jr. who was a 33rd over 95°'s. Both Grand Lodges are known today as Bogus and Irregular Grand Lodges.
So far we see a Man who is a Muslim, Moslem, Moor, from galaxy 19 of the 19th planet called Illiyuwm, who became a Shriner in Macon, Georgia. He was given what I know as a Nationality Card, which I am very well familiar as this is only given in the Moorish Science Temple of from a authorized Sheik of the same.

After receiving this information from Dr. York, I was compelled to respond as I felt there was more he would tell. So on June 6th, 2001 I replied:

Ezekiel Wrote: (6/07/01) Islam Brother Issa Al Haadi Al Mahdi, I am well aware of the Nationality Card issued by the Moors as I myself carry one on my person at all times. What is most interesting is your affiliation with King Solomon Lodge and Enoch Grand Lodge. Are you aware of legality in Grand Lodges? These Grand Lodges operate illegally when it comes to Masonic Authority. Enoch was a break off from Hiram Grand Lodge, which was set up by John G. Jones who was a suspended Mason from the Most Worshipful Prince Hall Grand Lodge. He was the original founder of the Shriners among people of dark complexion here in the States.

Speculative Masonic bodies must find the origin to the British Isles. That is if you are practicing speculative Masonry. Operatives are recognized as Stone Masons as were the Ancient Egyptians in their mystery schools of thought. Those Lodges you mentioned are speculative and considered spurious Lodges or what we know as irregular. I understand that this was back in 1970 well over 30 years ago.

One of my biggest concerns is the talk of you being from another galaxy. Is there some truth to this? And what about the extraterrestrial beings I have heard that exist on earth? I would like to know about this.

Here is where the Gold is tested by the fire to see if it's pure. Dr. York's response is not a direct one and avoids certain inquiries I made concerning the topic of extraterrestrial beings as some of his followers claim they were taught by Dr. York. This is explained by a student of Dr. York on her web site. He mentions Prince Hall in his reply but really does not explain who the man was as you will see later what he thinks he knows of Prince Hall, the father of our Fraternity here in America.

Dr. York's Reply: (6/8/01) "First of all when you speak of freemasonry and then jump into the subject of extraterrestrial you can become confused. I answered your question as to my affiliation with lodges in New York. Close observations I mention lodges and shrines in Virginia. If you are familiar with my family history as I hope you are, you will know of the family affiliation with Boston and Prince Hall. I like many accepted what you are calling European Freemasonry from Britain however, after entering Lodges in Egypt and Morocco, and the Grand Temple in Saudi Arabia I found that most if not all Freemasons in America haven't a clue of what real Shrinedom is. And where it originated they don't know who Hiram really was let alone the repeated mistakes stemming from a lack of fluency in the Arabic language. Things like Arabic Nobles of the Mystic Shrine in Arabic speaking countries. At the shrine it translate Arab Nobles of the Mystic Shrine the passwords are wrong as a result of Europeans receiving them in manuscripts from individuals who themselves were not Arabs. Rizk Allah Hassaan Effendee was a Turk and did not speak fluent Arabic. Louis Marracci did not speak fluent Arabic and never translated the Arabic Quran. He was Italian and translated from Castilian Spanish of Spain to Latin. Shaykh Alnasafi was a Persian; his native language was Farsi Albert L. Lawson an American, was not fluent in Arabic. Bro. Jones claimed to have received on June 1893 sanctioned from Noble Ali Rifest Pasha whose name Pasha alone reveals that he was not an Arab but rather a Turk. All of the above were not sanctioned by the (As Spayed) the blood line of the family we have and used in our temple translations from the Arabic which was brought back from the Egyptian temples and Shrines who got them from well preserved tents in the gold casket of As Spayed Al Hussein father of As Spayed Yacub, son of As Sayyid Ali, and Fatima daughter of as Sayyid Muhammad, Nabi (P.B.U.H.). The Masonic Lodge does not have its origin in Britain but in Babylon with Nimrod. Many people have been misled by a group of men called the Alberts. Peace!"

[E. BEY] *Notice that he never gives any reference to his information but at times places himself in an area of the world to have witness it with his own eyes. For the third time I asked the question of extraterrestrials.*
It is mind boggling to have learned in one of the website were the media reports that the Rev. Jesse Jackson attended one of there public functions and gives Dr. York and his followers credit for what they are doing in the communities. This is the deception and the views other Masons are blind to when one does not know the truth themselves. The illusions of doing for the communities are shadowed by the hypocrisies and lies of what looks good. We fail to pick up on falsehood when we dare not test the Gold with fire. The many sites that Dr. York has are somewhat ironic and shows an unstable mind controlling even weaker minds by the process of brainwash. Later you will see how misinformation can fool even the best of Men if we are not watchful.

Ezekiel Wrote: (6/9/01) Then Brother Mahdi Please explain what you see as extraterrestrials? And how you come from another galaxy or rather the 19th galaxy that you say. This indeed is an interesting subject as I have heard of many who say that they are from other worlds.
Dr. York is uncertain to whom he is talking to. He is unsure if he is talking to a human or some other being in what could be the enemy. He uses NASA as a sort of reference to answer my questions, but nothing that he will openly say that it is coming from his person:

Dr. York's Reply: (6/10/01) "I have written several books on this subject that are still available. One thing is for sure to date; the government has confirmed finding right outside of third solar system a tri- solar system. The same sheriff that hated legends. On which Caucasians, which include is deputy and friend admit of seeing craft hovering over the black pyramid in Tama. Anything that I would try to explain to you would sound like science fiction. The war in heaven still goes on and I never know exactly who or what I'm still talking to. Is there a Rizq? NASA thinks so. Is there an Illiyuwm? NASA found it. Are there such things as unidentified crafts? NASA has confirmed it. Are there people walking amongst you whose bodies are vessels for higher intelligence from other dimensions? It has been confirmed. Besides those things there is nothing more I can say."
I make one last attempt to see if he might explain his views on outer beings and try to direct the conversation back to Masonry and what his intentions

are as it relate to his International Shrine Order in Macon Georgia and abroad:
Ezekiel Wrote: (6/10/01) I do understand what you are saying Brother Mahdi. My question is, are you of that galaxy and did you come from that Galaxy? We all know that we have come from somewhere. I am asking did you come from this galaxy?

I am not interested in what NASA thinks. I am interested in what you think and the people who follow you. I myself know that there are other entities and other life form within our World. What I am asking is your explanation on how you see things. So, how do you explain extraterrestrial beings?

Back to Freemasonry, how do you relate the Shrine to Freemasonry? What is your concept in regularity in Freemasonry? And what do you think of Prince Hall Freemasonry? Prince Hall Freemasonry has been around longer than any other Black Fraternity in this country. What do you know of Prince Hall Freemasonry?

Dr. York's Reply: (6/12/01) "Subjects that I've discussed and made plain in books I leave at that, except for those who stand close enough to me to bring trust with how I feel about things. Prince hall had a white father and a half white mother. I did say if I'm correct my family was out of Boston. By that I thought I was making myself clear. Prince Hall Clandestine Modern Freemasonry is all confused. Reading the same books giving to them by Euro Freemasons. Prince Hall cannot establish an African Lodge when neither his mother nor father was African. Scottish Rites and the likes are Caucasian, being no Negro or Scottish. We have the in-depth history of the real teachings that was given to the Greeks, who gave it to the Romans, who gave to the Europeans, who the Negroes begged for charters from them for years. So we move and work on a much higher level than the sects that the original doctrine has divided into by self-righteous leaders. Something that must be done away with. After they finish their 32nd degree or their 12th degree to the Knights Templar they become Muslims anyway, so this is the civilizing of the Greeks and doesn't really apply to us the true seed of the Quraish tribe. The Black Arabs."

Again Dr. York ignores my question and now says he only discusses those things with those that he trusts and close to him. He places Prince Hall in a circle of a White Father and a half White Mother. He removes the Afrocentricity away from Prince Hall and calls him "beggars of Charters." What Dr. York is practicing is a mystery to me, but it sure does not sound like any Freemasonry I know nor any Shrinedom I have ever heard of.
The names he goes by are as mentioned, "Issa Al Haadi Al Mahdi, Dr. York, Chief Black Eagle, Dr. Malachi Z. York EL, Nayya Malchizodok EL, Al Mahdi, Dwight York, Rabboni Y'shua Bar El Haady and many others. I think this is the most far fetch controversial person I have ever known of. I have no idea how Freemasonry falls into any of his concepts. He has taken Islam, a pure religion of the East, and took his own twisted ideas, threw some Shrine twist into it, went to deep space nine, well in his case the 19th galaxy, took a trip to Egypt and became a Pharaoh, created his own Moorish group, and believes he is from a tribe of Indians called the Yamassee Native Americans. Now how can anyone follow him is beyond me. I get exhausted just dialoguing with him via E-mail. This Man is literally running his own Grand Lodge in Georgia, his own Shrine Temple called AL Mahdi Shrine Temple Ancient Egiptian Order & Arabic Nobles of the Mystic Shrine (A.E.O. & A.N.O.M.S). I guess he got tired of me asking questions,

> that he asked me to identify myself or the conversations with him will cease. I needed to know where did he get a Charter to operate or where did he receive his authority to practice Freemasonry. Well here is how it went.
>
> **Ezekiel Wrote:** (6/11/01) Where did you receive your Charter to give you authority to practice Masonry? That is if you are one who feels you need a charter. Why do you emphasize Shrinedom? Do you feel Shrinedom and Freemasonry are the same?
>
> **Dr. York's Reply:** (6/12/01) "If you truly read my books than you know my history as a Mahdi, and if you've read the web page you would have seen the blood link to the Prophet Muhammad and Ali. Need I say more? Again I repeat identify yourself, Lodge, Temple, Desert, Oasis, Potentate, or our conversation about Masonry and Shrinery has reached its end."

Clearly, Ezekiel. M. Bey was aware of York's reputation as a Scholar, and therefore fearful of being drawn into a head on debate, hence the statement ***"I am not Challenging you in any way"***. The prospect of having to contend with York's teachings clearly terrified the 'Orthodox' Prince Hall Masons, who like; Ezekiel. M. Bey are neither knowledgeable enough, or able to comprehend the depth of York's Knowledge of Freemasonry, which is obvious by the way Ezekiel. M. Bey shrewdly diverts the issue away from Freemasonry onto Extraterrestrials, in order to make York look Crazy, which is a common tactic often used by the Media. Ezekiel. M. Bey's strategy did not fool everybody, however, as most of his arguments were as one observer put it: *"sensationalized and laden with inaccuracies in much the same manner as the mainstream media exaggerates and misleads masses of people for dishonorable purposes"*. The following is an excerpt from Ezekiel. M. Bey's own chat room, and contains the opinion of one of Ezekiel. M. Bey's fellow Freemason's who saw right through his underhanded agenda against the Nuwaubian leader:

> Comment from: http://www.freemasonry.org/phylaxis/1guestlog.htm
> Greetings, Brothers: It is apparent that Bro. Ezekiel Bey has a personal grudge against Bro. York. This to me is sad and improper Masonic behaviour. In the discussion that Bro. Bey made available, the communication was sensationalized and laden with inaccuracies in much the same manner as the mainstream media exaggerates and misleads masses of people for dishonourable purposes. For example, there is no Masonic compound in Augusta, Georgia with armed guards, as Bro. Bey erroneously indicates. I live in Augusta, Georgia. I know. When Bro. York attempted to answer all of the questions related to freemasonry posed to him by Bro. Bey, the latter tried to change the subject away from the topic of freemasonry. Bro. York tried to be as humble as he could in stating that Bro. Bey did not have enough knowledge to dialogue about the other topics, but Bro. Bey used this as an opportunity to further degrade and denigrate Bro. York. Again, this is sad. Bro. Bey even went as far as to imply that there are "bogus" Prince Hall lodges in Brooklyn, New York. Personally, I never knew that there was such a thing as a "bogus" Prince

Hall lodge. Now the public knows too. But that just goes to show how far Bro. Bey would go to expound upon his personal grudge against Bro. York. And his grudge IS PERSONAL. Now there are and will be Prince Hall masons who believe the intentional lies that Bro. Bey has put forth and we have yet another division among masons of African descent. If I were an enemy of all people of African descent, I could rejoice because Bro. Bey has done my work for me and helped me to create more dissention among: (1) Children of God; (2) People of African descent and (3) Freemasons of African descent who are entitled to the real secrets of Freemasonry, not just the small portion that the Moors gave to the Europeans to keep them busy. I might suggest that Bro. Bey subdue his passions, and I suggest this respectfully, because I do not believe that one mason should put down another mason. Until my next communication, may you all travel peacefully. Respectfully submitted…

(Q. Parrain 2004)

We are not Freemasons, neither do we care for any such 'Secret Societies', therefore we are completely impartial to either side of the argument. However, we did notice that Ezekiel. M. Bey stated during the conversation with York that: *"Speculative Masonic bodies must find the origin to the British Isles. That is if you are practicing speculative Masonry"*. In other words, the real reason he opposes York's 'Nuwaubian Lodge' is because it is not sanctioned by any of the Head Lodges in the British Isles! York's supposition on the origins of what later became known as European Freemasonry are very thought provoking, but can they be verified?

The Origins of Freemasonry

British Masonic researcher Stephen Knight, substantiates York's theory of the Ancient Egyptian (African or at least Eastern) origins of Freemasonry, in his book *"The Brotherhood"*:

> Some Freemasons claim great antiquity for Freemasonry. This is reflected in the Masonic calendar, which is based on Archbishop Ussher's seventh-century calculation that the Creation must have taken place in the years 4004 B.C. For convenience, the odd four years are ignored and Anno Lucis (in the Year of Light, when Freemasonry is deemed to have begun) is four thousand years ahead of Anno Domini – so Masonic certificate of initiation bearing the date A.L. 5983 was issued in A.D. 1983. The implication is that **Freemasonry is as old as Adam**.
> Throughout the eighteenth and nineteenth centuries, Masonic writers produced vast numbers of books seeking to show that their movement had a continuous history of many hundreds, even thousands, of years. Some claimed that the ancestors of the Brotherhood were Druids or the Culdees; some claimed they were the pre-Christian Jewish monks, the Essenes. **Others insisted that Freemasonry had its origins in the religion of ancient Egypt**…

(Knight, 1983 p: 15)

Although Ezekiel. M. Bey was courageous enough to question York on what his beliefs were; he nevertheless acted deceitfully and exposed himself to be a hypocrite, by presenting himself as merely a 'Brother' *"simply seeking more understanding"*. Bear in mind that this conversation took place after Ezekiel. M. Bey made his damning condemnation of the Nuwaubian leader on the Dr. Charles. H. Wesley Masonic Research Society website in early 2001. It could however be argued that, York contradicts himself and exposes his own dishonesty as 'Imaam Isa', because in his book *"Secret Societies Unmasked"* Edition # 64 he claimed that Freemasonry is really 'Satanic worship' all the while knowing full well that he had been a Freemason since 1970:

> This is exactly what the Masonic order is all about! They tell the masses of people that they worship the Creator when in actuality they worship Satan, and they use their lodges to practice their belief
> (York)-Isa Al Madhi, 1990, p: 40)

> I was initiated in 1970 at Masonic, King Solomon Lodge No.4 1215 Bedford Ave. Brooklyn New York. Then I was pasted at Enoch Grand Lodge on Putnam and Nostrand Ave. in Brooklyn and raised at the same under Worshipful Master Charles Tensely 33rd degree.
> (York, 2001)

On the other hand, York's insight into Freemasonry as "Imam Isa", were as a direct result of being initiated into various Lodges, which placed him in the position to expose what he saw as 'Satanic' corruption of the pure Masonic teachings.

Figs.215, 216 & 217: Black Masonic Elite: Left- Right: *Imperial Potentate of The Nobles Mystic Shrine: William T. Pratt, Sovereign. Grand Comdr. Samuel Brogdon Jr. & Sovereign. Grand Comdr. S. J. Bennet of The Prince Hall Masons*

Prince Hall Freemasons and Black Shriners, are known to wield tremendous power in America as their members often include Judges, Government officials, Senators, Mayors, and high ranking Law enforcement officials, routinely listed in the Media as the most influential Blacks in the US. It is our opinion therefore that York's decision to 'Reform' Freemasonry, and reveal many of its secret rituals to be 'bogus' was very courageous, but clearly a step too far, and would have most certainly prompted them to take action against him, which may have been another one of the contributing factors which led to him being eventually imprisoned and discredited.

As a Freemason since 1970, which he admitted during his dialogue with Ezekiel. M. Bey, York would have been fully aware of the penalty for betraying any Masonic secrets, which he even makes mention of in his book *"Secret Societies Unmasked"*, as the final part of the *"Oath of The First Degree of masonry"* which states:

> "And I take a frank oath to all of these without concealment nor equivocation nor deceit. If I break this, my oath, I will deserve decapitation and crippling of my tongue..."

(Masonic Oath)

Fig.218: Threat To The Establishment:
Supreme Grand Master; Dr. Malachi. Z. York

It is doubtful whether any Freemasons actually suffer this fate for betraying the secrets, however, at the end of Ezekiel. M. Bey's denunciation of York in 2001, The Grand Master of the Georgia Prince Hall Masons, The Honorable Bro. Willie L. Williams, does make an intriguing indication of what action he planned to take to stop York, by stating: ***"I hope to launch a publicity campaign to educate the state about Bogus vs. Legitimate Masonic bodies"***. Could this 'Action', also have entailed alerting the Media & Law enforcement agencies of York's growing influence in the state of Georgia?

Figs.219, 220, 221 & 222: Nuwaubian Shriners & Masons: Top, Left- Right:
Dr. York accompanied by followers during Public Festival, Nuwaubian Shriners, Masons marching in formation during Parade
(Bottom) Veteran Ansaars: *Members of Al Mahdi Shrine Proudly representing The Nuwaubian Nation, at The Nation of Islam's 2006, Savior's Day Celebration*

Finally it is interesting to note that following the MWPHGL, Grand Master of the Georgia, Honorable Bro. Willie L. Williams' decision to publicly denounce 'The Nuwaubian Grand Lodge' as "Bogus" to state authorities, the Nuwaubians immediately began being investigated by the Georgia State authorities, for calling themselves Freemasons. The following is an article which appeared in several news media publications in December 2003, including, "News 4 Jaxs" news network, entitled *"Charges Considered against Nuwaubians in Christmas Parade"* 5:

BRUNSWICK, GA.
POSTED: 2:02 p.m. EST December 8, 2003
A prosecutor says members of a religious sect may face charges for lying on an application to participate in a city Christmas parade. Officials say United Nuwaubian Nation of Moors members who marched in Saturday's parade told the event organizer when they applied to participate that they were a Mason's group.
During the parade, Nuwaubians handed out literature and asked spectators about the guilt or innocence of their leader, Malachi York...Brunswick prosecutor Stephen Kelley says authorities are considering whether to charge the group members with submitting false information to a government agency, which is a felony.
Mayor Brad Brown, who was in the parade, said a document the group distributed entitled "Medical Records Don't Lie" contained profanity, and in some cases was given to children.

(Copyright 2003 by News4Jax.com*)*

Or the following article, which highlights that "Complaints", were actually made to the Mayor of Brunswick, GA, concerning the Nuwaubians claim of being a Masonic group: *"Nuwaubians Hassled By Police Over Parade Appearance":*

12/13/2003 7:49:43 PM
Brunswick, Georgia – The Nuwaubians, a black nationalist cult that combines Egyptology, Masonry and belief in space aliens, are being hassled by police in Brunswick, Georgia, who claim they made false statements on an application to appear in a parade.
Brunswick Mayor Brad Brown has ordered local police to investigate the group for "making false statement to a government" agency after the United Nuwaubian Nation of Moors stated on a parade permit that it was a Masonic organization. The basis for the **"false statement" complaint** is unclear, as Masonry takes many weird forms.
What has really angered the city is the fact that, during the parade, the group passed out fliers claiming that their leader, Malachi York, had been wrongfully imprisoned on charges of child molestation.

(LSN, 2003)

Chapter 15

New York to Georgia: The Great 'Nubian' Exodus

Fig.223 *Symbol of Chief Black Eagle*

"We moved to Eatonton Georgia, because we are the Yamassee, a branch of the Washitaw Moors, The Mound Builders. Our Ancestors built the Rock Eagle Mound and many others in such states as Wisconsin, Ohio, South Carolina, Louisiana and Tennessee. This is why we chose Eatonton to live…We are the Indigenous People of Georgia, Native American Moors".

unnm.com, 2002

Following the initial migration to Sullivan County in Upstate New York from Brooklyn in 1991, York now planned on one final gamble of the group's future, in the form of a mass exodus of the entire organisation, still known at the time as *"The Holy Tabernacle Ministries"*, to the state of Georgia. Throughout the years, York had always spoken of he's desire to move out of the Crime ridden Inner-Cities, to an environment more conducive to raising children and going back to nature. The group had previously owned and operated a large property in Upstate New York near the Canadian border since the 1970s, referred to as 'Jazir Abba', *"The Place of the Father"*, also known as 'Nubia'. This previous property encompassed a large woodland, described by the media as the group's Paramilitary Training camp, nevertheless it was also confirmed by eye witnesses to have actually functioned as a Children's activity Camp & Adult Hunting lodge during the Summer months, for the purpose of breaking up the monotony of urban life. There was also a fresh water lake, where the group's children often caught fish during holidays. Therefore, a new life in rural Georgia wouldn't have been too much of a culture shock to many of York's followers who had already become familiar with rural life, when the organisation eventually made their migration South. In fact, selected members of the group who were fluent in Arabic and proficient horse riders, had already been residing on the Upstate New York property with York for several years since at least the late 1980s, which rendered them more than prepared for life in rural Georgia.

Figs. 224 & 225 Jazir Abba: Top & Bottom: *Nuwaubians gathered on former Holy Land, located in Sullivan County, Upstate New York*

Another reason that prompted York's decision was the fact that since the late 1980s, increasing numbers of affluent Blacks began relocating to the State of Georgia, which was now fast becoming the new Black Utopia. Therefore York accurately predicted that a move to Georgia would bring many benefits. Above all York's belief was that the first real step towards true emancipated for African Americans was to not only be economically independent, but to also own their own land, which would get them away from the Urban 'Ghetto' mentality which was so counter productive. To further emphasise this point York often quoted one of The Honourable Elijah Muhammad's famous sayings which was: *"in order to be free the Black man in America needed: A Land, A Name & A Language!"* All three of which York appears to have finally provided for the so-called Blackman & woman in America, i.e.:

- A Land: (Kodesh) Tama-re / Wahanee
- A Name: Nuwaubian

■ **A Language: Nuwaubic**

Despite accounts of the draconian day-to-day regime by ex-members, it must be noted that York's followers had consistently lived together as a community for over 25-years, during which time, reports of serious violence or abuse towards members of the movement have never surfaced.

Southern Exodus & York's Attempted Overthrow

Other than those previously mentioned, it is unclear what York's real motives were for moving his entire organisation to rural Georgia. The most popular theory is that York may have been aware of the ongoing FBI investigation being conducted against him and his organisation, and decided to change his name, and move down South to avoid prosecution for a whole plethora of alleged illegal activities supposedly linked the Movement in New York. Aside from this, there are two other reasons purported by the Nuwaubian's for York's decision to relocate the organisation to middle Georgia. On one of the groups website's; unnm.com, there appeared an article entitled: *"Why did Malachi Move to Eatonton?!!!!"* 1, dated July 23rd, 2003, which stated the following:

> "We moved to Eatonton Georgia, because we are the Yamassee, a branch of the **Washitaw Moors, The Mound Builders.** Our Ancestors built the **Rock Eagle Mound** and many others in such states as Wisconsin, Ohio, South Carolina, Louisiana and Tennessee. This is why we chose Eatonton to live. It is close to Rock Eagle Mound." And if you read on pages 375-390; you will see how our seed was seeded in these parts. We are the Indigenous People of Georgia Native American Moors"
>
> (unnm.com, 2002)

Then there is a second far less romantic motive for York's move to Georgia, which involves his past relationship with the Orthodox Sunni Moslem World, also made mention of later on in the same feature article which stated: *"Yes, he was also moving because of...attempts on his life by certain groups that are known Terrorists"*. As we have explored in Chapter 4, there had already been several unsuccessful attempts made on York's life by Arab Extremists. Ironically it was the FBI, who first made public their discovery of a list, said to contain the names of several individuals targeted for assassination within the United States by Sunni Moslem Arab Extremists. This so-called 'Hit list' was said to include the names of:

- **Minister Louis Farrakhan (Leader of The Nation of Islam)**
- **Dr. Rashad Khalifah (Founder & Leader of the Submitters Perspective of Islam)**
- **Rabbi Mayer Kohen (Founder & Leader of The Jewish Defence League)**

And of course, **As Sayyid Isa Al Haadi Al Mahdi**, the much-reviled founder and leader of the Ansaaru Allah Community/Nubian Islamic Hebrew Mission, now known as Dr. Malachi. Z. York. The assassination attempts were successful on both Dr. Rashad Khalifah and Rabbi Mayer Kohen, who died as a result of multiple Gunshot & Stab wounds. Despite the attempt on York's life by Egyptian Terrorist El Sayid Nosier being aborted, the contract was known to still be active, which may have been York's reason for horridly leaving New York when he did. It has however been argued by many of York's critics that this was a cowardly move on the part of the Nuwaubian leader, for deciding to run away from the problem rather than confront it head on. Although, this explanation does not seem consistent with York's stubborn, 'Idealistic' personality, which would have prompted him to remain in New York, rather than retreat from a threat.

Increasing evidence now suggests that York may have been forced to leave New York after being betrayed by some of his followers, which included members of his own family. For example, former Ansaars have informed us of a Power Struggle within the organisation involving high-ranking members of York's security force the 'Swords of Islam' (S.O.I.), sometime during the early 1990's. Apparently shortly before York abandoned the group's Bushwick Avenue headquarters, certain powerful New York Ansaars had become disillusioned with York's Maverick-style of leadership, and increasing time spent away from the Community pursuing his music career, resulting in an attempted takeover of the Movement's headquarters by the disgruntled S.O.I. This attempted *Coup d'etat* was of course foiled by York immediately changing the name of the Organisation to 'The Holy Tabernacle Ministries', and relocating to Upstate New York, with those who were still loyal, leaving the renegades and troublemakers to fight over an abandoned headquarters and lifeless movement. This supposed attempted 'Overthrow' however would have left a serious breach in York's security arrangements, which could easily be exploited by his enemies most notably Arab/Islamic Extremists. Further evidence of this theory is the suspicious death of York's son Yadullah Muhammad in 1998. According to sources within the Nuwaubian movement, Yadullah was murdered by Sunni Moslem 'extremist' enemies of his father after being set up by his younger brother, Yacuwb or Jacob. In the previously mentioned Nuwaubian feature article entitled: *"THE FATHER, MALACHI YORK IS ACCUSED OF THE SON, JACOB YORK'S CRIMES"* 2, dated December 2003, it details York's son Yadullah's murder as follows:

> Jake is also suspected of being involved in the untimely death of his brother Yadullahi Muhammad in 1998 A.D. Jake was always jealous of Yadullahi because of the favor he had in his father's eyes. Yadullahi was very intelligent and was studying to be an ambassador for our nation. Yadullahi was sent to Morocco and Egypt to further his education to become well versed in the various languages. He returned home to become an

ambassador. Jake was envious of his intelligence and it is believed he is responsible for Yadullahi being shot in the heart at a party in New York.

(unnm.com, 2003)

Although the Sunni Moslems are not named as being directly responsible for Yadullah's murder, in a previous Nuwaubian rebuttal to an article in the Atlanta Journal-Constitution by Bill Olinski, dated July 7th 2002, entitled: *"Cult Leader ignored his own rules"*, the Nuwaubian's make mention of an incident which occurred in 1998, which is directly related to Yadullah's death and York's betrayal by his own son Jacob or 'Jake' York:

> Years later when his Son Yadullahi was shot he went to N.Y. for the funeral and couldn't attend because this same son Jake (Yaqub Abdullah Mohammed) had let the Moslem assassins know that he was there and they wanted to kill him so he had to stay away in order to ensure that they wouldn't miss and perhaps hurt another one of his children.
>
> (Nuwaubian staff writer, 2002)

If this account of treachery within the Ansaaru Allah Community is true, then York would have been left with no alternative but to immediately leave New York and purge the organisation at the time that he did, otherwise he would have almost certainly been killed.

Figs.226 & 227 Sibling Rivals: Left- Right:
Yadullah Abdullah Muhammad during a trip to Egypt & Yakuwb Muhammad aka Jacob York

Finally, the other theory of why York left New York is the most disturbing, and has been supported by both the Mainstream & Independent Media, and would later form the basis of his arrest and conviction for sexual abuse & molestation. This allegation claims that York travelled from New York to Georgia in 1993, for the sole purpose of *"Carrying Children Across State Lines for the purpose of Sexual gratification"*. Some reports even suggested that York and his accomplices abducted these children against their will. Although York would eventually be exonerated of this charge, it must be remembered that this baseless allegation formed the original pretext under which the F.B.I initially arrested the Nuwaubian leader, and later raided the Nuwaubian property in 2002. According to numerous online and newspaper media sources; Dr. Malachi. Z. York initially travelled to Macon Georgia in 1993 to carry children across State Lines for Sex, which would have naturally been without any of their parents consent. The following are articles, which first appeared in the media making these false accusations against York:

AA News, Title: *"Agents Sweep Religious Cult Compound, Charge Founder With Child Abuse"*, dated: 6/5/02 [3]

Dwight York, founder of the United Nuwaubian Nation of Moors and his girlfriend, Kathy Johnson were taken in custody on federal charges, which included **transporting minors across state lines for sexual purposes**...

(AA News, 2002, p: 1)

Atlanta News, Reporter: Mara Shalhoup, Title: *"Nabbing the man from outer space"*, dated: 6/5/02 [4]

...a federal grand jury indicted York on four counts of **transporting minors across state lines for sex**...

(Shalhoup, 2002)

Online Athens, Title: *"Innocent, pleads sect leader York"*, dated 6/5/02 [5]

Dwight York, 56, and companion Kathy Johnson appeared in U.S. District Court in Macon to face charges that they **transported minors from Sullivan County, N.Y. to Georgia for sex in 1993**.

(Online Athens, 2002)

The Black World Today, Reporter: Roy L. Parish: Title: *"Nation Under Distress"*, dated, 6/7/02, [6]

Dwight York, was arrested during African Liberation Month on May 8, 2002, and accused of **transporting children across state lines with the intent of sexual abuse**.

(Parish, 2002)

Macon Telegraph, Reporter Rob Peecher, Title: *"Opinions Mixed on York's arrest"*, dated, 12/5/02, [7]

York is accused in a four-count federal indictment of **transporting children across state lines for the purposes of engaging in sexual activity**. Johnson is accused as a co-defendant in only one of those counts.

(Peecher, 2002)

The Washington Times, Reporter Robert Stacy McCain, Title: *"Nuwaubian nightmare"*, dated, 2/6/02, .**8**

Nuwaubian leader Dwight York is in federal custody, charged with four counts of **interstate transportation of minors for sex,** and has also been indicted on 116 state charges involving child molestation.

(McCain, 2002)

The above articles are interesting for several reasons, firstly because they illustrate the fact that when York was initially arrested in 2002, the charge was for "**Transporting Minors Across State Lines**", for the purpose of sexual abuse. First of all, none of the witnesses who gave evidence against York, were brought by the Nuwaubian leader to Georgia during the group's mass exodus in 1993. In fact, as we shall see later, all of York's alleged victims have Parents within the organisation, who is known to have accompanied their children during the journey from New York to Georgia. Secondly it is simply inconceivable to think that Malachi York would transfer his entire organisation all the way from Upstate, New York to Georgia, which is 900 miles, just to have sex with children he already had access to since they were born. And also make note that all of these minors had parents, many of whom belonged to the organisation for over 20 years, who would have all accompanied their children on the long journey to Georgia with the rest of the group.

Then in a later article which appeared in the Athens Banner-Herald, dated 24th January 2004 entitled: *"Nuwaubian leader guilty"*, reporter Terry Dickson states the following:

The jury acquitted York of only one count of transporting minors for unlawful sex...

(Dickson, 2004)

Isn't it ironic that although York would eventually lose the case, the original reason for his arrest and subsequent indictment, which was of course "transporting minors across state lines, for the purpose of sex", he would be completely exonerated of, which clearly questions the very validity of not only the initial indictment, but the entire case, as we shall later examine in greater depth.

Arrival in Georgia

Prior to the group's arrival in Georgia, it is said York purchased 476 acres of Farmland, located at 404 Shady Dale Road, on Highway 142 in rural Putnam County, Eatonton, Georgia, from Arnie and Sandra Gay Lassen for an estimated value of $975,000 on January 15th 1993. According to the land deeds, the property, which would eventually become the Nuwaubian's new headquarters, was originally classified as a "Gaming Reserve". York first named the land 'Kodesh' which is Hebrew for *"Holy"*, then as the group progressed more towards Egyptology, the name was later changed to 'Tama-Re', which is the actual Hieretic (Ancient Egyptian) term for ***"Egypt"***. The property itself was a truly stunning piece of real estate, with almost 500 acres of breathtaking Green, Picturesque, Luscious landscape of rolling Hills & Savannas encompassing 4 entire 'Fresh-water Lakes', surrounded by thick wooded areas, and open fields set in Rural Georgia. York was said to be a been keen on Hunting & Fishing in his spare time, which was one of the reasons he chose the location to enjoy its many natural attractions.

Figs.228, 229, 230 & 231: Kodesh: Top, Left- Right:
Map of Putnam County & Luscious Landscape in Putnam County, Rural Georgia

To alleviate suspicions from local residents, York initially claimed to be a Blues/Country & Western singer from New York, who was simply relocating to rural Georgia with his extended family to enjoy a better standard of life in his retirement. York even released a Country & Western style 'Blues' LP under the name ***'Doc York and The Lewis & Clark Band'***, entitled: *"Live In Georgia at: 'On Stage'"*, in which the Nuwaubian leader made the following claim reaffirming his Native American Roots:

> **Doc York:** Whose Name Is Malachi. Z. York Is The Great Grandson Of Ben York (1770-1856) Of The Lewis & Clark Expedition, Referred To As The 'Louisiana Purchase' (1804-1806). He Was A Slave Turned Cowboy, And Acted As A Translator Of Indian Dialects And Scout. He Married A Native American Of The Shushuni Tribes. DOC YORK Is A True Black Cowboy.

And in order to further confirm this claim, members of the organisation were encouraged to continue wearing "Western" or Cowboy style clothing for the purpose of fitting in with the local surroundings. Again this was not too difficult, because the Nuwaubian's had already started wearing Cowboy Hats and Boots, Rayon & Denim Suites, with broad belt buckles, as far back as 1991 in Upstate New York during the Hebrew school, as we have already pointed out. According to eyewitnesses who were in the group at the time, those were very good times. A former Nuwaubian who asked not to be named, attended the group's saviours' day celebration from London in 1995, related the following account:

> When we arrived at Kodesh in 1995 for Saviours day it was amazing. This was long before the Pyramids had been built and all the trouble with all the authorities, and much of the land was still under construction. Everyone was so happy, walking around with Cowboy hats and boots on just shaking everybody's hands. We were like one big family, there were brothers and sisters from all over the U.S., England and the Caribbean all come to see 'Pops'. When we went to all the local shops, everybody knew who we were, and they were very nice to us, because they really respected Doc and his followers. In fact when we got to our Hotel, there was a huge banner in the middle of the street saying: ***"Welcome to the York Family Reunion"***. There were Nuwaubian's booked into a lot of the local hotels, so it was as if we had our own little town!
>
> (Ex-Nuwaubian)

Within the first few years of their arrival, the Nuwaubian's experienced what can now be described as a 'Honeymoon Period' with the local residents, and authorities. Prior to the eventual disputes over Zoning began with the Putnam County official's the group enjoyed a stage of relative harmony in rural Georgia. Although the group attracted a little interest and curiosity from members of the local Community including the media, they were initially afforded a good degree of balanced publicity. Of most interest was the group's mysterious leader Malachi York, whom the local media focused most of its attention towards. One of the first, was an article which appeared in the *Countryman* newspaper, in April 1993, written by Emory Lavender, entitled *"Malachi York"*, in which York was, shall we say slightly economical with the details of his past, in an attempt to dispel rumours that he was a Militant Black Muslim leader from New York.

On page 8 of the newspaper it stated:

> York, a direct descendant of Ben York, great medicine man to Lewis and Clark Expedition, confronts fears by asserting, 'I am not a black Muslim....Moreover, he notes that he is a registered teacher of Semitic languages and formerly pastured a church in New York. And he is a Freemason. York's Christian heritage is evident in his CD, "The Best of Dr. York". One of the songs is entitled, *"Let ME Be The One On Christmas"*...

(Lavender, 1993)

In the following month's edition of the *Countryman*, Emory Lavender wrote another article entitled: *"Malachi 'Dr.' York"*, which portrayed York from a more positive perspective, as successful entertainer who purchased a 450-acre ranch in Putnam County in order to simply enjoy country life in his retirement.

The next few years passed without much incident for the Nuwaubian's, who generally kept to themselves up until late 1997. They were still receiving favourable media coverage, such as the article which appeared in The Eatonton Messenger dated Thursday July 3rd, entitled: *"Thousands Attend Fraternal Gathering"*, in which the reporter, Roger Dotson, describes many of the positive aspects of the 4 day Nuwaubian event on Tama Re.

Figs.232, 233 & 234 Black Cowboys: Top, Left- Right:
York on the Cover of his 1993 LP 'Doc York'
& York accompanied by Bodyguards dressed in Cowboy Clothes in Upstate New York

Pyramid 'Hysteria' & Hypocrisy

Relations between the Nuwaubian's and local County officials eventually began to go sour a year later when local residents began complaining to Putnam County officials of hearing noisy outdoor religious ceremonies, and seeing strange structures being erected by the new occupants of 404 Shady Dale Road. Among the many peculiar buildings was said to be a Black, 40-foot Gold Tipped 'Pyramid' and giant Egyptian style Sphinx. What were a group of black people doing building an Egyptian Pyramid in the middle of rural Georgia? What could this all mean? No doubt the media soon began relaying images of these strange structures, to the astonishment of the outside world. Numerous magazine and newspaper articles began to emerge showing the Nuwaubian's in ceremonial Egyptian dress, in the midst of this huge Black Pyramid. Other than the fact that the group's beliefs seemed strange to outsiders, what was really the big deal about them building an Egyptian Pyramid, and dressing like ancient Egyptians for religious ceremonies? What was it that was so alarming about the Nuwaubian's and their Pyramid's? After all, there were several other modern Egyptian 'styled' Pyramidal structures which already existed in the U.S., including the famous Luxor hotel in Las Vegas, with its huge 350-foot-high (106 meter), 30-story pyramid of black glass Hotel complex, supposedly modelled after the Great Pyramid at Giza, complete with a Caucasian-looking Sphinx with 'Blue Eyes'. However not one journalist has yet called the designers or owners of the Vegas Luxor Hotel crazy. Was it because the Nuwaubian's were African American's that the idea of them building an Egyptian Pyramid was so abhorrent to both the Media & local residents? And was it also that as Southern Whites they felt threatened by the Nuwaubian's construction of what was after all an Ancient (African) Monument and therefore resented the fact that African Americans, whom they still considered their inferiors, could have the nerve to openly make such a bold statement, claiming kinship to the Greatest civilization the World has ever known, in such an audacious and unapologetic way.

Fig.235 Nuwaubian Pyramid Culture: *Malachi York Performing Religious Ceremony, With entourage around Black Pyramid*

Figs.236 & 237 Nuwaubian Pyramid Culture: Top & Bottom:
Nuwaubian 'Negroid' Sphinx & Black Pyramid

Figs.238, 239, 240 & 242 American Pyramid & Sphinx: Top, Left- Right:
350 ft Las Vegas Luxor Hotel, Pyramid Caucasian Sphinx & Black Pyramid

In 1999 New York Press reporter Adam Heimlich visited the property, and was able to gain unprecedented access behind the scenes into the inner workings of the community. The following are some of his impressions of what he witnessed, in an article entitled: *"Black Egypt"*:

> The Land rises away from the road in a series of hillocks, like little steppes, and the footpaths seem set up to accentuate this, lending pedestrians a sense of being enfolded within the landscape. The Egiptian structures (which don't look as magnificent up close as they do from Rte. 142, since most are made of concrete painted to resemble stone bricks), fit well within this scheme. That, and the bold-yet-tasteful use of color, make it clear that the Nuwaubian community boasts a number of talented artisans, and a planning commission wise enough to see their plans through for the good of all. "We are the ancient Tama-Reans," said Seti. "It's only right that we display craftsmanship and zeal."
>
> (Heimlich, 2000)

Although the Nuwaubian beliefs may be considered unorthodox, the ancient Egyptian culture was started in North East Africa, which therefore renders it part of African history and culture. Therefore all the Nuwaubian's were doing was practicing an extreme form of Afro-centrism, commonly referred to as "Egyptology", which is currently very popular amongst American blacks.

On the eve of the new Millennium, several newspapers and magazines featured articles which all referred to 40ft Egyptian Pyramids, with titles such as:

"Georgia Sect Alarms Neighbours"
"Reaction to Nuwaubian's Mixed in Putnam County"
"The Egyptians of Georgia"

When the Nuwaubian's first arrived in Putnam County, they often granted Journalists full access to their Land to conduct interviews and tour of the community. However they quickly realised that some of these Journalists, such as Bill Osinski of The Atlanta Journal-Constitution & The Macon Telegraph's Rob Peacher, had ulterior motives, which were to act as spies for Local County Officials & The Sheriff's Department, who were trying to undermine the group. Bill Osinski in particular, travelled to New York supposedly armed with a 'Secret' FBI report to carry out extensive background research into York and the Organisation's. After which he returned to Georgia to publish a series of damaging articles about the Nuwaubian's, and their supposed links to *"Organised Crime & Murder"*, which would eventually form the basis of his highly fictionalised book: ***"Ungodly: A True Story of Unprecedented Evil"***. In retaliation the Nuwaubian's formed the C.C.O.E (Concerned Citizens of Eatonton) to repudiate much of the damaging and inaccurate Media coverage of their group. York's response to this negative Media publicity, and growing hostility from local officials was highlighted in a rare interview given to an Independent Journalist, known to be sympathetic to the group's cause:

> I see the Game, They don't want a Positive Black Image here. They're making me out be a Monster...They Fear my growing Political Power, partly because I'm encouraging my followers to move down here, and participate in the Political process by Registering to Vote...This is our Paradise, this is our Mecca, in a sense...
>
> (York, 1997)

Throughout the group's history, York has always avoided contact with the media, and often to his own detriment, refusing to grant interviews to reporters. However, York and his followers were soon to discover that the more they evaded media scrutiny, the more they appeared obstructive and obtrusive to reporters, which in turn caused them to dig deeper in search of some background dirt on the Nuwaubian leader and his group's past.

Fig.243 Cult Buster:
Anti-Religious Investigator Rick Ross

As a direct result of all this negative Media publicity, it wasn't long before the group also caught the attention of the various Anti-Religious Government sponsored 'Watch-Dog' agencies, more commonly known as the "Cult Busters". Whose purpose it is to monitor all Independent Religious and Political groups, under the pretext of protecting the public from so-called "Dangerous Cults". Especially targeted were those group's whose beliefs differ considerably from those of the so-called 'Mainstream' and are therefore deemed a threat to the public. Such groups include The Nation of Islam, and all other such Black Nationalist/Religious groups. One such Anti-Religious Watchdog is known as: *"The Rick Ross Institute for the Study of Destructive Cults, Controversial Groups & Movements"*, led by, the self professed Crusader against Religious Cults Rick Ross, whose website <www.rickross.com>, lists a supposed A - Z of all groups deemed by him to be a threat to public safety. As soon as the Nuwaubian's began to appear in local headlines, Rick Ross' website started re-publishing many of the inaccurate Anti-Nuwaubian articles, which would eventually form a chronological archive of reference material against the group.

Why were the Nuwaubian's viewed as so different from the hundreds of Hindu & Buddhist Ashrams and Shrines located throughout the United States, housing huge Pagodas and Temples, such as the Malibu Hindu Temple, Las Virgenes Canyon or the Kadampa Buddhist Temple, San Francisco, which served the exact same purpose as the religious structures & monuments on the Nuwaubian property.

Figs.244 & 245 Eastern Religious Temples: Left- Right:
Buddhist & Hindu Temples in The United States

Was it simply because American Blacks were not supposed to have any religious beliefs of their own, outside of what is sanctioned by their former Slave Masters? Ironically during that period, the Nuwaubian Community were given a Spiritual stamp of approval by Buddhist Monks, who not only visited the group on several occasions but also Blessed the Community, and recorded religious chants, which would later be continuously played on the land via loud speaker during day light hours, and may have actually been the cause of many of the complaints from the groups neighbours.

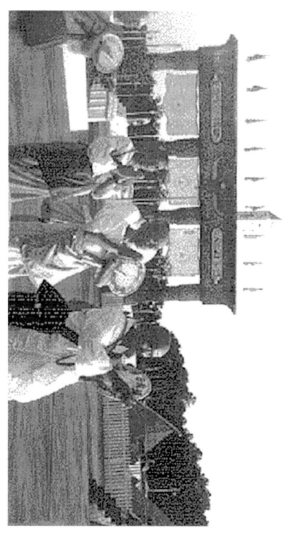

Fig.246 Spiritual Contemporaries: *Buddhist Monks Performing Religious Ceremony On Nuwaubian Property, Tama Re, Georgia*

Until that period the Nuwaubian's had never shown any violence or hostility towards any local residents of Putnam County, on the contrary; many residents often admitted that York's followers always showed respect and courtesy to their neighbours. In a *"Special Report"* published by the Macon Telegraph on the 16th Febuarury 2000, Anti-Nuwaubian reporter Rob Peecher asked a number of local residents on their feelings towards the Nuwaubian's. The following are the views of two different business owners in Putnam County:

> Ray Saltamacchio, who owns the photography studio Moments to remember in downtown Eatonton, said he shares some of the concerns with the rest of the community, but Nuwaubian's often come to him for their Nuwaubian-passport photos and have always been pleasant customers.
> "They've always been nice, never given me any problem whatsoever," Saltamacchio said. "As long as they don't come into town causing problems, I don't have any problem with them."
> Others in the community, like Vanessa Bishop, believe the Nuwaubinas have already caused problems.
> "I think that they are arrogant know-all who are out for self gain. Everything for them is race, and everything against them is race," Bishop said. "I'm sure not all of them are like that. I'm sure there are some good folks with that realm, but some are not".
>
> (Peecher, 2000)

Nation Sovereignty

If these were the views of local residents who had day-to-day dealings with the Nuwaubian's, then what was the basis for media anxiety towards the members of York's organisation, other than racism? The answer may lie in how the Nuwaubian's began to behave after York began unveiling his plans to declare the Nujwaubian Nation's Sovereignty status. Thereafter, some of York's followers got carried away, and embarked on a process of what can only be described as "Thumbing their Noses" at the Authority of White America like their predecessors in The Moorish Science Temple, almost a century before. Reports began to circulate amongst local Law Enforcement of York's followers being stopped during routine Police stops and claiming not to be subject to State Laws. However the 'Icing on the Cake' came during York's 1997 Saviours Day speech, in which he publicly disclosed the Nuwaubian Nation's intentions of becoming a Sovereign Nation:

> There are evil people who work their way into positions to hurt other people. People like Mr Adams, who is a building inspector in Eatonton, Georgia of Putnam County, who is trying to prevent our tribe, the Yamassee Native Americans from building on land that we own. This is what makes Indigenous Nations such as the United Nuwaubian Nation Of Moors declare our Sovereignty, our natural born right, our inalienable right, to exercise our right to Autonomy and Self Determination…I'm not talking about laws about American Indians, our sons.The Euro-American (Europeans) that came to these shores and set up a Government, do not

have the right to govern us because we were here before them. However according to United Nations Charters and documents, Indigenous people have the right to govern ourselves. They mistreat us in every way.

According To The Draft Declaration On The Rights Of Indigenous Peoples E/Cn.4/Sub.2/Add.1(1994) Article 31, it states:

"Indigenous Peoples, As A Specific Exercising Their Right To Self-Determination, Have The Right To Autonomy Or Self-Government In Matter Relating To Their Internal And Local Affairs, Including Culture, Religion, Education, Information, Media, Health, Housing, Employment, Social Welfare, Economic Activities, Land And Resources Management, Environment And Entry By Non-Members, As Well As Ways And Means For Financing These Autonomous Functions."

(York, 1997)

During the speech York went on to announce that he was going to declare the Nuwaubian Nation a "Sovereign Nation", with its own Government, which would no longer be answerable to the laws of the United States. In a move somewhat reminiscent of the Hon. Marcus Garvey before him, York even went to the extent of declaring himself; **'President'** of The Yamassee Tribe Of Native Americans & United Nuwaubian 'Nation' of Moors, and made reference to a Constitution of the United Nuwaubian Nation Of Moors, apparently drafted as early as June 26th 1992 A.D., at the back of one of the organisations publications. However unbeknownst to York, recording this speech, was an under cover reporter posing as one of his followers who was secretly filming the speech from a hidden camera in the crowd. His speech would later be aired over several Television networks including the Right-Wing Fox News Channel, which provides news to several other states, as far away as New York. In fact, Putnam County Sheriff Richard Sills, would later respond directly to York's comments on Fox Channel 5 News during a broadcast a year later on May 25th 1998:

> "I have some concerns about the rhetoric that is oriented towards an independent nation, "Sovereign" not subject to the laws of Georgia and the United States, and I have some concerns about that"
>
> (Sheriff Sills, 1998)

This excuse of York's organisation refusing to obey the law of the United States, was exactly the pretext Sheriff Sills needed to launch an all out attack upon the Nuwaubian Nation, even though there has never been any documented cases of where York has taught his followers to openly disobey the Law. On the contrary, York has been on record instructing members of his Movement the complete opposite. In The Holy Tabernacle *"Family Guide"*, it states the following:

> "Pledge no loyalty to any other country or government other than the United States of America, if you are an American. If you are in America from another country, follow our laws while here....You should have a

passport, driver's license, social security card, and you should have a proper identification card on you at all times. ... Pay your taxes. Don't let your religious beliefs; whatever they may be cause you to disobey the laws of America. Do not commit crimes or permit crime in your presence."

(York, 1993)

Fig.247 Sovereign Supreme Commander: *President: Nayya Malachi Zodok York-El Of The United Nuwaubian Nation Of Moors*

According to the Nuwaubian's, their cause was actually endorsed by none other than the former U.S President Bill Clinton & The United States Department of Interior, Bureau of Indian Affairs. Under U.S. Senate Joint Resolution 271, President Bill Clinton himself designated the dates; November 5th, 1994, November 2nd, 1995 & October 29th, 1996 as *"National American Indian Heritage Months"*. Then on January 19th 1999, during President Clinton's 'State of the Union address' he stated:

> We must do more to bring the spark of private enterprise to every corner of America, to build a bridge from wall street to Appalachia, to the Mississippi Delta to our Native American Communities with more support for community development...
>
> (President Clinton, 1999)

York's decision to declare The Yamassee Tribe Of Native Americans/United Nuwaubian Nation Of Moors a "Sovereign Nation" may have been one of the main reasons why the Putnam County officials and later the U.S. Government, under the new administration, began using every available means to undermine him and his Movement. To exasperate matters further, York was said to have developed a 'Nuwaubian Currency', and 'Passport-Visa' system, as well as issued official vehicle registration plates for the purpose of identifying 'Citizens' of the Nuwaubian Nation, which infuriated local officials and Law enforcement even further.

Finally, it is important to point out that York's vision of an independent sovereign state for African-Americans is in fact the fulfilment of The Nation of Islam's original goal for Blacks in America; namely the complete separation from White American society, which was initially developed by Noble Drew Ali during the 1920s for an "Independent" African American Nation, outlined in Part 4, of the Nation of Islam's *"Muslim Programme"* 9, in which The Honourable Elijah Muhammad states:

> 4. We want our people in America whose parents or grandparents were descendants from slaves, to be allowed to establish a separate state or territory of their own--either on this continent or elsewhere. We believe that our former slave masters are obligated to provide such land and that the area must be fertile and minerally rich. We believe that our former slave masters are obligated to maintain and supply our needs in this separate territory for the next 20 to 25 years--until we are able to produce and supply our own needs.
>
> Since we cannot get along with them in peace and equality, after giving them 400 years of our sweat and blood and receiving in return some of the worst treatment human beings have ever experienced, we believe our contributions to this land and the suffering forced upon us by white America, justifies our demand for complete separation in a state or territory of our own.
>
> (Excerpt taken from the 'Muslim Programme' by Hon. Elijah Muhammad, cited at noi.org, 2005)

Fig.248 Elijah Muhammad's Muslim Programme

Ironically, during his 2005 Washington D.C. address on the 10th anniversary of the Million Man March, Minister Louis Farrakhan, subtly laid out plans to begin implementing many of the steps necessary for the development of Elijah Muhammad's *"Muslim Program"*, such as the formation of various 'Ministries', which would cater solely for the needs of American Blacks. Washington Post reporter Matt Labash, in his critique of the March, entitled: *"The Second Time as Farce: Not that the first time was serious"* 10, suggests that Minister Louis Farrakhan may be aiming at the eventual development of an independent state or 'Territory' for Africans in America:

> The main event, of course, is Farrakhan himself. Mounting the stage with his Fruit of Islam security retinue…Farrakhan, to his credit, isn't short on specifics. **He essentially advocates a return to segregation, the need for blacks to grow self-sufficient and form a country within a country** by starting their own Ministries of Education, Defense, Art and Culture, Justice, and Science and Technology.
> Farrakhan students will recognize this as the Nerf version of "The Muslim Program," printed in the back of every issue of the *Final Call*. It advocates the "descendants of slaves" being "allowed to establish a separate state or territory of their own," with "slave masters" being obligated to fork over land that "must be fertile and minerally rich," while supplying "our needs in this separate territory for the next 20 to 25 years." Some of this, of course, would have to be done through reparations and the federal government turning back tax dollars.
>
> (Labash, 2005)

The notion of a Separate State, set aside within the United States exclusively governed and occupied by the descendants of African Slaves, should not be viewed as such an outrageous suggestion. After all, the Christian Cult, known as the Mormon Church of Latter-Day Saints, were permitted to form their own Separate-state in Utah by the U.S. Government for well over two centuries, after allegedly facing prosecution for their 'Documented' bizarre beliefs, which included 'Polygamy & Sex with Minors'. If for no other reason than Racism, American Blacks would have been allowed to run their own separate 'Sovereign State', as both Elijah Muhammad & Malachi York have envisioned. The events which took place in New Orleans, Louisiana following the devastation caused by Hurricane

'Katrina' in 2005, if nothing else, graphically demonstrated to the world, the real plight of African's living in America, and how they urgently need to take control of their own Destiny.

Besides York's declaration of Nation Sovereignty, the other motive for the Putnam county official's hostility and deep resentment towards the Nuwaubian's was because of the large amount of land controlled by the group. According to the Nuwaubian's, the residents of Putnam county or White America for that matter, have never been comfortable with the idea of African Americans owning their own land, which is why many of them were driven out of the South in the first place. In an article entitled *"They want our Land"*, released in 2002, York's followers correctly predicted that the local officials were after control of their land, and that this was one of the main motives behind all of the hostility towards them. The article goes on to illustrate in detail, the difficulties which have been faced by Negro landowners since the Reconstruction era in the United States, and how they were systematically brutalised and discouraged from owning large amounts of land and real estate. The article continues with an appraisal of a 3-part Television documentary which aired in the U.S. entitled: *"Torn From the Land"*, in which York's followers draw many historical parallels between their plight and that of African American Land owners of the past:

> "Torn From the Land", consists of a series of articles based on how African-American families were tricked out of their land and in many cases, their land just taken from them. In one of the articles titled, "Land Ownership Made Blacks Target of Violence and Murder," by Dolores Barclay, Todd Lewan and Allan G. Breed, it speaks of Anthony T. Crawford, an African-American who owned his own land up until 1916 A.D., when he was hung and killed by a white mob. It states, "The success of blacks such as Crawford threatened the reign of white supremacy, said Stewart E. Tolnay, a sociologist at the University of Washington and co-author of a book on lynchings. 'There were obvious limitations, or ceilings, that blacks weren't supposed to go beyond.' In the decades between the Civil War and civil rights era, one of those limitations was owning land, historians say...Racial violence in America is a familiar story, but the importance of land as a motive for lynchings and white mob attacks on blacks has been widely overlooked. And the resulting land losses suffered by black families such as the Crawfords have gone largely unreported. The Tuskegee Institute and the National Association for the Advancement of Colored People have documented more than 3,000 lynchings between 1865 and 1965, and believe there were more. Many of those lynched were property owners, said Ray Winbush, director of Fisk University's Race Relations Institute. 'If you are looking for stolen black land,' he said, 'just follow the lynching trail'...**Black landowners were put under a tremendous amount of pressure, from authorities and otherwise, to give up their land and leave,**' said Earl N.M. Gooding, director of Centre for Urban and Rural Research at Alabama A&M University. 'They became refugees in their own country'...It wasn't just Whitecaps and Night Riders

who chased blacks from their land. Sometimes, officials did it." In another article written by Dolores Barclay and Todd Lewan, titled, "Land Taken From Blacks Through Trickery, Violence and Murder," it states, "In an 18 month investigation, The Associated Press documented a pattern in which black Americans were cheated out of their land or driven from it through intimidation, violence and even murder. **In some cases, government officials approved the land takings; in others, they took part in them.** The earliest occurred before the Civil War; others are being litigated today…In 1910, black Americans owned more farmland than at any time before or since – at least 15 million acres. Nearly all of it was in the South, largely in Mississippi, Alabama and the Carolinas, according to the U.S. Agricultural Census. Today, blacks own only 1.1 million of the Country's more than 1 billion acres of arable land. They are part owners of another 1.07 million acres."

(Excerpt taken from UNNM, Newspaper, 2002)

As the Nuwaubian's correctly asserted, the agenda of the Putnam County officials was to create an atmosphere of hostility towards them which would eventually lead to them losing control of their land. This prediction would come true with terrifying accuracy 2 years later when the Nuwaubian's land, like many of their African predecessors, was illegally seized and sold by the United States Government, as we shall see later.

Since their arrival in Putnam County, the Nuwaubian's resided in relative peace with their neighbours. The FBI even visited the property on a number of occasions in the months leading up to the 1996 Atlanta Olympics, in order to asses the potential threat of 'Terrorism' to the Games posed by the Movement, as well as to question York about his Sudanese or East African Islamic ties. York even underwent a lie detector test, which he passed, ending with the FBI giving the Nuwaubian's a 'Clean Bill Of Health', as far as not likely to pose any kind of 'Dangerous Threat', with no further action taken. By all accounts, things remained like this during what can be viewed as a type of 'Honeymoon' period, despite the efforts of Sheriff Sills' predecessor former Sheriff of Putnam County, Eugene Resseau, who would subsequently be arrested and charged by the FBI for numerous 'Criminal Activities', which included:

- **1 count of Stealing from a Federally funded programme**
- **34 counts of stealing from those programmes**
- **1 count of conspiring to commit Money Laundering**
- **17 counts of Money Laundering**

Sheriff Eugene Resseau was eventually convicted and sentenced to 21 months in Prison in 1996, for stealing a total of **$52,595.09**, between February 1993 and July 1995. Before his arrest, Sheriff Resseau, accused the Nuwaubian's of being Criminals, on numerous occasions, and spent a long time spreading slander in Putnam County that they were *"Drug dealers, from New York"*. Although he gave the Nuwaubian's a hard time whilst in office, his efforts, and indeed his Criminal exploits would pale in comparison to the next individual who would succeed him to the office of Putnam County Sheriff.

Sheriff Howard. R. Sills

Howard Richard Sills, Badge # 1177, was appointed as Putnam County Sheriff on January 1st 1997 in replacement of the 'Disgraced' Sheriff Eugene Resseau, and so began a more concentrated effort against the Nuwaubian movement. The name Sheriff. R. Sills has today become synonymous with the Nuwaubian's, as the individual whose Zealous actions almost single-handedly brought down the entire Movement. So who is Sheriff Richard Sills, and why was he so determined to destroy York and the Nuwaubian Nation? According to the Nuwaubian's, all of their problems were the result of an ongoing vendetta against them by one man, Sheriff. R. Sills, who had been harassing

Fig.249 **Nuwaubian Nemesis:** Sheriff Howard Richard Sills

them ever since he took office in 1997. They claim Sheriff Sills is a violent racist who is up to his eyes in corruption, and even has connections to the Klu Klux Klan, through convicted felon Jesse David Langford, a known associate of Sheriff Sills' Deputy and lead Detective Noel Lee Wilson. Detective Wilson who was himself convicted of Drug Dealing and Falsifying information in 2002, is said to have been connected to Jesse David Langford prior to his arrest, for Trafficking Narcotics, and Transporting 'Illegal' Firearms, across state lines, while still on probation. However, rather than receive the mandatory custodial sentence, Sheriff Sills merely banished him from the county, which was seen by many as being far too lenient. Dr. York being a licensed 'Private Investigator', after having graduated from 'The Rouse School of Special Detective Training', was able to conduct a thorough investigation into corruption in Putnam County, and is even rumoured to having been responsible for uncovering information, which lead to the conviction of Sheriff Sills' predecessor Sheriff Resseau. York was also conducting investigations into illegal activities in Putnam County, allegedly involving Sheriff Sills. One of these according to the Nuwaubian's was Sheriff Sills' participation in the sale of property seized from Criminal Trials, the proceeds of which he is said to keep for himself. In an article on the Nuwaubian's website unnm.com, they quote an article which previously appeared in the **Eatonton Messenger** that stated:

In the **Eatonton Messenger, January 7, 1999 A.D.**, article titled, "*County Adopts 1999 Budget, Lower Expenses*" states: "Before adopting the budget, the Commission heard from Putnam County **Sheriff Howard Richard Sills** who asked???? the money and the property from a recent plea agreement be retained by the Sheriff's Office..." Does this sound familiar? That's right, he was doing it then and he's doing it now. It further says, "...**Sheriff Howard Richard Sills** told the commission that when the former owner of the lottery depot pleaded guilty to 11 counts of commercial gambling, he gave up the property where the store was located, along with some other cash and property...and asked that the Commissioners allow him to sell the property where the lottery depot is located and keep the money for the **Sheriff's Office and use it for capital expenditures. Sheriff Sills said he would use the money for patrol cars, to establish a marine patrol on Lake Oconee, help fund a joint Baldwin County's office marine patrol on Lake Sinclair and to buy "other" equipment...**" Was a **Marine Patrol** ever set up on **Lake Oconee? NO!** Did Sheriff Howard Richard Sills ever get new or more **patrol cars? NO!** So obviously the Sheriff spent your money on "**Other Equipment**". Just what was this other equipment used for. Remember when The Putnam County Sheriff's Office was selling seized and surplus property! In an article titled, "**Authorities Selling Seized Items**," by **Rob Peecher** on **September 8, 1999 A.D.** it states, "The Putnam County Sheriff's Office will begin selling seized and surplus property during a Sheriff's sale today at 10 a.m. Among the items to be sold are several John Deere tractors and automobiles that have been seized in now-closed investigations."

(Peecher, cited in unnm.com, 2003)

Figs.250 & 251 Convicted Felons: Left- Right:
Detective Noel Lee Wilson & KKK Member Jesse David Langford

> With Skilful Manipulating of the Press, they're able to make the Victim look like the Criminal, and the Criminal look like the Victim...It's the same Game going all the time...
>
> (Malcolm X)

Sheriff Sills is said to literally run Putnam County, with numerous officials in 'his pocket', such as Building's Inspector Jerome D. Adams, and Attorney Francis Nearn Ford. Sheriff Sills has also been accused of controlling a handful of 'Racially Biased' newspaper reporters on his Payroll, who have systematically written biased and un-factual articles aimed at vilifying the Nuwaubinas on Sheriff Sills' behalf, such as:

- **Bill Osinski of The Atlanta Journal-Constitution**
- **Rob Peecher of The Macon Telegraph**
- **Judy Bailey & Jena Frazier of The Union Recorder**
- **Rufus Adair of The Eatonton Messenger**

Another witness to many of the corrupt undertakings, is former resident of Putnam County, David F. Moreland Jr. Himself a victim of a scam involving $150,000 by County Officials, Moreland was eventually banished from Putnam County, for threatening to expose the same clique of corrupt Officials & Journalists who were involved in hostilities with the Nuwaubian's. Mr Moreland even wrote a book in 1999 detailing his experiences, and the deep level of corruption which exists in the County entitled: *"Chickens Come Home To Roost: A True Story in the Modern South"*, **ISBN: 0967176905**. Over the years David Moreland was able to acquire a substantial amount of information about many of the blatant dishonest and fraudulent misuses of power practiced at the highest level, by Putnam County Officials, which he was happy to hand over to the Nuwaubian's.

In retaliation to these and other accusations by the Nuwaubia's, Sheriff Sills issued a series of blistering attacks in numerous Media interview's allegedly that York was an ex-convict, and the organisation were nothing more than a dangerous "Waco type Cult". The following are statements made by Sheriff Sills referring to the Nuwaubian's as dangerous:

> <u>CNN</u>, Title: *"Religious rift brews in rural Georgia"*, dated, June 29 1999:
> The Intelligence I've gathered from other law enforcement agencies about criminal activity associated with Mr. York's group in the past is very alarming to me...Specifically, the sheriff claims that the Nuwaubian's are black separatists who may be stockpiling weapons.
>
> (CNN, 1999)

> <u>Time Magazine</u>, Reporter Sylvestor Monroe, Title: *"Space Invaders"*, dated, July 12 1999:
> Putnam County Sheriff Howard Sills, another object of Nuwaubian ire, says he fears that young people are being held against their will. "No one in

Georgia has ever dealt with anything like this," he says. "You only draw parallels to Waco, and I don't want a Waco. This is a cult.

(Monroe, 1999)

Atlanta News, Reporter: Mara Shalhoup, Title: *"Nabbing the man from outer space"*, dated, May 6 2002:
Sills says the Nuwaubian's' assertion that they're being picked on and that he's a racist are hogwash. The Sheriff and the county officials claim the Nuwaubian's, armed with guns, wouldn't allow zoning inspectors on the compound. And after the Nuwaubian's sued the county...a Nuwaubian named Bernard Foster was arrested in 2000 for slashing the tires of the attorney representing the county.

(Shalhoup, 2002)

Figs.252 & 253 Gutter Journalists: Left- Right:
Bill Osinski of The Atlanta Journal & Rob Peecher of The Macon Telegraph

By now, it was increasingly becoming clear that both sides were headed for a confrontation, with the Nuwaubian's alleging that Sheriff Sills was constantly harassing them by visiting their property under the pretext of inspecting building violations, to provoke them into a violent reaction. Following York's arrest, and the subsequent raid of their property in 2002, the Nuwaubian's again went on the offensive, claiming that Sheriff Sills was a fervent Racist with KKK links, typically representative of what are commonly referred to by African American's as **'Redneck-Cracker'** Confederate *"Good Old Boys"*, from the Deep South. According to them, Sheriff Sills wields tremendous influence in Putnam, and the surrounding Counties, and has often been overheard in the past making such statements as: ***"This is my town; I control the lawyers; I control the newspapers, nothing goes on that I don't know about. These are my Niggers; they move when I say move."***

The Nuwaubian's further antagonised Sheriff Sills by releasing a story in one of their independent newspapers; The Macon Messenger, entitled *"A John Gotti Hiding Behind a Badge"*, which featured an article exposing a disturbing aspect of Sheriff Sills' personality as a Violent wife beater:

> ...Richard Sills has been hiding something for years that would be revealed if his divorce records with his ex-wife Cathy Sills were not sealed. They are doing everything in their power to keep it from the public's scrutiny and if he wasn't afraid, or if he wasn't hiding something then he would allow this case to be open and made public. Why are they keeping secrets? Sheriff Howard Richard Sills Reportedly broke his wife's jaw with a baseball bat. In April of 1998 A.D., reports were received that Sheriff Sills was beating his wife. Everybody knows that Sheriff Howard Richard Sills repeatedly beat his ex-wife, Cathy Sills. But because he worked in the law enforcement, nothing was ever done about it. He almost killed Cathy Sills with a baseball bat and had the nerve to brag about it. She has an apparent broken jaw and her face will never be the same, and everybody wants to keep it hush-hush because of the law that states any police officer convicted of domestic violence can no longer carry a firearm. He divorced his wife in May of that same year. The divorce files of Howard R. Sills plaintiff verses Cathy Denise Sills, maiden name Taylor, Civil Action File No. 98-CV 151-5 and of course the county clerk, would be Chief Deputy Helen T. Kitchen who signed on his behalf, that are locked away should be opened for all to see how it affected Sheriff Howard Richard Sills' performance as a law enforcer, the stress and most importantly the reason for the divorce proceedings were locked away by court order by Judge William Prior Jr. (who is a close friend of Sheriff Howard Richard Sills and is now the judge in the Nuwaubian case where he denied them all bond.
>
> (Macon Messenger, 2003)

Then in an additional article released the same year, entitled: *"Where is the Taxpayer's Money Going Now!!!?"*, the Nuwaubian's highlighted a series of illegal activities, said to directly involve Sheriff Sills and the Putnam County Sheriffs Department, which included: Tax Evasion, False Accounting, Embezzlement, Property Fraud, Plundering Public Funds & Handling Stolen Goods. The Nuwaubian's made the major mistake of letting things get out of hand, by allowing themselves to become drawn into a feud with backward Racist Southerners, like Sheriff Sills and other County Officials, who held an extraordinary amount of Power, and literally make up the County's Laws as they see fit. As we shall see, the Nuwaubian's would embark upon a dangerous course by disclosing details of Sheriff Sills' private life in their literature, which he needed kept secret, and by doing so, threatened his position as County Sheriff. The Nuwaubian's had not only crossed the point of no return, but also placed their very lives in danger. The Kid-gloves were now off, in fact these revelations were said to be so disturbing to Sheriff Sills that he was apparently overheard threatening to attack the Nuwaubian property a second time, after York's arrest, this time to; **"Finish off The**

Job". In their January edition of The Macon Messenger, entitled: *"Putnam County Sheriff Howard Richard Sills plans to reattack Nuwaubian's land"*, they quoted Sills as saying:

> "I am going to clean up this mess once and for all, I have had enough of this Nuwaubian bullshit, I am going to do what the Feds were afraid to do, I am going to put an end to those flyers and books...I am going to have a Waco on them (Nuwaubian's)."
>
> (Sheriff Sills, cited in Macon Messenger, 2003)

Several years earlier in 1999, Sheriff Sills confirmed just how determined he was to destroy Dr. Malachi. Z. York, when it was reported that he began stalking York at his new residence in Athens Georgia. It all began after mounting pressure from the combined efforts of the Sheriff's department, the county officials and local News Media forced York to leave Putnam county, and re-locate to a different part of the state. It was decided that because York was the main target of Sheriff Sills and the County officials, that the best course of action would be for him to no longer reside at the property on 404 Shady Dale Road, for the interests of the organisation, and because it was said he feared for his own safety. So in 1998 York moved into a new residence, in Athens County, Georgia. The media had already verified that York no longer resided at 404 Shady Dale Road, since 1998, in an article describing York's new home as a 'Mansion' situated on Mansfield Court off Timothy Road, Athens. One of which was an article which appeared in Online Athens, on May 6th 2002 entitled: *"Innocent pleads sect leader York"* 11, in which it stated:

> York is also listed as the owner of a house assessed at $528,177 in Tony Mansfield Court area off Timothy Road. **He bought the house in December 1998** for $557, 000, according to Athens-Clarke County tax records.
>
> (Online Athens, 2002)

Fig.254: *York's Athens, Residence since 1998*

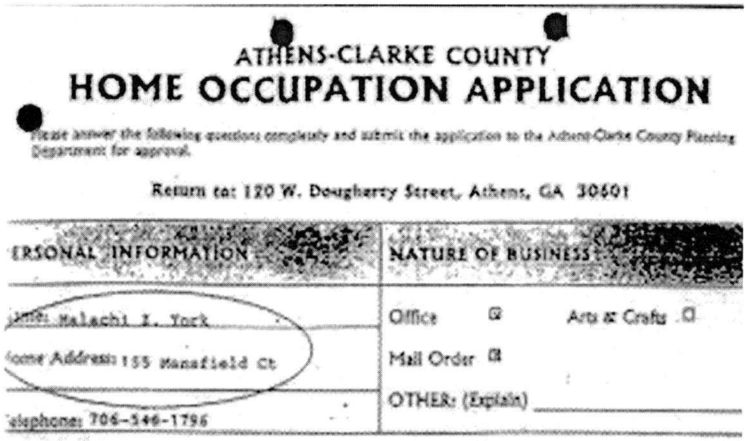

ATHENS-CLARKE COUNTY
HOME OCCUPATION APPLICATION

Please answer the following questions completely and submit the application to the Athens-Clarke County Planning Department for approval.

Return to: 120 W. Dougherty Street, Athens, GA 30601

PERSONAL INFORMATION	NATURE OF BUSINESS
Name: Malachi Z. York	Office ☒ Arts & Crafts ☐
Home Address: 155 Mansfield Ct	Mail Order ☒
	OTHER: (Explain)
Telephone: 706-546-1796	

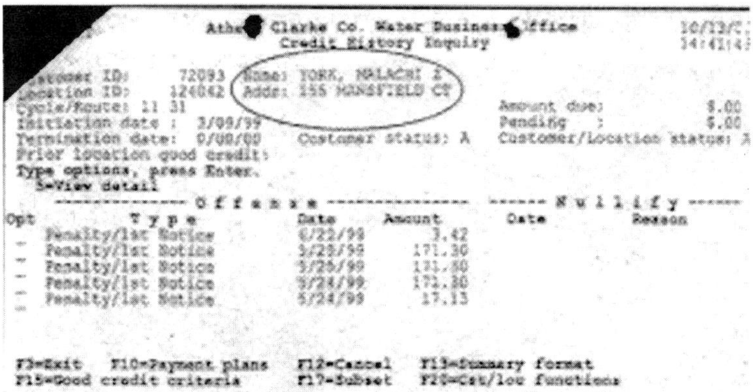

Athens-Clarke Co. Water Business Office — 10/13/C
Credit History Inquiry — 14:42:4

Customer ID: 72093   Name: YORK, MALACHI Z
Location ID: 124062   Addr: 155 MANSFIELD CT
Cycle/Route: 11 31
Initiation date : 3/08/99
Termination date: 0/00/00   Customer status: A   Amount due: $.00
Prior location good credit: Pending : $.00
Type options, press Enter.   Customer/Location status: A
  5=View detail

--------- Offense ---------   ------ Nullify ------
Opt Type   Date   Amount   Date   Reason
 _   Penalty/1st Notice 6/22/99   3.42
 _   Penalty/1st Notice 5/25/99 171.30
 _   Penalty/1st Notice 5/25/99 131.80
 _   Penalty/1st Notice 3/24/99 171.80
 _   Penalty/1st Notice 5/24/99   17.13

F3=Exit F10=Payment plans F12=Cancel F13=Summary format
F15=Good credit criteria   F17=Subset F20=Cut/low functions

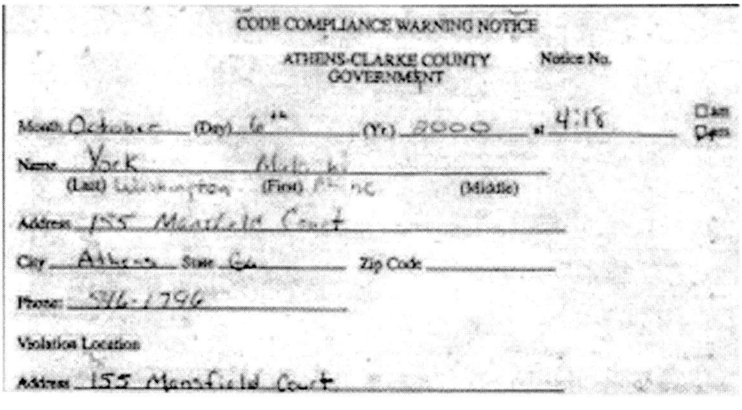

CODE COMPLIANCE WARNING NOTICE
ATHENS-CLARKE COUNTY GOVERNMENT
Notice No. _____

Month October (Day) 6th (Yr.) 2000   at 4:18   Clsn ___ Opn ___

Name: York   Malachi
      (Last) Washington (First)   (Middle)

Address: 155 Mansfield Court

City: Athens   State: Ga.   Zip Code: _____

Phone: 546-1796

Violation Location
Address: 155 Mansfield Court

Fig.255 & 256 Documented Evidence: Top & Bottom:
*Actual Documents, Verifying York's occupancy in the Property,
4-years Before Alleged Child Sexual Molestation took place*

193

Clearly these were 4 whole years that York had not resided at 404 Shady Dale Road, long before the raid upon the Nuwaubian's land by law enforcement officials. Therefore any evidence supposedly discovered by the police could not be linked to York for the simple fact that he had not lived there since 1998, as confirmed by the Media. York not only left the property, he also transferred complete ownership of the property from himself over to several members of his organisation. Which he did on January 24th 2000, signing what is called a **'Quit Claim'** deed, which effectively transferred the legal ownership of 476 acres of real estate at 404 Shady Dale Road, from himself, which at the time was part of Tama-Re Enterprises, to:

- Yvonne Powell
- Vincent Powell
- Donald McIntyre
- Michelle Mitchell
- Althea Shine
- Patrice Evans
- Anthony Evans

Fig.257 Proof of Ownership: *Document proving Transfer of Ownership of 404 Shadydale Road, from York to Board of Trustees in 2000*

It was these '7' individuals who became the new 'Legal' owners of the Nuwaubian property, which legally rendered it no longer the property of Dr. Malachi. Z. York. Despite this, on March 23, 1999, York was forced to call Auburn Avenue Atlanta Police Department, to complain about the presence of an intruder on his new Athens property. This intruder turned out to be none other than Putnam County Sheriff, Howard Richard Sills, who for some reason, now found it necessary to leave his jurisdiction in Putnam county, to harass the Nuwaubian leader in Athens County over 65 miles away. The officer that responded to the call was Officer David Bill, Badge # 2572, who reported seeing a fat bald Caucasian male fleeing the scene, near York's residence, fitting Sheriff Sills' description, at precisely 2:00 pm. Sheriff Sills apparently fled the scene when he saw the patrol car approaching the Nuwaubian leader's residence. Officer Bill informed York that if he was disturbed again, to call the station, and he would come back for York to file a complaint. Undeterred by the Athens County Police, Sheriff Sills was spotted on York's property on two more occasions, first at 2:35 pm, and again the next day on March 24. This time the incident was reported to Officer Gary Gullat, Badge # 2590. By engaging in such activity, Sheriff Sills reduced himself to the level of a common stalker, which is a criminal offence, and demonstrated the lengths he was prepared to go, to orchestrate York's down fall. This incident also raises the question of why Sheriff Sills lead the FBI, and other Law enforcement offices to arrest York at 404 Shady Dale Road in 2002, when he was fully aware that the Nuwaubian leader had not resided there for over 4 years?

Later that year, on April 20th, Superior Court Judge John Lee Parrott, ruled in favour of the Putnam County officials, issuing a permanent injunction upon the Rameses II social club, located on the Nuwaubian's' property on 404 Shady Dale Road. The Court order granted building inspector Jerome Adams Jr. and Sheriff Sills with the authority to enter the property "between certain hours" to ensure safety standards were being maintained. However Sheriff Sills is alleged to have contravened the court order by arriving unexpectedly at the property on several occasions with his deputy Noel Lee Wilson, holding a Video camera for the purpose of provoking the occupants of the land. Sheriff Sills and Wilson were repeatedly refused admission onto the property with the Video camera by the Nuwaubian security personnel, because the court order did not include Wilson or allow Sheriff Sills to film private property. This then, led to the two Nuwaubian security guards; Claude Turner and Henry Torres, being arrested for contempt of court. Clearly this little stunt was pulled by Sheriff Sills to further provoke the Nuwaubian's into a confrontation, so he could justify the use of force against them, which is what he appears to have desired from the beginning.

One reason for Sheriff Sills' vendetta against the Nuwaubian's is said to have been financial. Putnam County Sheriff's have often been accused of being involved in corruption, and Sheriff Sills, like his predecessor, Eugene Resseau, are no exception. The Nuwaubian's claim that Sheriff Sills began

demanding bribes from them not long after taking office in 1997, but when they refused, he began his campaign of harassment against the group.
There has also been the question over the ownership of the property at 404 Shady Dale Road. Sources claim that around the same time York purchased the property in 1993, a powerful conglomerate called the 'Reynolds Corporation', were also said to have been interested in purchasing the property to turn into Golf courses. As a result of having been beaten to the deal by the Nuwaubian leader, they were said to have been very angry, and vowed to stop at nothing to eventually get their hands on the property. Apparently it was Sheriff Sills' intention to harass York into putting the property on the market in order for those parties interested, to be able to purchase the land at a reduced price. The local authorities were also said to have been eager to curtail the activities of the Nuwaubian's after York unveiled plans to build an Egyptian 'Styled' amusement park on the property. In fact the Nuwaubian's were generating so much interest and revenue from their gatherings, which began to attract ever increasing numbers each year, that it was rumoured that several "Fast Food" giants including McDonalds, Taco Bell and Burger King expressed interest, and were looking into locating new restaurants near the Nuwaubian property. Fearing the rapid growth of the Nuwaubian influence in the county, local residents created what can only be described as a 'Vigilante Group' of hired thugs, calling themselves *"Citizens Against Nuwaubian's"* (C.A.N.), lead by Convicted Criminal Robert. L. Johnson. Clandestinely funded by County Officials, this group of local Criminals & White Supremacists are said to have been behind a number of Violent Attacks, Racial Abuses & Hate Mail campaigns against the York's followers residing on the property, the purpose of which was to intimidate and frighten members of the group into vacating the County. However, fearing for the safety of his followers, York immediately took the offensive by reinstating the groups Paramilitary wing, as a 'Private Security' force, contracted to protect particular, the group's most vulnerable members such as Women, Children & the Elderly, who were often victims of the vigilante group's attacks during trips to and from the property. Customarily the Media took the opportunity to routinely label the Nuwaubian Security, as an armed 'Militia', to make the group further appear to be a Dangerous Cult. Prior to his arrest in 2002, York had began preparing his followers for the inevitability of taking on, and defending themselves against the American Legal system, using 'Moorish Sovereign Law', which according to York would protect or 'Immunize' them from a system which he described as 'Evil' which treated blacks unfairly. The following is an excerpt taken from a lecture given by York entitled: *"Let's Set The Record Straight: No More God Games"*, in which he explains his view of the American Legal system:

> When you come down to 'Moorish' Law, the first thing you have to establish with them is, we do not except your King's James Version, or your St. Jerome's or New World Jehovah Witness Version.

We do not except this as fact, and so therefore in Court if I'm called to put my hand on this book, and swear to tell "The Whole Truth and Nothing But The Truth", I would be lying , by putting my hand on it, and pretending I would be telling the Truth because I don't believe in it.

We will not be able to institute, the articles of our Constitution, until you fully accept 'Yourselves' as Moors, and drop all of that other Crap, including the reference to be, "am I one of the 144,000?... Bible!!

You cannot expect to go up against a System of Evil, and it is Evil, while you're holding the Tool of Evil in your hand. And I'm telling you, you might not accept it, and say; "Yo! This Guy is Saying the Bible is a Tool of Evil". I'm saying the Bible has been used as a Tool of Evil. They use justification Laws to abuse us while they hold up the Bible. The KKK does not Burn Crescents, they Burn Crosses. For some reason, somehow the Christian World, I'm talking about the 'Ethnic Christian World', has over looked the Cross on the lawn for the 'White Hood'. You understand what I'm saying? They should be addressing the fact that the KKK is a Christian denomination, you with that?....Because, Organizations can be exceptions to the Rules. So they allow it, as long as they pledge to the Constitution, believe it or not, the KKK has their own Constitution. They have their own Laws, they have a Holy Book called the 'Koran', that they read. They have their own President, they have their own Chiefs, their own Imperial Wizards. They have a whole Government set-up, and they have become 'Immune'. The only time the system can bother them, is when they Violate the Laws of the System. As long as they stay within the Rules of the System, they cannot touch them. And this is why they have been able to exist.

The same thing applies to The Nation of Islam. The Honourable Elijah Muhammad, was a wise man, he knew how to work with the Rules and Regulations.

When we go to present to them, if you have a trial before you, say you want to pull-out a '3rd Article Judge', and what you're gonna see come in is a Judge in Cowboy Boots and a Cowboy Hat. Did you all notice on Television, in both of the Bombings in Okalahoma, both of the Judges that they selected, they ignored all the Okalahoma Magistrates, and they brought in a Cowboy. Did you notice it, he had to come all the way across the Country out of Texas, because Texas is a separate, and has never ever been registered as a State. And that's what them Fools, who took that Oath against the United States 6 months ago was trying to point out, they crushed it so quick. Because they were pointing out that Texas was never a part of the United States. And the Judges they pulled in, called '3rd Article Judges', come as Cowboys from Texas, another state. Why?, because they are dealing with you, as you are a Foreigner.

Now we have two approaches:

1. We are 'Indigenous' people of this Land, and we are the Descendants of Moors who came over here on their own.

2. We are the Descendants of those who were Kidnapped, and brought over here as Slaves from Africa.

Now we have to make up our minds which one of those paths, for the legal System are we going to stay on?

Are we going to continue to say that I'm an African, and therefore practice 'Dumb Ass' Islam, Christianity & Judaism and fall under Religious Law…Because the condition of mind, that makes it impossible for you to go right into a court in the middle of a Trial, and say "Give Me a 3rd Article Judge". They'll go: "Nigger Shut- Up, Get Out of Here, All of a Sudden, That Your Ass is in Trouble, You Want Answers!" And they'll just ignore you because they will want to know why you so articulate now?. Now all of a sudden, now you've read some book by some Nappy Headed Nigger in Georgia, and all of a sudden you all got all these intricate questions, and they'll just ''Dog' you, and it will be made to look like it's the right thing to do, because there'll be a Nigger sitting around them saying "That's right Mr Massa, that's right Sir, that Nigger's Crazy!!!

As Moors We've got to step out of Religious Law, until We like the Klan, can 'Unanimously' say We Do Not Accept This…

(York El, 1999)

During the years that followed, York and his organisation began to become involved in increasing Legal Battles with Local, State & Federal officials in which they would put many of York's complicated Sovereign & Common-Law strategies into practice, which were met with predictable responses from both the Media and the Legal Authorities, as we shall now examine in greater depth.

Legal Battles
& Victimisation by County Authorities

The Nuwaubian's legal problems in Putnam County can be best described as a series of incompetence and petty spitefulness, on both sides, which primarily began around 1997, culminating in a number of the Nuwaubian Community being directly targeted, and 'Racially Profiled' by Putnam County officials. The most well known incident began when Chief building inspector, Jerome Dean Adams, first visited the Nuwaubian property to carry out inspections of various buildings to assess whether they met the County's safety requirements. Following a series of legal altercations involving incorrect Zoning permits, inspector Adams was initially refused entry to the property by Nuwaubian Security personnel. However after being alerted by the Counties black Commissioner Sandra Adams, regarding the existence of other 'Illegal' building projects on the property, inspector Jerome Adams returned several days later with Sheriff Richard Sills. It was during this second round of inspections that Adams discovered a building under construction, which had not been issued the correct Zoning permit.

Several months later Adams cited Nuwaubian ground's man Victor Greig for being in violation of the necessary Safety and Zoning requirements for the structure, said at the time to be used as a 'Storage Facility. According to reporters at the time; Putnam County officials decided to Re-inspect the building after the Nuwaubian's foolishly allowed a TV Crew to film revellers at the building, in a Broadcast which advertised it as the **'Rameses**

II, Social Club', a Nightclub for members only. The building was not only deemed to be in contravention of the County's 'Safety Standards', but also had no Alcohol license, and therefore immediately padlocked with its power supply cut off. A month later Sheriff Sills again arrived at the property with an overwhelming force of over 10 squad cars of officers from a number of neighbouring Counties, to simply enforce the closure of the Club, which wasn't even opened at the time. Following this incident, the period of good relations between the Nuwaubian's & Putnam County authorities was over for good.

Figs.259 & 260 Left- Right: *Nuwaubain Grounds Keeper Victor Greg in Court with, Attorney Ronnie Jones & Rameses II, Social Club*

Then in May, Sheriff Sills together with attorney Francis Nearn Ford, took out a court injunction against York prohibiting the use of the Rameses II social club. Neither Sheriff Sills nor Attorney Ford, were building enforcement inspectors, which made their actions illegal. Nevertheless, the Nuwaubian's claimed that attorney Francis Nearn Ford also acted illegally by assuming the role of Putnam County Prosecutor, which was really his wife Dorothy Jean Adams' position.

As a result of the efforts of Sheriff Sills, Nuwaubian grounds keeper Victor Greig, would later be cited for Zoning Violations, and eventually fined $79,000, which was later reduced to $45,750, by Magistrate Judge Sylvia Huskins, for a simple zoning violation which is only classified by law as a "Misdemeanour", and should have been no more than $3,000. Victor Greig had to eventually file for bankruptcy to prove that he was unable to pay the excessive fine, after which, a long legal battle ensued, resulting in attorney Francis Nearn Ford making Victor Greig go to jail in order to force him to pay the fine.

The Judge during Victor Greig's bankruptcy hearing, Judge James D. Walker, later admitted that it was wrong for Victor Greig to be jailed for not paying a fine. The following is part of a court transcript taken from September 17th 1999, in which Federal Judge James D. Walker, criticised attorney Francis Nearn Ford for Jailing Victor Greig for a fine he had no way of paying:

> He's not going to pay the fine. He hasn't paid the fine and he's probably not gonna pay the fine. He's in bankruptcy. I don't suppose he is gonna be able to pay the fine. Why isn't it he wouldn't expect to serve a year? And how is it that you all can think he should serve a year when you don't have any authority to sentence him to a year? Unless you do it consecutively and so state?... Yeah. I think it's a fair reading of the ordinance. But I mean I don't know how you see failure to already done that. Evidence supports for the debtor's argument here. Basically, you're putting this guy in jail because he can't pay money. That's the problem with this on a fundamental level and he doesn't even know, not only does he not know how long he's gonna be serving. You're telling me that it hadn't even been determined yet.
>
> (Judge Walker, 1999)

Figs.261, 262 & 263 Putnam County Officials: Left- Right:
Jerome Dean Adams, Dorothy Jean Adams & Francis Nearn Ford

After losing the court action, attorney Ford attempted to make out to the media that he didn't lose the case against the Nuwaubian's, but that it was really his idea to release Victor Greig, even though he bitterly opposed Victor Greig's release. On September 30th 1999. Ford stated the following to the Eatonton Messenger, in an article entitled: *"Greig Released Following Change In Fine to $2,500"*:

> We thought it made sense to compromise. If he were incarcerated, it was going to cost the county money. Greig is not a hardened criminal. He was convicted of a zoning violation; it seemed the just thing to do.
>
> (Attorney Ford, 1999)

Finally on September 28th, after spending 11 days in jail, Victor Greig was released by Judge Cline, and ordered to pay the accurate fine of approximately $2,500. Attorney Francis Nearn Ford's insistence on taking the Nuwaubian's to trial, cost Putnam County Hundreds of Thousands of dollars and eventually lead to his wife Dorothy Jean Adams being fired from her post as Putnam County prosecutor in 2001.

According to the Nuwaubian's, Mr Thomas Chism, who had been acting as York's agent since 1993, had previously filed to the Putnam Zoning board, for 19 acres of the property to be Zoned, which was said to include all of the disputed buildings. However, these permits were either repeatedly ignored or denied by the Putnam Zoning board, which the Attorney leading the case against Victor Greig, Francis Nearn Ford, was already aware of. This even included a place of worship on their own property, which meant the group's members were forced to conduct religious services outdoors, which often meant being exposed to the elements. Some of the applications made by the Nuwaubian's, denied by The Putnam Zoning board were as follows:

- Application for Lodge Temple (Denied)
- Application for Hunting Club (Denied)
- Application for Office (Denied)
- Application for Church (Denied)
- Application for Fence Park (Denied)
- Application for Storage building (Denied)
- Application for Park buildings (Denied)
- Application for Museum (Denied)
- Application for Skating area (Denied)
- Application for Convenience Store (Denied)

To prove this, in 1999 the Nuwaubian's presented copies of the original applications made to the Zoning board, in another one of their newspapers *"Putnam News: We The People"* as evidence of a racial vendetta against them. These conflicts over zoning continued until mid 1999, when attorney Francis Nearn Ford and his wife, the real Putnam County prosecutor Dorothy Jean Adams, filed a lawsuit # 99-CV-1-1, which prevented the Nuwaubian's from using the property for anything other than its original purpose, which was agricultural.

Figs.264, 265 & 266 Denied: Left- Right: *Nuwaubian Applications for Church, Offices & Convenience Store Rejected by officials*

This lawsuit further escalated what became known as the *"War between the Nuwaubian's and the Putnam County officials"*, which culminated in York being summoned to appear before Circuit Judge Hugh V. Wingfield to give evidence over the zoning dispute. However, when York failed to appear, he was subpoenaed by the Judge, and threatened with arrest on charges of contempt of court. York finally appeared at the court on the June 29 1999, during the group's annual Saviour's day celebration. By this point, the whole situation had escalated completely out of proportion by not only the County official's, but also the Nuwaubian's, who helped to fuel speculations that they were indeed a 'Crazy' cult, when thousands of them stood outside the court room with their hands in the air, in a type of bizarre 'Prayer Vigil'. This strange demonstration by York's followers severely damaged their credibility in the eyes of outsiders, who would have otherwise been much more sympathetic and supportive of their cause.

The conflicts between the Nuwaubian's and Putnam County officials have been documented in a recent book written in 2001, by Rod A. Janzen, entitled: *"The Rise and Fall of Synanon: A California Utopia",* which examines the phenomenon of group's who are increasingly rejecting urban life, in the quest for a Utopian alternative:

> ...for example, of the 1993 confrontation in Waco, Texas, and the conflict in Eatonton, Georgia, involving the Yamassee Nuwaubian "utopia" in the late 1990s. Groups that early in their history managed to relocate to an isolated geographical region...

(Janzen, 2001)

Fig.267 Prayer Vigil: *Nuwaubians conducting Mass Prayer outside Courtroom*

Then there was the incident involving Thomas Chism himself, which resulted in him being charged with Fraud, and subsequently Banished from Putnam County for Life. It began in May 1999, when as Malachi York's acting agent Thomas Chism was wrongly accused with falsifying documents which he had delivered to Putnam County's 'Building & Zoning' office requesting the documents which were said to be pertaining to a request by the Nuwaubian's to set up a Circus & Theme Park on 404 Shadydale Rd. County building & zoning office administrative assistant Marianne Tanner, later testified in a court hearing that the documents brought by Mr Chism were forgeries. Although Thomas Chism's Attorney pointed out that Mr Chism was simply delivering the documents for an acquaintance, and that there was no evidence to prove that Thomas Chism actually falsified the documents himself, he was still found guilty and convicted to 3 months in Jail, and later Banished from Putnam County 'For the rest of his Life'.

However the most blatant example of this campaign of Racial Profiling against affiliates of the Nuwaubian Nation was the victimisation of Dr. William Thompson, M.D. by local Attorney Frank Ford, also in 1999.

Fig.268 Wrongly Dismissed: *Dr. Thompson*

Dr. Thompson, a Certified Physician who specialises in 'Emergency Medicine', such as Accident & Trauma victims, and is recognised by the American Board of Emergency Medicine (ABEM). Licensed to practice in over 47 states since qualifying in 1980. Dr. Thompson began working as an Emergency Physician in June 1997 at Putnam General Hospital, Eatonton, and was later contracted by the North Carolina Physician's Group (NCPG), which included Eatonton Hospital's Emergency Department. All was well until March 1999, when Dr. Thompson, was suddenly fired from his position in the Hospital's Emergency room without any prior warning or explanation. By way of the Freedom of Information Act (FOIA), Dr. Thompson and his Attorney's were able to discover the reason behind his sudden dismissal, and breach of contract by North Carolina Physicians Group. Through the (FOIA) Dr. Thompson's legal team were able to obtain evidence from the County Commissioner's office, and the Hospital's Administrators office which revealed that Eatonton Hospital kept a file on Dr. Thompson which contained a list of the names of all Dr. Thompson's patients at the Hospital, many of whom were affiliated with the Nuwaubian Nation, especially those who lived on 'Tama Re'. To his astonishment, Dr. Thompson also learned that the files revealed numerous references to a non-existent 'Medical Clinic' on Tama Re, which he supposedly helped set up. Most shocking of all was the discovery of a secret meeting which took place between Putnam county Attorney Frank Ford and Eatonton Hospital authorities, which concluded with a decision to remove Dr. Thompson from the hospital's emergency department, without any justifiable cause other than Dr. Thompson's Nuwaubian affiliation. Because of the activities of Attorney Ford, Dr. Thompson was unjustly fired without any due process, explanation or prior notice, only finding out that he no longer had a job by coming into work. Dr. William Thompson later filed a complaint with the United States Equal Employment Opportunity Commission (EEOC), after being refused consideration for other positions within the Hospital's Emergency Department.

Clearly these tactics of 'Racial Profiling' against the Nuwaubian's by the Putnam officials were designed to single out, and alienate certain key individuals within the Movement, in order to undermine and break the infrastructure of the Community.

The Nuwaubian's immediately responded by forming alliances with a number of International & National Political personalities. Throughout the entire episode, the Nuwaubian's must also be credited for their sheer tenacity and courage in fighting for their Civil & Human rights against Sheriff Sills and the other Putnam County officials. Indeed, until York's arrest in May 2002, the scales had begun to tip in their favour. In reply to what they claimed was constant harassment by Sheriff Sills and other County officials, the Nuwaubian's began "The Concerned Citizens Of Eatonton" (C.C.O.E), an organisation comprised of themselves and other Putnam residents who felt repressed by the corrupt county officials. The group also launched several Newspapers & Newsletters, which included **Putnam News & The Macon Messenger**, to rebuke many of the biased newspaper articles which ran unfavourable stories against them such as:

- **The Eatonton Messenger**
- **The Union Recorder**
- **The Atlanta Journal-Constitution**
- **The Lake Oconee Breeze**
- **The Macon Telegraph**

As previously stated, the Nuwaubian's were also forced to install 'Armed' Security Personnel to guard the gates of their property, after they claimed local racist thugs and bigots began driving past screaming obscenities, racial slurs, threatening them with violence and throwing objects at women and young children. Ironically these same security guards contracted to protect the law-abiding inhabitants of Tama Re would later be described as "Dangerous armed Para- militias" by the mainstream Media.

The last straw came in June 1999, during the group's annual "Saviour's Day" celebration, when York was forced to appear before Superior Court Judge Hugh V. Wingfield III. Although it was never made clear why York was called to appear in court. The obvious reason of which, seems to have been to draw him out into the open, and cut him down to size. Which was also apparent from the Police presence outside the courtroom, in a massive & unprecedented show of strength. Law Enforcement officials, lead by Sheriff Sills tried to intimidate York's followers, present outside the court. Alongside Sheriff Sills' own officers were almost 200 State Troopers, Department of Corrections officers & Georgia Emergency Management Personnel. On the opposite side of the street also stood 150 Sheriff's deputies from 13 different jurisdictions, including Eatonton County & Morgan County Dog patrol section, several armoured personnel carriers and Helicopters flying overhead carrying FBI and Justice department officials. So, why the huge Police presence for a few thousand unarmed people standing peacefully outside a court? To ensure their own safety the Nuwaubian's were now left with no alternative, but to seek outside assistance to help publicise their conflict with the Putnam County authorities.

One of the first Political figures to show concern on behalf of the group was State Senator Floyd Griffin, whose constituency encompasses Putnam County. A year before York's court appearance, on Friday May 8th 1998, Sen. Griffin's comments were featured in the Union Recorder newspaper, expressing his concerns about the heavy-handed tactics employed by against the Nuwaubian's. In the article entitled: *"Griffin Concerned About 'Overreaction' to Nuwaubian's"*, Sen. Griffin stated that he called a meeting with Putnam County officials, which was said to include Sheriff Sills, to voice his disapproval at the way in which the situation with the Nuwaubian's was being handled. The following is a complete transcript of the article expressing Sen. Griffin's concerns:

Griffin Concerned About 'Overreaction' to Nuwaubian's
State Senator Floyd Griffin said Thursday he is concerned that Putnam County Sheriff Howard Richard Sills is 'overreacting' to the Nuwaubian Community, and he urged both sides to "open up lines of communication".
Griffin, whose district included Putnam County, met Thursday with Sills, two Putnam County commissioners and attorney for the United Nuwaubian Nation of Moors. Griffin is running for lieutenant governor, but will hold the Senate seat until the end of the year.
I talked about my concerns as a Senator representing this area; I was concerned that there were some bad perceptions out there that could lead to some more things we don't need to have in our county. I said they needed to do all they could to get the thing under control. I told them I thought the sheriff could be overreacting, in my opinion, based on what I'm reading and people are telling me.

Sills said he listened to Griffin's observations, but he said he remains committed to enforcing the orders of the courts. It needs to be perfectly clear to everyone that the sheriff enforced the lawful order of the court, not the sheriff's order Sills said. "I enforce all court orders". He was referring to an order that he and a group of deputies served Wednesday at the Nuwaubian's Community on Shady Dale Road. Under the court order, which was obtained by a lawyer hired by Sills, the officers put new locks on a dance club that earlier had been operating in violation of local Zoning and Building codes. In April, a Nuwaubian Groundskeeper was fined $45,750 by a Putnam County magistrate for violations connected with the building. The

Fig.269 Nuwaubian Defender:
Senator Floyd Griffin

Nuwaubian Community, filled with buildings and statues reminiscent of ancient Egypt, has become a highly visible point of controversy in the county over the past few years. About 100 people live there and follow the teachings of a leader Malachi York.

Griffin said Putnam County's vigorous enforcement of county zoning and building ordinances against the Nuwaubian's could lead to perception problems. He said he is concerned that, 'if they keep moving in the direction they're moving in, then I think the perception is going to switch more to the fact that it could be a black/white thing, and that's what I'm trying to avoid as a state senator. We don't want a race problem in the 25th district."

The Nuwaubian community is predominately black. Sills said race has no part in his motives or actions. "That's not the case, and I stand absolutely by that", he said. Griffin said, "If they are breaking the law that should be dealt with. But they should not be harassed or their constitutional or civil rights violated." He questioned why Sills needed such a strong show of force to change a lock on a door.

Sills said it was because when he visited the centre last month an armed guard initially barred his way. He said a confrontation nearly developed then. Griffin said if the situation doesn't calm down. "I would have to take some action myself, and I don't want to do that. He declined to say what kind of action he might take". Along with Griffin and Sills, the meeting participants included county commissioners Bill Moore and Jimmy Davis. Commissioner Steve Layson was invited but he did not attend. Griffin said they scheduled the meeting well before this week's developments at the

Nuwaubian's county property. Afterwards, Moore would say only that the meeting focused on Griffins concerns. It's about the same as he told you. Any time anybody has a problem we need to try to work it out" he said. Asked whether he thought the "new lines of communication" might open up he said, "There's always hope". Davis said, "It was a good discussion." Commissioners will meet with the Nuwaubian's during the commission's May 19 meeting to hear their concerns.

Griffin said he made his own visits to the Nuwaubian's in recent months and found little reason for alarm. "They're my constituents just like anyone else in this district", he said. "And I wanted to get to know a little bit more about them and what they're all about, etc. So I visited with them about a month ago, and I met with Dr. York and talked with him about his organization, met with several of his key staffers, and then heard some of their concerns about what's going on up there with the staff and their code enforcement officials, the planning and zoning board." After hearing about alleged noise and crowd problems, Griffin said he made another surprise visit on Saturday night April 25th. "They didn't know I was coming. They let me in and showed me around where they were having outdoor music. I didn't stay that long. There wasn't a lot of people there at that time. I didn't see anything unusual. Plus it's way out in the country, and there's not that many people around so I don't see what's the big deal." He added, "There had been no indication in my opinion, based on my research, of any violence from those people over there, no matter what (Sills') intelligence told him."

Sills said he has tried to open up communication and has been rebuffed. Every time I've gone out to this place, I've asked to see Dr. York. I've talked to their attorney since this started and asked to see Mr. York. I've told him various public officials would try to meet with him. I never gotten one bit of response from him whatsoever."

Griffin said: he wants to do what he can to defuse things. "I wanted to do what I could if they needed me to try to help get that situation under control, because I was concerned about the Nuwaubian's being treated fairly and equally and that's the way everyone in the county should be treated: fair and equal." But Sills said, "This is not a matter that Floyd Griffin will decide. This is a matter that will be decided in the courts, that's what the courts are for."

(Article taken from the Union Recorder, 1998)

Several years earlier, during the group's 1997 'Saviours Day' celebration, held annually in celebration of Malachi York's Birthday on June 26th, the Nuwaubian leader threatened to inform The U.S. Congress, if the harassment continued:

> The Corrupt officials, who try to block you, like superintendent Mr. Lowe out of his own mouth tries to defame us by defamation of character and slander, which is against the law. We hear you and we will write to our Congress

(York, 1997)

Whether York fulfilled this threat is not clear, however, United States Attorney General, at the time; Janet Reno, somehow got wind of what was going on and had her office contact Putnam County building inspector Jerome D. Adams, directly on July 7th, 1999, to inform him that he had until July 13th, to approve all permits applied for by the Nuwaubian's, and end all hostilities. If his office failed to comply with this request, the matter would no longer be between Putnam County and the Nuwaubian's, but would be taken over by the U.S. Justice Department.

West African 'Diplomatic' Ties

After years of dismissing it as a lost cause, Dr. Malachi York finally re-established ties between his Movement and the African continent, around 1998, when a delegation of Diplomats from the Republic of Liberia, led by the then Minister of Justice Eddington Vermah, visited Tama Re during a tour of several Southern States. The visit was said to have been a resounding success resulting in the Liberian Delegation coming away very impressed with the hard work ethic, and high level of 'Self-Determination' and enthusiasm displayed by the Nuwaubian's in shaping their own destiny. So much so that several months later, the Liberian Government began the development of future ties with the organisation, beginning by bestowing upon Malachi York full Liberian Citizenship, and appointing him **'Consul General'** for the Republic of Liberia to the Atlanta, Georgia region of the U.S., which the Media have conveniently kept hidden from the public. In addition, York briefly assumed his rightful role as International Statesmen for the Nuwaubian Nation by overseeing the development of various Organisations, which would assist with the Re-construction of the West African Nation, whose infrastructure had been severely damaged during several years of Civil War. Amongst the bodies set up were:

The Nuwaubian Grand Lodge of Freemasonry Worldwide founded to recruit Architects, Brick Masons, Contractors, Electricians, Plumbers, Solar Energy Specialists etc, to travel to Liberia to restore and assist in the development of the buildings and structures that were destroyed by the civil war.

The Medical Association of America founded to provide much needed medical care, pharmaceuticals and vaccinations by African Americans licensed Medical Doctors, Nurses, Laboratory Technicians, Pharmacists and other Medical Practitioners, to travel to Liberia and assist with the country's medical needs.

The Amen Institute founded by African Americans with PhDs, Masters Degrees & Bachelors Degrees etc, to offer state of the art Education from Pre-Kindergarten to College courses and "exchange student programs" allowing students from Africa to study in the UK & U.S. and visa-versa.

The Egiptian Church of Karast Liberia founded to offer religious teachings and aid in the restoration of villages by donating food, clothes and other necessities that were lacking because of the Civil Wars.

Figs.270, 271, 272 & 273 Liberian Diplomat: Top: *Dr. York's Liberian Citizenship*
(Bottom) Left- Right: *York's Athens Residence, Liberian*
& York declaring his Liberian allegiance

Finally a **'Back to Africa'** Repatriation programme was set up by York, to provide his followers and other interested African-Americans with the opportunity to return to the 'Mother Land', to provide 'Western Professionalism' to their brethren on the beleaguered Continent. This included a desperately needed cultural-exchange between Nuwaubian's and African's on the Continent, leading to the possibility of full citizenship for American Blacks to the West African Nation. In return for the organisation's assistance, a number of lucrative business opportunities were rumoured to have been made available for the Nuwaubian's by the Liberian Government, in respect to various Building, Mining and other contracts. One such business enterprise was the 'Get Informed' financial consulting company set up by Dr. York and established in 2000. Other 'Key' Nuwaubian participants within the Corporation were:

- **Jay Davis, Chief Executive Officer (CEO)**
- **Maria Flores (Co-founder), Chief Financial Officer (CFO)**
- **Marcus Barnes, Chief Operations Officer (COO)**
- **Leroy Davis, Executive Operations Manager**

'Get Informed' was said to have been selected to provide 'Economic' advice to the Liberian Government by Minister Francis Garlawolu, in exchange for large financial investments in Liberian mineral resources once Garlawolu was re-elected. Minister Garlawolu is widely acknowledged to have strong Pan-African, Anti-Colonial sentiment's, which is why he chose York's organisation, because of this commitment towards assisting the plight of African-Americans. Born in rural Liberia during the 1930s, Minister Garlawolu was instrumental in the formation of the Liberian Government of National Unity, becoming its first Minister of Justice in 1996. During the World Conference on Racism held in 2001, Minister Garlawolu made an impassioned speech, which outlined many of his strong 'Afro-centered' beliefs and opposition to Colonialism/Neo-colonialism, Caucasian-Western Hegemony and the ongoing exploitation of African people, throughout the 'Diaspora':

Madam President, Ladies and Gentlemen

Madame President, My delegation would like to join previous speakers before us to congratulate you on your election to chair our deliberations. My delegation is convinced that with your wealth of experience we are expected to benefit from your chairmanship and that you can count on our fullest cooperation and support.

Consistent with its long standing policy and desire to rid the universe of every form of inhumanity, indignity, degradation and human suffering as evidentially and historically manifested in its undaunted campaigns and struggles for the absolute De-colonization and Total Liberation of Africa, Liberia unflinchingly supports further initiatives that would put finality to the abhorrent scourges of Racism and any concept or practice that would

reduce the natural status of the human person based on colour, religion or political ideology.
I am very glad that the God of conscience has inspired you great men and women of all races to gather here today to discuss the most decisive and appropriate means by which humanity may be totally redeemed from every form of injustice, which, if not immediately dealt with, shall place the destiny of weaker Nations and men into the vicious hands of powerful Nations.

It was through the efforts and dreams of great people like you that slavery, the worst form of injustice, was fought and debilitated; indeed, it was by the vision of men and women like you that colonialism found its untimely demise; yes, it was by the grace of God that apartheid was fought and finally defeated.
The questions which must be carefully considered and answered are:
Has slavery been totally banished from the face of the earth?
Are we sure that the surviving heirs of the slave Masters have not adroitly designed another chicanery to re introduce and maintain their slave estate?
Can we boast of the complete De-colonization of Africa when the colonialists have transformed themselves into business entrepreneurs?
My answer is No. A slave Master will always be a slave Master no matter the intricacy of time.
It is now clear that xenophobia, racial discrimination, sanction and the concept of Globalization are elements of slavery.

For example, let me take globalization from the African context. Our own African idea of a village is sample.
A village is run by a General Chief, Quarter Chief and a Council of elders. The overall Chief commands the Quarter Chief and influences decision of the Council of elders. Now with the creation of the envisaged global village, who is going to be the over all Chief - the Quarter Chief; and the Council of elders? We all know that America is going to be the General Chief while Great Britain the Quarter Chief with the Security Council as Council of elders. They are going to dictate the affairs of this village without any successful opposition. Today we see the United Nations endorsing the decisions of America and Great Britain to impose unjust sanctions on weaker Nations without due process of law.

Any African Leader who refuses to submit to their whims and caprices automatically becomes their target and is seriously victimized either by sanction or lack of economic aids.
Madame President, distinguished Ladies and gentlemen, I believe you have heard all sorts of negative things about Liberia and our President, Dr. Charles Ghankay Taylor.
These are all lies instigated by powerful Nations to purposely undermine the economic and social stability of Liberia.

Like some African Nations, Liberia has had a bitter experience of slavery. Some of our forefathers and mothers were forcibly taken from the soil of Liberia to the plantations of slave masters in the United States of America,

where they were treated as mere beasts. After the so-called emancipation, some of our people returned home and joined their indigenous parents to re establish a Nation called Liberia.
Hence, Liberia formally gained her independence on July 26 1847.

Since our independence, the World Powers had always manipulated our Leaders, treating them as mere surrogates, stooges or puppets. Hence, many considered Liberia a puppet regime, directly taking orders from Washington. Then came Mr. Charles Ghankay Taylor, a patriotic Liberian, who led a civil uprising in 1989, against the most powerful military dictator, Mr. Samuel K. Doe, and deposed him in less than six months. Ironically, this despot was supported by the World Powers at the expense of the Liberian masses.
Of-course, with the hidden hands of the World Powers, several Warring Factions emerged to stop Mr. Taylor, but the Economic Community of West Africa swiftly intervened and effected disarmament with great success.
Consequently, the most transparent democratic election was held in 1997, with International Observers attesting to the results, which declared Mr. Taylor as winner with 85% of the votes among 12 Presidential Candidates.
Immediately after his inauguration President Taylor formed a Government of Inclusion, thus appointing several opposition members including warring factions ` Leaders to key positions. A Human Rights Commission was established by Legislative Enactment.

Presently, for the first time in the history of our country, there are over 11 print and electronic media institutions freely operating in Liberia. Since our democratic Elections neither America nor Great Britain has contributed a penny toward our reconstruction. They have persistently told Investors that Liberia is not safe for investment. This has seriously undermined our young democracy. How can people say that America supports democracy - maybe democracy in that context means submission to the will of America or mortgaging the sovereignty of one's country to them.

Further, we were asked to burn all our arms and ammunitions as a Pre-condition to receiving financial aids from them for our reconstruction, which we did in good faith, only to be attacked by dissidents with British weapons, a week thereafter. We filed a formal complaint or protest with the United Nations but, to our utter dismay, the only response we got was to re-enforce the armed embargo against us. Is this not genocidal?
Is this not a crime against humanity? We are betrayed. Indeed we are betrayed. The war is raging in Lofa. Some of the dissidents are conspicuously living in America and prosecuting war against our people; quite against International Law. Is this not another form of slavery - you want our people to perish from the planet. When this is done then you are happy.
Ladies and gentlemen, compounding this evil, the Security Council has endorsed the decision of America and Great Britain to impose Sanctions on the dying people of Liberia. Liberia is blessed with natural minerals including diamond. The bulk of our people survive through diamond

mining. The unjust sanctions bars them from mining and selling their own natural gift. How do you want them to live?

The sanction further bars the President and Cabinet Ministers from travelling out of Liberia to conduct the affairs of Government. Is this not a special form of slavery, where the movement of the slave is restricted? What a travesty of justice.

The purported reason for the sanction was diamond smuggling and gun running to support rebels in Sierra Leone. There has been no iota of evidence to substantiate this false allegation. Prior to the imposition of sanction, Liberia never enjoyed the benefit of any hearing or to say the least due process of law - the law which hears before it convicts. This is against international principle of justice.

I also understand that these World Powers are trying to impose another sanction on the sale of logs from Liberia for the reason that the masses are not benefiting from the proceeds thereof.

This is not only false but malicious because the little taxes collected from logging Companies are used to recondition and build roads for the people - reconstruct or renovate their damaged and dilapidated public structures such as clinics and schools. The people of Liberia have been de-humanized. They love and support their President because he has refused to be a puppet and to mortgage their sovereignty for a penny.

This is why the Powerful Nations are using the International media and exiled politicians to Demonize President Taylor and Liberia. But the God that created the universe will not allow us to perish from the face of the earth.

Madame President, reverting to the subject of slavery, we seriously condemn, denounce, decry and deprecate every form of slavery, past or present.

Under the Universal principle of justice, every injury has a remedy therefore.

Hence, reparation is the remedy commensurate with the gravity of the incalculable injuries so unbearably inflicted on the people of Africa by slave Masters. I believe that reparation should also cover the depletion of our natural resources by Imperialists. - they must pay sufficient damages to those countries whose children were enslaved and natural resources unjustly exploited and depleted. They must also adequately compensate African Americans rather than just giving few of them little opportunity or token while the masses suffer.

We therefore recommend the following:

1. That the imposition of sanctions against any democratically elected Government or group of individuals be considered a crime against humanity. This is another form of slavery because it subjects the masses to great suffering, thereby reducing them to mere beggars and further divesting them of their human dignity.

2. That debt burden being an imperialist instrument often used to debilitate and economically strangle smaller Nation's, it should be waived against any Nation incapable of repayment, without pre-condition.

3. That refusal of any International Financial or Lending Institutions to grant loans to a needed country without any just cause, shall constitute a crime against humanity. We believe that every Nation should have the right to development and a Nation State that lacks the basic infrastructure to support its economic, social and political needs is incapable of providing the requisite enabling environment where individual development is ascertained.

(Minister Garlawolu, 2001)

Figs.274 & 275 Diplomatic Ties: **Left- Right:** *Liberian Minister Francis Garlawolu & Minister Garlawolu standing with Malachi York's Daughter Richelle York, Outside The Liberian Embassy*

Malachi York's other objective aside from the prestige of being Honoured by an African Government, may have also been to begin the cultivation of the Nuwaubian doctrine on the African continent, which would have had a tremendous effect in combating the dominant 'Colonial' or Slave Mentality held by many native African's on the Continent towards Whites as 'Culturally' Superior. Possibly fearing for the future security of the organisation in Putnam County, especially from the growing pressure from Federal Investigators and racist local officials, York may have probably began looking at other options such as Repatriation to Africa for possibly himself and his followers, should the need ever arise.

York also instructed his followers to get more involved with Political and Civil Rights organisations such as The NAACP and the Rainbow PUSH Coalition, to gain the support of these organisations. Therefore it was not long before some of the big names of the African American political spectrum began taking notice of the Nuwaubian's plight.

Rev. Al Sharpton

On the cloudy morning of September 15th 1999, veteran civil rights activist of the National Action Network, Rev. Alfred C. Sharpton, arrived at the Nuwaubian property to lend his support, accompanied by an influential entourage of distinguished individuals, which included:

- **Dr. Bill Howell of the Rainbow PUSH Coalition**
- **Rev. Alexander Smith & Rev. Thomas Oglesby of the NAACP**
- **Rev. Markel Hutchinson, President of the National Youth Connection**
- **Dr. Ander, Chairman of the United African Movement**
- **Attorney Alton Maddocks, Publisher and Entrepreneur**

Fig.276 *Rev. Al Sharpton*

Also present were a number of other key individuals more closely affiliated with York's Movement, such as: Attorney Lewis Clayton Jones, Renee McDade & Pastor Marshal Chance, National Spokesperson for the recently defunct Holy Tabernacle Ministries. As well as Dr. York's half-brother Oba Oyo Al Hajji, founder & leader of the New York based African Islamic Hebrew Mission (A.I.M.), a staunch supporter of York since the days of the Ansaaru Allah Community in Brooklyn N.Y.

This was a truly historic day for the Nuwaubian's, as it was the first time in the group's 30-year history, that York had made an alliance with such a high Profile African-American leader. After York had made a brief speech, it was the turn of Rev. Al Sharpton to address the crowd. Following an introduction by Rev. Markel Hutchinson, Rev. Al Sharpton took to the podium, and launched into a fiery speech in which he accused the Putnam officials of *"Racial Profiling"*. The following is the complete transcript of the speech made by Rev. Al Sharpton in 1999:

> I want to pick up where Brother Markel left off. We, in Black America or Blacks in America, come from different traditions, but from the same people. We have in our community different houses, but they are all in the same block. If they are allowed to violate your house, and mine is next door, it's only a matter of time before they use the violation of your house, to attack my house. They will tell you in the media the issue of what is

going on here. They say (that it's what you preach), but preaching is not illegal. You could say what ever you want to say, preach whatever you want to preach. What they have to answer to is where the law is being broken. If sheriffs run behind preachers, then I could show them a whole lot of preachers they need to be messing with. First of all, there are plenty of groups that have property in Georgia that we ought to be examining, that are up in those properties, planning the harm of people based on their race. This group is not planning anything, but trying to enhance their own people. With all those militia groups around Georgia, and you worry about a man that is preaching, rather than others that are plotting, planning and executing violence against people. Then you'll understand why many of us in the civil rights Community Say we are not going to sit by and allow you to target unlawfully. People based on you; disagreeing with what they say, when they have not violated the law. Because if you can do it here, you will do it everywhere. 'Well, Rev. Sharpton, what about the Nuwaubian's?' 'Well, it will be the Baptist tomorrow.' It will be 'the Holiness the day after tomorrow.

Once you begin to redefine the law, we got enough sense to know it can go from one to another. 'But we don't agree with what Dr. York says. 'Well that's why he bought enough acres to say what he wants to say, whether or not you agree or not. Dr. York is not busting up in folk's churches preaching. He is preaching in his church. And he has a right to do that. What I'm trying to say is. What the sheriff must do is deal with the letter of the law, and not allow the media to make the non-issue the issue. It's not Dr. York trying to stop affirmative action in Atlanta. You are on your own area dealing with your own ideology. That's your right. The people that are bringing hate to Georgia are the ones, after 300 years of slavery and 100 years of apartheid, trying to turn back the clock and deny us our civil and human rights.' That is not what he is trying to advocate. That is what they are advocating in Atlanta, Georgia. And the problem of racial profiling is not only on the highways. Racial profiling is when you look at a group that buys land to practice their religion. And you profile them differently than another group that you say has the right to do that, whether your name is York or Albanathy. They use the criminal justice system to profile us differently. And some of us don't care how much you criticize us. We gonna stand for what's right no matter what.

Young was telling me this morning. How some conservative White woman got on T.V. and called me a bigot. And I don't preach against anybody. I don't even call people devils, but I'm a bigot. Why? Cause I don't scratch where it don't itch. I don't laugh at what's not funny. And I don't ask for permission to go where I want to go. If they ask me to come down to see what they are doing here. Can't nobody in the United States tell me not to come. I'm going to go wherever I feel is necessary to go. And if Janet Reno can check out what happened to folks in Waco, Al Sharpton is going to see what's happening with his own people right here.

Now, Let me also clear up something else. Well. Markel said that Martin Luther King would be here and I am sure the media would say that's not true. Well, go back in your history. 1966, there was a march in Mississippi. James Meredith led the march. It was called, 'The March Against Fear.' As

James Meredith led the march, somebody shot him down. Dr. King flew in to Mississippi to his bedside. At his bedside was Stokely Charmichael later to change his name to Kwame Ture. And Floyd Magensin, and they all decided to finish that march. People said, 'Well Dr. King, you ought not to march with Stokely 'cause Stokely uses the term, Black Power. Stokely is a Black racist. 'They say Dr. King said, "I will continue to march; he can say what he say; I say what I say, but you cannot separate me from standing up for what I believe in and tell me who to walk with. Later that year, he went to Chicago to lead an open housing fight. One of the first stops, he went down to…Boulevard to meet with the Honourable Elijah Muhammad. Even though the Messenger Elijah Muhammad preached one thing and Dr. King preached another, there was mutual respect. It has only been in the last decade where people have tried to make us not like one another, and denounce one another. Like we can't sit down and understand where we agree and where we disagree. We are grown people. If you are a grown man or woman you can discuss your differences. If I got a disagreement with Dr. York's theology, we are intelligent enough to debate that. But we don't need somebody else telling us who to talk to. I am a grown man with children, I walk when I want to walk, talk to who I want to talk to, and back down to nobody.

Strange day, and this is Georgia. When I was growing up, they wanted Black folks to stay off by themselves. Now Y'all done that, it seems like they still ain't satisfied. They didn't want us downtown, so y'all have moved out of downtown. Out here. All the way out here. I don't even know where I'm at. You don't want us in the country, you don't want us in the city, you don't want us next door. You just don't want us at all. And we are not just going to walk away, kill ourselves so you can become satisfied. And if we stood back and allowed them to do wrong, then you would say 'where were all the people? That's why NAACP is here and Rainbow PUSH. Matter of fact, Rainbow PUSH called and invited me. Because people understand, as Markel says a threat of injustice anywhere, is a threat to injustice everywhere'.

Last point, Doctor, the media would say, "Well, Reverend Sharpton". Like they like me. They call us everything but a child of God and didn't want us to turn around and call each other names. And mad at us for what? Standing up for our rights. "What are they doing there with them pyramids? Because we built the first pyramids. The problem is that whether we approach it from different religions, approach it from different ideologies, we are the same people that understand that we must come into a consciousness of ourselves, and we must understand that we are not inferior Negroes of America. We are the original people of the planet. We are the people made in the image of God.

I can't love God and deny that God made me as a reflection of him. When God made man. God made us. When God said, let there be light, he was talking to us. When God said, let there be knowledge, he gave it to us, We had a conversation, and it became philosophy. We started counting, and it became algebra and mathematics. We gazed into the sky and it became astrology. I know why you are afraid, cause you know who we are. And you are afraid. We will not sit by and allow the rights of people to be violated. We will not allow the right to practice religion to be violated, or the right to free speech to be violated.

People have the right to practice their religion and their speech. If they are not violating the law they do not need a sheriff, unless the law is being violated. The sheriff needs to spend his time on those that are racially profiling Black folks 1-20. He needs to spend his time with those that are discriminating against employment right here in this community. But those that want to develop a sense of who they are, and return to the roots of civilization, by building their instruments and pyramids and depicted as criminals.

So, that is why we come and stand today to say we are not going to allow a double standard to occur. We are not going to sit quietly by and allow people's rights to be violated. Whether you and I pray the same way or not, we both have a right to pray. And there ain't but one God, and I leave you with this. 'As long as God is in charge, it doesn't matter who the sheriff is. If you don't believe God is in charge why is everybody running from hurricane Floyd. Tell the sheriff to turn the hurricane around. The God I serve can come through here and get everybody's attention. The God we serve has power and domination over the heavens and earth, and if you mess with his people. He will stand and give us the power to stand up for what's right.

So don't get weary. Don't back down. Don't buckle. Don't bend, Don't bow: stand up for your rights. Stand up for the rights to own your land. To raise your children in a moral and ethical manner. Not to grow up and be some Hollywood Negroes. But to be Egyptian African Princess and Kings and Queens that they are. Stand up in the name of Marcus Messiah Garvey. Stand up in the name of our fallen ancestors, because they depend on us, that they would pass the baton on to our generation. And we would be the warriors that will walk into the 21st Century with our shoulders thrown back. With our heads held high. With our fists lifted. "UP, YOU MIGHTY RACE; UP, YOU MIGHTY RACE; UP, YOU MIGHTY RACE! YOU CAN IF YOU WILL!"

(Rev. Al Sharpton, 1999)

Clearly, Rev. Al Sharpton was slightly overwhelmed by the unorthodoxy of the Nuwaubian's, however he did his best to raise their spirits during a very difficult time for the organisation, by giving a speech designed to encourage them not to give up. As one eyewitness commented after the speech, *"Even though the day started out cloudy, the sun was shining high and bright by the time both men finished speaking. Rev. Dr. Malachi. Z. York-El reminded the people of the strength they have and Rev. Sharpton brought the spirit down here and turn it around."*

Fig.277 United Front: *Dr. Malachi. Z. York walking with Rev. Al Sharpton during visit to Tama*

Interestingly, following he's visit to the Nuwaubian Village, Rev. Al Sharpton appeared in public for the first time in his career wearing a full-beard, almost identical to that worn by Dr. York. Although Sharpton would later remove it and return to his traditional 'Clean Shaven' look, there was definitely something different about him, after his encounter with York, which has lead some to speculate that Rev. Sharpton may have been influenced, at least to some small degree by the Nuwaubian leader.

Fig.278: *Bearded Al Sharpton speaking to reporters in New York following he's encounter With the Nuwaubian Leader*

Rev. Jessie Jackson

As time passed, York's organisation began to enjoy further support from the NAACP and Rainbow/PUSH Coalition. First former Augusta NAACP President Rev. Alexander Smith, pledged his support for the Nuwaubian's, along with Southern Regional Director of Rainbow/PUSH Coalition Joe Beasley, & GABEO President Representative Tyrone Brooks who often spoke on York's behalf. However, outside support for the Nuwaubian's reached its crescendo in August 2001, when former Presidential candidate and Rainbow/PUSH Coalition founder Rev. Jessie Jackson, made the Nuwaubian Village 'Tama-re' the first stop of his Southern Tour, to lend his support to Dr. Malachi. Z. York. Among the dignitaries present on this historic occasion were:

Fig.279 Rev. Jessie Jackson

- **Jack Ellis, Mayor of Macon Georgia**
- **Joe Beasley, Regional Director of Rainbow/PUSH Coalition**
- **Tyrone Brooks, Atlanta State Representative**
- **Alexander Smith, President of Augusta branch of the NAACP**
- **Jimmy Cliff, Legendary Singer/Song writer**

The event was marked by Rev. Jessie Jackson's speech, in which he pointed out, much to the displeasure of the Mainstream Media, that the ***"Nuwaubian's are Living the American Dream"***. Rev. Jackson also went onto state:

> We all have the right to expect in America equal protection under the law, equal opportunity, equal access and fair share...you have the right to own land and build and grow and register to vote and educate. This is the American dream...The South has harmed itself with laws of race division...we've learned to live apart, which in many ways is ungodly. We must now learn to live together, which is divine, and right and the intention...Nuwaubian's, you can define the new Georgia. A Georgia of love, a Georgia of caring, a Georgia free of drugs, free of violence, free of crime, free of hate...the new Georgia, the new South, the new land. Keep hope alive!
>
> (Jackson, 2001)

At the end of his speech, Rev. Jackson also encouraged all present, who were not registered to vote, to come to the front and fill out a voter registration form, which were also being distributed amongst the crowd.

After his visit to the Nuwaubian property Rev. Jessie Jackson, again reiterated to reporters *"It's a joy to meet with the Nuwaubian's. In many ways, they are living the American dream...They must have their rights protected...The federal government must protect their right to vote."*

Fig.280 *Rev. Jessie Jackson holding hands with York's Brother Oba York-Muhammad*

Fig.281 Murdered: *Sheriff Darwin Brown*

Another Georgian Official closely associated with the group was the late Sheriff of Athens County, Darwin Brown. Sheriff Brown, a decorated Police officer with over 22 years experience in law enforcement, was an open supporter and an initiate of York's teachings. Tragically Sheriff Brown was killed under suspicious circumstances on December 15th 2000. To this day no culprit has ever been brought to justice for Sheriff Brown's murder, however many of York's supporters suspect that his Murder may have been linked to enemies of the Nuwaubian movement within Putnam County's Sheriff's Department. At a banquet held by the Nuwaubian's in November 2001, the late Sheriff Brown was honoured and referred to by Dr. York as *"a great Nuwaubian...in the ranks of Dr. Martin Luther King Jr., Hosea Williams, and Medgar Evers..."*

Wesley Snipes

By now the conflict between the Nuwaubian's and the Putnam County officials appeared farcical to most outsiders. However events took an even more bizarre twist in early 2000, when it was reported that Hollywood action star Wesley Snipes had become a member of the Nuwaubian Nation. The story first broke after it was announced on the Nuwaubian website <www.factology.com>, that actor Wesley Snipes was now a Nuwaubian. Amongst other senseless boasts, the website claimed:

Fig.282 Wesley Snipes

> The Royal Guard of Amen Ra is an organisation owned by a Nubian, namely Wesley Snipes, who also owns Amen Ra productions and is a proud Nubian/ Nuwaubian...He is moving to Putnam County and with him comes more money and power...All Nuwaubian's will join his elite force for training. We will stop at nothing to drive the evil out of Putnam County
> (factology.com, 2000)

This vain outburst, by the Nuwaubian's, is customary of the group's political immaturity, and even to a large extent the movement's leader, Malachi York himself, who has often spoken first, before considering the repercussions of his words. The irresponsible threat to *"join his elite force for training"* and *"stop at nothing to drive the evil out of Putnam County"* was promptly used by the Media against Wesley Snipes, just like York's naïve announcement in the presence of undercover reporters in 1997, outlining his plans to declare the organisation's 'Sovereignty' from the United States. In the past, many of the problems encountered by the Nuwaubian's have been caused by their policy of talking too much. It is common knowledge that York's teachings have either directly or indirectly influenced many Black celebrities throughout the years, therefore there is no reason to entirely rule out Wesley Snipes' observance of the Nuwaubian philosophy. The names of the actor's Security & Film production companies; Amen Ra Films, Royal Guard of Amen Ra & Black Dot Productions do certainly reflected his adherence of Egyptology which York has been teaching since the late 1960s. However, because of the way members of the group handled the controversy surrounding Wesley Snipes' plans to purchase the property, the actor was left with no alternative except to publicly distance himself from York's organisation.

In an attempt to draw a connection between Snipes and the Nuwaubian's, Macon Telegraph reporter Rob Peecher stated in an article entitled: *"Snipes' Company may buy property: Actor's Amen-Ra films is interested in Putnam land adjacent to Nuwaubian's"*:

Snipes' production company, Amen-Ra films, owns The Royal Guard of Amen-Ra, the company planning to purchase the acreage, according to Snipes spokeswoman Justine Hah...

(Peecher, 2000)

The actor's intentions may well have been to relocate to Georgia, not to lead any type of Crusade, *"to drive all of the Nuwaubian's enemies from Putnam County"*, but simply to put into practice many of the positive aspects of York's teachings, such as doing for self, owning land and exploring different business opportunities, which many in Georgia would have benefited from, including the Nuwaubian's enemies. However thanks to the childish outburst by the Nuwaubian spokesperson, this could no longer be possible, nor could Snipes' business opportunities be perused.

Not long after the Nuwaubian announcement, the Enquirer magazine featured an article entitled: *"Wesley Snipes: I'm not a Nuwaubian"*, which described the Nuwaubian's as a type of wacky cult. In an attempt to immediately distance himself from the controversy the actor denied any involvement with the group in order to freely conduct his business. A spokesperson for Snipes went onto tell the magazine's reporter Patricia Shipp:

> Wesley is in no way involved with those lunatics, the Nuwaubian's. He was looking at property down there because he has family in town – not to be part of their Egyptian nonsense. Wesley wanted to start a security company for high profile personalities.
>
> (Shipp, 2000)

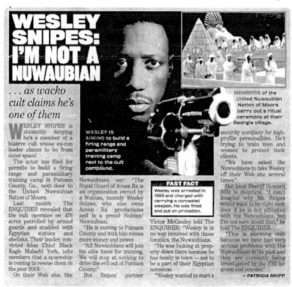

Fig.283 Afro-Centric Hollywood Action Hero:
Wesley Snipes in Enquirer Magazine Article

It later emerged that the actor's brother, Rudy Snipes had been instructed to buy 200 acres of land adjoining 404 Shady Dale Road in 2000, to be used as a **'Security Guard Training Facility'** for a Corporate security company, named 'The Royal Guard of Amen Ra'. Not dissimilar to The Nation of Islam's security companies, who have provided security for a number of 'A-list' celebrities such as R. Kelly and Michael Jackson. Also note that the NOI's security are viewed as one of the best in the business, and is kept completely separate from the group's religious ideology. Wesley Snipes' company even advertised vacancies on the employment website <www.cooljobs.com>, in which the vacancy was open to *"All Nationalities"*:

Security Officer
The Royal Guard of Amen Ra

The Royal Guard of Amen Ra, an international, multi-level security and protection company was founded by the world renown motion picture actor Wesley Snipes and is establishing an elite team of highly trained men and women who will provide the following services:
- International and Domestic Risk Management
- Intelligence and Protective Operations
- V.I.P. / Executive Protection to Dignitary and Celebrities
- Special Event Security
- Counter-surveillance and Counter Terrorist Measures

They are seeking approximately 200 Professional Security Agents. Those chosen will undergo an intensive training and certification program provided by the Royal Guard's Elite. The Royal Guard's Elite is a cohesive team of experienced, expertly trained security professionals from various backgrounds and continents. **Men and Women of all nationalities need apply**………

(www.cooljobs.com, 2002)

Fig.284 *Nation of Islam Professional Security Service*

Clearly the company was to be formed for the purpose of training 'Professional' Security Guards of "all racial backgrounds", not simply 'Nubians', as the Nuwaubian's foolishly suggested. Neither did the advert makes any mention of driving anybody out of Putnam County.

Despite the obvious professionalism of Wesley Snipes' company, his plans eventually became dragged into the petty racial quagmire of Putnam County. With Sheriff Sills, proving just how much of a threat he viewed York's organisation, and how racially motivated he really was when he personally involved himself in Wesley Snipes' business dealings. Even though the actor repeatedly denied any involvement with the group, Sheriff Sills stated to the Enquirer magazine:

> I can't imagine why Mr. Snipes would want to be right next door if he is not affiliated with the Nuwaubian's, but I'm not sure about that...This is alarming only because we have had very serious problems with the Nuwaubian's in the past and they are currently being investigated by the FBI for arson and murder.
>
> (Shipp, 2000)

On May 11th 2000 The Macon Telegraph featured another article by Rob Peecher, entitled: *"Snipes' Company may buy property: Actor's Amen-Ra films is interested in Putnam land adjacent to Nuwaubian's"*. In which, the Nuwaubian's further enflamed the situation by again claiming that Wesley Snipes was a member of their movement, in spite of the actor's wishes to remain publicly anonymous. Al Woodall, a supposed agent for the Nuwaubian's took the reporters bait, and by so doing destroyed any chances of Snipes' company purchasing the property at 290 Shady Dale Road by stating in the interview:

> Snipes is actually an avid Nuwaubian...what I'm hearing is there are a few Nuwaubian millionaires from the music industry, the movie industry, business, finance, from different aspects – but they're all millionaires, including Malachi York. And from what I'm hearing, they are planning on buying the property in Putnam County...
>
> (Peecher, 2000)

Even though Snipes' spokesperson Justine Hah denied any connection to the group, the persistent outbursts and empty boasts of York's followers, played right into the hands of those who did not wish to see any more Blacks purchasing land in the County, leading the actor's business dealings to become sabotaged by Nuwaubian nemesis Sheriff Richard Sills, who was as ever on hand to provide his opinion to the Macon Telegraph reporter:

> I had heard rumours about it, but I hadn't heard anything lately until yesterday, when I got a call from an inspector with the BAFT...He was following up on the application for federal firearms dealer licence that The Royal Guard of Amen Ra, Inc., had applied for back in December...Snipes stated that the business has complied with state and local laws, but does not take into account that property is zoned for agricultural purposes and "a for-profit security company and firearms dealer" is certainly not an agricultural business.
>
> (Peecher, 2000)

Notice how Sheriff Richard Sills pretended to have only recently heard a rumour concerning Wesley Snipes plans to buy the property, yet he had told the Enquirer magazine reporter Patricia Shipp, in a previous interview that:

"I can't imagine why Mr. Snipes would want to be right next door if he is not affiliated with the Nuwaubian's", proving that he was already aware of the actors plans to purchase the property next to the Nuwaubian's, and was clearly opposed to the idea from the outset. This is why he mentioned the issue of 'Zoning Restrictions', which was not any of his business as Sheriff, but the jurisdiction of the County Building inspector. The landowner Mr. Stanley Bishop, who is Caucasian, even admitted that when he was initially approached by the actor's agent Rudy Snipes, he had absolutely no idea of where the land was, or any connection to the Nuwaubian's.

Sure enough, a story later appeared on August 10th 2000, in Online Athens entitled: *"Wesley Snipes denied building permits"* 12, which demonstrated the power Sheriff Richard Sills has in the County, in influencing the racially motivated policy of Putnam County's decisions, which the Nuwaubian's had been suffering under for so many years:

> **EATONTON** – The Putnam County Commission has denied two of the three building permits that would be needed for actor Wesley Snipes to open a private security training centre in middle Georgia.
>
> The commission rejected permits last week for a weapons storage building and a 30-stall firing range. The county zoning board had earlier denied all three permits on grounds that the land is zoned for agricultural use. But the commission overruled the zoning board and granted one permit – for a guard shack at the front of the property.
>
> Snipes company, The Royal Guard of Amen Ra, had wanted to buy 257 acres in Putnam county from Stanley Bishop, a Lithonia contractor, for a camp to train security guards for celebrity protection, countersurveillance and counterterrorism.
>
> Bishop, who filed for the building permits, says Snipes' contract to buy the land has expired. But Putnam County Sheriff Howard Sills told the commission that Snipes' company is trying to sneak the school in by getting the building permits through Bishop.
>
> "It's about trying to backdoor something," said Sills. David Cooper, the attorney representing Bishop, charged that the county's motivation in denying the permits is racial.
>
> (Online Athens, 2000)

Wesley Snipes' security business would have brought job opportunities to both black and white people in Georgia, and probably helped the actor to earn good money out of the venture. The Company's expertise in 'Counter Terrorist Measures' could have even assisted the County to someday combat the menace of International Terrorism, should it ever arise. However, thanks to the immaturity of the Nuwaubian's, and the blatant racist bigotry of Sheriff Howard R. Sills and his cohorts at the Putnam Zoning board, the actor's plans had to be eventually abandoned in Georgia. This episode now proved beyond a shadow of a doubt, the lengths Sheriff Sills was prepared to go to destroy Dr. Malachi. Z. York and anyone even remotely connected with his organisation. Later that year, in one last desperate bid to rid themselves of Sheriff Sills, the Nuwaubian's heeded Rev. Jessie Jackson's advice, and attempted to remove Sheriff Howard R. Sills from office, by registering a block vote and encouraged the county's residence to vote in favour of Sills' opponent. Unfortunately for the Nuwaubian's, these plans were defeated, when Sheriff Sills was re-elected by a majority of 72 % of votes, and to make matters worse a three-judge panel later decided to purge the names of all Nuwaubian's from the County's voters roll.

Nuwaubian's Work on Public Profile

Sensing the imminent threat to himself and his followers, and possibly growing weary of the negative Media publicity, York launched what can be best described as a series of public and philanthropic (charity) engagements aimed at improving the organisation's public image and countering the negative portrayal the Nuwaubian's had been receiving from the media.

The new Millennium began on a positive note for the Nuwaubian's who amazed tourists and residents of the Nation's capital, when 500 of them lead by their Spiritual Leader; Dr. Malachi. Z. York descended upon Washington D.C., to conduct an Ancient Egyptian prayer ceremony at the recently refurbished Washington Monument. The monument, which is in fact an Ancient Egyptian Obelisk originally stolen from Africa and brought to the United States, was placed in Washington in honour of George Washington on July 1848. York accompanied by members of his Fraternity the **'Ancient Egiptian Order'**, referring to themselves as members of Atum Re's Royal Court, stunned onlookers when they appeared at the memorial dressed in an array of brightly coloured costumes, and began circling the 55 sq. ft. base of the 555 ft. ancient Obelisk praying and chanting in the groups own Nuwaubic language. The event was witnessed by number of journalists and news agencies, including CNN, but amazingly received absolutely no mention the next day in the media. However had the event attracted trouble, it would have almost certainly received wide media coverage.

During the ceremony York delivered a special prayer in Nuwaubic, and then asked for good fortune for Washington D.C and the entire United States, as well as health and prosperity for President William. J. Clinton as well as the First Lady, Hilary Rodham Clinton. After the event, Nuwaubian spokesperson, Ah Hotep Meduty Re, summed up the media attitude to the historic event as follows:

> For the media to record, but not report such a ceremony of great significance, is keeping the children of the ancient Obelisk and Mound builders hidden. This is a blatant disrespect to the Gods who control the elements that were asked to protect the monument...Those who witnessed this New Millennium Inauguration Ceremony of the Washington Monument may talk about it for years to come and is indeed one for the record books."

Fig.285 *Malachi York accompanied by followers, during Tour of Washington D.C. in 2000*

2001 proved to be one of the group's busiest years since their arrival in Georgia, with York's new strategy of making his followers come into more direct contact with the public in order to dispel the media's attempts at portraying them as a dangerous Cult. Fortunately for the Nuwaubian's these events received some coverage by the media, which did a lot to improve the organisations public image at the time. On Febuary 25th 2001, The Augusta Chronicle ran an article entitled: *"Parade Honors Black History"*. In it, reporter Lisa. M. Lohr described how members of The United Nuwaubian Nation of Moors held their annual "Nuwaubian" Black History Month Parade in Augusta Georgia, on the 24/02/01. Lisa Lohr went on to state:

> The Langey-Walker community was a sea of black and gold Saturday as the Ancient Egiptian Order paraded through the streets in honor of Black History Month.
>
> (Lohr, 2001)

In a subtle, yet spectacular show of strength, thousands of Nuwaubian's amazed and dazzled local residents and spectators by marching through the streets of Augusta, Georgia during the Black History Month Parade in their brightly coloured costumes, holding banners in a procession which literally lasted for hours, were incorporated into the movement, represented were the respective Fraternities, and Religious group's such as:

- **Arabic Nobles of the Mystic Shrines, Inc. Al Mahdi Shrine Temple No. 19**
- **The Grand Lodge Ancient Free & Accepted Masons Inc.**
- **The Ancient Egiptian Order of the World Inc.**
- **The Egiptian Church of Karast "Christ" Inc.**
- **The Brotherhood of Sutukh "Set"**
- **Eastern Stars**
- **Sisters of Aset**
- **Ancient Mystic Order of Melchizedek**
- **Daughters of Isis**

Other organisations invited to participate included:

- NAACP of Athens & Augusta
- Rainbow Push Coalition
- Belle Terrace Marching Units
- The Forte Gordon Dynamic Steppers
- Tobacco Road Elementary Gentlemen Steppers
- The Forte Gordon Marching Band

Figs.286, 287, 288, 289, 290, 299, 291, 292, 293 & 294 Show of Strength:
Nuwaubians during Black History Month Parade in Augusta, Georgia in 2001

Also present at the occasion was Rev. Alexander Smith, President of Augusta branch of the NAACP, who along with Malachi York's sister Grand Matron, Debra Jean York, and daughter; Hagar York, accepted awards on behalf of the organisation. During the event, the Nuwaubian's once again caused outrage amongst members of the White community, after they got the Mayor of Augusta, Georgia, The Honorable Bob Young to sign and authorise a "Proclamation" which basically expounded the Nuwaubian doctrine, and proved to be an excellent public relations stunt. The "Proclamation" officially presented to the Nuwaubian's on the 24th Febuary 2001 from "The City of Augusta", stated the following:

Proclamation

IN RECOGNITION of "Nuwaubian Black History Month Parade Day"

WHEREAS, the Nuwbuns were the dark, brown to black skin wooly hair original Egyptians (Egiptians). Who are confirmed on the walls of every temple, Mir (pyramid), Sebkhet (pylon, granite stone) and Tekenu (Obelisk needle) there is; and

WHEREAS, the Black race's greatness has been accepted in America and many books as people of Timbuktu Africa or the Olmecians from Uganda, Africa who migrated and walked here to North and South America to setup colonies way before the continental drift, and were accepted as running the richest trading expeditions ever; and

WHEREAS, Nuwaubian's are the indigenous people of Egypt, "Tahites" or the Tu'af, who are descendants from Tah who was called Ptah meaning "opener". Theses names proceeded Egipt, which is a Greek word, called Aheegooptos meaning "burnt faces" (black), as well as the word Kemet, which comes from Kham (Ham), the son of Noah, in late usage, collective name for Egyptians; and

WHEREAS, Imperial Grand Potentate Rev. Dr. Malachi. Z. York, 33 degree Deputy Grand Master of the State of Georgia and Rameses 2 Lodge No. 9, affiliated with the Most Worshipful Pride of Georgia Grand Lodge AF7Am.
And Noble of the Ancient Arabic Order of Mystic Shrine of Mecca Temple No. 1, 33-degree Inspector General of the Scottish Rite Freemasonry and Supreme Grand Hierophant of the Ancient Egiptian Order, who's brain child, was a whole Egyptian Village built in Eatonton, Georgia's Putnam County based on Egyptian Masonic Architecture, thus circumventing the plan eliminating the Nuwaubian culture, tradition and beliefs; and

WHEREAS, the first Annual Nuwaubian Black History Month Parade is aimed at recognizing all significant Great African-American Leaders, who have made a difference in the African-Americans lives and struggle for human equality in the past, present and future

NOW THEREFORE, I Bob Young, Mayor of the City of Augusta, do hereby proclaim February 24, 2004 to "NUWAUBIAN BLACK HISTORY MONTH PARADE DAY".
IN WITNESS THEREOF, I have unto set my hand and caused the seal of Augusta, Georgia to be affixed this thirtieth day of February 2001.

Figs.295, 296 & 297 Left- Right: *Mayor of Augusta, Bob Young, Mayor's Proclamation & NAACP President Rev. Alexander Smith*

The "Proclamation" prepared by the Nuwaubian's in advance, caused much embarrassment for Mayor Young, because many people mistakenly thought that it contained Mayor Young's own words, a point the Nuwaubian's seized the opportunity to exploit to great effect, and even thanked the Mayor in their flyer being circulated at the time, which stated:

> We would like to thank the Honorable Mayor Bob Young for not being part of the racism, hate propaganda, and slandering news of the media...
> (Nuwaubian's Parade bulletin, 2001)

Mayor Young now under Political pressure to distance himself from the "Proclamation" which contained his signature, told reporters that he had no prior knowledge of the contents of the Proclamation. In an article that appeared in Online Athens, entitled: *"Nuwaubian's' notoriety in Georgia growing"* reporter Vicky Eckenrode, explained Mayor Bob Young's position, on Tuesday, February 27th:

> Augusta Mayor Bob Young said he has had limited interaction with local Nuwaubian's. "The Nuwaubian people – whoever they are are – they contacted us, they made arrangements to have a parade in Augusta, and then they asked for a proclamation to recognize their parade," he said.
> That proclamation was not written nor seen by Mr. Young before being released...Mayor Young said it is not unusual for groups to write their own proclamation. "Typically, the organisation or individual that's asking for the proclamation will write up the information, and then what my staff does is put it into proper format," he said.
> (Eckenrode, 2001)

Figs.298 & 299 Left- Right: *York's Sister; Debra Jean York & Rev. Alexander Smith Accepting Mayor Young's Proclamation on behalf of Nuwaubian Nation during Parade*

By this stage York's influence began to spread and grow to many other parts of the State of Georgia, and according to the 'Georgia Informer' newspaper, the Nuwaubian leader was now recognised as: **'One of the 50 Most Influential Black Men within the State of Georgia'**, often aligning himself with many of Georgia's high profile Political Elite. This was mainly as a result of the Nuwaubian's activities under the name: Al Mahdi Shrine Temple No. 19, who were getting involved in various charity causes which included a 3,000 canned food donation to the Salvation Army. The generous donation was reported by Online Athens reporter, Jim Thompson, in an article entitled: *"Nuwaubian leader assists with canned food drive"*, dated Thursday July 12th 2001:

> The canned food drive was a cooperative effort of central Georgia's Al Mahdi Shrine Temple No. 19 and Black Men of Athens, a group whose community activities include mentoring youth.
>
> (Thompson, 2001)

Fig.300 *Malachi York shaking hands with Atlanta dignitaries*

Then on November 26th 2001, the Macon Telegraph featured an article entitled *"Help Wanted"*, which made reference to the plight of the "Atomic Star" track team, who desperately needed money to compete in the USA Track & National Cross Country Meet in Lincoln, Nebraska. When Dr. York heard about the plight of these young athletes, he was said to have personally provided a check of $4,000, under the name of Al Mahdi Shrine Temple No. 19, which covered all of the costs needed by the team.

Figs. Charity Work: 301 & 302 Top & Bottom: *Advert asking for donations to the 'Atomic Star' Track & Field Team & Malachi York with members of 'Atomic Star' Track & Field Team*

Despite these and other noble efforts made by the Nuwaubian's to improve relations, an incident occurred in 2001, which should have alerted the group to the danger they still faced, and serve as a warning to them to immediately leave both Putnam & Macon Counties, before its was too late. The incident began when the Nuwaubian leadership intercepted a "Bogus Flyer" being circulated to his followers and affiliates claiming that Dr. Malachi. Z. York had announced a "Special Alert" to all Nuwaubian's living in the State of Georgia to immediately make their way to New York. This was eventually uncovered to be nothing more than an insidious and cynical hoax perpetrated against York's followers by local County officials, allegedly thought up by Attorney Francis Ford Nearn and of-course, Sheriff Richard Sills. Clearly this was yet another attempt by these officials to rid themselves of the Nuwaubian's, and at the same time illegally obtain their Land & Real Estate; through a series of Liens, Restraining Orders, Intimidation & Deceptive tactics, and were now trying to gain control of the Land through fraudulent means, by attempting to trick them into leaving the County using this "Bogus Flyer". The Flyer, which was printed on cheap paper showed a fuzzy photo of Malachi York on the front and contained the following message:

> "This Is A Special Alert From Malachi Z York To All Members Of The United Nuwaubian Nation Of Moors. Important Changes Have Been Made. The Space Ships Which Were Originally Expected To Hover Over Tama Re Enterprises In Eatonton Georgia Will Not Be Arriving In Eatonton Now, But Will Come To New York And Hover Over Our Holy Tabernacle Ministries Building. I Have Received Definite Word That The Space Ships Will Definitely Arrive On Sunday December…After 12 PM. All Members Of The Nuwaubian Nation Of Moors Are Hereby Alerted To Move To New York. Any Nuwaubian Found In Athens, Milledgeville, Eatonton, Milledgeville, And Anywhere Other Than New York, Will Not Be Able To Board The Space Ships. All Nuwaubian's Are Alerted To Cease Purchases Of Mobile Homes, All Jobs, Present Land Holdings And Unimportant Possessions Must Be Given Up Or Sold Because These Cannot Be Taken With You…Since The Space Ships Are Coming, It Makes No Sense To Register To Vote, Purchase Houses And Purchase Land Since You Must Shortly Give Them Up When The Space Ships Arrive"
>
> (Bogus Flyer, 2003)

Although it is not known who the actual author of this "Bogus Flyer" was, it was clearly somebody quite familiar with Nuwaubian literature. Although a crude attempt, the aim of this Flyer was for the Nuwaubian's to leave the State of Georgia en masse, and does demonstrate the lengths Local officials were willing to go, to get rid of York and his supporters from Putnam County. As usual the Nuwaubian's dismissed the incident, and promptly released a 'Rebuttal' entitled: *"Officials Latest Desperate Attempts To Run Nuwaubian's Out of Putnam County!"* in which they simply brushed it off as yet another example of the desperate stupidity of local officials.

Dr. York's Nuwaubian philosophy, not only threatened to divide the County along racial lines, but his Secessionist plans of separate 'Sovereign' African American Nation-State, were viewed as such as threat to the internal or 'National' security of the United States that plans were already underway to destroy the Nuwaubian leader by the Federal Government.

Moreover, if the officials were willing to go to the extent of effectively breaking the Law by illegally delivering fake documents to people's addresses, constituting 'Mail Fraud', there was no limit to what they were capable of. This was clearly an indication of things to come, therefore at this point, the Nuwaubian's should have seriously began considering relocating their movement.

Nevertheless, unbeknownst to many of York's followers, there were a number of other far more serious internal issues brewing beneath the surface of the movement itself, which would make their previous problems with the Putnam authorities pale in comparison, and almost destroy the very fabric of the Movement in the months that followed, as we shall now investigate next.

Chapter 16

Southern Dream turns to Nightmare: The fall of Malachi York

Figs.303 & 304:
Left- Right: *Symbols of: The UNNM & The F.B.I.*

In May of 2002, the combined forces of Georgia Law Enforcement and the Federal Government staged a massive invasion of our normally peaceful village in Putnam County, Georgia. The invasion stemmed from allegations of child molestation directed at our Tribal Chief Black Thunderbird "Eagle" also known as Dr. Malachi Z. York...

Dr. Frederick O. Bright M.D., 2003

The beginning of York's demise suddenly occurred around May 2000, when reports began to surface of 2 women who were accusing the Nuwaubian leader of allegedly fathering their children. Although it had been common knowledge for many years amongst members of the organisation that York had sired many offspring from his numerous Wives & Concubines, which was acceptable at the time, according to Islamic/Hebrew & African Traditions. Nevertheless, throughout the years, York has often been accused by critics of constructing an artificial and secretive world around himself in which he has been able to wield absolute authority over the lives of his followers. Although York argued that these measures were necessary to protect his followers from the evils of society, what appears to have now emerged was an organization rife with corruption, incompetence, scandalous & undisciplined behaviour, mainly by Children & Young Adults who were given too much freedom, for which Dr. York must shoulder at least some amount of the blame.

Fig.305 Alleged Victim:
Pauline Rogers speaking on Montel Williams show

In several later allegations, the women claimed that York completely refused to take any responsibility for their children, with the first of these, 34-year old Pauline Rogers, claiming that York was the father of both her son and daughter. This Pauline Rogers would later be named as one of York's accusers during his Child molestation trial.

The second was 27-year old Sakinah Abdullah Muhammad, also known as Parham, who was raised within the Community from birth. Media reports claimed that she had filed a civil action or 'Law suit' against York, through the 'Department of Human Resources', child support recovery office for him failing to pay 'Child Support' for her child. Miss Parham would also be named as one of York's victims, but later denied being molested during the subsequent trial. However, since the trial, both women have subsequently reaffirmed their 'Sexual Abuse' allegations against York by recently appearing on The Montel Williams Show, in September 2007. Rumours were also circulating of a number of other young women living at the Nuwaubian property who were said to be visiting local hospitals, accompanied by adult male members to apparently have abortions carried out in secret. Although Sheriff Sills and others would later point the finger of blame at York for being responsible, it is a documented fact that York had been residing over 65 miles away in Athens County at the time, since leaving the property in late 1998. So how were these young women becoming pregnant, if not by York? For the answer to this, and indeed the basis of the Federal Government's entire case against York, we must first examine the structure of authority left in place at 404 Shady Dale Road by York, after he moved to his new luxury residence in Athens, Georgia in 1998.

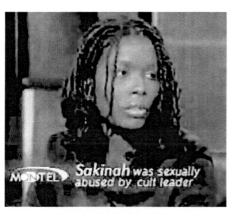

Fig.306 Alleged Victim:
Sakinah Parham speaking on Montel Williams

Increasing evidence now suggests that York may have made the disastrous decision of leaving the young people in the community under the supervision of Men & Women, who were barely beyond their teens. This in turn eventually led to a situation of teen lawlessness, widespread alcoholism & sexual experimentation amongst the young people within the Community. Most senior of those left in charge was a young woman known as Abigail 'Habiba' Washington, who we shall investigate in further depth later.

According to eyewitness reports, the young occupants of the Community quickly descended into mischief without adequate adult control. It was also rumoured that they often engaged in all night, alcoholic & group sex parties, whilst under the supervision of Abigail "Habiba" Washington. The following is the complete transcript of a handwritten letter by another young woman, 23-year old Nicole "Adah" Lopez, to a close confidant Krystal "Beluwra" Harden in 2000 1. It provides conclusive evidence that many of the young people accusing York of 'Sexual Molestation' were in fact, themselves having Sexual Intercourse with one another on the land:

"How are you doing? I missed you very much. I miss your mom she's cool, and cause you know I definitely miss Kuwsh. I wish I had the balls enough and left when you left. Instead of being here pretending. I want to experience things life, no worries, going places, smoking (and not cigarettes), getting drunk without guilt or stealing, finding new experiences. Its like our roles switched. I used to tell you live, have fun, stop being paranoid, while you was worrying about people say, now your telling me live, enjoy life, while I am here hoping Doc or Abigail isn't saying nothing bad about me. The only reason I haven't asked yet is I don't have the balls and I'm a little guilty because everyone has left him, but obviously something is wrong, we talk about Christians waiting in vain 2000 years for Jesus, as we sit on the land and wait in vain for Baba's return or a life. Both religion, both bull shit. The boys and girls have been giving their freedom to roam without anyone bothering them again from Baba, Kayuse was trying to put all these rules on them. Anyway Shababas party was funny. First Amanda and Beluwra got the "drinks" and not Zinfindile, the real shit, vodka and all. We were trying to find a good spot when Shelamoh and Isaam climb up to 103. It was them, the girls, me, Shababa, while sit Shaira was sleep in the attic. It was a friday night. We had music and no lights. Shelamoh was happy because he is always messing with Shababa. Shababa got wild, cursing, telling Isaam and Shelomoh don't mess with her unless their "ready". She cursed me out after she pulled me close and felt I had short hair. I tried to tell her I was growing it but she told me to get the fuck away from her and she played in Amanda's hair. At one point Shelomoh was trying to grab me tell me I was drunk (which I was) but I was pushing him back to Shababa, Beluwra got up and we were dancing together to Back that thing up so you could imagine how that looked. I was scared to death when Isaam tried to join in because I never danced with the opposite sex before. He was trying to get me to loosen up but I froze. I kept going back for Vodka and Whiskey. Beluwra was cutting up falling on people, grabbing people. At one point I was laying down and Isaam had came over and Shelomoh and Beluwra flew off the handle. She started Yelling at people and telling me why don't I find Kuwsh, of course I cursed her right back out, telling her, I don't want your man. Then she tried to jump off the balcony. Isaam tried to stop her, but she asked him to join her! She was really tripping. Amanda had an attitude because people kept getting on her bed and cause she was on her "rag" her bed is in front of the window. We kept trying to get Shababa to lay on the sleeping bag. But she was not having it. Then they had to carry her to the bathroom. She made so much noise Sit Shaira came out and told them to turn off the music, she must have been half sleep not to notice Shelomoh in the chair. **Shelomoh kept trying to get blow jobs from Amanda and them because he couldn't get**

it up. Isaam told him that can happen if he had to much to drink. Which he did. Because he tried to pin me to the bed 4 different times, Isaam had to tell him get off. I bearly had the energy to fight. Me and Amanda had to sneak them threw the front door at almost 4 in the morning and Athens had already been home. It was fun. We all over slept the next morning. Amanda had 3 Zinfindiles in a locked bag that the bitch Suhaila found while steeling stuff from Amanda of course she told Abigail, but Amanda said she found it cleaning up the Aset Fasha in the pyramid but she was to "scared" to drink it. She is doing okay. She is not planing on writing Doc, even though he sent a message as to why other girls wrote but not her. She is who he is expecting the letter from. She still wants to leave. I wrote Kuwsh and he didn't write me back, I had Solomon call him for me to say happy birthday. I also gave him a bunch of stamps. I don't know why he doesn't write me back when he was here. Beluwra would tell me a whole lot of shit, like he don't really like me like I like him or he calls me his bitch, or rips up my letters I give him without reading them. I was very hurt by that especially since I used to wait up until 5:30 in the morning waiting for him to come to Edfu when he was hanging with the girls in the sewing room. Shelomoh said he herad about me and Isaam, he probably heard about the party, because there is nothing for him to "hear". **Sometimes he is funny because he will assume I am doing stuff with someone without asking, and If I was, like he didn't do stuff with the girls or fuck Amanda after he fucked me, and I wasn't supposed to know.** But none of that can change the way I have felt, feel and will probably always feel for him. I gave him my heart."

(Nicole Lopez, cited in unn.com, 2000)

Figs.307 & 308 Disgruntled Follower: Left- Right: *Symbols of: Nicole "Adah" Lopez & Copy of Letter written to Krystal "Beluwra" Harden*

In her 'heartfelt' letter, Nicole Lopez, makes reference to no longer having to follow rules from **"Baba"**, which is a term often used for York by his followers. She also states that: *"They boys and girls have been given their* *freedom to roam without anyone bothering them…"* confirming that York would not have permitted such disgraceful behaviour, had he been present. During York's trial, the media often made mention of a number of the alleged victims who were diagnosed with various 'Sexually Transmitted Diseases (STDs), such as such as **Herpes Simplex II & Chlamydia**, which they were alleged to have all contracted from Malachi York. However after a number of thorough medical examinations by Federal Doctors, York was not only given a clean bill of health, but also found to have never suffered from any of these diseases in his entire life.

So where did these young people contract these Sexually Transmitted Diseases, if not from Malachi York, as Federal Prosecutors claim? In her letter Nicole "Adah" Lopez, who also recently appeared on **The Montel Williams show**, pretending to be an innocent victim; maked reference to engaging in Oral Sex, and having to share her boyfriend Abdul Salaam aka "Shelomoh", with her younger sister Amanda Noel. So could this then be the answer to the mystery of where these young people contracted these Sexual Diseases?

Figs.309, 310 & 311 Innocence Exposed: Left- Right:
Nicole Lopez on Montel Williams show & in Sexually Explicit photos in her real life

Family Feuds

Nicole "Adah" Lopez would later emerge as one of the Prosecution's key witnesses, so who is she, and what is her relationship to the Nuwaubian leader? Sources within the organisation say Nicole Lopez is the daughter of Barbara Noel also known as Shairia Muhammad, who is also the mother of 2 other of York's alleged victims, Amanda Noel aka "Amala" Muhammad & David Noel, aka "Taariq" Muhammad. A close examination of newspaper reports from the early part of York's case reveal that the Prosecution's case was based primarily upon the Testimonies of **3 children**, whose mother claimed that they were all Sexually assaulted, from as young as, 4 years old by Dr. York. The woman claims to have joined the group in 1986, when it was still known as The Ansaarullah Community, based in Brooklyn. After having travelled to Georgia, as part of the mass exodus in 1993 with her three children, the woman claims she was completely unaware that York had been sexually molesting her children until 2000, after which she immediately left the community.

The following are three interviews given by her to reporters, not long after York's arrest for Child Molestation:

> **Augusta Chronicle**, Reporter: Stephen Gurr, Title: *"Man sues sect leader, alleging child abuse"* 2, dated, 3/7/02:
>
> **Brother, sister speak out**
> The Brother and sister who claim York molested them joined the group with their older sister and mother in October 1986. The boy almost a year old, and his sister was 2. They are now 16 and 18. The mother says her daughters were separated and housed with other girls their ages, but initially her son lived with her...The family moved to Putnam County in 1993. Living conditions in the village were no better than in New York. "York lived in a nice house, and everybody else, they lived in broken down homes," says the sister who is now named in the indictment as one of York's victims...The brother and sister say their abuse ended about the time York moved to Athens in 1999. Their mother moved to Athens with York. She says she has two younger daughters, both fathered by York.
> (Gurr, 2002)
>
> **Macon Telegraph**, Reporter: Rob Peecher, Title: *"York's accusers describe years of sexual abuse"* 3, dated, 1/9/02:
>
> The Brother and sister's account form more than half of the 116 sexual child abuse charges in a state indictment issued May 14 against York, Lampkin and other members of the group...The two children and their mother joined York's group in Brooklyn, N.Y., in 1986, when it was called the Ansaru Allah Community, and followed York to Georgia in 1993. The mother thought she was joining a disciplined Islamic sect that would protect her kids from drugs and gangs. She says she knew nothing about the sexual abuse until late 2000. "I had no idea," she says. My main objective

of going there was the safety of my children, not knowing I'm walking them into the lion's den of a pedophiler.

(Peecher, 2002)

Macon Telegraph, Reporter: Debbie Rhyne, Title: *"York admits federal child-sex charge"* 4, dated, 24/1/03:

A former follower and the mother of three of York's alleged victims – all of whom are scheduled to testify if York's trial proceeds as scheduled next week – said Thursday that York's guilty plea is "an answer to my prayers...He just thought he could do whatever and get away with it," she said. But wrong is wrong. I don't care who you are – what planet he came from – it's still wrong. And for those Nuwaubian's that don't see it, it's unfortunate. It's very sad that they want to hold on".

(Rhyne, 2003)

The woman in question would later be revealed as none other than the Mother of Nicole Lopez', Barbara Noel Lopez, who is confirmed to have left the Community in 2000. During an interview conducted by one of our sources in 2003, Barbara Noel claimed to have been **"Peniless & destitute after leaving the community, with no money to feed her children"**. Prior to this, she claimed to have been intimately involved with the group's leader Malachi. Z. York, for whom she bore 2 children, which would have made leaving all the more painful. The Nuwaubian's claim that many single mothers in the community, often

Fig.312 York's Former Concubine: Barbara Noel Lopez

mislead their children into believing that York was their father in order to gain better positions within the movement. If this is the case, were single women permitted to remain single without being provided with husbands? The answer to this is provided by Anti-Nuwaubian Journalist Bill Osinki in his book *"Ungodly: A True Story of Unprecedented Evil"*, who comfirms that whilst in the Ansaaru Allah Community, Barbara Noel, whom he refers to as **'Nasira'**, had in fact been provided with a Husband, although as was so often the case, she walked out on the relationship after giving birth to 2 children, before eventually choosing to become one of Malachi York's Concubines. Barbara Noel has also been refered to as being of low moral character, and involved in various illegal activities, including Marriage to an illegal immigrant for $10,000, before joining the community in 1986. It has also been claim by York's followers that she informed her 3 children, Nicole Lopez, Amanda Noel & David Noel, that the Nuwaubian leader was their biological father. Again, how could York, the leader of the organisation, be confused with being the father of Barbara Noel's illegitimate children, if he was not in some way involved with her? And furthermore, how could a woman like Barbara Noel, whom the Nuwaubian's claim is of such 'Low Moral Character', be intimately involved with the leader of their movement? As we progress, it will increasingly become clear that the basis of many of Malachi York's problems have so very often unfortunately involved members of the opposite sex.

Barbara Noel's 2 daughters in particular; Nicole Lopez & Amanda Noel, were said to have been angered at discovering York was not their 'real' father, and as a result later provided testimonies which would form the basis of the Prosecution's case. In regards to the actual allegations, how was it possible for Barbara Noel, who was known to have been one of York's 'Concubines', to have not been aware of the alleged abuse against her children until 2000, which coincidentally happened to be the same year she was thrown out of the Community. Although it is a documented fact that York's policy was to separate children from their parents, this would explain the lack of knowledge other parents could claim to have regarding their children. Nevertheless, as someone intimately involved with York, to the point of having two of his children, or as the media put it; *".....two younger daughters, both fathered by York"* it's hard to believe that she would have been completely unaware of what was happening to her children. Augusta Chronicle's reporter, Stephen Gurr claimed that the endless sexual abuse to Barbara Noel's children only ended when; *"The brother and sister say their abuse ended about the time York moved to Athens in 1999"*. If this was indeed so, why did Barbara Noel's daughter Nicole "Adah" Lopez, not mention any of this abuse in the letter to Krystal "Beluwra" Harden back in 2000? In fact, she points out how much she looked forward to Dr. York's return whom she referred to as; "Baba", or 'Father'. If York were the cause of so much misery and pain through his constant Sexual Abuse, then why would she look forward to his return?

Upon leaving the organisation, Barbara Noel soon faced a problem often confronted by many long-term followers, which was how to survive in the 'Real' world, after being under the guidance of the group for such an extended period. Barbara Noel must have found that the world had changed a lot since 1986. Without adequate work experience or money, how would she survive in a City from which she didn't even originate? Although the Nuwaubian's claim that Barbara Noel and her children completely fabricated the entire story, which may well be true; however the question any rational person should ask is why? What would make somebody who was at one time intimately involved with York, even to the point of having 2 of his children, suddenly turn around after years of devotion, tell such horrible lies? The answer to this may again lay in York's treatment of his so-called "Concubines" or lesser wives. According to many ex-members, York seems to have adopted a policy of systematically impregnating numerous female followers. Although there is no evidence to suggest that any of these women were legally underage at the time, or forced to have Sex against their will, they all nevertheless, seemed to be women desired by the Nuwaubian leader within the Community. Although in Islamic & African traditions, it is accepted for a man to have more than one wife, and a number of "Concubines" or lesser wives, yet in York's case he seems to have taken this custom to the extreme. Even though his followers often try to deny this, there is overwhelming evidence to suggest the contrary. Most disturbing however, have also been the allegations that after leaving the organisation, many of these women have not been financially supported by the Nuwaubian leader. During his trial in 2004, State Prosecutors claimed that they discovered a family chart in York's home, containing the names of almost '200' illegitimate children, said to have been sired by the Nuwaubian leader from numerous women over the years. York has also been accused of discouraging the growth of the real family structures amongst his followers, and instead prompting members of the community to regard him as some type of father figure, or "Baba", who controlled almost every facet of their lives. If true, this policy of playing God was clearly dangerous, and would lead many members of the movement to eventually turn against him.

It has also been claimed by ex-members that York indiscriminately targeted any female in the community he desired. Despite York bitterly refuting this allegation, the evidence does suggest that there is some truth to this rumour, which has been reoccurring for more than 25-years.

If Barbara Noel was known to have joined the community as a single mother, how did she go from being the mother of 1 fatherless child in 1986, to eventually having 2 children for the organisation's leader? This was clearly a vulnerable woman, who should have been encouraged to get married and start a real family, instead of simply becoming another one of York's "Concubines". In spite of a husband having initially been found for her within the Community, for whom she bore 2 other children, Barbara Noel eventually rejected this individual, opting instead to become one of York's Concubines, of her own volition (or free will), because of Greed for York's perceived status & wealth. Could the eventual revelation that York was not their real 'Biological' father, and subsequent humiliation, have prompted Barbara Noel's children to turn against York, formed one of the motives for them eventually concocting the Molestation story, as an act of Revenge? Whether Malachi. Z. York Sexually Molested any of these young people cannot not be entirely verified, however other than 'Unrelated Adult' Pornographic material, supposedly recovered by investigators during the raid of the Nuwaubian property, to date no solid evidence of Sexual Abuse has ever been provided by the Prosecution, to incriminate the Nuwaubian leader. What Barbara Noel decided to do after leaving the community, may now shed some light on how the allegations of Child Abuse would later arise against the Nuwaubian leader.

It is often said that *"Birds of a feather flock together"*, and according to York's supporters, Barbara Noel did just that, by joining a group of disgruntled ex-Nuwaubian's under the direct influence of York's estranged son Jacob York, who Barabara Noal would also become sexually involved with, as we shall investigate in greater depth later.

York's Arrest & Invasion of Nuwaubian 'Holy Land'

We (are) engaged in what is clearly a War. A War of Survival. A War for Self Determination. A War for Economic Freedom. A War for Cultural Freedom, to be able to learn things of our Culture, to be able to regain Our Historical Identity...But when you begin to study ways in which to off-set, these Genocide-al attacks, and come up with ideas, Logical ideas, ideas that will work. Then you become the 'Greatest Threat' to the Internal Security of the United States. And if that **Organisation** is the Greatest Threat, then its (Militant) Ideological apparatus is up for grabs, its 'Fair Game'. *"All is Fair in Love & War"!* Then you get a COINTELPRO, a completely Illegitimate thing, and its thrown at you, and you can't cry, you know this was a War!

(Elmer 'Geronimo Ji Jagga' Pratt, FBI's War on Black America)

After federal investigators had collected all of the victim's supposed testimonies, it was now time to bring York in for questioning. On Wednesday May 8th 2002, FBI agents apprehended Dr. Malachi. Z. York whilst on a shopping trip to Milledgeville, Baldwin County, Georgia, accompanied by 4 female members of his organisation, who were; Kathy Johnson, Chandra Lampkin, Khadijah Merrit and Istir Cole. During the arrests, eyewitnesses describe an over excessive use of force by the FBI Agents against the unarmed Elderly Nuwaubian leader and he's 4 female companions, which included the vehicle's windows being smashed in with the butts of Automatic Weapons & Rifles. York along with the other occupants of the vehicle, were then all dragged out at Gunpoint, and ordered to lay on the baking hot 'Tarmac' with the weapons still pointing at their heads. Immediately following York's arrest, a combined force of Federal & State Law Enforcement officers from several Counties including Macon County Sheriff's Department, launched what has been described as a "Waco" style 'Invasion' upon the Nuwaubian property at; 404 Shady Dale Road. The property had previously been under surveillance by the authorities in the months leading up to the raid, which would later be confirmed by aerial photographic evidence taken months before the raid, which have recently come to light. The actual raid, described by Bill Osinski in his book *"Ungodly"* as a **"Military Operation"** was immediately broadcast to numerous Television & Online Media agencies throughout the US and said to be one of the largest ever carried out against civilians in the history of the United States, consisting of a combined Task Force of over 600 heavily armed Officers and Agents from a plethora of Law Enforcement jurisdictions including:

- The Federal Bureau of Investigation (FBI)
- The Georgia Bureau of Investigation (GBI)
- The Alcohol, Tobacco & Firearms Agency (ATFA)
- Federal Emergency Agency (FEMA)
- The Putnam County Sheriffs Department
- The Newton County Sheriffs Department
- The Jones County Sheriffs Department
- The Baldwin County Sheriffs Department

Figs.313, 314 & 315 **Under Surveillance:** *Arial Surveillance Photographs of the Nuwaubian Community before the Raid*

Eyewitnesses claim the officers were all heavily armed with Fully Automatic weapons, Assault Riffles, Head Masks, Body Armour, Shields & Tear Gas. Others described seeing stacks of Body Bags & 'Refrigerator' Trucks, designed for storing corpses. Combined with dozens of FBI Helicopters flying over head, with Snipers laying in wait, while Agents swarmed the property, Jumping out of Vehicles, Crashing through fences, Kicking Down doors and hurling Tear Gas canisters through windows, all simply to confront a peaceful Community of around 50 - 70 unarmed, mostly Women & Children. Sources say that a "No Knock Warrant" was issued by Federal Magistrate Judge Claude Hicks based upon information contained in a sworn affidavit submitted by FBI Special Agent Jalaine Ward, which supposedly contained evidence that Child Molestation & Weapons stockpiling were being carried out at the Property. The local authorities and Sheriff Sills in particular, knew full well that there were no weapons being 'Stock-Piled' at the property, from their previous raid in 1998, when Sheriff Sills along with Agents from the Georgia Bureau of Investigation (GBI) conducted a thorough search of the property, which produced not a single shred of evidence of any wrongdoing, and yielded no Hidden Cache of Weapons, except a few licensed small 'Hand Guns', which had hardly been used, and more importantly, absolutely no evidence of 'Child Molestation' or any other Criminal activity, have ever been discovered.

Figs.316, 317, 318 & 319 Government Invasion: Top, Left- Right:
Police Arial Surveillance Photo & Arial photo of
(Bottom) *Law Enforcement Officers outside Nuwaubian property and on Property*

Black Wall Street

The methods used against the Nuwaubian's during the Government raid under the pretext of searching for supposed 'Stock-piled Weapons', were a travesty and completely unwarranted, as at no point during the group's 30-plus year history of operating numerous properties, has there ever been any incidents of Crime or Violence directly connected to the Community. Whether from the Ansaaru Allah's property located at Liberty, Upstate New York, named 'Jazir Abba' to Tama Re in Eatonton Georgia, the Government was fully aware that York's followers have always maintained Crime free and Peaceful environments on their property. However the 'Heavy-Handed' scare tactics employed by the Authorities were designed to not only destroy the confidence of the organisation, but to also serve as a severe Warning to any other Black Political or Religious movement with similar ideas of 'Self Determination' & Independence from the United States. Many observers have drawn parallels between the tactics used against the Nuwaubian's and those used against the inhabitants of 'Black Wall Street' or 'Little Africa' in Tulsa, Oklahoma in 1921, that later became known as *"the Black Holocaust of Oklahoma"*. During the assault on **'Black Wall Street'**, local residents and Police officers motivated by Klu Klux Klan agitators attacked the peaceful black community in a night of 'Rampage', that left over 3,000 African-American Men, Women & Children dead and badly wounded, with over 700 successful Black businesses destroyed which included:

- **21 Restaurants**
- **30 Grocery stores**
- **5 Movie theatres**
- **An Independent Black Bank**
- **Post offices**
- **Libraries**
- **Private Schools**
- **Law offices**
- **Private Aircraft**
- **A Fleet of Buses & Transportation service**
- **Private Hospitals**
- **21 Churches**

Like the Nuwaubian's, the inhabitants of 'Black Wall Street' or 'Little Africa', Tulsa, Oklahoma, attracted the attention and jealousy of racist White local officials & residents, due to the success and remarkable prosperity their community had been enjoying. Following the attacks, all surviving residents of 'Little Africa' were either imprisoned or forcibly driven out of Tulsa, and left homeless and destitute whilst all their land and property, worth Millions of Dollars were 'illegally' seized and distributed amongst local White officials.

Figs.320, 321 & 322 Destruction of Black Wall Street: Left- Right, Clockwise:
*Bombing of Buildings & Businesses & Homeless Women and Children
Following Attacks by White Racists*

During the siege of the Nuwaubian property, important documents pertaining to the group's 'Nation Sovereignty' were purposely seized such as the so-called **'Blue Black Contract'** issued to the Nuwaubian's by the US State Department. As well as important other Documents, such Tax Returns & Bank records, which would have proven that the Nuwaubian leader was completely up to date with all of his Tax Returns, and therefore completely innocent of 'Money Structuring', which they would later accuse him of. Numerous other items were also confiscated including, Money, Religious books & Computers, as well as items of personal property such as Purses, Wallets, Drivers licenses, and Social Security cards. Included in the Government's search warrant was the name of York's former mistress "Habiba" Abigail Washington, who already had prior knowledge of the raid, being the Government's 'Key Informant', and whose job it was to plant certain "suspicious items" on the property which would appear incriminating, and could later be used by the Prosecution. These "items" were said to include Pornographic DVDs and the infamous "Pink Panther Doll" which Prosecutors claimed was found in York's Bedroom, which supposedly proved York was a Child Molester. Ironically the Warrant issued was for the name **'Dwight. D. York'**, the fictitious Government name given to Malachi York, which has never been proven to be one of his legal names, despite the Authorities full awareness that York was already in custody, from his previous arrest in Milledgeville, Ga. several hours earlier.

(Please Referrer to Appendix for further details)

Ms. Washington, who would later be granted complete Government 'Immunity' from Prosecution, eventually realised the damage caused by her co-operation with the authorities and attempted to make amends by completely 'Recanting' her Testimony against York as we shall see.

Despite numerous Media imaginary claims of the discovery of so-called "Home Videos" containing scenes of *"Sex Acts between York and Young children"*, nothing of the sort would ever be found either during or after the raid, probably because they never existed in the first place.

Immediately afterwards, long-time Nuwaubian foe, Sheriff Richard Sills who had made it his personal obsession to chase and harass Malachi York and his followers throughout Putnam County in true Southern Redneck; "Dukes of Hazards" fashion, was clearly delighted with the outcome of the raid, and stated to Atlanta Journal-Constitution's Journalist Bill Osinski:

> "The operation could not have worked better. There was no resistance associated with the raid…We made entry into that compound and we had control of that compound within five minutes. Five girls were taken into custody…They may testify later as victims in the case, they are being held today in custody of state Division of Children and Family Services…Some of the approximately 80 to 100 people on the Farm scattered when the raid began, but there were no incidents of Violence.
>
> (Sheriff Sills, 2002)

Also carried out, was the systematic forced removal of over 40 young children from their parents by Law Enforcement agents, who were then immediately placed under the supervision of Putnam County Sheriff's Departments lead Detective, **Convicted Criminal** Noel Lee Wilson, before eventually being taken into 'Protective' custody by the Department of Family and Children Services (DFACS). Whilst in so-called 'Protective' custody, none of the children were allowed any contact with their Parents, or permitted to have them present during weeks of forced questioning. However if Malachi York, their alleged Abuser was already in Police custody, what reason did the DFACS have for forcibly removing the Children from their Parents? Their motive soon became clear when it later emerged that these young people were coerced into testifying that they were abused by York, which resulted in over 13 of the Youngsters taken, being used to form the backbone of the Prosecution's case against York for Sexual Molestation. Despite the Prosecution's claims that these young people were being sexually abused on a 'Daily Basis', thorough medical examinations by Federal Examiners proved completely inconclusive. For example, the Prosecution claimed that many of the victims were diagnosed with various Sexually Transmitted Diseases, which they said were contracted from the 'Defendant' Malachi York such as Herpes Simplex II & Chlamydia. However after Government Doctors carried out extensive examinations on York in August 2002, during which numerous vials of his blood were tested, the results of the tests that came back astonished the Government Examiners, and proved without a shadow of a doubt that not only did Dr. Malachi York test 'Negative' for every known Sexually Transmitted Disease (STD), but was also shown to have never ever suffered from any of theses Diseases in the past, which means he couldn't possibly have given any of the victims these Diseases, as the Media claimed

For more information refer to: UNNM.com, article entitled: *"Medical Records Don't Lie".*

The Nuwaubian's also claim that during the raid 'Law Enforcement' officers pointed weapons at unarmed Men, Women and Children under the pretext that the organisation stockpiled weapons. Many Eye-witnesses claim law enforcement agents actually aimed automatic weapons at their heads, and the heads of their children during the raid in an attempt to provoke an armed confrontation, and were also seen laying out numerous body bags on the ground, and unloading 'Ice-Pack's from 'Refrigerated' trucks, which has caused many observers to speculate that there was a more sinister motive for carrying out the raid against the Nuwaubian's. The raid was quickly broadcast on various Television & Online News agencies, including Fox News Network, who later broadcast photographs of the raid. Of the 40 or so Children, some as young as 4 years old who were 'Illegally' forcibly removed from their parents during the raid, many being forced to undergo degrading examinations for signs of Sexual Abuse by the authorities, which included being shown photographs of Naked Adults, and asked if they had seen such images before. However to the disappointment of the Police and Prosecutors, absolutely no evidence was ever found of abuse to any of these Children. Sheriff Sills later told reporters that he had received an anonymous letter stating that children were being Sexually Abused by York, and others on the property, as early as 1998.

A separate raid was later carried out on York's Athens residence where no evidence of child abuse was found either. For some reason the media made constant references to a briefcase said to contain $414,000, supposedly recovered from York's Athens Mansion. Although this had no relevance to the charge, of Child Abuse at the time, it would later emerge why the Media constantly referred to this money, when York was later 'Indicted' for Racketeering and Money Laundering offences.

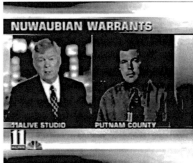

Figs.323, 324 & 325 Media Coverage: Top, Left- Right:
ABC Report on day of York's arrest
& ABC Reporter Walter Macintosh outside Nuwaubian property on the Night of the Raid

Authors Note:
Before we continue, it must be quickly pointed out that throughout York's entire Trial, his followers, particularly those within the higher echelons of the Nuwaubian Leadership have performed what can only be described as an outstanding job of raising the Public's awareness to their Leaders plight. This has been done by disclosing as much information as possible regarding every single shred of 'Evidence' and the many Inconsistencies and Lies used by the Prosecutors & Media agencies throughout the Trial. Their Leader, Malachi York should be very proud of this highly Educated, Perceptive & Courageous group of people who have Vehemently Fought his corner since his arrest, to clear his name and see Justice prevail.

Another intriguing theory regarding the conspiracy which was put forward by the Nuwaubian's soon after York's arrest, was that the FBI, State & Federal Prosecutors conceived or 'Patterned' the idea to set up Malachi York from a Movie entitled: *"Indictment"*, which was adapted from the true story of the McMartin Trial, which took place in 1983. Although this sounds pretty bizarre even for the Nuwaubian's, when you examine the many similarities between the Film and the actual case against York & his Co-defendants, you soon start noticing some interesting similarities.

To further verify their claim the Nuwaubian's published an article in 2003 entitled: *"Putnam County Patterns York Case after MOVIE! Charges So Shocking, The Truth Didn't Matter"*. In it, they point out startling similarities between the HBO

Fig.326 Fact Imitating Fiction: HBO Movie: "Indictment"

Movie *"Indictment"* starring: James Woods & Mercedes Ruehl, and the trial against Dr. Malachi. Z. York. For example, in the film the defendant is accused of molesting over 200 children, between the ages of 2 to 14. Like in York's case, there were no Parents present during questioning of the children, and crucial evidence was "Passed Over", and not shared with the Defence team by the Prosecution, much like in the Movie. According to York's followers this is not a joke, but they believe the case against their leader was actually a 'Copy-Cat Prosecution' based on a real trial that occurred in California during the mid 1980s. How ever strange or bizarre this may all sound, the Nuwaubian's maintain that it is the truth, and actually provided a list of similarities between events depicted in the Movie & Malachi York's case as follows:

"Indictment" the movie (McMartin trial)	York, Johnson and former co-defendants
Defendants were 5 females and 1 male	Defendants were 4 females and 1 male
Police Chief rallied and stirred up witnesses to file charges	Sheriff Sills rallied and stirred up witnesses to file charges
Children had Medical examinations which turn out to be inconclusive	Children had medical examinations which turn out to be inconclusive
Media frenzy causes public prejudice jeopardising fair trial	Media frenzy causes public prejudice jeopardizing fair trial
Media Reporter with suspiciously over invested interest to report false information (Wayne Satz)	Media Reporters with suspiciously over invested interest to report false information (Rob Peecher-Macon Telegraph and Bill Osinski- Atlanta Journal Constitution)
Female defendants had no prior criminal record	Female defendants had no prior criminal record
Ray Buckey had no prior felonious record	Rev. York had no prior felonious record
First, all defendants were denied bond	First, all defendants were denied bond
Second, all of the females received bond while the male (Ray Buckey) was still incarcerated without bond	Second, all of the females received bond while the male (Rev. York) was still incarcerated without bond
Mother and son were co-defendants (a man and a woman)	Husband and wife are co-defendants (a man and a woman, related by marriage)
State pursued case only to justify expenses	State is pursuing cases to justify expenses (May 8th raid and trial costs)

The McMartin Trial was launched during an election year which aroused suspicion	The York and Johnson trial was launched during an election year which aroused suspicion
Defendants had exactly 208 counts	Defendants had exactly 208 counts
Sheriff's Deputy trips defendant (Peggy Buckey) as he led her out of courtroom	Putnam Sheriff Sills trips defendant (Rev. Malachi York) as he pushed him out of courtroom which was caught on T.V.
Virginia McMartin received noble recognition awards from Chamber of Commerce and others	Rev. Malachi York received noble recognition awards from Putnam County Chamber of Commerce and organizations
Assistant D.A. knew case was wrongfully being pursued when faced with all the evidence	Assistant D.A. knew case was wrongfully being pursued when faced with all the evidence
Prosecution's claim of bizarre lifestyle used to justify charges	Prosecution's claim of bizarre cultural lifestyle used to justify charges
Prosecution claimed that defendant's interest in Pyramids justify charges	Prosecution claims that defendant's interest in Pyramids justify charges
70 year old Virginia McMartin was extremely sick elder	60 year old Rev York is an extremely sick elder
Virginia McMartin received medical neglect while incarcerated	Rev. York received medical neglect while incarcerated

(Source: unnm.com, 2003)

Child Molestation Charges
Dr. Malachi. Z. York, along with 4 of his supposed Co-defendants, Chandra Lampkin, Khadijah Merrit, Istir Cole & Kathy Johnson, were initially charged following their arrests with:

- 120 counts of Child Molestation
- 13 counts of Enticing a Child for Indecent Purposes
- 1 count of Rape
- 2 counts of Sexual Exploitation of a Child
- 9 counts of Statutory Rape

It is an interesting coincidence that many of the key witnesses in the Prosecution's case along with those arrested and charged as Malachi York's Co-defendants are mentioned, and even given acknowledgements in the original edition of the group's religious 'Scripture' the *"Holy Tablets"* first released in 1995. A number of the individuals listed below within the Tablets, are either directly or indirectly connected to the case:

- **Dr. Sakinah Aneesah Parnham (Prosecution, and later Defence Witness)**
- **Dr. Habiybah Washington (Prosecution, main Witness)**
- **Dr. Ishtir Cole (York's co-defendant)**
- **Dr. Ebony Hill (Prosecution, Witness)**
- **Dr. Hajar Abd-Allah Muhammad (Defence Witness)**
- **Nicole Rene Lopez (Victim & Prosecution, Witness)**
- **Khadijah Merrit (York's co-defendant)**
- **Atiyah Tatiyana Thomas (Victim & Prosecution, Witness)**

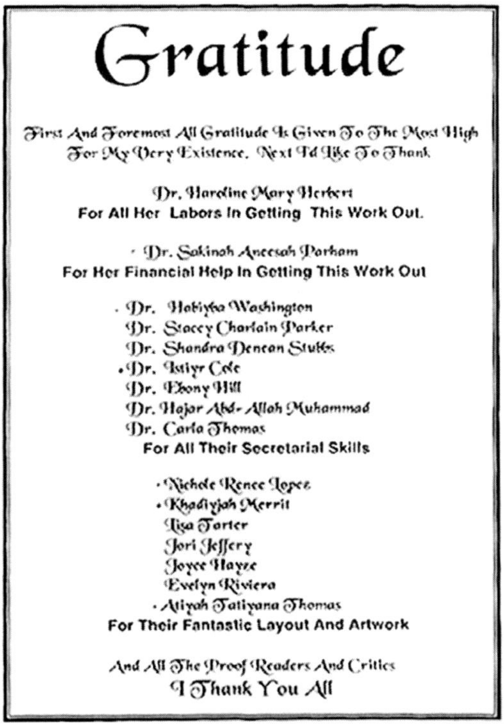

> # Gratitude
>
> First And Foremost All Gratitude Is Given To The Most High
> For My Very Existence. Next I'd Like To Thank
>
> **Dr. Haroline Mary Herbert**
> **For All Her Labors In Getting This Work Out.**
>
> **Dr. Sakinah Aneesah Parham**
> **For Her Financial Help In Getting This Work Out**
>
> Dr. Habiyba Washington
> Dr. Stacey Chorlain Parker
> Dr. Shandra Dencan Stuffs
> Dr. Istiyr Cole
> Dr. Ebony Hill
> Dr. Hajar Abd-Allah Muhammad
> Dr. Carla Thomas
> **For All Their Secretarial Skills**
>
> Nichole Renee Lopez
> Khadiyjah Merrit
> Lisa Jorter
> Jori Jeffery
> Joyce Hayze
> Evelyn Riviera
> Atiyah Tatiyana Thomas
> **For Their Fantastic Layout And Artwork**
>
> And All The Proof Readers And Critics
> **I Thank You All**

Fig.327 *Page of Nuwaubian Holy Text; The Holy Tablets*

Upon close analysis of these names mentioned in York's "Gratitude" of the Holy Tablets, it soon becomes startlingly clear, not only of the fragility of the case, but also the nonsensical leadership structure of the Nuwaubian Nation at the time. For example, the names of York's alleged victims are listed alongside names of the young women accused with York as 'Co-Defendants'. What the media failed to point out to the public was that York's victims and so-called Co-defendants were all roughly the same age group, and had grown up as 'contemporaries' within the organisation. However, what the media did do was portray York's Co-defendants: Kathy Johnson, Chandra Lampkin, Khadijah Merrit and Istir Cole, as adult women at the time of the assaults, and his victims mentioned previously as "Children", when in actual fact all of them are roughly the same age group, which means that York's co-defendants, particularly Chandra Lampkin, Khadijah Merrit and Istir Cole, sexually assaulted children their own age, whilst they were still children themselves, which is ridiculous, and makes absolutely **No Sense!!!**

Secondly, at the time of the Holy Tablets' release, all of the people credited with arranging the Holy Tablets, amusingly referred to as so-called "Doctors", were in fact young women, some as young as 16 years of age, which makes it hard to believe that they could have reached that level of authority & responsibility at such a young age within the Movement. Dr. Sakinah Aneesah Parnham (who allegedly financed the Printing of the 'Tablets') was aged 18, Dr. Habiybah Washington was 19 and Atiyah Tatiyana Thomas was 16. How could people so young be given such influential positions, when older more qualified people existed within the movement whom must have surely earned the right? Again why did York appoint such young women within the organisation to positions of such tremendous power? This was certainly true in the case of York's former 'Lover' and Mother of his children, Abigail "Habiybah" Washington, who was at one point in charge of the Finances of the entire movement. It is easy to see how York's policy of appointing young Women to positions of Influence and Authority, was eventually used to undermine him and the entire movement. The entire case began to appear to have been nothing more than a vendetta between young women, which got out of control. By 'Emasculating' all of the competent adult Men within the movement, opting instead to appoint young women to positions of authority, York permitted young women he favoured to wield far too much power, too young, setting in motion the series of events which resulted in him eventually being accused of some of the most Vile & Contemptuous crimes, by the same young women who had previously enjoyed his favour. This is verified by York's own acknowledgements in the "Holy Tablets" which clearly shows that many of the accusers, and accused were all once associated as contemporaries in leadership of the organisation. However to simply bolster the appearance of the case, the Prosecutors & Media pretended as if there was a huge age difference between the Victims and York's Co-Defendants, knowing full well that York's co-defendants were always innocent of any wrongdoing, which is why their charges were later quietly dropped, once York had been safely convicted.

It is also highly suspicious that although the case was purported to have been the **'Largest Child Sexual Molestation' case of its kind in US history,** hardly any mention of it was made on any of the main International Media outlets, such as CNN, SKY, BBC & Fox. Which has lead many observers to conclude that a tight lid was being kept on Coverage of the case, in order to hide from the World many of the irregularities in the case.

Figs.328, 329 & 330 Left- Right: *York's Main Wife; Kathy Johnson & Malachi York being led away from Court by F.B.I. Officers*

The day after his arrest, on Thursday May 9th, York and his Co-defendants appeared at an 'Arraignment Hearing', held in Macon. In the presence of Federal Magistrate Judge Hicks, the same Judge who had previously issued the *"No Knock Warrant"* used to raid the Nuwaubian's Land the day before. During the Arraignment, York's original Plea was entered in the presence of hundreds of witnesses as **"Not Guilty"**. On Monday 13th of May, York again appeared before Judge Claude Hicks, who decided to refuse York bail. However, Kathy Johnson who was considered his "main-wife" at the time was granted $75,000 Bond.

Then on Tuesday 14th, exactly 6 days after his arrest, Malachi York along with his 4 Co-defendants were indicted by a Grand Jury, which took just 2 days to reach its decision, after hearing Testimonies from 4 of York's alleged victims; Nicole "Adah" Lopez, David "Taariq" Noel, Amanda "Amala" Noel and Khalid Eddington. It must also be pointed out that not a single shred of 'Physical' evidence was produced during the indictment hearing, from either the raid on the Land or York's arrest. For example, York was actually originally charged with *"Transporting Minors Across State Lines for Sex"*, which included the supposed trips to Disney World, Florida, where he was accused of taking young children for the purpose of Sex. We will now show that York was completely innocent of this and other charges against him, which State & Federal Prosecutors were well aware, yet still decided to go ahead with the Trial knowing full well there was never any evidence against him. After the indictment hearing, State District Attorney, Fred Bright stated to the Press:

> "It's a Voluminous case, we intend to Prosecute it to the fullest extent of the Law...Whether York will be tried first in Federal court or State Superior Court is undetermined...York arguably faces a Longer Prison term in State

court, where each "Aggravated Child Molestation" charge carries a 30-year sentence. The Federal charges each carry a Maximum 15-year sentence...Although I must add that this is not an Indictment against the Nuwaubian way of Life or Culture."

(Attorney Bright, 2002)

Figs.331 & 332 Co-Defendants: Top & Bottom: *Malachi York sitting in Court with Kathy Johnson, Chandra Lampkin, Khadijah Merrit & Istir Cole*

Sheriff Sills, however was much less diplomatic in he's treatment of the Nuwaubian's, and immediately criticised what he felt were the group's unnatural practices, and distinctly un-American "Sovereign Nation" identity to the Reporters present:

York has Multiple Concubines, with Kathy Johnson currently cast in the role as "main-wife", according to many of his victims, interviewed by our investigators…There's really no such thing as a Nuwaubian Nation…We're in the United States of America. That's the 'Only Nation' I know of that I live in…

(Sheriff Sills, 2002)

York's Arrogant Confrontational approach towards other Black movement's & Leaders, could now be exploited by the authorities to maximum effect, with very few within the Black Community speaking out in Defence of the Nuwaubian leader.

Nevertheless, following York's arrest, several high profile Black 'Political Figures' did express their concern, not only about the lack of evidence against the Nuwaubian leader, but also the heavy handed tactics employed by Federal & Local 'Law Enforcement' officials against York's unarmed followers, who up to that point had no prior history of violence or 'unlawful' behaviour within either Putnam or any of the surrounding counties. One such

Fig.333 *Senator Tyrone Brooks*

individual was Atlanta Democrat, State Senator Tyrone Brooks, who is known to have visited the Nuwaubian property on several occasions prior to York's arrest, and had first hand experience of many of the progressive activities undertaken by the group. Sen. Brooks a Veteran of the 'Civil Rights' era, marched alongside Dr Martin Luther King Jr, and was instrumental during his 20s in De-Segregating Georgia's school system, as well as being a campaigner for the Southern Christian Leadership Conference (SCLC), which encouraged Blacks to vote during the 1960s. Elected to the State House of Representatives on a Democratic Ticket in 1981, Brooks was part of a delegation of dignitaries who accompanied Rev. Jessie Jackson to the Nuwaubian's rural retreat; 'Tama Re' in August 2001. The following is a complete transcript of a letter written by Sen. Brooks in response to the negative Media publicity surrounding York's arrest, and the subsequent raid of the group's property which appeared in the Atlanta Journal Constitution, exactly 14 days after York's arrest entitled: *"Culture of Harassment Victimizes Nuwaubian's"* [5]. In it, Sen. Brooks outlined many of the favourable aspects of the Nuwaubian movement, and more importantly his concerns and criticisms regarding the circumstances of York's arrest, and the ongoing campaign of 'Politically & Racially Motivated' injustice and discrimination being directed at the Nuwaubian Community by State and Federal authorities:

To understand fully who the Nuwaubian's are, you just study the Ancient land of Nubia in North Africa. If you can't do that, then visit Tama Re 'Egypt of the West' Ga. 142 outside Eatonton in Putnam County, Ga. It's been my pleasure to work with the Nuwaubian's during the last three years. To be in their surroundings is to be in peace and harmony – No Cussing, No Fussing, No Drugs, No Alcohol, No Tobacco products. There is a strong work ethic, and entrepreneurial self-help philosophy throughout the Community.

They don't believe in welfare, but believe in getting their fare share. They have been registering to vote and joining our progressive organizations such as the N.A.A.C.P. and Southern Christian Leadership Conference.

Now, the charges against Malachi York, the group's leader, and his wife, Kathy Johnson, are serious and will be addressed in the court of Law, by two highly respected and able Attorney's, former State Sen. Leroy Johnson and Ed Garland but the conduct of Law Enforcement in making these two arrests is insulting and disgraceful. Why do we need more than 300 Law Enforcement officers to make two arrests? Maybe the U.S. Attorney General thought Eric Rudolph or Osama Bin Laden was living at Tama Re. This was not just about the arrest of York and Johnson. It was an attack on the Nuwaubian's to force a confrontation so that Georgia could have itself a Waco. But it wasn't going to happen because, upon my first visit, the first message I delivered was: "Before your enemies can destroy you, they first must make you angry"… Thank God. The Nuwaubian's heard me.

The current political climate in Georgia is cold and calculating. The mean-spirited political Manoeuvring and divisive catchphrases are reminiscent of the 1930s and 40s. Wearing titles such as 'Segregationist' as a badge, these self-centred and manipulative politicians found a clever strategy to ride into public office. Unfortunately, that free ride was always on the backs of African Americans, now Nuwaubian's.

Unfortunately, there is a new generation of politicians who hope to win elected office by playing on the fears of Poor and Middle class White voters. They have no other platform throughout the years the "Red card" has been played well by Republicans and Democrats however in recent years Republicans have taken the lead in using these guerrilla tactics. Why more than 200 FBI agents and another 100 local and state Law Enforcement officers to arrest two people?

After 10 years of constant harassment and racial profiling and overuse of Federal Law Enforcement, the U.S. Attorney General should conduct an internal inquiry and some brave soul in Congress should initiate a full-scale investigation. The Southeastern Legal Foundation and the National Rifle Association should be consistent and support these requests. Black people are not the problem or the enemy. Crime, Drugs, Illiteracy, Poverty, Hunger, Homelessness, Violence, Disease, Inadequate Health care, hopelessness and cynicism are the cancerous weeds strangling this society. These problems affect us all.

The second half of the 20th century brought much change and progress in this society. Progress in black America was hard won. Black people have had to Slave; Pray, Work, Struggle, Strike, March, Boycott, Picket, Sit in, Walk out, Go to Jail, Sue, Cry, Bleed and Die for every single right

achieved in this Nation. As an African-American voter, I am tired of unscrupulous White Politicians riding the wave of victory on the backs of minorities. On the other hand, intelligent White voters should be equally weary of being used and manipulated like puppets in a calculated race game that nobody wins.
Don't let them ride the backs of the Nuwaubian's to win positions of power.

(Sen. Brooks, 2002)

Fig.334 *Rep. Tyrone Brooks, Defending The Nuwaubian on ABC News, following York's arrest*

The next series of Pre-Trial hearings began in October, with a new Trial Judge appointed; Ocmulgee Superior Court Judge, William A. Prior, whose turn it was to now preside over the next phase of Pre-Trial hearings. Things got off to an awkward start for York and his legal team when it emerged that Judge Prior had been a close friend of Sheriff Richard Sills for over 20 years. Because of this fact, York requested that his Attorney's put forward a motion to have Judge Prior remove himself from the case, due to the fact that he had not only been involved in cases against the Nuwaubian's in the past, but was closely associated with Sheriff Sills, who was known to be an adversary of the group, and part of the investigation against Malachi York and his 4 Co-Defendants. Judge Prior denied the motion on the grounds that he could be completely fair and impartial during the trial. However as the trial progressed, Judge Prior demonstrated that he was anything but impartial by denying several motions presented to him by York's Defence team without any just cause, and by so doing, exposed himself to be blatantly biased in favour of the Prosecution. One of Judge Prior's first rulings was to agree to have the Trial moved to a neutral County, which had little or no past involvement with the Nuwaubian movement. On October 25th 2002, York's Defence 'Legal Representative' Attorney Ed Garland suggested Fulton or Chatham Counties, where it was felt Jurors *"Would have never heard or read about, or even talked about the case before"*. However Prosecution Attorney, Fred Bright recommended the case be re-located to a County with "a similar racial Demographic make-up as Putnam County". Attorney Bright's reasons for making this request was because Putnam County was predominately Caucasian, which is why the Defence were trying to have the case moved to a county with an equal amount of African Americans and Whites to ensure a balanced Jury pool in order for York to receive a fairer trial. The Counties Attorney Bright chose were:

- **Glynn (60% White, 30% Black)**
- **Bulloch (70% White, 25% Black)**
- **Tift (65% White, 30% Black)**
- **Spalding (60% White, 30% Black)**
- **Troup (75% White, 18% Black)**

York's fear was that in these counties the Jury chosen would more than likely be racially biased against him and his and 4 Co-Defendants. To alleviate the Defence's anxieties, Judge William Prior said that he would take all Counties into consideration, and examined the possibility of each one upon its own independent merits, and promised to make a fair decision.

On the morning of the same hearing, a very disturbing incident occurred which provided observers of the case, with a glimpse into the issue of "Brutality & Inhuman Treatment" against Malachi York by Law Enforcement officials, which would later resurface during the course of the Trial. It all began when Sheriff Sills caused outrage by publicly physically abusing York as he left a court hearing in the Putnam County Courthouse. At around 11am, as York was being led out of the Courtroom, Sheriff Richard Sills attempted to deliberately cause York to stumble and fall down the Courtroom stairs, whilst his Hands and Feet were bound and shackled in "Leg Irons". In the presence of hundreds of eyewitnesses, Sheriff Sills placed his foot in York's path almost causing him to lose his balance and fall. At which point York looked towards the crowd of onlookers which included many of his supporters and members of the Media, at which point, a few of York's followers shouted *"Sills pushed him!"*, causing Sheriff Sills to nervously grab York and forcefully drag him down the rest of the stairs and into an awaiting Police vehicle.

Figs.335 & 336 Public Humiliation: *York being Dragged by Sheriff Sills outside Courtroom*

Fortunately the entire incident was caught by York's followers on camera, and documented as concrete evidence of the 'Inhuman & Humiliating' treatment York was being subjected to on a daily basis by Law Enforcement officials whilst in custody, as we shall further investigate.

On November 26th, Judge Prior announced that the case would be moved to either Newton County (Covington) or Spalding County (Griffin). He stated that he decided to choose these Counties based on first their "Racial Demographics", which were ironically almost identical to Putnam County, and secondly whether or not these Counties would accept the case. The Judges ruling was final, and therefore York and his 4 Co-defendants realised that there was no way they would now receive a fair and impartial trial in any of these Counties. As soon as the Judge's decision was announced, the Newton County (whose racial statistics were 75% White), local Media immediately went into action, with their newspapers The Newton Citizen & The Covington News, printing negative articles about York & the Nuwaubian movement. As if by magic, Newton County's Newspaper and TV Stations seemed to know when to begin publicising negative information about the Nuwaubian's as soon as the Judge's decision was announced to re-locate the trial to their county. This strange occurrence left many observers questioning whether there was somebody actually leaking information to other Media agencies who had intimate knowledge of the trial, with some even suggesting that maybe Sheriff Sills or one of the Anti-Nuwaubian Journalists such as the Atlanta-Journal Constitution's Bill Osinski or the Macon Telegraph's Rob Peecher were actually travelling to other Counties to become acquainted with local Reporters & Law Enforcement Officials, in order to spread 'Dis-information' about York and the movement to influence the trial. Evidence of this was finally confirmed by Assistant District Attorney Dawn Baskin's statement which was reported in a Covington Newspaper article entitled: *"Newton May Host Nuwaubian Trial"*, where she stated:

> "Whatever final location is chosen, a Putnam County Judge will preside over the case. Putnam County will just take over your Courtroom".
> (Baskin, 2003)

What she was actually saying was, no matter where the Trial was to be re-located, it will be subject to the same bias as in Putnam County, and the outcome of it will be exactly the same for the Defendant's. Another tactic of the Media and the Prosecution was to always label the case **"The Nuwaubian Trial"**, which by definition is 'Racial Profiling', because the term "Nuwaubian" is the name of the organisation which also denotes the group's African ethnicity, as well as 'Religious' affiliation, therefore this would be exactly like the Newspapers and Prosecution referring to it as **"The Negro Trial"**, which is what they were really implying. After all if the Defendant's were all of a more recognised faith, would they call it The

Catholic Trial, The Jewish Trial or The Mormon Trial? Obviously not! The case should have been against each individual by name. Therefore by doing this, the Media & Prosecution effectively made the admission that the entire organisation was on Trial, which therefore made it 'Racially' motivated, as we shall also demonstrate in further depth.

Finally, a second separate 'Indictment' hearing was conducted solely against the Nuwaubian leader on November 21st, in the presence of a Grand Jury for the Middle District of Georgia (Macon Division). This second superseding indictment containing a list of 13 counts of Sexual Child Molestation, would eventually form the basis York's 14-day trial in January 2004.

York's Guilty Pea & 'Secured Party' Defence

Early during the Pre-trial hearings, York began what can only be described as a series of very Unorthodox, 'Complicated Defence Strategies' or Intellectual & Legal Acrobatics against the Prosecution, using "Common Law". These tactics appeared to many observers as confusing, and were therefore quickly written off by the Media as ridiculous, the first of which was York's declaration of being "a Secured Party".

On January 16th 2003, during a hearing for Pre-Trial motions in the U.S. Federal District Superior Court for the County of Putnam State, Georgia, in the presence of Judge William A. Prior, York stated for the record: *"I'm a secured party, and I do not give permission to anyone to use my name."* According to the Nuwaubian's, what York meant by this statement, was that he was a 'Private Citizen', and as such, the court did not have any Jurisdiction over him. In other words York was saying he did not recognise the legitimacy of the Court, and refused to participate any further in the court proceedings. Naturally, York's response left many observers perplexed. So in order to further clarify the meaning of York's legal tactics, his followers released an article, dated 16th November 2003 entitled: *"Maku is a Secured Party"* 6 which stated the following:

> A **secured party** is a party in whose favor a security interest is created/provided for under a Security Agreement (UCC 9-102 (a) (72). A **security agreement** is a consensual agreement whereby a debtor transfers a security interest in collateral in exchange for valuable consideration, and is defined as "an agreement that creates or provides for a security interest". A security interest is an interest in property that secures payment/performance of an obligation and is UCC-equivalent of a statutory lien. Following execution of the Security Agreement the creditor is known as the "**secured party**" because he has the benefit of a security interest in the property of the debtor; i.e. he is secured in the event the debtor does not make payment as agreed. To understand what a secured party is you first must realize that all courtrooms in America today are commercial marketplaces dealing in matters bearing exclusively upon private, commercial scrip known as **Federal Reserve Notes**. Today's courtrooms are impersonal businesses

under jurisdiction of a foreign, occupying, military power that are managed from the bench (from the Italian banca: **bank**) by merchant bankers called "judges" and "magistrates" who enforce private, copyrighted, corporate policy (known as code) wholly owned by **British corporations**. The "business of the court" consists of admitting attorneys wishing "to conduct business", and adjusting and balancing accounts between debtors and creditors transacting in Federal Reserve Notes who come before it and consent to have disputes resolved in this, America's modern judicial forum.

(UNNM.com)

The meaning of York's Common Law strategy would remain perplexing to many observers, until much later in the trial when he would again utilised this tactic in the presence of the new Judge, Federal Judge, Hugh Lawson. Nevertheless, despite these and other 'Legal' complexities, York had still been indicted on almost 50-Count's of Child Molestation, for which he seemed to have a strong chance of winning at the time, however the events that now followed would confirm to many York's guilt, and forever damage not only his, but the credibility of entire Movement. On Friday 23rd of January 2003, in U.S. District Court for the Middle District of Georgia Macon Division, after having been in Federal Custody for almost 9 months, York shocked the World, by **'Pleading Guilty'** to all 47 Counts of aggravated Child Molestation against him. After Assistant District Attorney Dawn Baskin read out the list of charges, it was the turn of the Defence to submit their Plea. In a closed court session, in which neither the Jury, nor members of the Public were admitted a completely dishevelled looking Dr. Malachi. Z. York, Spiritual Leader of the United Nuwaubian Nation of Moors, was brought before the recently appointed Trial Judge, Hugh Lawson, with his legs Bound & Shackled, dressed in an Orange jail 'Jump Suit' with his Hair and Beard un-kept, shoulders hunched over, and head bowed. York shuffled towards the bench to confirm his name, and enter his plea. In the presence of his acting Attorney Manubar Aurora, along with District Attorney Fred Bright, Assistant District Attorney Richard Moultrie & Sheriff Howard Sills. The following is a complete transcript of the proceedings that took place on that infamous morning:

> **Judge Hugh Lawson**: Mr. York are you now under the influence of any alcohol drugs or narcotics?
>
> **Malachi York:** No
>
> **Judge Hugh Lawson**: You understand you are charged with 40 counts of aggravated child molestation, and that you could receive a maximum sentence of 30 years in confinement, for each count. That you're charged with 34 counts of child molestation, that you could receive a maximum sentence of 20 years in confinement, for each count. That you're charged with 1 count of sexual exploitation of children, and you could receive a maximum of 20 years in confinement. And you're charged with two counts of influencing

witnesses, and you could receive a maximum of 10 years in confinement for each count.

Malachi York: (Closes eyes and bows his head)

Judge Hugh Lawson: And that you could receive, a minimum sentence of 10 years on Probation.

Malachi York: (Opens eyes and looks at Judge)

Judge Hugh Lawson: I'm telling you the most and the least do you understand that?

Malachi York: (Nods in acknowledgement)

District attorney Fred Bright: Actually your Honour, for "aggravated child molestation" the minimum is 10 years in confinement

Judge Hugh Lawson: The sentence minimum would be 10 years in confinement do you understand that?

Malachi York: (Nods in acknowledgement)

Judge Hugh Lawson: Do you understand that you have the right to an attorney and in fact, your lawyer Mr. Aurora is here with you and representing you is that correct?

Malachi York: (Nods in acknowledgement)

Judge Hugh Lawson: I'm going to inform you of certain other rights that you have Mr York, and inform you of the fact that if you plead guilty you give up these rights. You have a right to trial by Jury, you're presumed to be innocent, you have a right to confront any witnesses the state brings against you. You have a right to subpoena any witnesses you want to testify for you. You have a right to testify in all the evidence if you want to. You have the right to the assistance of an attorney during the trial. You have a right not to incriminate yourself. You have a right to plead not guilty, and remain silent, not enter any plea…

Malachi York: (Closes eyes and bows his head)

Judge Hugh Lawson: Do you understand these rights, and understand if you plead guilty, you give up these rights?

Malachi York: Yes.

Judge Hugh Lawson: You heard the recommendation the state made, is that the recommendation you understood the statement made?

Malachi York: Yes.

Judge Hugh Lawson: Did you in fact do what the District attorney Mr Bright told me you did?

Malachi York: Yes.

Judge Hugh Lawson: How do you plead Guilty or Not Guilty?

Malachi York: Guilty.

Judge Hugh Lawson: This is to all the indictments said by the District attorney?

Malachi York: (Nods in acknowledgement)

Judge Hugh Lawson: Did anybody force you or threaten you to enter this guilty plea?

Malachi York: No.

Judge Hugh Lawson: Did anyone promise you anything to cause you to enter this guilty plea?

Malachi York: No.

Judge Hugh Lawson: Are you satisfied with the services of your attorney's not only Mr Aurora but also your other attorney's?

Malachi York: Yes.

Judge Hugh Lawson: Were you able to hear and understand my questions to you?

Malachi York: (Nods in acknowledgement)

Judge Hugh Lawson: He's under oath let him enter his plea

District attorney Fred Bright: Ahhem, Your Honour we've drawn up this withdrawal of a not guilty plea, to enter a guilty plea, and it comes down to the defendant withdraws his not guilty plea and enters a guilty plea…places his constitutional rights…and pleads guilty as charged to all of the offences above, I've already made note of those on record. There the same ones I made mention of before your Honour, I signed on behalf of the state…

Figs.337, 338, 339 & 340 Plea Bargain: Top, Left- Right:
Malachi York being read agreement, by Judge Lawson **(Bottom)** *York Signing Plea Agreement in the Presence of Attorney Aurora, Judge Lawson & Sheriff Sills*

District attorney Fred Bright, hands 'Guilty Plea' over to Malachi York, who then signs the document, after his Attorney Manubar Aurora.

Sheriff Howard. R. Sills, then looks over at Judge Hugh Lawson in Approval, as Malachi York is signing the 'Guilty Plea' bargain agreement.

> **Judge Hugh Lawson**: Malachi Z. York, I find your guilty plea was freely voluntary, knowing the factual basis of your plea, and I accept your plea.

Immediately following York's Guilty Plea, those present which included Assistant D.A. Dawn Baskin and other parties involved with the trial, either directly or indirectly, including York's Defence Attorney Manubar Aurora, Sheriff Richard Sills and Putnam County Commissioner Sandra Adams, all made statements to the Media who promptly circulated the latest developments to News Networks throughout the United States. First off was York's long-time nemesis Sheriff Richard Sills, who had come into conflict with York and the Organisation on many occasions who stated:

> "York's Guilty Plea finally puts an end to this charade that has gone on for 30 years…There is real evil in the world, but this whole matter was the first time I've seen it on such a scale"

(Sheriff Sills, 2003)

Assistant District Attorney Dawn Baskin, who helped to spearhead the investigation against York, by cataloguing statements from all of the victims stated,:

> "The molestation of at least three of the victims began before they were 10 years old; one of them was 4 or 5. Two of the victims were twin sisters, and there were two sets of brothers and sisters. Ten of the victims were girls, and three were boys...The state has identified fourteen other victims of York, whose incidents of molestation were beyond this case's statute of limitations. And with the number of victims who did not come forward, experts estimate five or six other victims for every one who comes forward, is considered the number York actually molested would become 'astronomical'...The scope of this case is overwhelming, there was a concern that a jury would find it unbelievable that something like this could go on for so long...These crimes went on for 30 years, without anybody saying anything. Today, it came to an end"
>
> (Attorney Baskin, 2003)

Then former County Commissioner, Sandra Adams, who had frequently been the object of the Nuwaubian's indignation, and had subsequently been fired from her position for Corruption following a Nuwaubian investigation into her affairs, expressed her satisfaction at the outcome of the proceedings, by stating:

> "It's not a Victory, because of what happened to those Children...But at least the Truth is out!"
>
> (Adams, 2003)

Finally, Attorney Manubar Aurora, who was acting as York's 'Legal Representative' until that stage of the trial, seemed to be relieved at the outcome, and surprisingly spoke disparagingly about his client, by stating:

> The Plea, was a fair deal for York...He got 14 years, when he was facing a Thousand...York was distraught, apologetic and accepting of responsibility...
>
> (Attorney Aurora, 2003)

Following the 'Guilty Plea', State and Federal Prosecutors recommended that Malachi York be imprisoned for 15 years, and serve an extra 3 years of supervision. However, U.S. District Judge Hugh Lawson later rejected the Federal Plea Bargain as being too lenient, and recommended that York be given a more severe custodial sentence. Naturally this plea bargain by York sent shockwaves through the Black community on both sides of the Atlantic. To many, it was seen as a final confirmation of the Nuwaubian leader's guilt, whilst others who had previously supported the Organisation throughout their hostilities with the Putnam authorities, viewed it as a slap in the face. For example, Georgia State Representative, Sen. Tyrone Brooks, a strong supporter of Malachi York & the Nuwaubian movement, who had previously expressed concern, and been "Highly Suspicious" of the charges against the Nuwaubian leader from the outset, was clearly angered and disappointed at learning of York's Guilty Plea, but fell short of withdrawing his full support for the movement in a statement to Macon Telegraph, reporter Rob Peecher:

> "I am surprised because so many of his supporters have called me and said that he is maintaining his innocence. I spoke to two of his associates last week. They were calling around trying to get people to be character witnesses. I told them I didn't have time to be a character witnesses for anything like that because I didn't know anything about any of those charges...If he's pleading guilty to those charges, obviously they've got to look for new leadership...I hope the Nuwaubian's will stay together, get organized, stay focused and continue to build on their land in Putnam County...They don't use profanity, they don't smoke tobacco products...We have bishops in the Catholic Church who've been charged with molesting children, I don't think we're going to give up on every Bishop or the Pope. You have to deal with that particular person who would do such a horrible thing to a child and then move on".
> (Senator Brooks, 2003)

Sen. Brooks went on to add that he would *"continue to be a staunch supporter of York's followers, and hoped they do not disband."*
Naturally York's Guilty Plea was also met with jubilation by many of his other enemies not directly connected with the case, such as ex-follower Saadik (Alan) Redd, otherwise known as Siddiq Muhammad, who seized this as another opportunity to attack York's credibility by stating the following to Journalists:

> "I hope that they can see the fallacy in him and understand that the whole thing was a lie and that they can put their lives back together and become functioning human beings.............What's sad about a guilty plea is that now the Nuwaubian's won't get to hear for themselves the evidence and the details, and see all the victims "
> (Redd, 2003)

Fig.341 Televised Trial: *TV Broadcast of York being lead away from Court by U.S. Marshals*

It appeared blatantly clear at that point, that York made a Plea-Bargain with the Prosecution, in an attempt to receive the minimum sentence for the crimes he had been accused of, which seemed to be further confirmation of the his guilt.

However a hard-core element of York's followers, including the group's leadership based in Putnam County, stayed loyal and maintained his innocence, unfortunately many of the local leadership coward in the face of mounting public criticism, by subtly trying to disassociate themselves from the Case, through fear. Nevertheless York's more staunch supporters, including many of those from the Old School 'Ansaaru Allah' era, came out in his Defence and held rally's in several major cities, including: Atlanta, New York, Philadelphia, and as far away as London, in attempts to raise public awareness of he's innocence. Sadly many Nuwaubians who were simply too afraid to face the wrath of public questioning, stayed away, and failed to support these initial efforts.

Fig.342, 343, 344 & 345 Unwavering Support: *Some of the numerous Rallies Held, Immediately after York's Arrest by York's most Staunch Followers*

At this point, Federal Prosecutors and Putnam officials were confident of a swift victory, and an end of the Nuwaubian's troublesome activities in Georgia. However, Judge Hugh Lawson later decided to reject York's guilty plea, on the grounds that the sentence he would receive would be too lenient. This decision by Judge Lawson actually did the Nuwaubian's a favour, because it now bought them more time to restructure York's Defence team before the case finally went to trial.

It was unclear at the time why York pleaded Guilty, especially when taking into consideration that the Prosecution have never been able to produce a single shred of solid evidence since the trial began. This was later confirmed at the beginning of York's eventual trial in Brunswick County, Ga, by Assistant District Attorney Richard Moultrie, who admitted on two separate occasions that the prosecution had **"Little & Scant"** evidence to support the charges against the Defendant, Malachi York. Therefore if this were the case, why would York accept a "Plea Bargain" when he knew that the Prosecution had nothing on him, especially after having gone on record, as pleading "Not Guilty", in his original Plea on May 9th 2002? One answer to this was later provided by York's followers, who claimed that York's actions were the result of his Defence team, Edward Garland & Manubar Aurora, who were actually working against his interests, and had agreed to a deal with the prosecution, behind his back. However, it was rather difficult to believe that a man of such intelligence and resources as Malachi York, could be manipulated in this type of way by his own legal team, however this cannot be entirely ruled out, when you take into consideration how the American legal system actually works.

The Plea Bargain System

"**The Plea is the centrepiece of America's Judicial process**: the right to a trial by jury system that places a defendant's fate in the hands of a jury of one's peers. However…nearly 95 percent of all cases resulting in felony convictions never reach a jury. Instead, they are settled through **plea bargains** in which a defendant agrees to plead guilty in exchange for a reduced sentence. **Other defendants in "The Plea" describe being pressured by Prosecutors and Judges into accepting plea bargains that resulted in them spending years behind bars for crimes they say they didn't commit**"

(Excerpt taken from, PBS Special *"The Plea"*, June 2004)

To keep down court costs, and at the same time maintain and justify receiving enormous amounts of Tax Payers money, the American legal system closely followed by that of the United Kingdom, has developed an ingenious new strategy called the 'Plea Bargain'. Its Official/Legal name in the U.S. is Rule 35 or 51K, and applies to people who agree to cooperate with the Prosecution to 'Make a Deal', by pleading guilty to avoid going to trial. This new tactic is aimed predominately at Black, Ethnic and Poor defendants, and has been proven to be unconstitutional in complete violation of the 5th Amendment of "Title 18 USC sections 241 & 242" of the U.S. Constitution.

In reality this system is nothing more than a form of legalised 'Entrapment', particularly in cases where the defendant is known to be innocent. To save time and demonstrate to the public that they are defeating crime and continuing to maintain a high rate of convictions, the legal system, frequently resorts to forcing people to Plead Guilty in exchange for lower sentences. In Great Britain, the system is not as blatant as in the US, however it is commonly known amongst experienced Criminals that they'll receive a more lenient sentence if they plead guilty, and avoid going to trial. In exchange for a less severe sentence, the defendant must plead guilty to all of the charges presented before him or her, even ones they are completely innocent of, and also forfeit their right to a 'Trial By Jury'. By utilising this system, Police and Prosecutors are able to 'Fast-Track' literally thousands of cases through the system, and by so doing save Millions of Dollars. It is a procedure which has proven to be beneficial to the courts, and the entire legal system to simply rush 'Plea' agreements or bargains through, in order to prevent them from paying the combined costs of:

- **Court Fees**
- **Lawyers Fees**
- **Witness Provisions**
- **Jury Provisions**

When you take into consideration that the Police arrest people everyday for major or minor offences, imagine if every single one of these people arrested, were brought to trial, the Legal System would simply buckle under the strain of so many cases, literally grinding to a halt.

According to Judge Caprice Cosper, of Harris County, Houston, Texas:

> "The system would Collapse if every case that was filed in the criminal justice system were to be set for trial...The system would just entirely Collapse"
>
> (Judge Cosper, 2004)

To avoid this from happening, throughout the entire Legal System, from the Defence Lawyers to the Judges, there is a common consensus or agreement that those defendant's who refuse to bow to pressure from their Defence lawyers, and refuse to cut deals with the Prosecution, choosing instead to stand up for themselves and fight for their freedom are usually 'Found Guilty', and given much harsher sentences as a deterrent or lesson to others. As previously pointed out, this policy of 'Plea Bargaining' is aimed predominately at Black, Ethnic & Poor defendants, and is nowhere more apparent than when it comes to defendants being coerced into becoming Government Informants or 'Snitches'. It is said that the Jails are literally full of innocent people whose friends & associates a have informed against them, often for a crime they didn't commit, simply to receive a reduced or no sentence for themselves. This has led to many dangerous criminals such as Murderers, Rapists & Drug Dealers, who are willing to work with the authorities being let back onto the streets to often commit worst crimes against the unsuspecting public in exchange for testifying against innocent people in court. The truth is, when it comes to certain sectors of society, the system doesn't really care who is innocent, as long as someone is convicted of the crime, and thereby ensuring an endless supply of new people to be incarcerated.

Finally, another strategy known to be associated with Plea Bargaining, are 'Private Meetings' which often take place between the Prosecution & Defence Attorney's. It is in these 'Private' or Secret meetings which are actually 'Illegal', that deals are usually ironed out between both sides, often with the Prosecution convincing the Defence that there is absolutely no way his or her client, the Defendant, can possibly win the case, and that it would best if the client is persuaded by the person he trusts; his Lawyer to plead guilty. This is not always guaranteed to work, however in cases where the Defence Lawyer has lost several similar cases, the Prosecution plays on his insecurities by suggesting that it would be best for his or her reputation as a Defence Attorney, to get their client to compromise or 'Roll Over' and take a plea bargain.

In the case of Malachi York, the Prosecution were so desperate to secure a conviction that they were willing to resort to any means necessary. Prosecutors are known to often work with Defence Attorney's in order to come to 'Arrangements', which would be best suited for both sides. There was no better way of securing York's conviction, and having the matter resolved as quickly as possible, than to have him sign a Guilty Plea Bargain. This would not only satisfy their objective, but also Destroy Dr. York's standing or credibility as a Leader in the Black Community. Which is why York's Attorney Manubar Aurora was not only known to having had several 'Secret Meetings' with the Prosecution behind York's back. But encouraged his client that it was in his best interests to take a guilty plea, in exchange for a reduced sentence.

However none of this really justifies why Dr. York should have pleaded guilty, especially being a man of such high intellect and education. How could York allow himself to fall victim to a legal tactic, which is often used against Poor & Uneducated Petty Criminals? York's admission could only mean two things: either he was Guilty and took the plea to avoid the full consequences of his actions, or at best he was very weak and buckled under the slightest amount of pressure from the Prosecution and his Defence Attorney. Or was it actually the slightest amount of pressure, which made York talk, and just how far were the Authorities really prepared to go to secure a conviction against the Nuwaubian leader?

Coercion & Human Rights Abuses

Intense pain is quite likely to produce false confessions, concocted as a means of escaping from distress. A time consuming delay results, while investigation is conducted and the admissions are proven untrue. During this respite the 'interrogate' can pull himself together. He may even use the time to think up new, more complex "admissions" that take still longer to disprove.

(Excerpt taken from, KUBARK, 'Declassified', Counterintelligence Interrogation, 1963)

Throughout the trial, York's followers maintained that he was being Tortured and placed under extreme duress by both Law Enforcement & Prison authorities. Many of the details of York's treatment or mistreatment in custody were outlined by his followers in an article entitled: *"A NATIONAL****ALERT****, Illegal Detention: A Plot for Destruction"*, dated July 16, 2003. Indeed as we shall see, York himself confirmed this when he finally received the opportunity to address the public at the beginning of his trial, after his 'Plea Bargain' agreement was rejected by Federal Judge Hugh Lawson. According to York's followers, immediately after his arrest in 2002, Malachi York prior to his 58th birthday, eventually decided to Plead Guilty to over 47 counts of Child Molestation after being subjected to almost a full year of extreme coercion whilst on remand or 'Pre-Trial custody'. This included hundreds of hours of Forced Questioning & Interrogation and Sleep, Food & Water Deprivation by Prison officials. All this coupled with the allegation, by his followers that he was categorised as a "High Risk" Inmate, and placed into general circulation in The Federal Penitentiary of Atlanta, Georgia, with Convicted Murderers, Rapists & Drug Dealers, despite being a "Pre-Trial" detainee, meaning he was not yet convicted of the alleged crime. Which according to William Daniel in his book *"Criminal Trial Law Practice"* is against the US Constitution:

> "The level at which states provide pre-trial detainees with basic necessities, in addition to being "reasonably related to a legitimate governmental objective must meet standards applied under the 8th Amendment prohibition on cruel and unusual punishment i.e. states must furnish detainees with a reasonably adequate diet and living space and with reference to medical needs they must not be deliberately indifferent to detainee's serious medical needs"

(Daniel, 1989)

Even worse was the allegations by York's followers that he was being repeatedly Beaten, Tortured and Humiliated by Law Enforcement officers & Prison guards in order extract a guilty confession. At first this sounded a little far-fetched. After all, why would the authorities go to such extreme lengths to get York to confess? And if so how could they expect to get away with this against an American citizen. Are there not Laws in place, which protected people against this type of treatment? Weren't these kinds of extreme methods such as 'Torture' only used against Foreign or "Political" Prisoners? Let us examine the term "Political Prisoner" for a moment, and see whether it can be adequately applied to Malachi York. According to The Collins English Dictionary regarded as *"The most comprehensive single-volume dictionary,"* the term **'Political Prisoner'** is defined as follows:

> **Political Prisoner** *n.* someone imprisoned for holding, expressing, or acting in accord with particular political beliefs
> (Collins English Dictionary, New Edition)

Although York was not arrested, or for that matter, ever indicted for any of his Religious or Political views, it is no secret that throughout the case the Media often draw the public's attention to what they interpreted as many of York's extreme teachings such as: Being Head of an Independent Nation; *"Not subject to the Law of the United States"*, Being: Anti-American, Anti-Semitic and Teaching & Promoting: Black Nationalism and Supremacy. This by definition and confirmed by the Media, rendered Malachi York a 'Political Prisoner', and therefore outside of the Laws which protect normal citizens. The moment York decided to pursue the idea of an Independent 'Sovereign' Nation-State for American Blacks, he effectively 'Sealed his own Fate'. Therefore we can safely conclude that the case against Dr. Malachi. Z. York was never ever about Child Molestation. If it were, the children of the organisation, York's supposed 'Victims', would not have eventually been forcibly evicted, and made homeless by the very same Authorities, after York was convicted in 2004. If this were really the case, they would have instead been provided with compensation and counselling which none of them have ever received. The case, which was also against the entire Movement, was a Political one, and meant to serve as a warning to any other Religious or Political group with similar ideas in the future.

Whilst proclaiming to the World that they were an Independent 'Sovereign Nation' recognized by the United Nations, York and his followers may have overlooked one crucial fact. Although the United States Government may have been forced to recognise the Nuwaubian Nation as a 'Sovereign' entity, what then was there to stop the very same United States Government from mounting an Invasion of the said 'Nuwaubian Nation', anytime they saw fit? Which is exactly what the Government did, under the pretext of looking for evidence of Child Molestation, when they raided the Nuwaubian property in May 2002, with an overwhelming Force of over 600 heavily Armed Federal Agents & 'Law Enforcement' Officers. The moment an individual or group step out of the relative security and safety of being 'Domestic Citizens', they effectively enter into the Political arena, where the rules automatically change, and the 'Kid Gloves' as it were, immediately come off. This is probably why Minister Louis Farrakhan won't bring himself to openly declare The Nation of Islam an 'Independent Nation', even though this is what the Honourable Elijah Muhammad's actual Manifesto states, because Minister Farrakhan understands what repercussions the Nation of Islam will face, the moment they declare their complete 'Independence' from the United States.

Anyway back to the point, we have already established that York, by *de facto* is classified a 'Political Prisoner', which made the case one of Political significance, particularly because it concerned America's most valuable Resource namely; the future control of the Hearts & Minds of its Black population, whom Malachi York, was now offering an alternative to being (Modern) Slaves. However, for those unwilling to accept that York is a Political Prisoner, the following is an excerpt taken from a 2005 interview with Attorney Malik Zulu Shabazz, 7, Leader of the New Black Panther Party, and Rising Star of the Black Nationalist spectrum in America, who lists **'Dr. Malachi York'** as one of the many Political Prisoners currently being held by the United States:

> The two cases I would have to bring up right now are Imam Jamil Al-Amin and Dr. Malachi York. I'm working on the appeal of Dr. Malachi York, the former leader of the Ansar Allah community in Brooklyn or the Nuwabian Nation. Dr. York has received a sentence of 1,620 years on alleged charges of child molestation and other tax evasion charges. But the trial was a trumped up trial. It is currently on appeal, I'm assisting on the appeal and we expect Dr. York to be victorious on his appeal. I would ask those who read this interview to support the case of Dr. Malachi York, even if we may disagree with some things that Dr. Malachi York has written. He has a following around the world and he deserves our support. Imam Jamil Al-Amin's case is tougher, but we must support him, because he has given us so much and fought for us on the frontlines. We cannot let him just languish in jail. I would also like to advocate for the cause of Mumia Abu Jamal, of course, as well as the cause of Dr. Mutulu Shakur, Brother Sekou Odinga, Sundiata Acoli, Brother Mufundi Lake and all of our other **political prisoners** who have fought for us. Many are being persecuted behind bars. Many don't ever receive a letter or words of inspiration from us. So, in our paper, we always have a page for the **political prisoners** with their information and their addresses. As an attorney, I am fighting as many cases as I can, but I want to ask all of the other attorneys who will read this article to take some time out of your work to give back to those who helped us get where we are.
>
> (Shabazz, 2005)

To further confirm Dr. York's current status as a Political Prisoner, his followers have asserted that whilst at New York's MCC-(Correction Facility), undergoing a supposed 'Psychological Evaluation' in 2003, the Nuwaubian leader was briefly transferred to a facility called '10 South' where Terrorists are usually held while awaiting trial, where he was said to have encountered Arabs, and other Foreign Political Prisoners. Therefore due to the Political significance of the case, this meant greater emphasis would have had to be placed on securing a conviction against the Nuwaubian leader.

Figs.346 & 347 Freedom Fighter: Left- Right: *Attorney Malik Zulu Shabazz With Members of The New Black Panther Party*

Figs.348, 349 & 350: Political Prisoners: Left- Right: *Dr. Malachi. Z. York, Imam Jamil Al-Amin & Mumia Abu Jamal*

Figs.351, 352 & 353: Political Prisoners: **Left- Right:** *Sundiata Acoli, Sekou Odinga & Dr. Mutulu Shakur*

The consequences would have been disastrous for all involved with the investigation, with over 30 years of investigative which included the 1993 report which described York's teachings as: *"Extremely Militant Black Nationalism"*. It was Clearly the FBI who we're really leading the investigation against York, but let Sheriff Sills, (who in reality, had as much chance of bringing down Malachi York as a Snow Flake has of surviving in a Molten Lava) take the credit. Not to mention the Millions of Dollars of Property & Real Estate belonging to the Nuwaubian's, which were being systematically stolen and illegally distributed amongst the respective agencies, would all have to be returned. No, this was a Trial of immense political significance, and would therefore have to be won at any and all costs. Speaking of which, a brilliant strategy of the Media, was to keep a firm lid on the case, making it appear as only a localised issue, which kept the trial away from the scrutiny of the International Media, and therefore relegating Dr. York's plight to much less significance than it actually was.

Startling new Concrete Evidence has also come to light confirming the lengths the authorities were willing to go to, to secure a conviction, in the form of 'Eye Witness' accounts of Physical & Mental abuse used by Prison staff against the 68-year old Nuwaubian leader. The three witnesses; **Robert Daniel, Gary Tatum & Dexter Thomas** not known to be affiliated with the Nuwaubian movement, were all inmates at Jones County, Correctional Facility, at the same time as Dr. Malachi. Z. York, have bravely come forward to describe how Nuwaubian leader was Physically Abused & Tortured on an almost daily basis by Correctional officers, in the months leading up to his Guilty Plea.

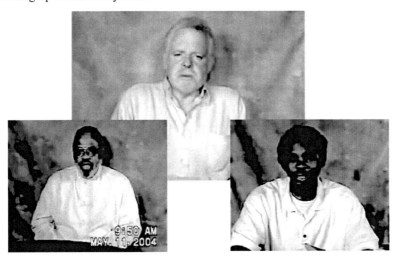

Figs.354, 355 & 356 Human Rights Abuses Witnesses: Top: *Former Jones County Jail Inmate, Robert Daniel* **Bottom, Left- Right:** *Former Jones County Jail Inmates; Gary Tatum & Dexter Thomas who all witnessed Abuse against Dr. York*

With this in mind, let us now turn our attentions to some of the actual "Interrogation" methods, which may have been employed to make Malachi York 'Falsely' confess to almost 50 Counts of Child Molestation.

During the scandal at Iraq's 'Abu Grade' Prison, and subsequent Torture & Human Rights Abuses carried against Political detainees, the issue of "Interrogation" tactics briefly came to light with certain 'Declassified' documents being made public for the first time. One such document was the former CIA, now 'Declassified' manual from the mid 1960s entitled: *'KUBARK COUNTERINTELLIGENCE'*. Although we are not accusing any US Correctional Officer's of actually using this particular manual to Interrogate Malachi York, there are some upsetting similarities between the Nuwaubian's descriptions of their leader's treatment at the hands of Federal Investigators & Prison Authorities for almost '1 Year' leading up to his Trial, and those found within the *"KUBARK"* 'Interrogation' Manual. The following may 'Theoretically' highlight many comparisons to how Dr. Malachi. Z. York may have been forced to confess to Crimes he did not commit, using some of the 'Coercive Interrogation Techniques' listed below.

Authors Statement & Disclaimer:

Before we continue, let us just make it Absolutely clear that we are not accusing any US Government Agency mentioned within this book of any of the following "Torture" or "Interrogation" methods. These procedures listed below have been 'Declassified', and have therefore been made available for Public scrutiny. Once again we would like to make it clear that we are not accusing any US Government Agency or Organization of practicing any of the Interrogation methods mentioned below, but simply making comparisons between the numerous accusations by the Nuwaubian's of: *"torture, cruel and unusual punishment & mental anguish"* **supposedly inflicted upon their leader Dr. Malachi. Z. York by Law Enforcement & Prison Officials, and those outlined below.**

KUBARK. *'Declassified'*;
(CIA) *Counterintelligence Interrogation*:

B. Coercion

Coercive procedures are designed not only to exploit the resistant source's internal conflicts and induce him to wrestle with himself but also to bring a superior outside force to bear upon the subject's resistance.

... All coercive techniques are designed to induce regression. As Hinkle notes in "The Physiological State of the Interrogation Subject as it Affects Brain Function", the result of external pressures of sufficient intensity is the loss of those Defences most recently acquired by civilized man: "... the capacity to carry out the highest creative activities, to meet new, challenging, and complex situations, to deal with trying interpersonal relations, and to cope with repeated frustrations. Relatively small degrees

of homeostatic derangement, fatigue, pain, sleep loss, or anxiety may impair these functions." **As a result, "most people who are exposed to coercive procedures will talk and usually reveal some information that they might not have revealed otherwise"**
One subjective reaction often evoked by coercion is a feeling of guilt. Meltzer observes, "In some lengthy interrogations, the interrogator may, by virtue of his role as the sole supplier of satisfaction and punishment, assume the stature and importance of a parental figure in the prisoner's feeling and thinking. Although there may be intense hatred for the interrogator, it is not unusual for warm feelings also to develop. This ambivalence is the basis for guilt reactions, and if the interrogator nourishes these feelings, the guilt may be strong enough to influence the prisoner's behavior.... Guilt makes compliance more likely...." Psychologists and others who write about physical or **psychological duress** frequently object that under sufficient pressure subjects usually yield.

(KUBARK, 1963)

Comment:

Malachi York's followers have always maintained that their Leader was subjected to extreme forms of cruelty especially during the 9 months between his Arrest in May 2002, and Guilty Plea in January 2003. These included him being forced to endure Hours, upon Hours of endless Questioning without being allowed to Sleep, and Forced to wear the same Clothes for weeks, without being allowed to Wash, Shave or Brush his Teeth.

C. Arrest

The manner and timing of arrest can contribute substantially to the interrogator's purposes. "What we aim to do is to ensure that the manner of arrest achieves, if possible, surprise, and the maximum amount of mental discomfort in order to catch the suspect off balance and to deprive him of the initiative. One should therefore arrest him at a moment when he least expects it and when his mental and physical resistance is at its lowest…

(KUBARK, 1963)

Comment:

York's dramatic Arrest by Federal Law Enforcement Agents was purposely intended to cause maximum trauma or "Shock & Awe", in order to shake him up and "catch him off balance". The overuse of excessive force which included, Smashing the windows with Machine Gun butts, deliberately causing broken glass to temporarily impair (effect) York's sight, along with forcefully dragging him out of the vehicle to the ground at Gunpoint, may have all been designed to unnerve him before being taken into custody, as part of the first stage of the 'Interrogation' process.

D. Detention
If, through the cooperation of a liaison service or by unilateral means, arrangements have been made for the confinement of a resistant source, the circumstances of detention are arranged to enhance within the subject his feelings of being cut off from the known and the reassuring, and of being plunged into the strange. Usually his own clothes are immediately taken away, because familiar clothing reinforces identity and thus the capacity for resistance. (Prisons give close hair cuts and issue prison garb for the same reason.) If the interrogate is especially proud or neat, it may be useful to give him an outfit that is one or two sizes too large and to fail to provide a belt, so that he must hold his pants up.

The point is that man's sense of identity depends upon a continuity in his surroundings, habits, appearance, actions, relations with others, etc. Detention permits the interrogator to cut through these links and throw the interrogate back upon his own unaided internal resources.

Little is gained if confinement merely replaces one routine with another. Prisoners who lead monotonously unvaried lives "... cease to care about their utterances, dress, and cleanliness. They become dulled, apathetic, and depressed."(7) And apathy can be a very effective Defence against interrogation. Control of the source's environment permits the interrogator to… determine his diet, sleep pattern, and other fundamentals. Manipulating these into irregularities, so that the subject becomes disorientated, is very likely to create feelings of fear and helplessness. Hinkle points out, "People who enter prison with attitudes of foreboding, apprehension, and helplessness generally do less well than those who enter with assurance and a conviction that they can deal with anything that they may encounter.... Some people who are afraid of losing sleep, or who do not wish to lose sleep, soon succumb to sleep loss...."

In short, the prisoner should not be provided a routine to which he can adapt and from which he can draw some comfort or at least a sense of his own identity…

(KUBARK, 1963)

Comment:

Again this is very consistent with reports from York's followers that he was not allowed to have any Correspondence with Family or Friends. In the months leading up to his Trial, York was said to have been moved to no fewer than **10 separate Prisons**. His Head was often left un-kept and he was given Prison clothes, i.e: Orange Jump-suit designed to humiliate, despite him still being an "Un-convicted" Inmate. When he requested a Shower a bucket of Cold water would be thrown over him, which meant he was not permitted to wash at regular intervals. York was also said to have been Kept in Cells with 12inch Rats & huge Cockroaches, Chained to a Stone Bed for Hours, and Forced to endure extreme Cold at Night or temperatures of up to 98-degrees during the day in unventilated cells, Forced to Eat Unclean/Unhealthy Food & Deprived of Sleep.

E. Deprivation of Sensory Stimuli

The chief effect of arrest and detention, and particularly of solitary confinement, is to deprive the subject of many or most of the sights, sounds, tastes, smells, and tactile sensations to which he has grown accustomed..."The symptoms most commonly produced by isolation are superstition, intense love of any other living thing, perceiving inanimate objects as alive, hallucinations, and delusions."

The apparent reason for these effects is that a person cut off from external stimuli turns his awareness inward, upon himself, and then projects the contents of his own unconscious outwards, so that he endows his faceless environment with his own attributes, fears, and forgotten memories... In summarizing some scientific reporting on sensory and perceptual deprivation, Kubzansky offers the following observations:

"Three studies suggest that the more well-adjusted or 'normal' the subject is, the more he is affected by deprivation of sensory stimuli. Neurotic and psychotic subjects are either comparatively unaffected or show decreases in anxiety, hallucinations, etc."

These findings suggest - but by no means prove - the following theories about solitary confinement and isolation:

1. The more completely the place of confinement eliminates sensory stimuli, the more rapidly and deeply will the interrogate be affected. Results produced only after weeks or months of imprisonment in an ordinary cell can be duplicated in hours or days in a cell which has no light (or weak artificial light which never varies), which is sound-proofed, in which odors are eliminated, etc. An environment still more subject to control, such as water-tank or iron lung, is even more effective.

2. An early effect of such an environment is anxiety. How soon it appears and how strong it is depends upon the psychological characteristics of the individual.

3. The interrogator can benefit from the subject's anxiety. As the interrogator becomes linked in the subject's mind with the reward of lessened anxiety, human contact, and meaningful activity, and thus with providing relief for growing discomfort, the questioner assumes a benevolent role.

4. The deprivation of stimuli induces regression by depriving the subject's mind of contact with an outer world and thus forcing it in upon itself. At the same time, the calculated provision of stimuli during interrogation tends to make the regressed subject view the interrogator as a father-figure. The

result, normally, is a strengthening of the subject's tendencies toward compliance.

(KUBARK, 1963)

Comment:
York's followers have also revealed that he was Kept in Solitary confinement for up to 24 hours a day, in Cells without any windows or Light, so he would go days without being aware of whether it was Night or Day. They claim he was repeatedly Hoodwinked, Bagged, Blindfolded and made to walk backwards in Shackles, designed to Humiliate and Unnerve him, as was witnessed by Hundreds of observers when Sheriff Sills 'Physically Abused' him outside the Courtroom in 2002. To ensure he was unable to develop any kind of normality, he was constantly being moved to different Correctional facilities to break-up any type of routine or contact with followers or fellow Prisoners.

F. Threats and Fear
The threat of coercion usually weakens or destroys resistance more effectively than coercion itself. The threat to inflict pain, for example, can trigger fears more damaging than the immediate sensation of pain.

G. Debility
...If this notion were valid, however, it might reasonably be expected that those subjects who are physically weakest at the beginning of an interrogation would be the quickest to capitulate, a concept not supported by experience... In brief, it appears probable that the techniques of inducing debility become counter-productive at an early stage. The discomfort, tension, and restless search for an avenue of escape are... followed by withdrawal symptoms, a turning away from external stimuli, and a sluggish unresponsiveness.

H. Pain
....people react very differently to pain. The reason, apparently, is not a physical difference in the intensity of the sensation itself..."The sensation of pain seems to be roughly equal in all men, that is to say, all people have approximately the same threshold at which they begin to feel pain, and when carefully graded stimuli are applied to them, their estimates of severity are approximately the same.... Yet... when men are very highly motivated... they have been known to carry out rather complex tasks while enduring the most intense pain."... **Intense pain is quite likely to produce false confessions, concocted as a means of escaping from distress. A time-consuming delay results, while investigation is conducted and the admissions are proven untrue. During this respite the interrogate can pull himself together. He may even use the time to think up new, more complex "admissions" that take still longer to disprove.**

(KUBARK, 1963)

Clearly 'Interrogation' is nothing remotely like what is depicted in the Movies with sweaty-muscular men, with dodgy moustaches hitting people over the head with Telephone Directories while attaching Electric Cables to the toes of screaming prisoners. Unlike Hollywood's depiction, actual Torture & Coercion tactics are based upon detailed and sophisticated 'Scientific' rules of "Mind Manipulation",

Fig.357 *Extreme Interrogation Method*

in other words forms of Brainwashing aimed at altering the mindset of 'Interrogates', which in this case may have been Malachi York's, in order to obtain the required 'Confession'. These Interrogation methods when applied to any individual are known to usually produce False Confessions.

Following York's trial in 2004, the issue of the cruel treatment he suffered in custody was raised in the Eatonton Tribune, dated 29th June 2004, in an article by Emily Lawson, entitled *"International Criminal Court picks up York Torture Suite"*. In the article numerous parallels are drawn between the treatment of "Iraqi Detainees" at the infamous Abu Grade Prison, which highlighted many of the Torture and Interrogation tactics allegedly used against York in custody. These included being **Hoodwinked, Blindfolded, Forced to Walk-backwards, and Shackled & Chained to the ground**.

Meanwhile, as a result of actions by his followers, York's case was also being investigated by the International Court of Human Rights, who were said to be concerned and actively looking into the case, in particular allegations of: *"Human Rights Violations, against him such as Torture, Arbitrary Detention & Interrogation"*, as of the 23rd March 2004.

Finally, to further confirm the Nuwaubian's allegations that their leader suffered Cruel Interrogation whilst in custody at the hands of both, Police & Prison authorities preceding his Guilty Confession. Recent evidence has came to light exposing many of the same Human Rights abuses, 'Torture & Unusually Cruel Interrogation' tactics previously mentioned, allegedly practiced by so-called 'Rogue' elements of the Chicago Police department, in order to forcibly extract 'False Confessions' from suspects within the Black Community. The revelations came as a result of evidence provided by several wrongfully convicted inmates, following a lengthy investigation, which resulted in the subsequent acquittals of numerous innocent African-American males. The following is an excerpt taken from an article which appeared in Reuters International news agency, authored by New York based Journalist, Oliver Burkeman, entitled: *"Chicago Police Torture Black Suspects"*, dated July 21 2006, which stated:

> A rogue Chicago police unit routinely tortured black suspects in the 1970s and 80s with **electric shocks, beatings, near-suffocation, and mock Russian roulette**, according to a four-year investigation. Though investigators found evidence of torture in at least half of 148 cases examined, it was too late to bring charges because of the statute of limitations.
>
> The scandal exacerbated racial tensions in Chicago for years, and centred on Jon Burge, a former police commander, and his so-called "midnight crew". He was fired in 1993 when torture claims surfaced, but nobody has been charged with a crime, prompting condemnation from the UN committee against torture in May.
>
> One case was Andrew Wilson, accused of killing two officers in 1982. He said police had administered electric shocks and "put a plastic bag over his head, and burned him on the arm with a cigarette", according to the investigation. Mr Wilson had earlier testified that Mr Burge, holding an electric-shock device, "ran it up between my legs, my groin area…then he jabbed me with the thing and it slammed me…into the grille of the window. Then I fell back down, and I think that's when I started spitting up blood and stuff."
>
> Mr Wilson was convicted, but his death sentence was subsequently reversed on the basis his confession had been obtained by torture…
>
> (Burkeman, 2006)

As if this were not enough, most shocking of all is the accusation that Dr. Malachi. Z. York was actually denied Medication for an alleged **"Life Threatening Medical Condition"** by Prison authorities, supposedly under the orders of the Prosecution & Law Enforcement Officials.

York's Medical Condition

Malachi York is said to have been diagnosed in 1999 with a severe form of 'Hereditary Angioedema'. This genetic condition is said to occur in 1 in 10,000 to 1 in 50,000 people, and has no cure. In an article entitled: *"Medical Records Don't Lie"* [8], the Nuwaubian's outlined the details of York medical condition:

> The disease is characterized by episodes of 'edema' (swelling) in body parts, mostly notably the hands, feet, face, and airway passages. In addition, patients often have bouts of excruciating abdominal pain, nausea, and vomiting that is caused by swelling in the intestinal wall. These attacks occur spontaneously usually due to stress and anxiety. Dr. Malachi Z. York was diagnosed with Acute Hereditry Angioedema in 1999. He had been having attacks since as early as 1997, but the condition went undiagnosed. During this time period, he was having 4-6 attacks per week.
>
> (unnm.com, 2003)

It is said that individuals with this condition often suffer excruciating pain, which can even lead to fatality without the prescribed medication, as a result of blockages of the person's airways from the throat passage contracting during attacks. Apparently, without adequate medication York may have been faced with the decision of either signing the Plea Bargain or face possibility of death. In response to York's predicament, his daughter Richelle Davis York, aka "Little Feather" circulated an urgent e-mail to members of the organisation, highlighting the danger to York's life. The following are excerpts from a 'Confidential' e-mail that we were able to obtain a copy of, sent out on the 1st of August 2003:

Fig.358 *Richelle Davis York*

> Since May 8, 2002 A.D. Maku has not received proper medical care for his current health conditions. He suffers from a life threatening illness called Angioedema and with stress this condition can cause Maku to have seizures. His personal physician has been eagerly trying to cooperate with the prison facilities in regards to his current health care but has been denied any right to pertinent information in regards to his medication and general well being...The prison facility he was placed in May of 2002 is Atlanta Federal Penitentiary. At this facility he was physically and mentally tortured. He had to sleep on the floor with 5 other inmates in a cell that is properly housed by 2 inmates. The place is infested with rats and other rodents. The facility temperature is kept below 20 degrees and inmates are only allowed a thin piece of cloth they call a blanket to keep warm...He was placed, while being detained during pre-trial, with convicted murderers, and drug dealers...The Atlanta Penitentiary is the worst facility in the country.

The following sections of 42 USC 1983 have been violated:

- **2.2.6 Conditions may not pose risk to health**
- **2.2.7   Deliberate indifference to course of medical treatment, excessive risk of health**
- **2.2.10 Deliberate indifference to health and safety**
- **2.2.11 Unreasonable threats to health**
- **2.2.14 Deliberate indifference to Standard**
- **2.2.16 Medical care must be provided**
- **2.2.20 Right to Jail Housing Apart from felons and danger**
- **2.2.21 Affirmative duty to protect inmates**
- **2.2.43 Cursory Medical Care Insufficient**
- **2.2.48 Treatment below professional Standard, Denial of treatment Option maybe deliberately indifferent**
- **2.2.58 Duty to review prisoner files. Ignoring inadequate treatment**
- **2.2.61 Solitary confinement prolonged**

2.2.62 Solitary Confinement as mental health

These are the codes they have continuously violated while our Maku has been incarcerated unjustly. He has been denied his medication and has been placed in solitary confinement for an excess of a year being incarcerated. His illness requires that he be monitored continuously and this was ignored. This malpractice has continually placed Maku's life in jeopardy...He has gone three days without his medication for which he needs to take three times a day...

(Davis York, 2003)

It must again be noted that this e-mail was confidential, and never meant to be read by the public, therefore judging from the urgency expressed by Richelle Davis York, it can only be concluded that the Nuwaubian's were not lying, and Malachi York who is often affectionately referred to as 'Maku' meaning "Chief" was indeed in real danger of Death during that period. Around the same time, the Judge presiding over the case, Judge Hugh Lawson, would eventually be replaced due to his blatant bias, incompetence and close relationship with Sheriff Howard Sills. During the Pre-trial Hearings, Judge Lawson also made a series of mistakes including his decision to discuss York's plea negotiation with the Prosecution team in secret to determine a suitable sentence for the Nuwaubian leader, which was in violation of US Law, which states:

"*If the court rejects a plea agreement containing provisions of the type specified in Rule 11(c)(1)(A) or (C), the court MUST DO THE FOLLOWING ON THE RECORD AND IN OPEN COURT!*".

The secret meeting was held on May 28th 2003 in collusion with York's Defence Attorneys who increasingly appeared to be working against York's interests. Present at the meeting aside from Judge Hugh Lawson were:

- **Ed Garland (York's Attorney)**
- **Manubar Aurora (York's Attorney)**
- **Richard Moultrie (Assistant District Attorney)**
- **Maxwell Wood (U.S. District Attorney)**

Despite being only 15 minutes away in Gray County, Georgia, Dr. York was never informed of the meeting by his Attorney's and only learned of the illegal meeting after seeing a news report on Television in prison, which mentioned the Judge's decision to reject his guilty plea. It was even claimed that another Attorney acting on York's behalf, Attorney Robert Ratliff of Mobile, Alabama, tried to gain access to this "Private Meeting", after learning of its existence at the last minute, but was flatly refused admission by Judge Lawson, which is also against the US Law.

It must also be noted that York's legal team at the time, Garland, Samuel, Loeb Law Firm, were the ones who originally encouraged him to take the 'Guilty Plea' bargain in the first place. The Nuwaubian's claim that Judge Hugh Lawson decided to reject York's plea bargain because the plea had been prepared too hastily by both the Defence and Prosecution, and should never have been accepted by the Judge in the first place. In actuality, the Plea would have benefited York more, because according to the sentencing guidelines, York could have qualified for the "22 – Offence" level, which means he could only be sentenced to a maximum of 4.5 years in prison. In other words the plea bargain would have eventually worked in his favour, which is why Judge Lawson quickly realized his mistake and promptly decided to reject the guilty plea he had already accepted. Both the Prosecution team and the Judge overlooked this fact because of their eagerness to see the Nuwaubian leader convicted, and quickly destroyed.

There also appeared to be some confusion as to whether York had any prior convictions. Throughout the trial the Nuwaubian's maintained that York had no prior convictions, however this is untrue because York himself has admitted in the past, in his book *"The Ansaar Cult in America: Rebuttal to the Slanderers"* that:

> Yes, as a teenager I did belong to a gang and I did get into squabbles...And yes I did get arrested but that is the best you can do. I was a youthful offender...**during my brief stay on Rikers Island in the 60's before I was sent to the rehabilitation centre for youths**...
>
> (Isa Al Mahdi, 1989, p: 59-60)

Although nowhere near the severity of what he was now being accused of, York clearly had a criminal record which probably eliminated him from falling into Criminal Category I, offence level of 22 points, which carried the maximum of 3.5 to 4.5 years in custody, which taking into consideration time already spent on remand, would have made the Nuwaubian leader eligible for 'Parole', or early release as early as 2004.

The other error Judge Lawson made was to hold York longer than the '90'-day period, which is required under 18 U.S.C. § 3164 of U.S. Law, which states: *"persons who are being held in custody solely because they are awaiting trial shall be brought to trial within 90 days"*. Judge Lawson failed to enforce this, in order to buy the Prosecution more time, due to the weakness of their case. This was only part of a series of blunders and dirty tricks by both the Prosecution & Defence Teams used against the Nuwaubian leader, such as York's Attorney Garland's request for a 2 week continuance, which later turned into an extra month, in which time he failed to pay a single visit to his client, despite being only 15 minutes away from where York was being held. For making these and other blunders Judge Lawson, would eventually be 'rescued' or removed from the case, otherwise there was a strong possibility that he could have eventually lost his seat on the bench for incompetence. Before his removal from the trial, one of Judge Lawson's last acts was to sign an order to have York transferred over to the U.S. Attorney General to be sent to New York, for **"Psychological Evaluation"** to asses whether York was "Mentally Competent" to stand Trial. On June 26th 2003, a motion was put forward for York's Psychological or Psychiatric Evaluation pursuant to 18 U.S.C.A. § 4241, which stated: *"It is the belief of counsel that the defendant is unable to assist in his own Defence and that he does not and cannot appreciate the nature and consequences of the proceedings against him"*. However York's followers assert that this was simply another ploy to further assist the Prosecution with their flimsy Case after most of their witnesses began to either recant (retract) their Testimonies or in many cases disappear. In an article entitled: *"Judge Helps Prosecution Buy Time"* 9, dated July 5 2003, the Nuwaubian's stated the following:

> The only reason they are pushing for this psychological evaluation to see if Dr. Malachi Z. York-El © TM is competent, is to delay the case further because the Prosecution has lost all of their witnesses. After a whole year of this circus, the witnesses the federal prosecution coerced into false testimonies have all told them they want to move on with their lives. There are even some that want to tell the truth about the allegations but are being threatened by FBI agents and the Federal Prosecutors that they will go to jail for giving false statements and that it is in their own best interest to cooperate with them.
>
> (unnm.com, 2003)

Before being transferred for Psychological Evaluation, York briefly received an opportunity to address the Public, and confirm in his own words, why he had now decided to reject his previous 'Guilty Plea' and fight the Case. In the presence of a packed Courtroom, York finally got the chance to have his say on June 30th 2003. However unlike when he signed the Guilty Plea, this session was open to the public, and provided York with the opportunity to finally reveal to the World how he was being treated whilst in custody. It began by Judge Lawson asking him whether or not he wanted to retain his Guilty Plea. Then after being repeatedly questioned on the witness stand by Judge Lawson regarding his plea, York eventually responded to the Judge by informing the court that he was in fact 'Forced' to take the guilty plea on January 23rd 2003, by being placed under extreme 'Duress' & 'Coercion. Then, when asked what he meant by this, York replied that: ***"it was legal jargon, and Judge Lawson was well educated enough, and was sure that he knew what that meant."***

York's 'Common Law' Defence

> ...It appears that y'all want to proceed on in your system with our lives. We are Native Americans. We have our own lives; we have our own inalienable rights; we are Indigenous people; and we are Sovereign. I am to be tried, by a Jury of 'My Peers'. Among my People...
>
> (Excerpt taken Dr. Malachi. Z. York's, Courtroom Statement, 2003)

Throughout much of his Ministry, York emphasised the importance of using 'Unorthodox' legal strategies to combat the American legal system, which he accuses of being biased towards the interests of Blacks. In particular, the Nuwaubian leader makes references to what he describes as 'Moorish Law', which he advised his followers to use as **'Sovereign Law'** to combat the "Racist American legal system". As the trial progressed, York employed some of these legal strategies with interesting yet disastrous consequences, as we shall now observe.

In the presence of U.S. District Judge, Hugh Lawson, York again resorted to the tactic of instructing his Attorney, Manubar Aurora, to inform the court that Garland, Samuel & Loab Law firm, were no longer his Legal Representatives, and that he wished to 'Defend' himself using "Common Law". According the Media, the use of "Common Law", is a tactic frequently employed by *"Anti-Government and Militia groups"*, and is not real law recognized by the American Judicial system. However, throughout the years, York has taught that "Common Law", is in fact the original Law upon which all American Law is actually based. To best explain the relevance and complexities of "Common Law" in the American Legal system, let us again quote an excerpt from the Nuwaubian article entitled: *"Does Common Law Still Exist?"* 10, dated 16th November, 2003 which outlines the legal strategy York decided to utilise at this stage of the Trial:

> There are three types of law: Statutes or written law, Common Law and Administrative Law...Common Law does indeed exist and is fully recognized by the State and Federal Courts. The term "common law" is itself very common but most people do not know exactly where it stems from or even when to use it. Common Law is simply unwritten, judge-made law (as opposed to written, or statutory, law). The Courts always likes to act like Common Law doesn't exist or that it is some kind of rhetoric...Now, let's take a look at where **Common Law** originated and how real it is: Common Law is a term used to refer to the main body of English unwritten law that evolved from the 12th century onward. So keep in mind that Common Laws are the laws that the English Settlers brought over here and still do recognize. According to **The Black Law's Dictionary, Editor in Chief Bryan A. Garner, Common Law** is defined as: *"The body of law derived from judicial decisions, rather than from statues or constitutions;"* So you see, Common Law does exists. If it did not; then why is there a law that states that if a couple lives together for a certain amount of years, the two are considered married? According to The Black Law's Dictionary, Editor in Chief Bryan A. Garner **Common Law Marriage** is defined as, *"A marriage that takes legal effect, without license or ceremony, when a couple live together as husband and wife, intend to be married, and hold themselves out to others as a married couple. Common Law marriages are permitted in 14 States and in the District of Columbia."* And yes Georgia is one of these states...in an recent article titled, "**The streets and squares of old Brunswick**" written by **Todd Gwynn**, he states, "**The State of Georgia operates today on the basis of English Common Law and has very few statutes of its own.**" See, these are the things that they don't want you to know. But earlier, **Judge Lawson** termed Common Law as *"frivolous or spurious"* meaning *"Lacking authenticity or validity in essence or origin."* **Georgia recognizes Common Law.** As a

matter of fact, **Black Law's Dictionary is copyrighted British law and like all the rest, private, non-public-domain property. In other words, all Law is British Law and British Law is Common Law.** The courts are rarely made to recognize Common Law, and apparently they don't really want to. Common law consists of the rules and other doctrine developed gradually by the judges of the English royal courts as the foundation of their decision and added to over time by judges of those various jurisdictions recognizing the authority of this accumulation doctrine. Law of common jurisdiction applied by these courts. And they cannot deny that Common Law exists, and GEORGIA STILL RECOGNIZES COMMON LAW. Furthermore, in an article titled **"The Law of the United States"** by **Ronald Rodriguez** in the **Loredo Morning Times on January 5, 2003**, it states, "*In addition to England those countries colonized by the English also operate under the common-law system. Thus the colonists brought the system of common law and equity courts to the United States.*" It doesn't stop there, did you know that if you own any property that it is automatically sovereign! **Transition to the Colonies: An Example the Due Process Clause Dictionary of the History of Ideas Volume III Philip P. Weiner,** "*According to the Common law doctrine, the common law originated in the Middle Ages to protect property rights. The American Revolution destroyed allegiance to the British crown, but kept common law rights of property. This situation made every man "sovereign" over his own property. Neither Congress nor state legislatures nor county or city ordinance nor judicial ruling by any courts could deprive people of their common law rights, including their rights to "allodial" property (an ancient concept describing property that could not be lost for failure to pay taxes; it never applied in the United States, although some states did enact "homestead" laws.)*" So The Common law is still in full force and effect today. People just don't know it because they have been conned into believing it doesn't exist, and unwittingly consent and grant jurisdiction with virtually every single advance made against them by government and legal entities. In fact, our legal system and its billions of pages of codified law, including the UCC has been developed over the last millennia by the creditors for the express purpose of circumventing the protections afforded debtors by the common law. This is attested by on of the world's most respected authorities on the Uniform Commercial Codes, Anderson on the Uniform Commercial Code (1981): 1-103:6 Common Law - "The code is complementary to the common law which remains in force except where displaced by the Code (North Carolina Nat. Bank vs. McCarley & Co. (1977) 34 NC App 689 SE2d 583, 23 UCCRS 455. In attempting to codify a large body of law it is almost impossible to anticipate all the factual situations that may arise. And it is for this reason that courts have adopted the principle of statutory construction that a statute will not be construed so as to overrule a principle of established common law, unless it is made plain by the act that such a change in the established law is intended. A statute should be construed in harmony with the common law unless there is a clear legislative intent to abrogate the common law.

(unnm.com, 2003)

Clearly **'Common Law'** is not only recognised by the American Legal system, it is the basis upon which all U.S. Law is actually formed. Unfortunately for York, the response of the Trial Judge Hugh Lawson, was one which would permeate throughout the entire trial, and that was to simply dismiss "Common Law" as more of York's nonsensical Court-room rhetoric, or "Side-showing", in the words of Sheriff Sills, and therefore over-ruled by the Court. For example, when asked by Judge Lawson, if he hired his Legal representative Mr Ed Garland of Garland, Samuel, Loeb Law Firm, York's response was "No! I didn't hire Ed Garland". When questioned by Judge Lawson on whether he hired Attorney Manubar Aurora as his Legal representative, York again answered "No! I didn't."

Under "Common Law" York asserted his right as a "Private Citizen", not to participate any further in the court proceedings. Unable to get a satisfactory answer from the Nuwaubian leader, Judge Hugh Lawson then turned to York's former Attorney, Manubar Aurora, and asked him questions concerning York's new position:

> "Well, let me ask you this, Mr. Aurora: Are you telling me, as counsel for this man and as an officer of this Court, that you believe these positions you are presenting the Court have legal merit?"
>
> (Judge Lawson)

To which Attorney, Aurora immediately replied:

> "Judge, based on what I've seen in my limited time reviewing these documents, I know the Court made us aware of some of these documents. A lot of them deal with UCC and common-law type issues that I'm not familiar with. I do not know if there's merit or not merit with these positions".
>
> (Attorney Aurora)

Then Judge Lawson, who was by now becoming increasingly agitated, abruptly interrupted Attorney Aurora halfway through his sentence and angrily pointing his finger at him, stating:

> "Mr. Arora, you have a duty to this Court not to present frivolous or spurious matters in support of the position of your client ...I'm warning you you're going to be in serious trouble with the Court if you violate that rule..."
>
> (Judge Lawson)

It later became clear, what York's "Common Law" tactics were designed to do, which was to 'halt' and frustrate the court proceedings. Although Judge Lawson, referred to "UCC and Common-Law" as "frivolous or spurious", in reality he knew he was forced to recognise it as legitimate Law, which is why he reacted with such anger, and resorted to threatening York's former Legal representative, Attorney Manubar Aurora, with disciplinary action if he chose to continue **"Violating the Rule"**. This was the un-written rule of the Court agreed between Judges & Attorney's to deceive the public by ignoring "Common Law", which they are well aware is 'Real Law'. For example all crimes including murder are categorised and classified as 'Commercial Charges'. This fact is officially acknowledged in Title 27 Code of Federal Regulations Sec. 72.11. This single Sec. of Title 27 confirms the undeniable supremacy and applicability of the UCC or "Common Law" in all legal matters in every American courtroom. By York utilising 'UCC or Common Law', he was able to rid himself of his unproductive Legal representatives of the Garland, Samuel, Loeb Law Firm, who were working in 'Cahoots' with the Prosecution against his interests as well as bringing the Legal Proceedings to a "Grinding Halt", by refusing to use what Judge Lawson referred to as "an officer of this Court", which was his former Attorney, Manubar Aurora. The matter was eventually resolved, when York eventually hired a new Legal representative, Attorney Frank Rubino for the next phase of the Trial, which began after he returned from so-called "Psychological Evaluation", almost 6 months later. Upon Malachi York's return from New York, where he had previously been ordered to undergo "Psychological Evaluation" simply to help the Prosecution buy more time, a new trial Judge had been appointed to the case in his absence. The new Judge now presiding over the Trial, would prove to be far more efficient, yet even more biased against The Nuwaubian leader and his Organisation than his predecessor, Judge Hugh Lawson.

The case against York is very unique because despite Media claims, there has never been a shred of 'Physical' Evidence presented by the Prosecution, which support any of their claims of alleged Child Molestation. One major culprit of this malicious campaign of 'Misinformation' is freelance Journalist Joanna Soto Carabello, who wrote a scathing attack in the Athens Banner-Herald, published Sunday 6th July 2003, in which she accused York of a whole barrage of 'Sexual Offences' against Children, and made references to supposed **'Video Evidence'** without having actually seen it for herself:

> While staying with York, the children had to ask for the most minor things through written requests. If the children refused to engage in sex acts with York, he would deny their request. Some of the children were also photographed and videotaped engaging in sexual explicit acts or in provocative poses...
>
> (Carabello, 2003)

Needless to say, these alleged Videos & Photographs of York engaging in Sexual activities with children, have never materialized, probably because they never existed other than in the imaginations of the Prosecution, Federal Investigators & the Media. Maybe Ms. Carabello, and the rest of her Journalistic cohorts should have first made sure the Video evidence actually existed before participating in a vicious campaign of Slander by misleading the public about what was nothing more than 'Hearsay'.

Fig.359 *Joanna Soto Carabello*

It was known from the outset, by State & Federal Investigators that their was a lack of evidence against York, prompting Assistant D. A. Richard Moultrie to openly admit on not one, but several occasions during the trial that: *"the Prosecution has Little, Scant evidence to support the Charges against the Defendant"*. And it was for this reason that the Prosecution, with the assistance of the various Law Enforcement officials used every available means at their disposal to secure a conviction against the Nuwaubian leader. These ranged from tampering with the Jury selection to threatening 'Uncooperative' witnesses with imprisonment; also by working closely with the Macon Sheriff's Department, led by the Nuwaubian's long-time Nemesis, Sheriff Howard Sills, who was working in concert with a number of very unsavoury and Unscrupulous Journalist's like Bill Osinski of the Atlanta Journal-Constitution, who have long been suspected of being on the payroll of Putnam County, to write un-factual and biased articles about York and the Nuwaubian Movement.

Judge Ashley Royal

York's first encounter with the new Trial Judge, Ashley Royal immediately got off to a wrong start when the Nuwaubian leader openly refused to stand when the Judge entered the courtroom, and had to be physically raised to his feet by two U.S. Marshals. From this moment on, it was clear to all that it was all or nothing, either York would win this case beyond a shadow of a doubt, or there would be very dire consequences for him. However, not even York would have predicted how server the consequences would be for not only himself, but the entire Movement, should he be found 'Guilty'.

One of Judge Royal's first actions as new Trial Judge was to immediately move the Trial venue 225 miles from Macon, Ga, to so-called "neutral location" of Brunswick County, also within the state of Georgia, immediately setting a Trial date for January 5th 2004. Judge Royal's explanation for making this decision was according to him, as a result of "negative Pre-trial publicity", by the Media. Judge Royal's ruling was announced on October 29th 2003, and appeared at first, to be a fair decision made for honourable reasons after the plethora of biased publicity York & The Nuwaubian's had been receiving from the Media.

The following statement was released to the Media by Judge Royal, outlining his motives behind the ruling:

"...the court has carefully considered the problem of media saturation and potential bias involving not only allegations against Malakai York, but also reports about the Nuwaubian's because York is the leader of the Nuwaubian's. The court regularly reviews and has reviewed both Macon Telegraph and the Atlanta Constitution for many years. Over the years the Court has noticed in both newspapers coverage of the Defendant's criminal case and articles that reflect unfavorably on the Nuwaubian's that could adversely impact the Defendant at trial. The Court has grave concerns about trying to select a jury in this case in any division in the Macon and Atlanta media markets."

(Judge Royal, 2003)

However, upon closer analysis of the ruling, there emerged what appeared to be far more sinister motives behind the Judge's new choice of venue. According to York's followers, Brunswick County, Georgia, falls directly under 'Confederate Jurisdiction', as a result of the 1791 Treaty between the U.S. Government and the Creek Indian & Yamassee Native American Nations, which ruled that the entire Eastern part of what is now the State of Georgia, should be under British Sovereignty before being completely taken over by Settlers following the treaty over 115 years ago. It was for this reason in particular, according to the Nuwaubian's that Judge Royal, who was well aware of the United States recognition of Malachi York as Sovereign Head of the Yamassee Native American Nation, decided to re-locate the trial to Brunswick County, which is under 'Confederate Jurisdiction'.

The second more straightforward reason for changing the trial venue may have been because of the County's Racial Demographics. Race and Racial Demographics are issues which regularly dominate many high profile African American trials, as we have witnessed in recent years with the O.J. Simpson & Michael Jackson trials. Unlike Macon, Brunswick County has a predominately White population of just under 70,000 residents:

71% Caucasian (White)

27% African (Black)

Under 1% Native American

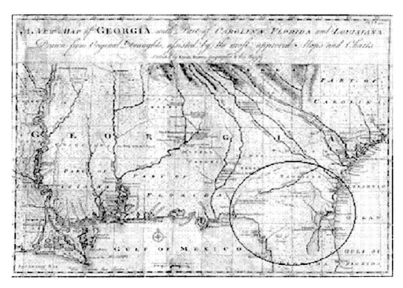

Figs.360 & 361 Top: *Current Map of Georgia-showing Brunswick County*
(Bottom) *1791, Map showing location of 'Confederate Jurisdiction'*

Racial Demographics appear to be the obvious reason for the change of venue, to ensure the 'Jury Pool', was comprised of the majority White population, which would almost certainly deny York a fair trial. To further ensure the outcome of the trial, the local Media immediately set about tainting the Jury Pool, with more negative and inflammatory publicity about the Nuwaubian organisation, guaranteeing that the trial remained 'overtly' Racially & Politically motivated.

Next Malachi York resorted to another of his audacious Legal tactics. During a Pre-Trial hearing held on October 6th, York's new Legal Representative Attorney Frank Rubino, put forth a Motion on his clients behalf to dismiss all charges against him due to "Lack of Jurisdiction". Because York, otherwise known as 'Maku' *"Chief"* Black Thunderbird 'Eagle' was: *"a 'Secured Party' and an indigenous person who does not give anyone jurisdiction over him"*. In other words, York was requesting that the Prosecution immediately drop all charges and release him, as he is a 'Head' of a Sovereign Native American Nation, which the Court lacked "Jurisdiction" over. In actuality, York was probably fully aware that eventually none of his 'Legal Tactics' would be successful. However, realising that he was going to be 'Sent Down', he probably decided that he would do it on his own terms, by raise the issue of 'Indigenous' Nation Sovereignty in the process.

Fig.362 York's New Defence:
Attorney; Adrian Patrick

Then on November 21st, after a series motions, York's fortunes took an even further turn for the worst when a Federal Grand Jury Indicted him on a new charge of **"Racketeering & Money Structuring"**, otherwise known as a Federal 'RICO' violation. This meant that York was not only fighting the Child Molestation charges, but now a Federal 'Racketeer Influenced & Corrupt Organisations' or (RICO) charge, which was usually used to combat organised crime syndicates such as The Italian Mafia & Colombian Drug Cartels. York 'wavered' his right to personally appear at these arraignment hearings, and a plea of "Not Guilty" was entered on his behalf by his Defence Attorney, Frank Rubino, and newly appointed Attorney Adrian Patrick, Bar # **1044**. It was now clear that the U.S.

Authorities were determined to destroy Dr. York one way or another, and if found guilty on all of these charges, he was certainly going to go down for a long period, if not the rest of his life. In December, a series of further Pre-Trial hearings were held leading up to the end of 2003, and repeated motions which were filed by the Defence to dismiss counts 1, 2 & 3 of the prevailing Indictments were again denied by Judge Royal. Also during these hearings Judge Royal ruled that an anonymous Jury were to be chosen for the trial, who were not to be sequestered during the course of the trial except perhaps for the duration of their deliberations. The Defence team were also informed that the court gallery would not be accessible to the public, except members of the Media, and those directly connected to the trial such as Sheriff Sills. Judge Royal claimed this decision was made because followers of the 'Defendant' had distributed flyers outlining information about the case during a Christmas Parade in Brunswick proclaiming York's innocence, and even 'Intimidated' the Prosecution's witnesses. Judge Royal added that during the course of the trial he would be monitoring what the residents of Brunswick were reading concerning the case.

In retaliation to the flyers that were circulated by York's followers, Judge Royal also ruled that the Nuwaubian's were prohibited from further demonstrations outside the Court.
Before the close of 2003, York subsequently sacked his entire legal team, except Attorney Adrian Patrick, who now became York's lead Attorney throughout the duration of the Trial. Seemingly upbeat and optimistic about the approaching trial Attorney Patrick told reporters:

> "We're confident its going to be a very intense trial...There are Strengths and Weaknesses on both sides, but we will be prepared for January...We'll be ready to aggressively defend our client...
>
> (Attorney Patrick, 2003)

The Trial

What was supposedly purported to be **"The largest case of Sexual Molestation against Children in United States history"**, finally got underway on the morning of Monday January 5th 2004, at The Anthony A. Alaimo Court Facility, Brunswick Federal Court House, Brunswick County, Georgia. With the confirmation of Judge Royal's previous rulings that the Trial Jury would remain anonymous throughout the duration of the case, and the entire Trial was to be completely closed to spectators, with only "Properly Credentialed" representatives of the Press permitted to enter the Courtroom. Judge Royal had previously expressed his concerns about disruption to the Trial to the Prosecution Attorney's, and promised to avoid a repetition of previous hearings by closely monitoring all material distributed by York's followers to people in the immediate Brunswick vicinity:

> I was extraordinarily unhappy that members of the Nuwaubian's went down...and tampered with the jury pool...Whether Mr. York directed this or not makes no difference to me. Its going to make it difficult to pick a jury...
>
> (Judge Royal, 2003)

An alternative part of the court was made available to members of the public, which included York's followers to view the progress of the Trial via 'Closed Circuit Television'. An order denying any further motions to dismiss counts VI & II of the Racketeering Act was also signed by Judge Royal himself, in order to avoid any further delay to the Trial proceedings.

Following the Jury selection-process, opening arguments began by the Prosecution and Defence teams, with Prosecutor's immediately going on the offensive by claiming that York used his status as religious leader solely for the purpose of having Sex and making Money, enriching himself over 30 years, marrying numerous women, and abusing young Boys & Girls in the process. They even went as far as to suggest that York's co-defendant Kathy Johnson molested her own son during supposed Sex rituals with York, involving dozens of other children.

The Prosecution team was comprised of Federal and State Prosecutor's who regularly interchanged with each other throughout the duration of the Trial. Heading the investigation against Malachi York was an A-list list of individuals whose names had already become very familiar with those observing the case against the Nuwaubian's. The group responsible for 'Spearheading' the investigation was a combined force of Federal & State Attorney's and Federal & Local Law Enforcement officials, which comprised of the following:

- **United States Attorney Max Wood**
- **Assistant United States Attorney Richard Moultrie**
- **Assistant United States Attorney Stephanie Thacker**
- **District Attorney Fred Bright**

- Assistant District Attorney Dawn Baskin
- FBI Special Agent Jalaine Ward
- FBI Special Agent Joan Cronier
- Putnam County Sheriff Dept. Sheriff Howard Richard Sills
- Putnam County Sheriff Dept. Detective Tracey Bowen

Figs.363 & 364 Prosecution Team: Left: *Assistant U.S. D.A. Richard Moultrie, FBI Special Agent Jalaine Ward, Att. Dawn Baskin & Sheriff Sills* **(Bottom):** *Detective Tracy Bowen, Atty. Stephen Bradley & Sheriff Sills*

Straight off the mark, District Attorney Fred Bright picked up from Judge Royal's lead by moving to silence York's followers, accusing them of attempting to disrupt the Trial by turning it into a circus, by previously staging a series of 'Peaceful' demonstrations outside the court, and distributing flyers, the purpose of which were to rebuke the negative Media coverage against their leader Malachi York. Attorney Bright stated to Reporters before the trial:

> "It's like living in bizarre world…They cannot stand being told no, and they cannot stand being ignored".

(Attorney Bright, 2004)

In order to enforce his ruling Judge Royal ordered an unprecedented force of Law Enforcement personnel to be deployed comprised of Officers from several Jurisdictions which included: Black clad SWAT teams from nearby Glynn County, along with Machine & Automatic weapon carrying, armed Federal Protective Service Officers to form a "Ring of Steal" around the court's perimeter, to ensure that no demonstrations took place by York's followers. Naturally the massive Police presence affected the mood outside the court which became a far more subdued affair, than the previous hearings in which hundreds of York's supporters made their presence felt by waving banners, and loudly proclaiming their leader's innocence. This time instead of large numbers, most of York's supporters were advised to stay away from the proceedings with just a handful of around 30 allowed to watch the trial on the 3rd floor of the Courtroom via CCTV.

Towards the end of the first day, Judge Royal finally chose a panel of 16 'Anonymous' Jury members, with another 4 more to be later designated as alternatives. The Jury panel was said to be comprised of 5 women and 11 men, of whom 3 were Black and 13 were White. However, before they were allowed to continue, Judge Royal led them all out of the courtroom for a private "one to one" meeting, to asses their prior knowledge of the case away from the scrutiny of both Legal teams and the Press.

Of the Jury members selected by Judge Royal, York's Attorney Adrian Patrick stated:

> "It's hard to tell about the Jury, before you give them the case, but I think we have the best jury we can get...
>
> (Attorney Patrick, 2004)

Seemingly pleased with the Judge's choice of Jurors, Prosecution U.S Attorney Maxwell Wood stated:

> "It is a very difficult thing to do with a high-profile case...but with his one to one questioning of the jurors, I think Judge Royal was fair to both sides...
>
> (Attorney Wood, 2004)

In opening statements Attorney Adrian Patrick told the Jury that the basis of the Prosecution's case against York for "Sexual Abuse" was a "Conspiracy", entirely fabricated by a tiny group of York's former followers. This group were led by a woman formerly responsible for the group's Finances, who he claimed was eventually kicked out of the organisation for dishonesty, and would later be revealed to the court as the Prosecution's key witness Abigail Washington. During the first few days of the Trial, the Court heard from numerous Prosecution witnesses who claimed to have been Sexually Molested by York, some claiming from as young as 5 years old. First of which was one of the Prosecutions' 'key' witnesses, 19-year old Amanda Noel, aka "Amala" Muhammad, daughter of 49 year-old Barbara Noel. On Wednesday 7th January, Amanda Noel testified that York had begun molesting her since the age of 8, and claimed that for the next eight years, she was forced to perform 'countless' sexual acts upon the group leader. She also claimed that she saw York have sex with at least 10 other girls, whose names and ages she provided as well as the times the abuses were said to have occurred.

In his opening argument Defence Attorney Adrian Patrick, tried to convince the jurors that the Prosecution's case was only based on 'emotions' and no solid evidence. Attorney Patrick urged the Jurors not to judge York on the basis of his religious beliefs and lifestyle, which he admitted were "different". Attorney Patrick also argued that the 'Child Molestation' charges were started by disgruntled ex-members of York's organisation, and that out of over 60 children living on the group's land during York's arrest in 2002, none brought charges against the Nuwaubian Leader of any Molestation.

In response, U.S. Assistant Attorney Stephanie Thacker, informed the jurors that York maintained what she described as a *"carefully orchestrated system to sexually abuse children, and recruit new victims"*, and that York manipulated his victims into recruiting and introducing younger victims, who were often times their own siblings, to be abused which was done by gaining their confidence. She Added that York's method of manipulation was a *"well developed process of steps, that often began with innocent rubbing"*, later progressing into oral and full intercourse. She continued by claiming that York was able to do much of this because of his policy of 'Isolating' the group's children from their parents, often in Spartan dwellings, whilst York lived in opulent surroundings containing Televisions, Good Food, Beverages and other such luxuries, which were said to be used to entice and reward those who agreed to have Sex with him.

In her testimony, Amanda Noel reaffirmed many of the grievances (as you may recall) which were outlined in her elder sister Nicole Lopez' letter to her best friend Krystal "Beluwra" Harden in 2000, testifying that she rarely saw her Mother, and that she believed for many years that York was her actual Father. Adding that; *"York was taking away my childhood, and that we didn't get a chance to be like other children"*. Then she made an interesting announcement during her testimony that when she reached age 16, she finally decided to leave the compound, and went directly to the FBI, when she heard that they were investigating York. This statement was surprising for two reasons. Firstly, if you recall during the early part of the investigation there was nowhere that either she or any of her siblings admitted to going to the Authorities themselves to reporters during numerous interviews. Secondly as we shall later see, it was York's son Jacob York, who claimed to have first contacted Sheriff Sills, who in turn contacted the FBI, concerning York's activities. Amanda Noel was clearly lying, and must have added that part into her testimony to make it sound more authentic, as was the case with most of the other witness testimonies, as we shall later see. Attorney Adrian Patrick again reasserted his claim that the allegations against York were essentially made by four family members in particular, who had fallen out of favour with York and were out to get even. Defence Attorney Patrick added that the Prosecution's other main witness namely, Abigail Washington aka "Habiba" Abdullah Muhammad "ran the organization for many years and was ousted in February 2001 because she was out of control." Attorney Patrick also blamed Ms Washington for being solely responsible for the group's Financial transactions, which Prosecutor's were trying to accuse York of misappropriating. During the course of the Trial, a pattern soon began to emerge of a Conspiracy against York, which many of the witnesses, including Abigail Washington were at the centre of.

On Thursday the 8th, another one of York's alleged victims, Amanda Noel's sister, 28-year old Nicole Lopez, aka "Adah" Muhammad, took the stand to testify against York. Nicole Lopez you may recall was the young woman who wrote the letter to her confidant Krystal "Beluwra" Harden, in which she expressed her desire to leave the community due to tedium or 'Boredom'. In her testimony, she pointed out that York gained their confidence by first giving them special privileges such as Soda, Pizza & TV. She added that herself and other children were later introduced to Pornographic Movies and Sex Toys, in preparation for actual Sex with York, whom she said taught all of them that it was tradition for group members to have Sex with the leader in order to learn about intercourse to later please their husbands. Nicole "Adah" Lopez, claimed that she finally left the Community when she was 23 in 1999 and later assisted her sister to escape. However this was another blatant lie because when she wrote to Krystal Harden, she was still on the land in 2000. During the hearing it also emerged that Nicole "Adah" Lopez had agreed to testify as part of a **'Deal'** with the Government to avoid Prosecution. However, if she were merely an innocent victim why would she need to make a deal to avoid Prosecution? Well the answer to this again lay in her own letter where she openly admitted to being in 'Love' with, and having regular Sexual Intercourse with fellow Nuwaubian Abdul Salaam aka "Shelomoh" LaRoche. LaRoche was born 1984, making him 11 years her junior and therefore an underage 'Minor' when she started having Sex with him, making her Guilty of 'Child Molestation' herself. This point was also raised by York's Attorney, Adrian Patrick in his opening arguments, but was quickly 'swept under the carpet' by the Prosecution who stated that Nicole Lopez had 'Complete Immunity' from Prosecution, and was soon disregarded by the Jury.

During his cross examination, York's Defence Attorney Patrick also pointed out a number of other contradictions in the transcripts of Nicole Lopez' testimony such as the fact that in her original statement to the FBI, she claimed that her first full Sexual encounter with York occurred in his trailer, however under oath, the day before she stated that the assault first occurred at his House. To which Nicole Lopez immediately responded:

> "I wasn't lying intentionally. They were asking me a lot of questions....it was a mistake, I'm sure now that it happened at his home...I must have mistakenly said 'trailer' instead of house".

(Lopez, 2004)

Undeterred by her outburst, Attorney Patrick continued his cross-examination by also bringing to the court's attention a report from an examination carried out in a New York Children's hospital in 2003, when the FBI's investigation first got under way. In her testimony, she told Medical Examiners that York first had vaginal intercourse with her at 8 years old, however during her later testimony on the 6th of January, she stated that she was 13 when the assault first occurred.

To this Nicole Lopez again replied:

> "That's not true, That's not what I said,..."

(Lopez, 2004)

Next, Attorney Patrick pointed out that she again contradicted herself, when she told the Grand Jury, during York's Indictment that she had no money when she left the Nuwaubian Compound. However in her testimony on the 6th, of January, she told the Jury under Oath that she had $300 when she left the group, to which her reply this time was:

> "I must have lied by accident…"

(Lopez, 2004)

The next witness to take the stand for a second time was Nicole Lopez' younger sister Amanda "Amala" Noel, who began by testifying that while the organisation was based in Brooklyn, New York, the Defendant began to encourage her to perform Sexual acts on him using a 20-year old "Sister" (female follower) within the Community named Nathada, who told her when she was 13, *"that all Girls in the Community, should be taught Sex by males 'in the Family'"*. She continued that this Nathada asked her; *"would I mind if York taught me different things about sex,."* Adding that this "Sister" later showed her how to perform "Oral Sex Techniques" on a 'Sex Toy', and then asked her if she was "ready for the real thing", at which point Amanda Noel claimed that she 'chickened out', but later performed Oral Sex on York on a different occasion. Finally, Amanda Noel claimed that Nathada later made a Video of her completely naked, which was given to York, which he was said to have liked. Then the Prosecution called former Milledgeville Wal-Mart employee, Juanita Tomlinson to give evidence who testified that the Defendant visited her store with a young woman, who appeared to be between the ages of 12 to 14 at the time. Ms. Tomlinson claimed that York purchased a Diamond ring for the girl, adding that the Nuwaubian leader returned on another occasion with a different girl around the same age, whom he also bought a ring for. At the time, the Media immediately made a big deal out of Miss Tomlinson's Testimony, as concrete evidence of York's guilt. However when later put under cross-examination by York's Attorney Adrian Patrick, Ms. Tomlinson admitted that the girls did both resemble York, and quite easily could have both been his Daughters.

The Prosecution then raised the issue of 'living conditions' amongst members of the Community, and even suggested that York formed the organisation in the 1960s solely for the purpose of exploiting people and "Molesting their Children". Claiming that York's followers resided in "squalid & horrid living conditions", and were forced to work from morning until night without receiving any wages for their labour which was all done, according to Federal Prosecutors "to support York's lavish and opulent lifestyle." Some of the money Prosecutors asserted, was used to maintain many of the young boys & girls York used as "Sex Slaves", who were apparently "Segregated by Sex" from their parents within the Community. Adding that, life for those living at "the Compound" under York's dictatorial regime was a hellish nightmare where York was regarded as a "Living Deity or God" to his followers. To make things worse, the followers were often forced to endure shortages of basic everyday necessities such as Food, Deodorant, Toothbrushes, Toothpaste, Combs and Baby-Diapers, which all had to be requested by written application form. It was further alleged that York was able to do this by subjecting his followers to a form of 'Brainwashing', commonly used by Paedophiles known as *"Child Sexual Abuse Accommodation Syndrome"*, claimed the Prosecution's so-called expert witness, Dr. William Bernet, director of Forensic Psychiatry at Vanderbilt University, who continued by stating:

> "What happens is, the child just comes to expect what she has learned within that small culture, and if kept in that isolated place that child will accept and adopt whatever she is told…'What (York) seems to have done is develop a very deliberate, sophisticated grooming process that involved many factors, including keeping the children isolated so that they become compliant and expecting that (the alleged abuse) will happen to them,".
>
> (Dr. Bernet, 2004)

Beverly Hills, California based Psychologist, Dr. Carole Lieberman, who was said to have provided 'Expert' Testimony at "several high-profile cases", also added for the Prosecution:

> "Because he was able to manipulate people into believing he is a god makes him very powerful,…For the victims, it becomes an honor to be able to serve him"
>
> (Dr. Lieberman, 2004)

Nicole Lopez continued that she once had to be admitted into intensive care due to a "Potassium Deficiency" in her diet which almost left her "Paralysed". On another occasion a woman in the community resorted to boiling rice in the morning and giving the water to her baby, and used 'Towels' & Old Stockings' as substitutes for Diapers and 'Sanitary Napkins'. And when something broke at "the girls house" such as windows and floorboards, they often went months without being repaired. However things were a lot different said Nicole Lopez, where York resided with "China & Fillet Mignon" and plenty of "Hot Water" in stark contrast to his followers. Whenever something was damaged or needed fixing at York's home it would be done immediately, without delay. To verify Nicole Lopez' testimony, Federal Prosecutors presented so-called 'Photographic Evidence' of York's residence which contained many signs of opulence which included Ornate Decorations, Gold Fixtures, Plush Furniture and a Gilded staircase bearing a sign which read: "Do Not Go Upstairs".

Despite the Prosecutor's attempts to suggest that the source of York's wealth and obvious affluence were the result of some type of forced 'Slave Labour' of his followers, it must however be pointed out that in spite of the revenue generated by the Organisation, Malachi York had been a Multi-Millionaire in his own right for over two decades, from a very successful career as a Singer/Songwriter/Producer & CEO of various Independent Records labels and Publishing businesses since the early 1980s, as we saw in Chapter 7. Not to mention the hundreds of publications he had authored, under various names since the late 1960s which have earned him anywhere from Hundreds of Thousands to Millions of Dollars, a fact that the Media and Federal Prosecutors conveniently chose to evade, and instead concentrate on the 'venomous' and exaggerated incessant ramblings of a handful of disgruntled former followers whose descriptions of life within the Community are contradictory to accounts by the majority of the group's members. Certainly if York wanted to, he could have made life a lot more comfortable for his followers, which he had promised to do years earlier in New York. Despite the Prosecution's description of life within the Community, it must be remembered that many of York's followers joined the Community 'Penniless' and often 'Destitute', as Bill Osinski, himself admits in his book *"Ungodly: A True Story of Unprecedented Evil"*. None were never at any time forced to stay against their will, and certainly always welcome to leave at anytime they pleased. In fact, York's policy was to immediately throw dissatisfied and trouble makers, out of the Community, without hesitation. The Nubian (Nuwaubian) Nation has always been a self-sufficient organisation since its formation during the late 1960s, never reliant upon Government 'Hand-outs' or assistance, therefore what York's followers built, they did out of a sense of shared ownership to be inherited by their children in the future. York was never the sole owner of the Nuwaubian assets as the Government falsely asserted, which was confirmed in 2000 when York signed a **'Quite Claim'** relinquishing all legal ownership of 'Tama Re' to his followers. Nevertheless in order to fulfil the day to day running of the Community, members were simply required to work in return for food, clothing, shelter and any other necessities. If conditions within the Community were really as bad as the Prosecutor's and so-called victims had suggested, surely all of the lands occupants would have been severely malnourished and unhealthy, which is again contradicted by the happy, healthy and vibrant Community members, particularly Children; photographed on numerous 'Public' occasions during the many Nuwaubian Festivities.

Figs.365, 366, 367, 368, 369, 370 & 371 Happy & Healthy Children: Top, Left- Right, Clockwise: *Various Photos of Healthy Nuwaubian Children before & After the Government Raid in 2002*

Surely if conditions on the land were as harsh as the Prosecutors maintained, why then, didn't Nicole Lopez make mention of any of these so-called "Hellish" conditions as her reason for wanting to leave the Community in her letter to best friend Krystal Harden, whilst still resident on the land in 2000? On the contrary, instead of harsh living conditions, what Nicole Lopez described was an environment of abundant Food, Alcohol and Sexual enjoyment between young people within the Community, completely devoid of discipline and any types of 'Rules'. And as we shall see, once York's trial was over, the living conditions for his followers would really worsen, following the Government's sudden forced eviction of over 50 families in 2004.

Next to testify was 23 year old Khalid "Eddie" Eddington, born 8th June 1980, who described in graphic detail to the court how York often forced him and other youngsters into numerous rooms in the upstairs part of the house, where they were forced to have Sexual intercourse with the Defendant, beginning when he was 13.

When asked by the Prosecutor's if he considered himself *"A Homo Sexual"*, Khalid Eddington replied:

> "No Sir, I wouldn't consider it being Gay, It was supposed to be secret between me and Mr. York. A lot of things went on that I didn't think were wrong because that was just the way we lived,"
>
> (Eddington, 2004)

Khalid Eddington went on to describe how after being born in Brooklyn, New York, he travelled with both his parents and other members of the group, during the Mass Migration, first to Sullivan County, Upstate New York, in 1991, then eventually to Putnam County, Georgia in 1993. He described how at the age of 13 he was taken to York's 'Trailer Home' at night, where he had sex with Nicole Lopez in front of York, and was later forced to engage in anal intercourse with the Defendant. Khalid Eddington claimed that he was eventually kicked out of the Community after being accused of not doing his share of the work.

The final set of testimonies for the day were provided by various FBI agents who claimed to have discovered, during a search of the group's so-called "Compound", what they described as 'Adult Pornographic' material, in the form of Videotapes & DVDs, amongst an assortment of other Sexual paraphernalia. It was also claimed that Videos containing naked images of children on the 'Compound' were apparently destroyed by one of York's sons prior to the raid. Also included amongst the items discovered was a 'locked brief case' which was said to contain over $270,000 in $50 & $100 bank notes, the significance of which had absolutely no relevance to the case at the time, but would later form the basis of a new charge the Prosecutors were gradually trying to build against York. Which was best exemplified by Assistant U.S. Attorney Stephanie Thacker's opening statement to the Jury: *"At its core, this case is about power,…the Defendant abused that power to engage in criminal sexual activities with minors, **and to structure financial transactions in a criminal manner.**"*

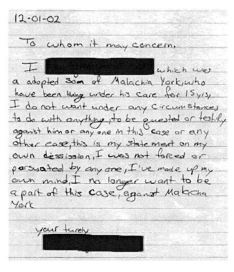

Fig.372 *Brave Confession Letter by David Noel*

The next day, Friday the 9th January kicked off with controversy when York's lead Attorney Adrian Patrick accused Judge Royal of showing blatant bias on the side of the Prosecution, and requested that he "Remove" himself from the Trial. After approaching the Judge's bench, Attorney Patrick asked the Jury to excuse themselves from the court, before accusing Judge Royal of making a series of "Improper" suggestions to U.S. Assistant District Attorney, Richard Moultrie during the trial. Attorney Patrick's accusations were made against Judge Royal as the result of a report provided by the Government's medical examiners before the trial, in which one of the Prosecution's main witnesses, 18 year-old David "Taariq" Noel, born 25th October 1985, repeatedly denied being molested by York to the FBI's medical examiners. Despite the Prosecution's insistence that he was also a victim of Sexual Abuse, David Noel had always maintained the contrary. It quickly emerged that David Noel, had been a reluctant witness from the outset of the investigation. David Noel was the youngest son of Barbara Noel, and the half brother of the Prosecution's two main witnesses Amanda Noel & Nicole Lopez. David Noel was so distressed by the allegations against York that he contacted his two older siblings; Afifa Taylor & Bakhita Taylor who were not associated with the movement, to complain about how he was being forced by their Mother Barbara to falsely testify against Malachi York because of Money. In an act of desperation, David Noel went to the extent of actually writing a letter shortly following York's arrest, denouncing all of the allegations of Molestation against York, dated 1st December 2002, which stated the following:

> To Whom It May Concern,
> I David Noel, which was adopted Son of Malachia York, who have been living under care for 15 yrs, I do not want under any circumstances to do

with anything, to be questioned or testify against him or anyone in this case or any other case, this is my statement on my own decision, I was not forced or persuaded by any one, I've made up my own mind, I no longer want to be a part of this case, against Malachi York.

> Yours truly, (David Noel).
>
> (Noel, 2002)

David Noel's letter was to be the first of many testimonies made by the majority of York's alleged victims, denying ever being molested by the Nuwaubian leader, who all eventually retracted or 'Recant' their forced, 'False' confessions of abuse against the Defendant after the trial. Sensing that the case was on the verge of collapsing, Judge Royal and the Prosecutor's again began resorting to more dirty tricks by suppressing evidence and intimidating witnesses. For example, undeterred by the overwhelming facts in York's favour, FBI special agent Joan Cronier actually questioned the validity of the Government's own Medical report, and Khalid Eddington's original statement which clearly stated that York was innocent. Instead Agent Croner claimed the report was inaccurate, immediately prompting Judge Royal to quickly seize the initiative by instructing the Prosecution to use an alternative part of the report which didn't contradict the witnesses 'new' accepted testimony.
It was for this blatant interference that Attorney Patrick again requested Judge Royal remove himself, by stating in a raised voice:

> "The court prompted the government to introduce evidence…The court is overstepping its bounds!"
>
> (Attorney Patrick, 2004)

In response, Judge Royal denied Attorney Patrick's allegation and flatly refused to remove himself from the position of Trial Judge by replying:

> "I can present evidence, and I can question witnesses. You are incorrect in that".
>
> (Judge Royal, 2004)

The Government's medical report was part of a series of Medical Examinations which were made with a number of young people taken into 'Protective Custody' after the raid on the Nuwaubian property in 2002, in which a handful of York's so-called victims were diagnosed with "Sexually Transmitted Diseases", said to have been contracted from the Defendant. However as we have seen, these allegations contradict Medical reports made by Government examiners who found that it would have been impossible for the Defendant Malachi York to have been the source of the Diseases. It is also interesting to note that none of the Children originally seized during the raid and illegally questioned without the presence of their Parents by FBI agents & Medical Examiners, ever admitted to being Molested by the

Nuwaubian leader. This was exemplified by the testimony provided by the next female witness to give evidence to the court. Amanda Noel admitted when questioned by the Defence that she originally denied being molested when first interviewed by Medical Examiners and the FBI. Attorney Patrick was able to establish that in her original testimony when asked by Federal investigators if she knew why she was being interviewed she replied: ***"Because of the lies they have been saying about Mr. York."*** However in court she claimed that she made that statement through fear, after being warned by senior members of the organisation not to tell about Sexual activity with the Defendant. Either she had originally lied to protect the Defendant, or she was now lying for the Prosecutors. Whatever the case, something just didn't seem right about her testimony, which as we shall later discover was completely fabricated as a result of being coerced and threatened by the authorities and the Prosecution to say what they required to obtain a conviction against the Nuwaubian leader.

Towards the end of the week's proceedings, York's Attorney pointed out to the court many of the inconsistencies between the previous testimonies of **all of** the Defendant's accusers, which were hugely significant to the strength of the Prosecution's case, also adding:

> "I think the way it was set up, the defendant was going to come into court and get slaughtered. It seems as if the witnesses are changing their stories. I see substantial inconsistencies."
>
> (Attorney Patrick, 2004)

In response to Attorney Patrick's allegations, Prosecution Attorney Wood said he was happy with the outcome of the first week's testimony and could see no problem with any of the evidence given by the witnesses, and added:

> "It's not unusual in child molestation cases to have inconsistent evidence because you are dealing with children. We'll have more than the victims' testimony."
>
> (Attorney Wood, 2004)

Attorney Patrick closed by promising to provide Defence witnesses in the forthcoming week, whose testimonies would repudiate both the 'Child Sexual' Molestation allegations, as well as the allegation that the Defendant forced his followers to live in 'Squalid' conditions on the Nuwaubian Ranch. Outside the courtroom, many of the group's staunchest adversaries began to gather like vultures at the end of the first week of the Trial. One of whom was Georgia Benjamin-Smith, head of the Eatonton chapter of the National Association for the Advancement of Coloured People (NAACP), who told Atlanta Journal-Constitution reporter Bill Torpy how delighted she was that the group's founder Malachi York had finally been brought to Justice. Mrs Benjamin-Smith claims to have been repeatedly harassed and intimidated by York's followers for opposing their attempts to dominate the local NAACP chapter, adding:

> "It's been a nightmare, but we did something New York couldn't do...We stayed on it and didn't back up. This little town didn't back up...I was told more than once, 'Leave him alone. He's just a black man trying to have something...But I had a gut feeling something was wrong. I'd say, 'What's wrong with you? Don't you see what's going on?...With the king bee gone, [the followers] will scatter like ants"
>
> (Benjamin-Smith, 2004)

There was also former Putnam County Commissioner Sandra Adams, who was subsequently fired on corruption charges, stemming from investigations made by the Nuwaubian's into her fraudulent practices as County Commissioner. Mrs Adams commented to reporters about her feelings towards the group's activities in the County:

> "This was made a racial thing and it tore the community apart...Al Sharpton, who is running for president, came down here and attacked us".
>
> (Adams, 2004)

As always, on hand and ready to add his 'two pennies worth' was the Nuwaubian's No.1 enemy Sheriff Sills, who was naturally happy with the outcome of the first week's proceedings, and expressed his suspicion about the Nuwaubian's staging some type of incident on their leaders behalf during the forthcoming stages of the trial:

> "The only thing predictable about this group is that it is totally unpredictable. They could all be dressed in clown outfits tomorrow and it wouldn't surprise me a bit".
>
> (Sheriff Sills, 2004)

Meanwhile according to several eye-witness accounts, Sheriff Sills conducted a continued insidious campaign of covertly 'Tainting' the Jury Pool by spreading and circulating inflammatory information regarding Malachi York to local residents & Journalists as well as members of the Jury, and by so doing severely damaged the Nuwaubian leader's chances of a fair trial.

Nevertheless the Trial resumed on Monday 12th January, with testimony from more of the Government's supposed 'expert witnesses, which included Psychiatrist Dr. Cheryl Collins, who claimed to have treated one of York's female victims Amanda Noel at the National Children's Hospital in Washington, D.C. Dr. Collins said the girl she treated had been suffering from "Post-Traumatic Stress Disorder, which Dr. Collins claimed was as a result of "Child Abuse". Dr. Collins went on to add that the girl suffered from a number of behavioural problems such as Nightmares, Depression, and described her abuse in a "Detached Monotone, flat effect" voice, which Dr. Collins claimed is commonly associated with child abuse victims, and was supposed to prove that she had been Molested by the group's leader.

However as the trial progressed, the court would soon learn of the true cause of many of the young people's trauma.

Also to testify was one of the Prosecution's 'Key' witnesses, York's former Concubine Barbara Noel, the Mother of the prosecution's two main witnesses; Nicol Lopez & Amanda Noel. During her testimony, Barbara Noel told the court how York threatened to kill one of her children, if she exposed his Sexual activities to the authorities, adding that the Defendant threatened to *"throw her daughter's body behind the deer pen"*, an area often used for hunting located on the group's Putnam Ranch. As we saw earlier, during the time of the supposed Sexual Assaults against her daughters, Barbara Noel was living with York, at his Athens residence, which she later admitted during her testimony.

Next came another round of accusations of foul play by the Defence, after Judge Ashley Royal resorted to more of his old tricks, by taking it upon himself to assist the Prosecution, by summoning both legal teams to his bench before Amanda Noel's testimony, and specifically instructing the Defence not to mention Amanda Noel's mother's testimony at any time during her questioning, because Amanda Noel *"had a problem with details."* Enraged by Judge Royal's constant interference on the side of the Prosecution, Attorney Patrick again called for Judge Royal to remove himself from the trial for displaying blatant bias on the side of the Prosecution. According to York's Attorney, Amanda Noel had a problem remembering the details because of the many lies previously fabricated by her mother and sister, and would have simply contradicted her Mother's account if questioned. Being fully aware of this, Judge Royal again seized the opportunity to aid the Prosecution, which Attorney Patrick highlighted:

"The court is clearly acting defacto as a Prosecutor"
(Attorney Patrick, 2004)

Unrepentant, Judge Royal simply dismissed Attorney Patrick's allegations, and again refused to "Step Down" or removes himself from the proceedings stating in retaliation:

"I'm surprised you don't understand the role a judge has in a trial," he said. "You simply don't understand basic rules of evidence".
(Judge Royal, 2004)

On Tuesday 13th, one of the Prosecution's other main witnesses Miss Nicole Harden, took the stand to give evidence against the Defendant. Born August 1969, 35-year old Nicole Harden is the sister of another one of York's accusers, 19-year old Krystal Harden, and has often been accused by York's followers of Sexually Molesting numerous youngsters within the Community including 16-year old Abul Salaam LaRoche also known as Shelomoh. As we shall see, Miss Harden, like many of York's other accusers was 'Blackmailed' and manipulated into giving evidence against the group's founder because of things they had previously done to Minors within the Community, in return for complete **'Federal Immunity'** against Prosecution. Following her testimony, Nicole Harden was cross-examined by Attorney Patrick regarding the Sexual Molestation accusations against her, and the accusations made against his client. The following is a transcript of Attorney Patrick's Cross-Examination of the Prosecution witness Nicole Harden:

Attorney Patrick: Do you know who Abdul Salaam LaRoche aka Shelomoh is?

Nicole Harden: Yes I do!

Attorney Patrick: How old are you?

Nicole Harden: You mean now

Attorney Patrick: Yes now

Nicole Harden: 34!

Attorney Patrick: And you know a Boy named Abdul Salaam LaRoche aka Shelomoh LaRoche is that right?

Nicole Harden: Yes

Attorney Patrick: How old would you say he is?

Nicole Harden: I don't know around 15

Attorney Patrick: How old was he in 1998?

Nicole Harden: I guess around 11 or 12

Attorney Patrick: Have you ever had Sexual Intercourse with him?

Nicole Harden: Umm, Yeah

Attorney Patrick: Is that Yes or No?

Nicole Harden: Yes I did

Attorney Patrick: How old were you in that year when it happened

Nicole Harden: Let me think, 29

Attorney Patrick: How old was he then

Nicole Harden: Around 11

Attorney Patrick: Now I want to ask you are you a Paedophile?

Nicole Harden: A what?

Attorney Patrick: I am sorry. Are you a Child Molester?

Nicole Harden: Nope!

Attorney Patrick: You are not?

Nicole Harden: No!

Attorney Patrick: But didn't you just tell this Jury, before this Judge, before this Court that you had Sex with an underage Boy named Abdul Salaam LaRoche aka Shelomoh?

Nicole Harden: Yeah, yes but I'm not a Child Molester

Attorney Patrick: Do you know what a Child Molester is?

Nicole Harden: I think so

Attorney Patrick: You think so? So you don't know

Nicole Harden: I didn't say that

Attorney Patrick: Well you know when an adult has sex with a minor that is Child Molestation. Now again did you have sex with Abdul Salaam LaRoche aka Shelomoh when he was 11 years old and you were 29?

Nicole Harden: Yeah

Fearing that their witness was about to incriminate herself, the Prosecution abruptly interrupted Attorney Patrick's Cross-Examination of Nicole Harden, in an attempt to protect her and prevent the court from further discovering about her 'Illegal' relationship with Abdul Salaam LaRoche.
After all of the Prosecution witnesses had provided their testimonies, two more witnesses gave evidence. The first of these was 27 year-old Sakinah Parham, born 30th April, 1976, who was a last minute addition to the Prosecution's list of witnesses. Sakinah Parham claimed that York had begun having sex with her at the age of 14, and eventually decided to leave the Community after finally falling pregnant for him in 2000. Miss Parham, who you may remember was one of the original 2 women to first accuse the Defendant of fathering their children, claimed York continuously refused to pay Child Support for any of his numerous children born to women within the Community. Miss Parham testified that she was told as a girl that it was a privilege to have Sex with York, and that soon after leaving the Community she quickly became penniless and destitute.

Abigail Washington

Sakinah Parham's testimony was followed by 28-year old Abigail "Habiba" Washington, the Federal Prosecution's main witness, who began by testifying that York was also the father of her 2 children. Adding that he once informed her that he enjoyed having Sex with younger women because: *"His purpose for doing it was to keep the girls loyal to our culture, and that if you have a girl when she is a virgin, she is more likely to remain loyal to you"*. In the Prosecution's opening statements, Miss Washington it was claimed was key to the investigation against York, because she was not only molested by him, but was also formerly responsible for the organisations finances, and therefore of vital importance to the new charge the Government were also building against York which was for **"Money Structuring and Racketeering"**, which fell under the RICO statute that carried sentences of up to life imprisonment.

Fig.373 *"Habiba" Washington*

The RICO act stands for 'Racketeer Influenced & Corrupt Organisations', and was originally designed by the Federal Government to combat organised crime syndicates such as the Italian Mafia, Colombian Cartels and Russian Mob. However, recently the 'RICO act' has been used to target any organisation or business deemed to be engaged in illegal activities, as was recently witnessed in 2005 after the Indictments and subsequent Trial of Chris & Irv (Lorenzo) 'Gotti', Co-founders of Rap label, 'Murder Inc' Records, which eventually fell flat on its face due to insufficient evidence. It has often been stated that a RICO or 'Racketeering' charge is very difficult to substantiate because *"Racketeering activity essentially requires a plaintiff or prosecutor to prove a crime within a CRIME"*. In other words, in order to secure a conviction for 'Racketeer Influenced & Corrupt Organisations' (RICO), Prosecutor's essentially have to establish that the Organisation or Corporation in question, is not only a 'Criminal Enterprise', but also run for strictly 'Criminal Purposes', which the Nuwaubian movement has absolutely no proven history of being.

During her testimony Miss Washington provided in detail, primary evidence relating to the so-called 'Money Structuring and Racketeering' charges against the Defendant, stating that York always instructed her to separate the "Bank Deposits", to prevent them from going over the sum of $10,000. The reason, she said York instructed her to do this was to avoid making 'Transaction Reports', which are compulsory by Law every time any transaction exceeded the sum of $10,000. She described to the court how York's books and other products, printed on the Putnam Property were distributed and sold through a sophisticated network of outlets or "Nuwaubian Stores", located in several major cities throughout the U.S. and abroad, which she claimed generated between $20,000 to $70,000 fortnightly. It was becoming increasingly apparent why the Media and 'Law enforcement' investigators continually kept placing great emphasis on the so-called 'Black Briefcase' discovered underneath a bed at York's Athens residence, supposedly containing over $250,000 in cash, since the beginning of the case. During her testimony, Miss Washington claimed that "every other Wednesday" the monies brought in from book sales would be sent to York, all in $50 & $100 bills, which she claimed he kept in a **'Black Briefcase'**. After which, a certain amount would then be deposited into a "Holy Tabernacle Ministries Business account", which she verified by producing a number of "Deposit Slips". It was clear from her detailed description of the inner financial workings of the organisation that; Abigail Washington was of far more significance to the Prosecution's case than any of the other witnesses.

After the Prosecution had completed their questioning of Miss Washington, York's Defence Attorney Adrian Patrick cross-examined her in an attempt to establish what incentives she may have been promised by the Prosecution to testify against his client, and more importantly, asses her involvement in what he was trying to prove was a conspiracy against the Defendant. The following is a transcript of part of Attorney Patrick's cross-examination of Abigail Washington, regarding her 'Immunity Agreement' with the Federal Government to falsely testify against the Nuwaubian leader:

> **Attorney Patrick:** Ms. Washington have you reviewed your Immunity agreement?
>
> **Abigail Washington:** Umm. My Immunity agreement?
>
> **Attorney Patrick:** Yes, your Immunity agreement for you to testify here today for the prosecution
>
> **Abigail Washington:** Yes I have reviewed my Immunity agreement
>
> **Attorney Patrick:** Are you aware that on paragraph 2, line 3, it states that you will be given *"Favourable Concessions"* for your testimony here today?
>
> **Attorney Moultrie:** Objection!! Objection!! Your honour her Immunity agreement does not say that. That is nowhere in the agreement, and Mr. Patrick should be strongly reprimanded by this court for brining up this frivolous information in his client's Defence before the Jury

Attorney Patrick: Your honour, may I approach the witness so that she may read this section of her Immunity agreement to refresh her memory and the prosecution's memory?

Judge Royal: Yes go ahead

Attorney Patrick: Ms. Washington would you please read paragraph 2, line 3 for the Jury?

Abigail Washington: "You will be given favourable concessions in return for your testimony at trial and cooperation in the investigation against Malachi York".

At this point Defence Attorney Patrick, then turned to the Jurors, and showed them the piece of paper previously read out by Abigail Washington, and stated: *"The Government just said this statement was not in the agreement and it has been read in open court that the Government lied, in fact Ms. Habiba Washington is on the government's payroll and has been paid to testify against Mr. York. What is the Government trying to hide from you, the Jury? I would like to tender this document into evidence".*
According to Attorney Patrick, the Prosecution's case against his client was essentially based upon a conspiracy orchestrated by disgruntled ex-members of the organisation, one of whom was Abigail Washington who was initially in charge of the group's finances and was eventually thrown out for matters involving dishonesty with the organisations finances, and Sexual impropriety with youngsters under her care. From the detailed testimony provided, Abigail Washington certainly fitted many aspects of Attorney Patrick's description, so who is she, and how was she able to wield such influence within the organisation? For the answer, let's divert our attentions away from the actual trial for a moment, and examine in further depth the background of the Prosecution's key witness Abigail Washington.
Born 8th October, 1975, within the Ansaaru Allah Community, "Habiba" Abdullah Muhammad, was the daughter of one of York's closest followers, Nathaniel Washington otherwise known as Brother 'Yusef' Abdullah Muhammad. Noted from a young age for her exceptional intellect, this woman was actually at one time said to have been in charge of the finances of the entire Nuwaubian movement, and enjoyed a great deal of power within the movement. Shortly after his guilty plea in 2003, York's followers issued a press release entitled: *"The Set Up: The Truth Behind The Plea"*, in which Abigail Washington was first vilified and accused of stealing money from the organisation, as well as being the 'Mastermind' behind the conspiracy to falsely imprison the group's leader. The following is an excerpt from this press release:

> We all know that this was a well thought out plan and instead of reporting the money properly Abagal Washington, a/k/a Habiba Washington, a/k/a Gaile Washayton or Watch-Shayton, a/k/a the Dwarf illegally stole money

to put it aside for herself. She even admitted this openly to the Federal Government. Did you know that she was even studying a book called **CONSPRACY AND BUTTERFLY**. And get this: This Book <u>Butterfly</u> is about children getting together to plot against a minister saying that they were molested. That's right she actually studied this and plotted this. Don't Believe Me Check it Out for yourself. She has been setting this up for years.

(Nuwaubian staff writer, 2003)

Even though there is absolutely no doubt about Abigail "Habiba" Washington's involvement in the conspiracy, there is however, a lot more to who Abigail Washington actually is, than the Nuwaubian leadership would like York's 'rank and file' followers and indeed the general public to be aware of. A regular tactic used by the Nuwaubian hierarchy is to often vilify and tarnish the character of anyone against Dr. Malachi. Z. York in order to gloss over York's shortcomings to make him appear completely faultless. This is often necessary in cases of those who deserve it such as Sheriff Howard Sills, and numerous other racist officials & Journalists, such as the Atlanta Journal-Constitution's Bill Osinski. However in the case of Abigail Washington the issue is much more complex than York's followers would like to admit.

As we have already observed, most of York's problems going back to the 1970s, in the Ansaaru Allah Community, almost always seems to involve members of the opposite sex. What the Nuwaubian's initially failed to make mention of was that York was not only intimately involved at one point with Abigail Washington, but that they have two children together named; 'Enlil', and 'Setra'. According to insiders within the movement, York's relationship with Abigail Washington began in 1992, when she was just 17 years of age. There is no account of them ever being married, although she was said to have been one of York's favourite "Concubines", and it is precisely for this reason that the young woman was able to eventually reach the position of such authority within the organisation. Therefore at one stage Abigail Washington must have possessed some good qualities, for York to have been intimately involved with her, ultimately granting her such authority within the Movement. Either that or the Nuwaubian leadership are admitting that York is a very poor judge of character to have placed this Evil young woman in charge of the entire organisations finances? After all, she was raised in the Community from birth, so they can't claim that the Nuwaubian leader was not aware of her character.

To further confirm the close relationship between York and Abigail Washington, let's find out from the man himself. The following is an excerpt taken from an interview with Malachi York conducted from Prison in 2004, in which he illustrates what his feelings were towards Abigail Washington, even after discovering how she had betrayed him:

"Ok first of all, when you speak about "Habiba" Washington, Habiba Abdullah Muhammad, right, She was more than just part of the case. She was somebody I was very close to, trusted a great deal, and loved a lot. We have two children, a Son named Enlil, and a Daughter named Setra, two Beautiful Children. I'm close to the whole family, I know her Mother, I know her Father, in fact her Father Nathaniel Washington, named "Yusef", was on the stand to Testify on my behalf. Never to bad mouth or talk bad about his daughter. He did never say anything bad about her, it's just that he said he knew that when she came to him she was 17, about me and her relationship. And then the Prosecution tried to make him look bad by saying, didn't he think it was strange that a 40-year old man was trying to Marry a 17-year girl. And he said, well she came to me, and then he came to me and talked about it. And he said that we live by the Bible Law, we don't live by what you call, your system of things. We live by the Bible Law, and our Tribal Laws. In our Tribal Laws we don't have the same Principles where you'll pretend you have all these Ethics, and you'll pretend you'll have all these Morals for the Public, but behind closed doors, all kinds of things like the Clinton situation is going on. And I can go on and on and on like the Catholic Churches etc etc etc.

Alright, so let me leave it like that there, **as far as I'm concerned, Habiba Abdullah Muhammad was threatened by People, and coerced that they was going to take our Children away from her, and they put her on the spot. She's really a beautiful person.** They put her on the spot, and I could tell, cause when I was in the court, looking into her eyes from the stand after knowing her since She was a Kid, right, I knew that they were manipulating her, against me. You follow, and I could see the regret in her eyes, at a certain period in her eyes. It hurt me just to sit there, but I could feel her touch me Heart to Heart! You follow what I'm saying? I said this is ridiculous, this is out of hand. I said there's nothing in our life, that involves this much that needs to go this far, where they're trying to put me away, the Father of her Children away for Life!

I don't see her as a Bad Person, at all, as people would like me to be, I'm not 'Mad' at her, I'm not Angry. I'm hurt somewhat. But I realized after I saw her, I needed that, when I was down in Brunswick when I was in Court, and I saw her Eye to Eye, I needed to see that, for me to be able to look inside and say, they have cornered Her. I may have been mad when She left, cause I distrusted her for certain things, you know what I'm saying? But in actuality I could see that She didn't mean for it to get like this, or go this far. They all got tricked by (Sheriff) Howard Richard Sills, and by Jacob who was threatening them on what was going to happen to them if they didn't cooperate with the Government, and all that kind of stuff. And I understand that. They received what they call 'Favourable Concessions', they paid them, all kinds of things to coerce them to topple the organization. But I don't think those people really thought it was going to go this far, especially I don't think She would have thought it would go this far, that they were gonna try to put me away for Life, or as many times as they were going to try to Kill me, and Torture me since I've been incarcerated, I don't think She anticipated all that happening.

> Well as far as the RICO and all that stuff, they threw the RICO together at the last minute, it wasn't even in the original Indictment, they just threw that together because they needed someway to hold this case together. Then went to them and told them, what we need you to say, is he told you to structure Money or whatever, you know at a certain amount of time, and they give them the dialogue, and they gotta say it on the stand, and that's it. Because by the time she was requested after the Prosecution finished, by the time She got before the Defence-Prosecution, the whole thing changed. Then they start putting the receipts up, She was saying I'm not saying he told me that day to do this. But the Judge and the Jury, and them were all already Pre-stacked, you know what I mean, it was already set up anyway, so they was going to go on regardless of what was coming down, but we got all that on the minutes, and everything is down, and we're getting the Transcripts, so that could be exposed for the 'Appellant'.
> **But I don't have any hard feeling against Habiba Washington,** or I call her "Habiba" at all, Right!....
>
> (York, 2004)

At the age of around 23, Abigail Washington was left in charge of not only the group's finances, but also many of the young people in the community, after York had relocated to Athens, Georgia. For reasons unknown, Abigail Washington later fell out of York's favour over some financial irregularities, which is when she may have decided to take revenge by eventually becoming Malachi York's estranged son, Jacob York's 'recruiter' within the Community. Because of York's policy of blatant nepotism in appointing family members and 'Female Favourites' to key positions within the organisation, it was very easy for York's enemies to manufacture his downfall. Clearly, all Jacob had to do was target Abigail Washington to gain access to the inner working of the movement. During the trial, there had been mention of some Video-tapes allegedly showing sex between children made at the Nuwaubian property, which were said to have been destroyed by one of York's other son's before the trial. In an article, which appeared in the Macon Telegraph, dated January 9th 2004 entitled *"Woman testifies she groomed younger victims for York"*, reporter Wayne Crenshaw states the following:

> According to a woman, York once told her to fondle a male toddler. "(York) said his aunt did that to him when he was a boy," the woman said. After she testified, the government called a string of FBI agents to identify numerous items of evidence they recovered from a search of York's compound. Though the contents of several boxes were not discussed, one agent identified a briefcase found in York's home as having contained $279,450. Another agent identified a case of DVDs as containing several pornographic movies, including such titles as Debbie Does Dallas. He said the case was recovered from York's bedroom. The woman said she was told that pornographic videos made of children on the compound were destroyed by York's son.
>
> (Crenshaw, 2004)

Could this woman have been "Habiba" Washington herself, whose name is known to have appeared on several receipts for Pornographic DVDs, ordered by her credit card, and addressed to **"Gail Washington", PO Box 6769, Athens?** This material was later recovered by law enforcement officials during the raid of the Nuwaubian property in 2002. Which could be why the Agents refused to divulge the contents of the other boxes, because it may have proven that they really belonged to their own lead witness Abigail Washington? Were these Pornographic films mentioned, actually destroyed by one of Malachi. Z. York's son's, in an attempt to hide the evidence of Malachi York's guilt, or were they destroyed by Abigail Washington herself to hide her own guilt? These were also the same boxes of Pornographic DVDs, she testified belonged to Dr. Malachi. Z. York, during the trial.

It has also been claimed that Abigail Washington used this Pornographic material to introduce many of the young people to Sex, before eventually encouraging them to leave the community to join York's son Jacob, in his so-called "Halfway House", as we shall see shortly.

Whatever her actual role, it is fair to say, despite all of the things Abigail Washington was responsible for, she was eventually proven not to have been the 'Mastermind' behind the conspiracy, but in actual fact merely a **'Pawn'**, because of her own dishonesty and arrogance, which made it easy for her to be controlled by the Powerful Forces who were really behind the conspiracy to destroy the Nuwaubian leader, and who, as we shall now see, recruited Malachi York's estranged Son, Record Producer Jacob York, to be their 'key' individual in the conspiracy.

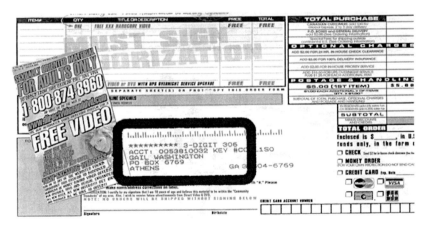

Fig.374 Receipt of Pornographic DVD's addressed to York's former Mistress Abigail Washington

Fig.375 *Pornographic DVD's discovered by F.B.I. during Nuwaibian Raid*

On Friday 16th January, the Defence summoned several witnesses who were still loyal to the organisation to provide evidence on York's behalf. First up was Evelyn Rivera, who claimed to have been one of the Defendant's followers for over 23 years. In her testimony Evelyn Rivera stated that she "wholeheartedly" believed that the entire case was a conspiracy to destroy her leader's credibility. She went on to add that none of York's so-called victims were at all trustworthy stating *"They are all liars...I knew them as children. They all lie."* Evelyn Rivera's testimony was followed by eight more individuals, some of whom were actually the parents of many of York's accusers, who all asserted that York had not "Sexually Molested" their children or any other young people within the Community, and that these prosecution witnesses must have been coerced or forced to lie against the Defendant. Another Defence witness was Samiyra Samad, who like Evelyn Rivera, was well spoken and smartly dressed. Mrs Samad a middle-aged qualified Nurse, with slightly greying hair was a complete contrast to many of the Prosecution witnesses who were all brash and arrogant adolescents. Mrs Samad was an impressive witness who gave the court a glowing account of life in the Community and of the Defendant whom she described as *"Someone who always spoke the Truth."* Mrs Samad says she joined York's Movement in 1977, whilst it was known as the Ansaaru Allah Community, based in Brooklyn, New York, later migrating to Georgia with the rest of the group in 1993. Mrs Samad claimed to have carried out Medical Examinations on up to 1,000 children within the organisation over the years, and never once saw or heard any signs of

'Sexual Molestation' against any of the youngsters, adding that she had three children of her own, and originally joined York's movement to provide a safe environment for them. Mrs Samad ended her testimony by stating:

> "I am a mother. I would not lie for something like that...And I would not lie for him!!"
>
> (Samad, 2004)

Once again the Media were on hand to cynically play down all of the positive testimonies provided by numerous witnesses for the Defence, which contradicted the evidence given by York's accusers, especially regarding the group's living conditions and the Defendant's Sexual depravity against children. Whenever York's so-called victims described brutal acts of Sexual Molestation, the media described the witness's testimony Verbatim, or word for word, in graphic detail, however in cases where the witness spoke on York's behalf, the reporters usually seemed uninterested.

During the final week of the trial, things took an even more disturbing twist when the Prosecution actually showed members of the Jury a copy of the group's Religious manifesto **'The Holy Tablets'** as evidence of York's guilt, which had absolutely no relationship to any of the charges against him, and have subsequently left many observers of the case wondering whether Dr. York was actually on trial for his teachings, rather than any supposed Sexual Molestation. This presumption was consequently confirmed by Journalist Bill Osinski in his book *"Ungodly: A True Story of Unprecedented Evil"*, in which he asserts that the groups Holy book *"The Holy Tablets"*, was one of the things which initially 'Frightened' local residents, and alerted County officials towards the supposed perceived dangers of York's teachings not long after their arrival in Putnam County.

Attorney Patrick called a series of 'Special' witnesses who spoke up in favour of the Defendant, which included "Habiba" Washington's father Nathaniel Washington, who described his daughter as "usually trustworthy", which the Prosecution tried to manipulate to mean she was honest about her accusations against the Defendant. When asked about his daughter's relationship with York, Mr. Washington replied that he was fully aware of when it started, and prior to this he had never seen any signs of Sexual interference on his daughter. Again the Prosecution tried to twist Nathaniel Washington's words by enquiring whether he didn't think it was strange for a Middle-aged man to have that kind of relationship with a 17-year old girl. However, Mr. Washington made his position clear by explaining that it was what his daughter wanted, and before the relationship actually begun, himself and York both sat down and discussed the matter, according to the Law's & Customs of the Nuwaubian beliefs which were in line with Ancient African & 'Semetic' traditions found within the scriptures.

Attorney Patrick then attempted to repudiate the Prosecution's claim that York exploited his followers and "Brainwashed" them into believing that he was some type of 'Demi-God', by asking each witness individually if they believed York was God. Naturally this question was treated with amusement by many of the Nuwaubian's who clearly did not believe this. One of the Defendant's followers in particular, Raymond Valentine, answered by saying that York was "like a father" to his devotees. York's Attorney pointed out that all of those that stayed within the Community testified in favour of York, while those outside the Community testified against him. The Jury then heard from a succession of witnesses who provided further testimony in York's Defence, including five young women whom the Federal Prosecutor's insisted were Sexually Molested by York, however one by one, these young women all fiercely contradicted the Government's claim, by denying that they were ever molested by the Defendant.

Next to take the stand was a member of the United Kingdom's Nuwaubian Community; Horace Wright. Wright provided Testimony regarding the Prosecution's claim that York's followers worshipped him as a kind of Deity or 'God'. Wright, a former successful Reggae Dance-Hall DJ, known as 'The Dub Bug', who through hard work & diligence, had taken leadership of the movement in London, not long after joining the late 1990s. 'Dr' Horace Wright or Montu Ptah, who was often refered to as 'Imam' of the London congregation, eloquently refuted the Prosecution's allegation that York compared himself to 'Jesus Christ' in his publications, by presenting the Court with a very detailed account of Dr. York's teachings.

Fig.376 *Bruce LaRoche aka Brother Wali*

Finally the court heard the testimony of 18-year old Safaa'a LaRoche, the sister of Abdul Salam LaRoche, born 13th May 1985 in Brooklyn, New York. Safaa'a was the daughter of York's former Driver and 'Best Friend', Bruce Lucious LaRoche, otherwise known as 'Abdul Wali', or Brother Wali who was one of York's original followers to have joined the Ansaaru Allah Community during the late 1960s. Bruce Lucious LaRoche is accused of subsequently becoming an FBI informant against the organisation and assisted Federal Investigators to compile a detailed dossier of evidence against the Nuwaubian leader.

Safaa's testimony was a heart-moving account of how 'Law Enforcement' officials 'Invaded' the group's peaceful Community in May 2002, and how she and many of the other young people were left mentally scarred and "Traumatised" by the Federal agents and Police Officers storming of the group's property aiming "Automatic Weapons" at everybody, shouting and ordering them to the ground. Safaa'a LaRoche ended her testimony by adding:

"To this day, I still have nightmares about it,...It's scarred on my soul...I heard glass breaking and orders being shouted...I don't think anybody realizes what we went through that day...It was horrible"
(LaRoche, 2004)

Shortly before the close of proceedings, Attorney Patrick showed the court photographs of York's female accusers in intimate poses with the Defendants son Jacob York. Attorney Patrick brought it to the court's attention that all of York's alleged victims travelled to "South Beach", Florida with the Defendant's son, before going to the FBI. York's Attorney concluded by promising to unveil the source of a conspiracy against the Defendant, which he claimed was entirely orchestrated by the Defendants "estranged son", Jacob York.

Jacob York and the Child Abuse Conspiracy

You may recall at the beginning of this chapter the name of Jacob York being mentioned in connection with Barbara Noel Lopez, the mother of 2 of York's accusers. Also anyone remotely familiar with early Media reports of the case will recall numerous interviews, conducted by an anonymous young man claiming to be Malachi York's son, who professed to be responsible for exposing his father's activities to the authorities. Whilst in reporter Bill Osinski's 'highly fictionalised' book *"Ungodly: A True Story of Unprecedented Evil",* this same individual is referred to as **'Malik'**, one of the story's central characters, most responsible brining the Nuwaubian leader to Justice.

The 3rd week of trial began on Monday 19th, which also happened to be designated as a Public holiday in honour of 'Dr. Martin Luther. Amidst marching bands and numerous other festivities that morning, York's trial got under way inside Brunswick County Federal Courthouse, which now included the new indictment of 'Racketeering', recently added to the Sexual Molestation charges. The first motion by Defence Attorney Patrick was for the Judge to permit several witnesses to illustrate to the court details of a Conspiracy supposedly led by the Defendant's son Jacob York, and dozens of disgruntled former Nuwaubian's to frame the group's leader of Sexual Child Molestation, adding that:

"Jacob York clearly has a grudge against his father...Jacob is in the music business and asked his father for money...He didn't give it to him...Jacob has told several people that he's going to get him."
(Attorney Patrick, 2004)

Naturally the Defence's assertion of a Conspiracy was flatly dismissed by the Prosecution, and referred to by US Attorney Maxwell Wood as nothing more than **"Classic Hearsay!!"**
Next York's Defence used the Testimony of 21 year-old Sakina Woods, whom Investigator's initially claimed was also Molested by the Defendant.

However Miss Woods immediately got on the stand and firmly repudiated the Prosecution's allegations by denying ever being the victim of any Sexual Assault by York, adding that the Federal investigator's tried to force her to accuse the Defendant:

> "It seemed they wanted me to say something that didn't happen…They kept asking me over and over and I kept telling them, 'No, No, No."
>
> (Woods, 2004)

Sakina Woods' claim was also verified by 18 year-old Hanaan Merritt, who testified to the court that Federal investigators tried to coerce her to accuse the Defendant by continuously putting her and others under pressure to admit that they were Sexually Assaulted. Miss Merritt added that: ***"the investigators basically told us that he molested us. They kept saying, 'No, you're lying".*** Clearly frustrated by the Prosecution's attempt to trivialize her testimony, Hanaan Merritt admonished Attorney Maxwell Wood by informing him that the raid on May 2002 left her and many of the young people severely 'Traumatized and Distressed', and asked if he would like for his child to go through the same experience?

The Prosecution with the assistance of the Media simply poured scorn over all of the claims by York's Defence, that the Nuwaubian Nation was a deeply Spiritual organisation, which had been dedicated to the 'Upliftment' and progress of the downtrodden, throughout its 30-something years of existence.

On Wednesday 21st, the issue of a Conspiracy against the Defendant re-surfaced when one of York's other daughters, 23 year-old Leah Mabry, testified that she had encountered her brother Jacob, who was accompanied by several of her father's accusers in May 2001. During a conversation, he had apparently tried to persuade her to go with him to the FBI, to inform them that she was also Sexually Molested. Rubbishing the notion that she was herself Molested by the Defendant, Miss Mabry continued by claiming that Jacob had a bitter vendetta against his father. Following Leah Mabry's testimony, a string of witnesses for the Defence took the stand claiming that the entire Sexual Molestation charge was nothing more than a lie concocted by a group of disgruntled members of the organisation encouraged to do so by the Defendant's son Jacob York. Leading up to, and throughout the duration of the trial, the name 'Jacob York' kept coming up in relation to a conspiracy against the group's founder. So who is this intriguing individual, and what are the basis of these allegations against him, and what is, if any, is his actual role in this alleged "Conspiracy"? For the answer to this, let us again divert our attentions away from the Trial for a moment and investigate this Mysterious character known as Jacob York.

The entire Conspiracy against Malachi York is said to centred around two individuals, namely; Barbara Noel, the Mother of 2 of York's main accusers Nicole "Adah" Lopez, & Amanda Noel and Jacob "Jake" York, the estranged son of Dr. Malachi. Z. York. It was these two, who are said to have been the "Masterminds" and Primary Conspirators, behind the plot to bring down the Nuwaubian leader.

Compelling new evidence now suggests that aside from Barbara Noel, Jacob York was also in cahoots with another young woman within the organisation namely Abigail Washington aka "Habiba" Abdullah Muhammad, who as we have seen, also acted as the Prosecution's Key witness during the Trial, for not only Sexual Abuse charges, but the additional 'Money Structuring & Racketeering' charges.

In December 2003, York's followers published an exposé of Jacob York entitled: *"THE FATHER, MALACHI YORK IS ACCUSED OF THE SON, JACOB YORK'S CRIMES"*, in which they accused Jacob of being behind a conspiracy to destroy his father which involved coercing young members of the movement to accuse the group's leader of 'Sexual Molestation'. The article describes in detail, how it was in fact Jacob who had been molesting underage Girls and Boys in the community ever since the group were based in Brooklyn, New York. The conspiracy is said to run to the very core of the Movement, and reveals a catalogue of Lies, Sex, Manipulation and Greed, all centred around one Jacob York.

Jacob, whose real name is Yacuwb Abdullah Muhammad, and known by numerous other names including: Yacuwb, Jacob Johnson & "Jake York", was born in 1973, the 3rd son by York's former Wife/Concubine, the late Dorothy Mae Johnson otherwise known as Zubadah Muhammad or *'Sister Zubadah'*.

The true source of Jacob's resentment towards his father is said to be his late mother, who died as a result of an aneurysm or 'Brain Tumour' in 1995, after a painful separation from Malachi York. For many years Dorothy Johnson was regarded as York's main or 'Chief' wife, however following the group's arrival in Georgia, the relationship between Jacob's mother and father appears to have suffered. However, York's followers now assert that he was never actually legally married to her, which would have made her simply another one of the Nuwaubian leader's many "Concubines". Nevertheless, numerous reports have also indicated that Zubadah had indeed been with York since the very beginning, and would have therefore regarded herself as 'Head' wife, or what Pimps often refer to as the 'Bottom Bitch'. Despite York's followers insistence that he was in no way responsible for her untimely death, it does however stand to reason that she would have naturally felt a great deal of animosity at no longer being recognised as York's No.1 wife, after having bore 5 of his children, and spent many years of her life devoted to the Nuwaubian leader. Like many of York's other shortcomings, his followers try to gloss over this issue, as if York was completely blameless, nevertheless the evidence suggests that Dorothy Johnson felt deeply unhappy with York's endless appetite for different, often much 'Younger' women, which naturally lead to tensions between the two, finally causing her to abruptly leave the community in 1995, returning back to New York alone. Dorothy Johnson would have almost certainly informed her children of her feelings towards their father, which appears to have sown the seeds of the bitter resentment between Jacob and his father. The Nuwaubian's even acknowledge that Jacob holds his Father responsible for his Mother's death, and that he swore to stop at nothing to destroy him. However, another reason for Jacob's hatred, was his Father's apparent refusal to financially endorse Jacobs music career, because of Jacob's promotion of 'Filth Music' particularly Sexually explicit & Violent 'Gangster Rap', which Malachi York has always been strongly critical of, as we saw in Chapter 7. Whatever the motive of Jacob's animosity, he was now determined to destroy his father, by whatever means necessary.

As we saw in chapter 7, Jacob like a number of his other siblings, followed in his father's footsteps by pursuing a career in the music business, and had many successes, producing Rap artists like Lil' Kim & Junior Mafia. In fact, many within the organisation who know Jacob, actually claim that he is the child with the most in common with his father. Interestingly, many of the character traits exhibited by Jacob, are almost identical to many of the accounts made about Dr. Malachi. Z. York, by many of his ex-followers in Bilial Philips' book: *"The Ansar Cult In America"*. Some of which include:

- **Exceptional 'Intelligence Quotient' (I.Q.)**
- **Determined will to Succeed**
- **Criminal Mind**
- **Insatiable Lust for Power & Money**
- **Shrewd business sense**
- **Manipulative and Controlling Nature**
- **Charismatic Personality**
- **Pathological Love of Women**
- **Extraordinary Entrepreneurial Talents**

Although it would be fair to say that Jacob is the complete opposite of his father, it is not as clear cut as York's followers would have the public to believe, by portraying Jacob York as an Evil monster, and his father as a Saint, when he is clearly 'a chip off the Old Block'. The only obvious difference between the two is that Jacob has used his intelligence for Evil & immoral purposes, unlike his Father, who has used his many talents to raise the condition of his people throughout his many years as a Leader.

Music Mogul with Fraudulent Business Dealings

As a youngster growing up within the Ansaaru Allah Community, Jacob would have been heavily influenced by the constant flow of Hip Hop luminaries such as Afrika Bambaataa & the Soulsonic Force, Ice T, LL Cool J, Stetsasonic, JAZ, Sweet Tee & DJ Jazzy Joyce & The Jungle Brothers, who were not only affiliated with his father's organisation, but often frequented York's Brooklyn recording studio. Following in his father's footsteps from a very early age, Jacob decided to pursue a career in the music business, and is widely recognised within the industry as the driving force behind Rap Star Lil Kim's early career, with first Junior Mafia then later the launch of her Solo career. Jacob York received International notoriety when his name, along with that of Lance "Un" Rivera, and the late Christopher Wallace aka Notorious B.I.G. appearing as 'Executive Producers' of Lil Kim's Multi-Platinum selling début LP *"Hardcore"* released in 1997, which was one of the first to amalgamate Pornography with Rap music. In fact, Jacob York is acknowledged to have been the architect behind the whole 'Sexually Explicit' theme of the hugely successful album.

In his book *"Ungodly"*, Bill Osinski attempts to mislead the public by portraying Jacob York, whom he refers to as: **(Malik)**, as a struggling 'Party Promoter', trying to break into the music industry, who wanted nothing to do with his father.

> During those years, Malik [Jacob] told few people that he was the son of a man who demanded to be treated as a god. Rather he tried to sever all connections with his past and with the people he'd grown up with...from Ansaru Allah
>
> (Osinski, 2007, p: 225)

Nevertheless, this is complete rubbish, and could not be further from the truth. As we have seen, Jacob was not only a prominent record producer as far back as 1994, behind many of the early successes of Notorious B.I.G., Junior Mafia & Lil Kim. But actually used his Father's influence in New York, to open many doors on both the Street, and the Industry. For example, if Jacob was trying to hide his identity, why does he publicly use the name 'York', and not Johnson, which was his mother's maiden name. And why did he also 'Christen' his first record label; **'Yorktown'** record's, in honour of his Father Dr. York, if he was so ashamed of his connection to the Nuwaubian leader, as Osinski attempts to falsely contend.

Fig.377 *Jacob's 'Yorktown' record label*

Fig.378: *Label of Lil Kim's 1996 Debut LP showing the name Jacob I. York*

However despite many early successes, Jacob ran into serious problems in 1999, when his production company, "Untertainment" hit the headlines after the National Basketball league (NBA), filled a law suit against them for illegally using the NBA logo for the cover of one of the label's artists, Cam'ron's debut LP: *"Sports, Drugs & Entertainment"*. The advert depicted the NBA logo, the silhouette of a Basketball player, shown holding a gun whilst dribbling a basketball. On April 19th, 1999, residents of Malcolm X Boulevard, Harlem NY, were outraged when a huge billboard featuring the disturbing image appeared in front of several High schools. A number of local leaders including Mayor Rudolf and Rev. Al Sharpton, immediately called the offices of Untertainment to demand that the ad be removed. Rolling Stone Magazine covered the story in an article entitled: *"Cam'ron's Ad Is Pulled: Cam'ron's album advertisement violated NBA trademark and was removed"*, which explained the NBA's reaction to the advert:

> The NBA responded by filing suit against Untertainment on April 22, claiming an infringement of their trademark. The league sought damages

and an immediate injunction against any further use of their logo, which required that the billboard be taken down and an end to all print ads.
(Rolling Stone, 1999)

Figs.379 & 380 Left- Right: *Record Producer Jacob York With Industry Heavyweights: Jermain Dupree & Terrence Howard*

An article which appeared in the New York Metro on May 10th 1999, by reporters Beth Landman Keil & Deborah Mitchell, entitled: *"NBA Says Rapper's Got No Game"*, demonstrated how serious the NBA took the misuse of their logo by Untertainment, and provides some insight into the 'Depraved' mindset of Jacob York:

> Apparently the league that brought you the likes of Dennis Rodman and Chris Webber doesn't want to be associated with bad behaviour anymore. The NBA has filed a lawsuit against Untertainment, which is distributed by Sony's Epic Records, over a billboard for rap artist Cam-Ron that features an apparent rip-off of the NBA logo. The ad, which was posted directly across from a boys' high school in Harlem, replaced the acronym NBA with the more sinister SDE (sex, drugs, and entertainment). Cam-Ron himself appeared with a basketball and a gun. The ad was removed amid pressure from the NBA and from district councilman Bill Perkins, fresh from his successful February crusade to remove malt-liquor billboards from the same neighbourhood. "I was outraged that they would dare promote gun violence, sex, and drugs as something so positive for young people as basketball," says the councilman. Jacob York, president of Untertainment, is also contrite: "We apologize if we caused any harm," he says. **"We were just trying to get an image colourful enough to describe Cam-Ron's new album, one that would impact the kids."**
>
> (Keil & Mitchell, 1999)

The ad-campaign was a gamble, which went terribly wrong for Jacob, eventually costing his record company Millions of Dollars in litigation with the NBA. Notice also, Jacob's comment concerning his motive for deciding to use the logo: *"We were just trying to get an image colorful enough to describe Cam-Ron's new album, one that would impact the kids."* Why on earth, would Jacob want to use such an image to reach school kids? This statement speaks volumes, and exposes the depraved mentality of Jacob York. As a result of this marketing fiasco, Jacob and Cam-ron later parted company, with the Rapper going on to sign to fellow New York based Roca-Fella Records becoming one of the labels leading artists.

It is also alleged that not long after the disastrous advertising campaign, Jacob ran into serious financial problems with the IRS, later going on the run to avoid payment of outstanding taxes, of over a $100,000. Nevertheless, it has been Jacob's involvement with a number of fraudulent Bank and Mortgage transactions, which have been the cause of much controversy. The following is an excerpt from the previously mentioned article which appeared on the Nuwaubian website, containing an eyewitness testimony by Jacob York's former best friend Damon Pryor also known as 'Baasil Abdullah Muhammad', outlining Jacob's shady business dealings:

> Recently an eye witness and bestfriend of Jake York, who was asked by Jake to forge bank statements came forward to give the details of how he was able to purchase the house located at 5179 Meadowbrook Chase in Stone Mountain, GA, for $139, 000. "Jake said he needed to falsify Bank of American bank statements for the months of October and November to read higher than the stated balance of $9,416.51, it needed to be in the range of $50,000 - $60,000. His reasons were that he was trying to buy a house and needed proof that he was financially capable.
>
> (unnm.com, 2003)

Jacob is said to have illegally obtained a House, by forging bank statements to appear that he was earning 3 times more money than he actually was, which automatically qualified him for a Mortgage from any Bank or Finance company. The following is a transcript of a statement made by a former associate of Jacob York, detailing how he purchased the property, and who he had living with him:

> He said he needed a bigger house for more people and asked if I could falsify 6 documents by changing the checking balances with higher additions and fewer subtractions giving the final balance a higher sum." (excerpt from an eye witness' affidavit) **"This is the house that was mentioned in the statements that he gave to the FBI that was used as a "half way house" for girls who were leaving the 404 Shady Dale Rd. property. Our witness states in a legal affidavit that, "Jacob boasted about the girls he had living at his current house with him with graphic details of his sexual encounters with most of them if not all were banaats that were mentioned by name. They were hinting around the allegations supposedly from the young females."**
>
> (Excerpt from an eye-witness' affidavit) (unnm.com, 2003)

Jacob has also been implicated in another massive Mortgage Fraud, involving more than $280,000,000. In 2003, 3 men; William Carroll, Robert

C. Dukes and Darius Sampson, known to be linked to Jacob York, were arrested in DeKalb County Georgia, for their role in a postal service scam involving the purchase of millions of dollars of real estate situated in the much sought after Suburban 'Stone Mountain' section of Georgia. The story which appeared in WMZ, Eye Witness News, entitled *"Nuwaubian's Charged in Multi-Million Scheme"* dated 10th February 2003, stated the following:

> Three members of the Nuwaubian Nation of Moors are accused of trying to steal more than $280-million dollars from the U.S. Postal Service, as part of a scheme to buy land in Bibb County. That's according to Sergeant K.K. Jones with the DeKalb County Police Department. William Carroll is accused of identity theft and theft by deception. Robert C. Dukes and Darius Sampson are both accused of theft by deception. A press release from Sergeant Jones says, the three men tried to purchase two homes in a Stone Mountain subdivision using fake documents. A release from Sergeant Jones says Carroll filed a lien for more than $280-million dollars against the United States Postal Service. All three men are either current or former employees of the U.S. Postal Service. The investigation found the three men planned to defraud the postal service and an Atlanta area builder to buy land in Bibb County. Sergeant Jones said the land would be used to re-establish a home base for the Nuwaubian's religious organization.
>
> (WMZ, News, 2003)

Figs.381, 382, 383, 384 & 385: Property Fraudsters: Left- Right:
Police Mugshots of: Robert Dukes, Darius Sampson & William Carroll
(Bottom) Exclusive *Stone Mountain Real Estate, Properties*

The media immediately pointed the finger at the Nuwaubian's, falsely implying that the 3 Criminals were acting on the instructions of the organisation. In an article written by Macon Telegraph reporter Rob Peecher, he alleges that the properties were fraudulently purchased to launch the "Rebirth of the Nuwaubian Nation."

However this has been proven to be untrue, because sources close to Jacob York admit that he was the actual 'Mastermind' behind the entire scheme. In fact, the location of many of the properties in question in the same Georgia residence of 'Stone Mountain' is where Jacob had already illegally acquired a number of other properties using the very same method. In response to the allegations made by Rob Peecher, the Nuwaubian's answered with an article entitled: *"There Is Only ONE Tama-Re "AL TAMAHA"!!!"*, dated 23rd October 2003, in which they state:

> The fact of the matter is that the United Nuwaubian Nation of Moors has thousands of members worldwide who have read our literature or may even have joined one of our fraternal organizations. To make the nation accountable, as a whole, for these individuals own criminal activities is ridiculous. Is the Pope held responsible for all the Catholics who commit crimes in the world? No he is not. So why is that every time someone who says they are a Nuwaubian is arrested it automatically becomes an alleged crime that the nation as a whole…is involved in committing. This is a blatant defamation of character and a libellous statement that the Macon Telegraph writer, Rob Peecher is guilty of time and time again. It is called Yellow Journalism. Yellow Journalism according to the *American Heritage Dictionary is journalism that exploits, distorts, or exaggerates the news to create sensations and attract readers*.
>
> (unnm.com, 2003)

Liberator of Victims

Not long after Dr. Malachi. Z. York's arrest in 2002, reports soon began circulating in the media of one of York's sons who was helping the FBI with their investigations regarding his father's abuse of children. This son would later be revealed as being none other than Jacob or "Jake" York. Please remember to bear in mind that in various interviews with the media, Jacob took credit for not only witnessing his father Sexually Abuse young girls in the community, but also taking the steps necessary to help York's victims escape, by providing them with a type of "Safe Haven", after leaving the community. In an article which appeared in The Atlanta Journal-Constitution entitled: *"Cult leader ignored his own rules"*, dated July 7th 2002, reporter Bill Osinski, who had coincidentally first broke the story regarding York's supposed Sexual Abuse of Minors, describes Jacob York's account of his Father's activities within the Community, and how he was the one initially responsible for contacting the authorities, later providing safety for his Fathers victims:

York's son said, he learned York was continuing to have sex with underage members of the community. **Some of the children were ones he remembered from when he was growing up in Ansaru Allah**, he said.
Some of these children had grown up and had children by York, he said.
He came to Georgia to confront York, and he said York admitted that he was sick, but he thought he could control his sexual predations, he said.
But the son was not satisfied with his father's explanations, so about two years ago, he moved to metro Atlanta. **His home soon became a sort of halfway house for people leaving the Nuwaubian community.**
He recalled a time about a year ago when he told the young people staying with him about the hard times he'd had after leaving Ansaru Allah. Some of the girls in the group started to cry, he said, because they'd been told he and others who left had deliberately abandoned them.
Then the girls started to tell him about the extent of sexual abuse, **York's son said. At that point, he called Putnam Sheriff Howard Sills and said he had some information about his father.**
The next day, the son met with Sills and FBI agents in Atlanta. He brought with him a young woman who has become one of the key witnesses in the investigation.

(Osinski, 2002)

Clearly the above establishes that this son of Malachi. Z. York, who we now know to be Jacob York, had known all of his father's victims since childhood, whom according to Bill Osinski he knew as: *"Some of the children were ones he remembered from when he was growing up in Ansaru Allah."* Secondly it was he who provided sheltered accommodation for his father's supposed victims at his home, which Bill Osinski again confirmed as: *"His home soon became a sort of **halfway house** for people leaving the Nuwaubian community. He recalled a time about a year ago when he told the young people staying with him about the hard times he'd had after leaving Ansaru Allah."*
Finally it was this son, who admitted to first alerting the authorities to his Father's crimes, which Bill Osinski further corroborates: *"York's son said. At that point, he called Putnam Sheriff Howard Sills and said he had some information about his father. The next day, the son met with Sills and FBI agents in Atlanta".*
Another article which later appeared in The Macon Telegraph entitled: *"York's accusers describe years of sexual abuse"*, dated September 1st 2002, by reporter Rob Peacher, also highlights Jacob York's connection to the victims and indeed Jacob's 'Pivotal' or central role in the investigation against Malachi York:

> **York's son says he saw a videotape of York having sex with a child a number of years ago,** but waited before going to authorities. He knew his father had government connections and feared he might be able to quash any investigation.
> He says he decided to go to Putnam County Sheriff Howard Sills after seeing some Nuwaubian-produced pamphlets about the sheriff. If

Nuwaubian's hated Sills as much as the fliers suggested, the son says, he believed he could trust the sheriff. Sills brought in the FBI. **A year before York's arrest, the son was introducing Sills and federal agents to children later named in the indictment.** Others also claimed they had been molested by York, but the cases were so old that the statute of limitations had expired, according to law enforcement sources.

York's son is involved in what he calls a kind of underground railroad to help former members get out of the group and straighten out their lives.

(Peacher, 2003)

This article again verifies how important Jacob York was to the investigation. By his own admission to the media, Jacob York was central to the entire case against his father, as Rob Peecher stated: *"York's son says he saw a videotape of York having sex with a child a number of years ago"*. By initiating the initial contact between the victims and Sheriff Sills, as Peecher also pointed out: *"A year before York's arrest, the son was introducing Sills and federal agents to children later named in the indictment"*. Then providing sanctuary for his father's victims, which again Peecher described as: *"York's son is involved in what he calls a kind of underground railroad to help former members get out of the group and straighten out their lives.*

Therefore, if Jacob York was, as all of the evidence suggests, the central figure in the case, then it stands to reason that the Prosecution would certainly use his testimony during the Trial against his father, after he had been so instrumental in assisting the investigation. **However this never happened!!**

So is there any solid evidence to prove that Jacob York knew the victims, and what if any, is his real relationship to them? In the above mentioned article entitled: *"THE FATHER, MALACHI YORK IS ACCUSED OF THE SON, JACOB YORK'S CRIMES"*, actual photographs were provided of Jacob in intimate poses with several of the Prosecution's Key witnesses, whom he had admitted knowing to AJC reporter, Bill Osinski.

  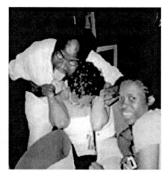

Figs.386, 387 & 388 FBI Informant & Sexual Predator: Left- Right: York's Son, Jacob York enjoying Intimate Moments with Prosecutions Witnesses: Atiyah "Tatiana" Thomas, Adah "Nicole" Lopez & Nicole Harden

Pimp & Exploiter

After leaving the Community in 2002, Barbara Noel met Jacob and the two quickly formed a Sexual relationship, eventually purchasing a house at 5179 Meadowbrook Chase in Stone Mountain, Ga. Not only did Jacob know his father's alleged victims, several sources claim that Jacob was also having Sexual Intercourse with them in the same house he described to the media as *"a sort of Halfway House"*. According to another associate of Jacob's, he often boasted about how he used to practice Anal Sex with many of the young girls within the Ansaaru Allah Community, many of whom were known at the time as *"Al Banaat"* which translates from Arabic as '**The Girls**', a kind of female Islamic 'Gospel' group, formed by Malachi York during the 1980s. More shocking however is the testimony of an eyewitness simply known as "Bud", who claimed that: *"...in the late 1980's and early 1990's Jacob York sodomized young Boys on Bushwick Avenue and one of these young boys is related to me."* The witness also went on to maintain that Jacob was part of a Gang, of Homosexual young Homosexual Men, who routinely raped & sodomized underage Boys & Girls within the Community. Because the girls were routinely checked for signs of vaginal intrusions, Jacob is said to have often entered them 'Anally' to avoid being discovered and punished by his Father for violating girls in the Community. Ironically, information that has also recently come to light actually exposes Jacob York as being guilty of many of the offences for which his father has been imprisoned.

For example:

Malachi York (Father)	Jacob York (Son)
Accused of Sexual Molestation against minors.	Admitted to friends to having had sex with minors in the 'Ansaaru Allah Community' during the 1980s & 90s.
Accused of Transporting Minors across state lines for Sexual purposes.	Travelled to "South Beach" Florida with group of underage females to indulge in Sex and Drugs in 2001.
Accused of Fraud and Financial Irregularities.	Confirmed by witnesses to have acquired numerous properties in Georgia by 'Deception', and Mortgage Fraud.

York's followers also claim to have acquired numerous other photographs of Jacob in Erotic and Sexually explicit situations with many of the minors who would later give evidence against his Father.

As Jacob was no longer part of his father's organisation, the means by which he is now known to have gained access to the young people within the Community, is through the Mother of two of his Father's children, and the Prosecution's witness, Abigail "Habiba" Washington. Leading up to the York's arrest, Jacob's house in Stone Mountain began to attract ever increasing numbers of young Nuwaubian's, including Barbara Noel's daughter Nicole "Adah" Lopez, who had already begun to express her discomfort at being on the land, as we saw in her letter. Among the occupants of Jacob's house was another of Dr. Malachi. Z. York's accusers, his daughter; Fatimah Muhammad-York, who was said to have been thrown out of the Community, after her Father discovered that she was a Lesbian. According to insiders, aside from Jacob & Fatimah, a number of York's other children are wayward, spoilt, renegades, who also have nothing to do with their father or the movement. In complete contrast to many of York's other positive children, such as Rachael & Hagar whom are identified by many, as now being the Backbone of the organisation. One reason, which may explain the behaviour of some of York's children, may be as a result of them being from different Wives or 'Concubines', resulting in natural animosity and rivalry, between them. Another clue may lie in the way many of them were brought up in the Community. The Children's upbringing in the Ansaaru Allah Community is key factor to our understanding of the events that led to York's eventual downfall. For example, it has already been established that Jacob was familiar with many of the Prosecution's key witnesses since childhood. The Nuwaubian's further corroborate this by asserting that Jacob was eventually thrown out of the movement after years of Sexually abusing some of these same youngsters, when the group was still based in Brooklyn, New York. Again the question any rational person should ask is, how was Jacob able to get away with so much in the first place? The answer may lie in eyewitness accounts of life within the Ansaaru Allah Community in Bilial Philips' book: *"The Ansar Cult In America"*, which describes how York's children were often spoilt from a very young age, and given special privileges which other children in the community were denied.

Fig.389 Lesbian: *York's Daughter: Fatimah Muhammad-York*

York may have often been too busy to adequately discipline his numerous children, whose Mother's were only preoccupied with competing with each other for the position of 'Top' wife, and often used their children as bargaining tools in their constant Power Struggle for the coveted position. The following is an account from Bilial Philips' book by an Ex-York follower, Abdul Muta'aal Muhammad, who describes the extra privileges York's Children received from the rest of the kids in the Community:

> Dr. York (Isa) lived at 743 Bushwick Avenue in the apartment, which was in the back, and his wives in 745, in the building on the corner with his children. The apartment of his wives was decked up. They had their own kitchen and they had their own time schedule. They were responsible for all the brothers. They ate better and had the freedom to do whatever they wanted to do. His children would be playing around and other children would be ordered to bed.
>
> (Philips, 1988, p: 163)

Because of the "Autocratic" nature and centralised structure of the movement, York's authority could never be questioned and therefore this account of the privileged status of York's children may shed some light on Jacob York's later mistreatment and 'Sexual Abuse' of other children in the Community. The privileged status of York's children within the Community, caused many of them, including Jacob to grow into selfish and conceited individuals, whom would eventually threaten the stability of the very organisation their father built. Therefore by simply failing to discipline his children, Malachi York may have unwittingly helped to sow the seeds of his own eventual downfall. York's policy of segregating children by themselves also appears to be one of the causes of the abuse, which took place between the Children, many of whom were literally left at the mercy of Jacob York, and his gang of Molesters, which went on undetected for many years.

The atmosphere at Jacob's so-called 'Halfway-House' was a dangerous cocktail of adolescents between the ages of 14 to 20, which led to what has been described by eyewitnesses as a "brothel" type environment, in which Jacob York played the 'Central' role of a 'Pimp' and Barbara Noel the role of 'Madam'. As well as being Sexually involved with many of these young people, it has also been alleged that Jacob decided to produce "Video" recordings of his sexual exploits with these young Men & Women, and later introduce many of them in to Prostitution. After having lived in the sheltered environment of the Religious Community all of their lives, these young people now found themselves being exposed to Pornography, Sex, Alcohol and even Drugs. According to Nichol "Adah" Lopez's letter, many of them had already begun experimenting with Sex at 404 Shady Dale Road, whilst under the supervision of Abigail Washington, whose job it appears to have been to initially corrupt them. The difference now was, they were under the direct control of Jacob York, who intended to now "Turn them out" and use them primarily for his own Sexual gratification, then ultimately to destroy his father.

When the story first broke, the media tried to misinform the public by portraying all of York's victims as children between the ages of 4 and 14. However what is now known is that not one of these so-called "Children" was under the age of sexual consent at the time of the accusations. It is also known for certain, that Jacob was in deep financial trouble, and may have even been facing a lengthy Custodial/Prison sentence for 'Tax Evasion', from his ongoing lawsuit with the NBA, for the misuse of their logo in 1999.

It's unclear exactly what happened next, however sources claim that Jacob, being fully aware of the ongoing investigation against his Father by the various law enforcement agencies, which included the FBI, decided to try and capitalise from this situation, for 3 reasons. Firstly to avoid prosecution and even jail time, for things he had done. Secondly, for the generous financial rewards which could be obtained in the event of his father's conviction, then finally, to get revenge against his father for the death of his mother, Dorothy Johnson.

Jacob York told Rob Peecher of The Macon Telegraph, that his reason for initially going to Sheriff Sills was because *"after seeing some Nuwaubian-produced pamphlets about the sheriff. If Nuwaubian's hated Sills as much as the fliers suggested, the son says, he believed he could trust the sheriff."* In other words Jacob admits he approached Sheriff Sills, not because of his father's guilt, but because he was aware of the hatred Sheriff Sills had for his father.

According to York's followers, both Jacob York and Abigail Washington had both been on the FBI's confidential payroll for some time, prior to York's arrest, and knew exactly what was required of them by this stage of the alleged conspiracy. In fact during an audio-recorded interview conducted from prison in 2004, Malachi York states the following concerning his son's involvement with the FBI:

> ...I did everything I could to shape him into a better person, but down inside he had this desire to go his own way. He became a avid hater of me, and he became one of the campaigners behind this whole case, of launching this whole thing, to get these people together, and threatening them. He was on the payroll of the FBI, now a witness got on the witness stand who was his best friend who was there when the deal was made with the FBI agents, and he was also the one who was going to testify that Jake came to him, because he knew he was good at forging checks, to try to get him to forge checks for him, so he could use those forged checks to buy a house, because his credit was not strong enough. His credit was around 2,000, he needed it to be around 24,000 to get cover from the bank. And the guy refused to do it, which is a friend of his called Damon Pryor, who was going to go up the court to testify about this, in his testimony, he testified how Jake York was on the Government payroll, they got to Jake York with things he had did in the past, right and then turned him. He already had a dislike for me, and they used that, they used that as an excuse to try to topple our organisation, and topple me, then they told him to solicit people, then he went around getting people...
>
> (York, 2004)

Exactly a year before Malachi York's arrest, Jacob is alleged to have arranged a trip to **South Beach, Florida**, for all of those involved in the conspiracy, on May 26th 2001, where their stories were to be finally rehearsed in preparation for the case against Jacob's father for Child Sexual Molestation. On May 30th, 4 days into the trip, Jacob York & Abigail

Washington made contact with the FBI, to begin providing statements, which would be used to arrest and indict Malachi York. As we have seen, Jacob openly admitted to reporters that he was the one who introduced his father's victims to Federal Investigators, beginning with Abigail Washington, whose statement, was made on May 31st.

The following are the names and dates of birth of witnesses referred to by the media as **"The 13 Child Victims"** at the beginning of York's trial in 2002:

1) Khalid Eddington, Date of Birth: 6/8/1980, Aged: 23 (Alleged Victim)

2) Kiturah Eddington, Date of Birth: 01/06/1977, Aged: 26 (Alleged Victim)

3) Amanda "Amala" Noel, Date of Birth: 01/26/1984, Aged: 19 (Alleged Victim)

4) Zaiyda LaRoche, Date of Birth: 01/15/1978, Aged: 25 (Alleged Victim)

5) Abdul Salaam aka Shelomoh LaRoche, Date of Birth: 3/20/1984, Aged: 17 (Alleged Victim)

6) Safaa'a LaRoche, Date of Birth: 05/13/1985, Aged: 18 (Alleged Victim)

7) Nicole Harden, Date of Birth: 08/19/1969, Aged: 34 (Alleged Victim)

8) Krystal "Beluwra" Harden, Date of Birth: 02/14/1987, Aged: 19 (Alleged Victim)

9) David "Taariq" Noel, Date of Birth: 10/25/1985, Aged: 18 (Alleged Victim)

10) Sakinah Parham, Date of Birth: 4/30/1976, Aged: 27 (Alleged Victim)

11) Atiyah Tatiana Thomas, Date of Birth: 9/27/1979, Aged: 24, (Alleged Victim)

13) Nicole "Adah" Lopez, Date of Birth: 04/19/1975, Aged: 28 (Alleged Victim)

Pauline Rogers, Date of Birth: 11/27/1965, Aged: 38 (Witness)

Abigail "Habiba" Washington, Date of Birth: 08/10/1975, Aged: 28 (Victim & Main Prosecution Witness)

Throughout the trial, York's followers maintained that all of he's accusers were lying, and that their Testimonies were encouraged by Jacob York for offer of huge financial rewards from the State & Federal Investigators. After the trial, this claim was confirmed when the Prosecution team launched their so-called 'Restitution Hearing' on April 1st 2004, aimed at providing York's alleged victims with generous financial settlements. Professor of Psychiatry at Mercer University, Richard Elliott, provided a so-called 'Expert' testimony for the Prosecution, on behalf of the Victims during Compensation Hearings. Depending upon the outcome of these Restitution Hearings, the financial compensation to York's accusers could run into Hundreds of Thousands or even Millions of Dollars, which would in turn bankrupt the movement, which was to be the Government's initial pretext to seize the group's assets, and would have naturally included their land; Tama Re.

Baasil Abdullah Muhammad, aka **Damon Pryor**, who grew up in the Ansaaru Allah Community with Jacob York, claims that Jacob had in fact been on the FBI's payroll as an informant several years before his Father's arrest. In a previously unseen interview conducted by 'Key' Defence witness Damon Pryor who described in detail, how Jacob York, was initially approached by FBI agents several years before his Father's arrest in 2002. Damon Pryor's account of how Jacob was recruited by the 'Feds' is very reminiscent of the scene from the movie "Belly", starring Rappers DMX & NAS, in which the central character 'Tommy' played by DMX, is approached on the basketball court by an undercover 'Agent', and given a choice of either working for the 'System' or going back to Jail. The following is a complete transcript of a secretly recorded conversation, which took place on the 8th June 2004 between Damon Pryor and Jacob York, in which Malachi York's son reluctantly admits how he initially became part of the Conspiracy to destroy his father:

> **Jacob York:** What you up to?
>
> **Damon Pryor:** What do you mean what am I up to you know what I am up to! One thing, and that is letting the world know the truth about the conspiracy and freeing our 'Chief' (Malachi York). Did you see the tape of Habiba?
>
> **Jacob York:** Yeah they mailed it to me personally.
>
> **Damon Pryor:** Jacob, everyone is coming forth you can't possibly sit here and deny all of the truth that is coming out and you already know what I testified to, everyone is coming forth now, Farrah the underage minor who you took on the trip to South Beach, she has come forth to tell the truth.
>
> **Jacob York:** She's a liar; it's an insult to think that I would want to Fuck her.
>
> **Damon Pryor:** You act as if its unusual for you to want to Fuck with underage girls, I know you, we have pictures of ya'll down there in

South Beach. We have a whole conspiracy DVD out now, with everyone's testimony on it? Did you know we also have a tape?

Jacob York: A tape of what?

Damon Pryor: The orgy y'all had down there on South Beach, we have it.
Jacob York: I am not on it!

Damon Pryor: We also have Hakeem

Jacob York: Hakeem who?

Damon Pryor: 'Hakeem Black' who went down there for a day and will testify to the conspiracy while he was there and how you were telling the girls they should go to the Feds about these allegations, namely Adah (Nicole Lopez), Istiyr (Istiyr Cole) and Kariyma (Areline Hamilton) you know who was there. Come on how can you deny the fact that Habiba (Habiba 'Abigail' Washington) said that you told her that she should go to the Feds with these allegations because some people had implicated her in some illegal activities. So everyone is lying on Jake. Habiba (Habiba 'Abigail' Washington) has more to lose coming forth with the truth going up against the Feds than she did sticking with those lies having them on her side. But you best believe that we are going to protect her with our lives and anyone else that recants their lies to tell the truth.

Jacob York: The only ones I was having Sex with was Adah (Nicole Lopez), Istiyr (Istiyr Cole) and Atiah (Titiayana Thomas). I stopped Fuckin with Kariyma (Areline Hamilton) after I found out that she had Fucked Cush, I cut her off.

Damon Pryor: But didn't you know that Atiya (Titiayana Thomas) was Hakeem's girlfriend?

Jacob York: Well, I used to see him with her. He used to bring her by the House.

Damon Pryor: What was the point of you involving yourself in the case, what satisfaction did you get out of being the axis of the whole conspiracy?

Jacob York: They approached me in New York City. I was coming out of a Club and a White dude approached me and questioned me later about everything I knew about the community, I felt like I had an obligation to those children, innocent children.

Damon Pryor: Hold it were you down there in the trial?

Jacob York: No

Damon Pryor: Of course you weren't there, I was, and my testimony was blocked. No underage children got on the stand, no 10-year olds; 5-year old got on any stand and said anything. These were all adults with testimony of hearsay. No medical experts testified that there was any physical evidence, no DNA, no pictures or photos that was factually recorded or reported. Now you mean to tell me with over 1,100 sex acts a year for over 10 years, on young kids; 5 to 10 years of age, including anal, oral and vaginal sex there wasn't any reporting to any medical facility?

Jacob York: Well what about the 'Pink Panther Doll' that kids testified that they had to perform with?

Damon Pryor: Are you serious, that was up the hill found in the silo and that was on property that Doc doesn't even own and it hasn't been his legal residence in over 5 years. Jake it's nothing you can say right now in my face that wasn't addressed in the trial down there in Bushwick. If you felt so strongly about innocent kids or if you felt so surely about all the allegations why didn't you testify in court if you were so concerned?

Jacob York: Because of the statue of limitations had expired, you know about that?

Damon Pryor: That's Crap, the whole purpose of the superseding indictment was to allow the hearsay testimony in the courtroom. The Feds knew that the statute of limitations was over that's why they needed Habiba to say that she was also involved in the money structuring so they could try and stick the molestation charges. Everyone saw in court what they were up to. We all know and they know they didn't prove their case.

Jacob York: They got a conviction didn't they?

Damon Pryor: You know that the Judge picked the Jury that was not even the peers of 'Pops' we know what the Judge did. Come on man, you have been following the case and I know you have been on our website. You playing stupid as if you can sit here and honestly say that you don't know that the Feds are using you to try and bring down Pops. You know that they have been trying to bring him down for years.

Jacob York: So why did he take the guilty plea?

Damon Pryor: He took the guilty plea because they woke him up at around 4 o'clock in the morning, taking him through several tests and questioning him. Keep in mind that this was without food, or water and he has a life threatening disease called 'Hereditary Angeiodema' that's triggered when put in stressful situations. At this point his ex-attorneys who we later found out was working with the other side along with Sills, and the Prosecutors and Psychiatrists were negotiating a Plea and after he maintained his innocence they tortured him, wouldn't allow him to look over the agreement. They threaten to send him to prison for 1,000 years. And Sills told him, "We are putting the other co-defendants through the same thing. They will never get to see their children again. And your wife Kathy you best believe is not doing too hot with the disease and all. It's you we want. We will let the others go if you take this Plea". All this along with sleep deprivation, starving him, he was imprisoned with convicted killers threatening his life at sixty years of age, that's why he took the Plea! He sacrificed himself for others.

Jacob York: Everybody knows that when you go to prison you don't sleep like you normally would.

Damon Pryor: Jake you have never been in prison I was tortured in prison so I know what its like being starved eating one meal a day. Fed frozen meat and a small juice for weeks at a time, don't tell me Shit about torture!

Jacob York: The Feds have a 90% conviction rate

Damon Pryor: The have 90% conviction rate because of guilty pleas those dudes take, they are not convictions by trial and ninety percent of the time when you take it to trial if you lose then it will get overturned in an appellant court.

Jacob York: You mean to tell me you know people who have been convicted of crimes that have gotten turned over?

Damon Pryor: I was in Federal Correctional Institute, it happens for those that do go to trial. So I guess you feel good that Pops got sentenced to 135 years?

Jacob York: Noah saved my life he pulled me out of a hail of bullets in New York City when niggas was trying to kill me man. I grew up with that nigga, we slept on the floor together shared food, everything. I felt like I owed him something. When he came to me and asked me what he had done what could I say.

Damon Pryor: Just because you hear Shit about people doesn't give you the right to create a case around hearsay. If that's the case everybody would be guilty of things that have been said about them.

Jacob York: They came to me, I didn't go to them, remember when Ayyuwb got locked up for those bank schemes, the Feds knew that I was involved. They threatened me with that. They also threatened me with 'Tax Evasion' and that I would have charges brought up against me for 'Money Laundering'. They froze my accounts and all my assets, I couldn't get to my Money and they shut down my business, do you know what that is like? They had me in everything I was looking at a lot of time.

Damon Pryor: So that's why you did it because you, couldn't get your money and you couldn't stand up to your own Shit along with the hate you have in your own heart. So you help deliver your own father to the 'White Man'? Don't act like you don't know that the 'White Man' is the Devil, you know the 'White Man' is the Devil, don't you?

Jacob York: Yeah he is!

Damon Pryor: If nothing else other than that he is your father and without him you would not be here, you should have been willing to protect him, knowing that they have been trying to get him since day one. What are you going to say when he gets out, what are you going to say?

Jacob York: What do you want me to say, you think he's getting out?

Damon Pryor: I know he's getting out, you know where I stand.

Jacob York: You know where I stand.

Damon Pryor: We'll see in the end.

Ironically, Damon Pryor's assertion that Jacob York was initially approached and recruited in New York by the FBI, as early as 1998, is 'Unwittingly' verified or Confirmed by Anti-Nuwaubian reporter Bill Osinski's in his book *"Ungodly: A True Story of Unprecedented Evil"*, in which he states:

> **One night, Malik (Jacob) was in a nightclub, and he was approached by a man who identified himself as a federal agent.** The agent asked him, "What's going on with your father?" Malik didn't know, but he figured it was time for him to find out.
>
> (Osinski, 2007, p:226)

Figs.390 & 391 Left to Right: True Ansaar: *Damon Pryor photographed in 2005 & During Testimony on WNUB Nuwaubian TV in 2007*

The second day of the 3rd week of the Trial continued with York's Attorney Adrian Patrick, making repeated attempts to subpoena Jacob York for cross-examination to establish a connection between him and his Father's accusers. However Jacob could not be located anywhere, and Judge Royal immediately overruled the suggestion of a conspiracy involving Jacob York and his Father's accusers.

Undeterred by the numerous Defence witnesses, the Prosecution proceeded to accuse York of a number of financial irregularities including earning 'Hundreds of Thousands' of dollars without paying his followers any wages, and concealing his finances in order to evade reporting requirements. They continued by portraying the Defendant as a kind of 'Despotic Ruler' who earned in excess of $850,000 from 1996, over a 5-year period, whilst practically enslaving his followers to work day and night for no pay.

To refute the Government's claims of Racketeering & Financial irregularities, the Defence called upon the testimony of Malachi York's accountant, New York based Neil Dukoff, who presented the court with copies of Federal Tax returns filed on behalf of his client. Mr Dukoff, and his Father before him had been York's accountants for over 30 years, and presented his client's Tax returns, which showed that between 1996 & 2001, the Organisation grossed $5.9 million, from sales of literature and other merchandise. The Tax returns also revealed that after expenses were deducted, York reported a 'Net Taxable Income' sum of $857,236 over the 5-year period in question, with a figure of $303,746 paid in Federal income Tax. York's accountant stated that his client never even claimed Tax exemption for his movement as a Religious organisation, which he was perfectly entitled to do by U.S Law. Mr Dukoff added that his client was very prompt in paying his Taxes, and his finances were always completely 'Transparent' with every Tax payment made on time; *"We considered everything...for-profit and the client paid taxes on his profit every year".*

At this stage of the trial the hypocritical Media in particular, again made a big fuss about how York's followers laboured long hours as Carpenters, Security Guards, Electricians, Groundskeepers and Plumbers for the organisation, with some as young as 10 years old working up to 12 hour shifts, packing 'Incense & Soaps', as if they were really concerned about the movement's followers whom they had been busy vilifying since the group arrived in rural Georgia in 1993. The truth is whatever the arrangement York's followers had with him, they made of their own free will, offering their services 'Voluntarily', through a sense of shared ownership, as nobody was ever held captive on the Property. York transferred ownership of the property back to his followers by signing the 'Quite Claim' back in 2000. And besides if the Media and Prosecutors cared so much about the injustices of **'Unpaid Labour'** against Blacks, maybe they should consider lending their support to the 'Reparations' movement for compensation for over 400 years of real forced 'Slave' labour carried out by their ancestors against the forbearers of many of York's followers, whose welfare they suddenly seemed so concerned about.

In response to Mr. Dukoff's testimony, Assistant U.S. Attorney Richard Moultrie, tried to trap York's accountant by asking him whether he didn't think it was strange that his client never reported paying any wages in his Tax returns. In York's Defence Mr. Dukoff's replied: *"Everyone runs their business the way they want to run it…We were not provided with wages paid out"*. Attorney Moultrie then preceded his cross-examination of Mr. Dukoff, with a series of questions designed to further trap him into incriminating the Nuwaubian leader:

Attorney Moultrie: Mr. Derkoff

Mr Dukoff: It is Dukoff

Attorney Moultrie: Oh. I apologize. Dukoff. You have been filing Mr. York's tax returns for over 30 years is that correct?

Mr Dukoff: Well, yes our firm has handled Mr. York's accounting for yes I would say about 30 years.

Attorney Moultrie: Have you ever filled tax returns under the name of Dwight D. York?

Mr Dukoff: No never. I have only known the defendant as Isa Muhammad or Malachi York.

Attorney Moultrie: So you have never known him to go by the name Dwight D. York?

Mr Dukoff: No. I do not recognize that name!

Attorney Moultrie: Well if he had done business under the name of Dwight D. York would you have known that?

Mr Dukoff: No of course not.

Attorney Moultrie: So he could have done business under the name of Dwight D. York?

Mr Dukoff: Anyone can do business under a different name and the accountant may not know it. But I know this man and my father knows this man and we have never known him to go by the name of Dwight D. York and we have been working with him for well over 30 years.

Mr Dukoff then reiterated the point in his Client's Defence, that a great many Religious & Educational organisations similar to the Nuwaubian Nation also known as the 'Holy Tabernacle Ministries', often declared themselves to be 'Non profit' to avoid paying high Taxes, which although

York was perfectly entitled to do by Law, he never chose to, and instead opted to pay the full income Tax contributions to the Federal Government each year, preferring to register his organisation as a 'Business', rather than declaring it a 'Tax Exempt' Religious movement.

Dr. Fred Bright 's Review of the Medical Evidence

Next York's Defence called Georgia based Gynaecologist Dr. Fred Bright M.D. a Professor from the 'Morehouse School of Medicine, who testified in York's Defence to establish whether there was any physical evidence to determine whether or not York had 'Sexually Molested' any of his accusers. Despite Dr. Bright's insistence that his testimony was completely 'objective', Assistant Prosecutor Stephanie Thacker, quickly discredited Dr. Bright as a credible witness by presenting the court with a copy of his Nuwaubian application form, for the group's A.E.O (Ancient Egiptian Order) which read: *"I have tremendous respect and love for the 'Master Teacher' of our Day and Time"* Although Dr. Bright's testimony was used by the Defence, he was simply dismissed as a 'biased' witness by the Prosecution, because of his affiliation with and the group, and immediately lost all credibility. However, unperturbed by the Prosecution's tactic, Dr. Bright later released his own Video recorded statement examining in-depth, many of the "discrepancies, irregularities and flaws" in the Prosecution's evidence against York for 'Child Sexual Molestation'. The following is a complete transcript of a letter released by Dr. Bright outlining many of the inaccuracies in the case against the Nuwaubian leader:

To: All Concerned Civil Rights Advocates, Religious Leaders and True Defenders of Justice
From: **Frederick O. Bright M.D.**

Dear Concerned Persons,

Firstly I'd like to thank you for taking the time to read this letter. I am writing this letter to inform you of an ongoing situation that is threatening the very foundation of American Society. We the people of the Yamassee Native American Moors of the Creek Nation who are recognized in United States History as indigenous people of America are facing a critical situation. The United States, which has been founded on principals of Liberty, Freedom and Justice for All is becoming the enemy of All peace loving people. The threat to freedom is no longer confined to so-called Terrorist backed Nations. The threat to freedom is raising its ugly head in the Heart of America. People of all walks of life are being falsely accused of crimes whenever one turns on the television. The recent plight of the Yamassee Native American Moors of the Creek Nation in Georgia, USA is a modern example of how racism, prejudice and the unfair administration of injustice by persons with governmental authority is being used to prevent minority people from uplifting themselves. The current racism that we are experiencing although disguised as justice, is nothing short of judicial lynching. Having been a witness to many of these injustices, and now facing a near complete loss of respect for the current Justice System, It is clear that the time to bring our plight into the forefront is now!

In May of 2002, the combined forces of Georgia Law Enforcement and the Federal Government staged a massive invasion of our normally peaceful village in Putnam County, Georgia. The invasion stemmed from allegations of child molestation directed at our Tribal Chief Black Thunderbird "Eagle" also known as Dr. Malachi Z. York. During the serving of the so-called warrant, nearly 300 Law Enforcement Officials forcibly entered the small village. Young children had fully automatic weapons pointed at them, homes were broken into and at least 5 teenagers were forcibly removed from their homes without pre-existing evidence of any molestation having occurred. Dr. York was taken into custody after being arrested at a location outside of the village. Subsequent to the invasion, I was asked to review medical information from the case in support of Dr. York. On the Martin Luther King Day Federal Holiday 1/19/2004, I testified in Federal Court on behalf of the defendant about findings in my review of the case. The description of my testimony in a brief article by the Atlanta Journal Constitution was woefully deficient in the description of my 2 hour testimony. As they did properly state, the entire medical evidence collection was indeed sloppy. Nevertheless they failed to mention the details of my testimony, which prompted my characterization of the majority of the government's investigation as sloppy. Additionally the fact that the details in this case have been almost completely hidden from the scrutiny of the public by judicial orders, makes it clear that a cover-up is being perpetuated by government officials.

As an individual who has always tried to strive for the American Dream, I feel it is time to reveal the atrocities taking place to my extended family so that others may avoid a repeat of these incidents in their lives. At this time I will merely focus on medical evidence irregularities in the case as other details are to date being summarized for the appeal, which will be filed soon.

In cases of sexual molestation or assault, alleged victims usually undergo examinations within 72 hours of an alleged assault. This examination window of 72 hours enables forensic evidence to be obtained that can ascertain whether an accused has had body fluid exchange with an alleged victim. Additionally in most assault cases, victims can identify a specific time when the assaults took place. When a medical examiner evaluates an alleged victim, the history of the events is critical in determining the extent of evaluation that is necessary. In my review of the evidence in the Malachi York case it became clear that either the government examiners had no interest in accurately recording any of their findings or the alleged victims were giving unreliable statements. The details that stood out as abnormal were the following:

1. There were no recorded interviews or statements (written, audio or video) from alleged victims that could be independently evaluated by defendant's experts. This deficiency allows the government officials to make any statements necessary to bring charges against an accused. They can make statements without having to prove they actually obtained the

information accurately. The absence of recorded victim interviews prevents scrutiny of the official's statements. In the event that contradictory information is identified, the contradictions can easily be dismissed or explained away by the government.

2. There were no specific times ascertained for any of the alleged acts. The assaults were simply generalized to a wide time frame such as in the summer of 1999. This lack of detail allows considerable leeway for the government to mischaracterize the alleged assaults. This is especially true when it comes to sexual contact with persons on the cusp of adulthood as many of these alleged victims were.

3. None of the alleged victims were examined within 72 hours of the alleged acts. This absence of examinations near the time of any alleged acts allows a jury to only consider the alleged victims testimony in order to arrive at their verdict. It limits the ability of a defendant to be found innocent by an absence of body fluid on or within an alleged victim's body.

4. There were no past medical reports of genital injuries to any of the alleged victims despite allegations of repeated traumatic injuries. This absence of historical injuries requiring medical care is not consistent with the extent of molestation being alleged by many of the accusers.

5. Prosecuting detective(s) stated they "knew" that certain adolescents had been molested despite denials of molestation by half of the alleged victims. In fact many of the so-called victims to this day deny they were ever molested. For an official to state they know an individual was molested would suggest that they were a witness to the act. These statements demonstrate clear bias on the part of the detectives.

6. Child protection service examiners made statements that alleged victims had histories consistent with molestation. These statements were made even when the historical statement was a denial that molestation had occurred. This fact shows that the child protection services had the intent of finding the defendant guilty no matter what the evidence was. Many of the official summaries were obviously based on preconceived opinions, not based on the evidence available.

7. Child protection services made statements that the physical examination in many cases demonstrated no evidence of molestation. They went on to state that no evidence is consistent with molestation. They could not answer the question of what evidence is not consistent with molestation. In other words any findings whether present or absent will be used to draw the conclusion that an alleged victim has been molested.

8. Many of the alleged victims were mistakenly described by the wrong gender. (Females referred to as male) This fact casts doubt on the accuracy of the entire child protective services reports.

9. The Child protection services stated that video or picture evidence was obtained during their forensic evaluations. Despite requests for the government to produce this evidence, no such evidence was ever produced. This fact in and of itself suggests that evidence was either obtained or destroyed or evidence never existed but was wrongly reported to exist.

10. The government assumed that all parents who lived within the village were aware of the alleged molestations and would wilfully conceal those acts. This fact was evidenced by the finding of no parental consent for

examinations of alleged victims who resided in the village at the time of the invasion. In fact the guardians of alleged victims who resided in the village were completely detached from their guardianship by Georgia Law Enforcement. This is in contrast to alleged victims no longer residing in the village whose guardians were involved in the examination process. This is a form of prejudice on the part of Law Enforcement officials who assumed that every guardian residing in the village was aware of the acts or would cover up the acts. Additionally this behaviour removed parental rights from some parents simply because they lived within the village.

11. The multiple allegations of sexual molestation which were described suggests that a 50+ year old man suffering from a life threatening medical condition could engage in sexual acts 4-5 times each day. He can perform in this manner without any resultant pregnancies, injuries to adolescent victims or forensic evidence ever being obtained. Additionally this total absence of forensic evidence occurred despite a 3-4 year ongoing investigation by law enforcement officials.

12. Finally in this case, the most unusual fact in evidence was that approximately half of the alleged victims denied under oath and when initially examined, that they were ever molested.

Despite the inconsistent histories about these alleged acts, and the total absence of medical evidence, the Federal government was able to secure a conviction by an anonymous jury not of the defendants peers, and prove the accused committed these acts beyond a reasonable doubt. From this case, it has become clear to many people who have followed the proceedings that one no longer has to be proven guilty. An individual merely has to be accused in a court where any evidence (whether consistent with or not consistent with a crime) is used to prove a crime occurred. This reality is even more striking when any evidence which is beneficial in ascertaining one's innocence can be conveniently excluded by judicial order. It is the hope of our people and myself that bringing this injustice into the light will result in increased scrutiny of government officials who for too long are able to hide their actions from public view using judicial authority.

(Dr. Fred Bright, cited in UNNM.com, 2004)

Fig.392 Key Defense Witness:
Official Nuwaubian Physician, Dr. Fred Bright

In total, the Testimonies of over 80 witnesses were heard throughout 3 week trial, with approximately 49 witnesses for the Prosecution, and a further 44 called by the Defence, culminating on Wednesday 21st January, with the testimony of 9-year old Elijah 'Ilyas' Hibner, a young eyewitness present when the 'Law Enforcement' officials raided the group's property in 2002. Prior to their closing arguments the Defence ended with a moving eye-witness account by Elijah Hibner, who related to the court how he and the other children within the group were subjected to Physical and Mental abuse by FBI agents and officers from local 'Law Enforcement' departments during the raid which included; Weapons being pointed at the heads babies to stop them crying, Toys and other property smashed, as well as their food being Eaten and Thrown away by the officers carrying out the raid.

Finally, the next day during closing arguments the Prosecution reiterated to the Jury their claim that York's sole purpose for re-locating his organisation to rural Georgia was to 'Sexually Abuse' children and exploit his followers. U.S. Assistant District Attorney Richard Moultrie, added that York was a corrupt leader who abused people's trust.

Attorney Adrian Patrick, argued in York's Defence that it was unfeasible for the Defendant to have carried out Sexual abuse against so many victims without there being any 'Physical' evidence to support the allegations. Attorney Patrick used the victim's Testimonies to demonstrate to the court the absurdity of the Prosecution's claim, which asserted that the Defendant Sexually assaulted children within the organisation over 12,000 times between 1993 to 2001, which calculates as York, who was approaching the age of 60, having carried out **1,446 sexual acts a year, or 121 times a month**. Attorney Patrick again raised the issue of York's Son's involvement in a conspiracy, whom, York's followers claim was protected throughout the entire duration of the trial from giving evidence by the FBI. Which leads us to question: why Jacob York was not present during the Trial if he had played such an Important & Central role in helping the victims prepare their evidence for the case? Why was the issue of a conspiracy involving the Defendant's Son so quickly dismissed by the Prosecution, with the assistance of the Judge who overruled any suggestion that this individual be subpoenaed to appear to provide evidence for the Defence? And why when interviewed by reporters after the Trial, did Jacob York deny ever knowing any of the victims contradicting his previous statements to numerous reporters? Such as the following statement made to Bill Torpy of The Atlanta Journal-Constitution, dated January 24th, in the article entitled: *"Sect leader guilty of molestation"*, in which he cynically lied to the Media regarding his earlier involvement with his Father's supposed victims:

> The jury did not buy Defence contention that York was framed by a conspiracy concocted by his son, Jacob, a music producer who'd had a falling out with his father. **Jacob said Friday he did not know most of the victim witnesses and had not talked with them,** much less conspired with

them. "But I'm flattered that he thinks I'm that smart," he said. "Justice for the innocents has finally been done."

(Torpy, 2004)

Attorney Adrian Patrick completed by providing the court with various photographs of Nuwaubian Children enjoying themselves at numerous festivals held at the group's property, and then asking the Jurors if these looked like the faces of Children who were suffering any kind of 'Abuse', and if so, would they be so Jubilant and happy in their surroundings, which the Prosecution attempted to portray as a miserable 'Slavery' existence?

The Verdict

The Slave-Master, never likes the Slave to get into a Defensive position. He's called an "Uppity Nigger", and he's Lynched...
(Elmer 'Geronimo Ji Jagga' Pratt, *"FBI's War on Black America"*)

Dishonour or disgrace a Nation's Heroes, and you can demoralize its people...the "Politics of Personal Destruction," the Defeat of causes by disgracing their flawed champions. It has become standard operating procedure in American politics.

Patrick J. Buchanan, *"The Death of the West"*

On Friday the 23rd January 2004, the Jury, comprising of 9 Men & 3 Women were initially 'Deadlocked' 11 to 1, following 7 hours of deliberations after one of the Jurors point blank refused to convict the Nuwaubian leader, through insufficient evidence. This impasse constituted what is known as a 'Hung Jury' where not all of the Jurors can decide whether to convict or acquit, which should have been grounds for an immediate **Re-Trial**. However to alleviate the problem, Judge Ashley Royal again intervened by passing a note to the Juror instructing her to convict. After which the Jury subsequently returned with a unanimous verdict of 'Guilty' against the Nuwaubian leader, thereby concluding the 3-week trial. The Jurors eventually found Malachi York Guilty of all, except two of the original 13 related charges against him. Although the 'Burden of Proof' was never sufficiently met by the Prosecution, the end for York came swiftly, after the Jury members were again instructed to return to consider whether the two remaining counts of 'Property Forfeiture' of York's assets should also granted, which was this time unanimously decided in less than an hour. York was eventually found Guilty on all charges except the charge, which initially formed the basis of the original Indictment against him, which was; ***"transporting minors across state lines for the purpose of unlawful Sex".***

As if expecting the worst, a small group of 40 of York's loyal supporters quietly observed the trial proceedings via a private 'Televised' screening in a separate room. As the 'Guilty' verdict was read out against their leader, there was very little reaction from the group of Nuwaubian's present.

In the end, Dr. Malachi. Z. York 'took it on the Chin' like real Man, and dignifiedly stood, expressing little reaction as the 'Guilty Verdict' was read out by the Jury foreman, keeping silent throughout the entire proceedings, and was not as Bill Osinski falsely described in his book, *"trying to grovel for sympathy"*. Instead Attorney Patrick spoke on York's behalf, describing his client as 'Upbeat', and *"Relieved the trial was over"*. He added that York would immediately begin proceedings to appeal against the verdict, and instructed him to inform his followers that everything would be fine and none of them were to worry about him. Somewhat reminiscent to the scene outside U.S. District Court for The Middle District of Macon, following York's previous Guilty Plea in 2003, a group of Nuwaubian detractors and supporters again gathered to give their final comments to the Media once the trial had concluded. Gloating after his victory, U.S. Attorney Maxwell Wood who headed the Prosecution's case referred to the Nuwaubian leader in less than complimentary terms:

> "He sent a 9-year-old boy in to testify and he didn't have the guts to testify himself...He is Dwight York, a con man from Brooklyn, New York."
>
> (Attorney Wood, 2004)

U.S. Assistant District Attorney Richard Moultrie, who also helped lead the Prosecution's case against York, stated:

> I'm very proud of the victims...I admire them and I'm very pleased for them...It is their victory...
>
> (Attorney Moultrie, 2004)

Head of the local NAACP, Georgia Benjamin Smith, who often conflicted with the Nuwaubian's for their Political activities in Putnam County, was clearly jubilant at the outcome of the trial and stated:

> "The more I think about it, the more it seems like a dream...This man was going to take over this county...He was going to take it over."
>
> (Smith, 2004)

Never one to miss an opportunity to express his loathing for York, embattled Putnam County Sheriff, Richard Sills made a triumphant rambling statement, declaring the final defeat of the Nuwaubian (Yemasse) Nation:

> "I know what happened in 1861, when my ancestors did the same thing...When a group of people declares, 'We're a sovereign nation, we're not subject to the law' and blood is getting ready to be spilled...This has been an ordeal, not just for me personally but for my office, my staff and the people of my county...Today the authorities have sent away not a saviour but one of the most heinous criminals of the history of this nation."
>
> (Sheriff Sills, 2004)

However, in response to the Sheriff's comments, local resident Charlie Dorsey who witnessed the Law Enforcement's underhand 'Jim Crow' tactics and the Government's eventual 'Kangaroo' Trial against the Nuwaubian leader stated:

> "The sheriff ain't never been with them…They were the only black race that stood up against the sheriff."
>
> (Dorsey, 2004)

Finally, Baptist Pastor & Regional NAACP leader, Rev. Omer Reid, lamented at the verdict against Malachi York:

> "He put Egypt in the middle of Putnam County…There were a lot of people who would have paid good money to see what he had built."
>
> (Rev. Reid, 2004)

Following a series of further legal manoeuvres by York's Defence team, along with numerous adjournments of York's sentencing, the date was finally decided and set for March 26th 2004, by Federal Judge Ashley Royal. Despite the date set by Judge Royal, the actual sentencing did not take place until a month later on Thursday April 22nd 2004, when Judge Royal finally got the opportunity to 'Throw the Book' at the Nuwaubian leader, with an obscene sentence of 135 years in custody for the combined charges of 'Sexual Child Molestation & Racketeering'. Sentencing the Nuwaubian leader to 'the Statutory Maximum' for each count to run consecutively for each count, which according to Attorney Malik Shabaaz actually calculates into a total amount of **1,620** years Imprisonment:

Count 1 - 240 Months
Count 2 - 240 Months
Count 3 - 60 Months
Count 4 - 180 Months
Count 5 - 180 Months
Count 6 - 180 Months
Count 7 - 180 Months
Count 9 - 120 Months
Count 10 - 120 Months
Count 11 - 120 Months

Concerned at the length of the sentence, York's Defence Attorney Adrian Patrick questioned the Judge regarding the legality of the sentence, to which he responded: ***"The statutory maximum was life"***, as if to suggest he had not given the Nuwaubian leader a life sentence. With this astronomical sentence of 135 years, Malachi York would not actually be eligible for Parole or 'Early Release' until the year 2119, at which time he would be almost 200 years old, which means it was obviously a life sentence handed down by Judge Royal.

Fig.392 Fallen Icon: *Nuwaubian Leader; Dr. Malachi. Z. York being lead away from Court by Sheriff Sills & Armed Police*

Prior to Judge Royal passing sentence, Dr. York commented that he'd **"Probably get life anyway, and that the entire case was neither about Child Molestation or Racketeering, but more about destroying him and his organisation because of their different Religious beliefs".** Following York's sentencing, U.S. Attorney Max Wood praised the Judges decision of giving the 'statutory maximum', and stated: "We're very pleased with the sentence". The Guilty verdict now also entitled the Government to seize the group's 476-acre property under the RICO statute.

Witnesses 'Recant' False Testimonies

On Wednesday, February 4th 2004, before sentencing the Nuwaubian leader, Judge Ashley Royal granted a preliminary order of forfeiture against all of Malachi York's assets, which the Prosecution insisted included the 476-acre property in Putnam County, now controlled & owned by members of the organisation.

Next the Defence submitted a series of motions to try and delay the court's decision to seize the group's land, which began with a Motion on Thursday, 19th by the Defence to postpone the forfeiture until after York's appeal. The Defence even presented to the court actual documentation proving that Malachi York had not been the owner of 404 Shady Dale Road since signing a "Quit Claim" back in 2000, which effectively transferred complete ownership of the property over to several members of the organisation, who were not part of the Indictment. This Motion was filed on behalf of the actual owners of the property by Attorney Robert Ratliff on March 5th 2004, an entire month before York was sentenced.

Then on April 23rd, exactly a day after York was sentenced to 135 years imprisonment, the Prosecution's main witness Abigail "Habiba" Washington, along with several other former Prosecution witnesses, broke their silence, by making a series of remarkable 'Video-Taped' confessions, which finally exposed the 'illegitimacy' of the entire case against the Nuwaubian leader. In a 'Sworn Affidavit' in the presence of her Attorney Dwight Johnson, lasting over half an hour, Ms. Washington finally admitted that the entire case against Dr. Malachi. Z. York was based on a complete pack of lies, and part of a 'Conspiracy' conceived by the Federal Bureau of Investigation (FBI) to discredit York and destroy the Nuwaubian Movement. In it, she describes how she was tricked by Jacob York into first being part of the conspiracy against his father Malachi York. Habiba Washington also explained how she was often Threatened, Pressured, Coerced & 'Manipulated' by Jacob York, who was assisted by the Macon & Putnam County Sheriff's departments & FBI Special agents Jalaine Ward and Joan Cronier, who spearheaded the entire investigation against Malachi York, and how York's son Jacob was able to skilfully manipulate her and the other witnesses into falsely testifying in order to take revenge against his father, by playing the central role in the conspiracy.

Fig.393 Repentant Witness: *Malachi York's former Concubine Abigail "Habiba" Washington, Retracting her Previous Statement against York, Following the Nuwaubian leader's Sentence*

The following is a complete transcript of Abigail Washington's sworn Testimony filmed in a 30 minute Video, recorded in the presence of several witnesses including her Attorney Dwight Johnson on Friday 23rd April 2004:

> Hello my name is Habiba Washington, and I came here to put on record the Truth behind all of the Lies, brought up in the case against Malachi York. I'm gonna start of by saying that I haven't been Forced, Threatened, Coerced or Pressured to do this tape. I am also gonna state that as you can tell I'm not under any kind of influence, Alcohol or Drug.
> I wanna begin with all of the events that lead up to the final verdict in the case against Malachi, I wanna start of with how it started, where it started, when, and the reason why.
> I left the Community in February of 2001. I moved from Georgia, and went to New York, and went to live with my Family. In about March of 2001, I was contacted by Jacob, Jacob is the son of Malachi York, he's also an ex-member. Jacob contacted me, and our conversation was basically about the Good times that we had in the Community, what we went through, how we grew up, just making up for 'Old times'. Two months after that Jacob called me, this was in May, Jacob called me about a trip to Florida, a trip where a lot of some of the Boys and Girls, that were going down ex-members, that were going to go down to Florida, just to hang-out to have Fun, whatever. I agreed to go on the trip, I told Jacob that I would come on the trip. I left down, umm I left from New York, went to Georgia, we all met up at Jacob's house, it was Me, Jacob, Nicole Lopez, Anwar Rasheed, Iyse, Istyr, some other Boys and Girls that I don't remember.
> Umm, before we actually went down to Florida I had a conversation with Jacob, outside of his house, and Jacob brought up some feelings that he had about his Father, Jacob was really upset with his Father. He stated that he hated his Father, that he felt that his Father does not need to be alive, that he should not even be given life. Umm, he felt that his Father needs to just 'Rot in Jail'. Jacob wanted all of us to, all of us meaning me Nicole, Karima he was talking to a couple of people. Different people that left the Community he wanted us to bring a Case against his Father. Jacob told me that some of the Girls and Boys that left the Community went to the Government about different things that was going on in the Community, meaning "Child Molestation". Before I left the Community I was the main person in charge of the Finances as well as in charge of anything that went on with the Community living, umm eating anything financial anything that happened regarding any of the members in the Community I dealt with that, so I was basically in charge. Jacob told me that the FBI knew who I was, and that they were told about certain things that I had done in the Community, and some of those things I could be incriminated for. Jacob told me that if I don't go to the FBI first then they would come after me, they would incarcerate me, they would take my Children away from me because there are things that they were told about me that could incriminate me.
> When Jacob first talked to me about that I was not interested in bringing out any charges against his Father, I didn't see any reason, I didn't believe that anything was going on, I didn't believe that anything was wrong, we

wasn't doing any Criminal acts, Jacob brought up the fact that I had a son by his Father at 17 years old, I told Jacob that my son with his Father was never, it never came about because I was forced to have Sex with his Father. Yes I was 17 years old, and yes I did agree to having a child with his Father at that age, I understood my age, I understood his age. I didn't see anything wrong with it, I consented to it. So I told Jacob that that's the way that I felt. I didn't feel that anything wrong happened. We both agreed to it, I felt that I was an adult, it was my decision, and I went with it. Jacob proceeded to say that there were some things that some of the other members, the other ex-members, had went to the Government with, and that I should really, really talk to them and see what's up, and see how I can clear my name, so that I'm not Prosecuted for any of those things. We all went to Florida after that conversation, and during that trip to Florida we had several conversations in the car with Jacob. There were several other Boys that were there, and Jacob started talking about going on the Land, and taking some of the Kids, and just 'Kidnapping' some of the Children off the land. He was talking about my sister, my sister, my younger sister 'Iyster' was still there and he wanted us to just go up there and just take her, and some other little Girls and Boys off the land, because he felt that they shouldn't be living on the land with his Father. But we had all agreed that that was not going to happen, you know none of us was interested in going up on the land, and kidnapping anybody, so we just said that we can just do it the legal way. He started bringing up different things in the Community like how we grew up, how we lived. He brought up the fact that he was in Love with Nicole, and he felt that because Nicole liked his Father that it was a betrayal, that his Father was the one that was responsible for it. Jacob felt that his Father was responsible for his Mother's Death, and his Brother's Death, and he really, really felt that he needed to take Revenge on his Father. And he was not able to do it, but we were able to do it, because we were there longer, we were umm closer to his Dad than he was. So Jacob had a conversation with me and Karima and Nicole, Nicole had a lot of disgruntled issues, talking about Nicole Lopez had a lot of issues with Jacob's Dad because for one she was kicked out, and she felt that it was wrong that she was kicked out because she didn't have anywhere to go, she didn't know anybody, after all of the years that she lived in the Community, he kicked her out, meaning Malachi kicked her out, and umm she had nowhere to go, so she was kind of Mad about that.

Everybody started venting in the car about different things we didn't like, it didn't have nothing to do with 'Child Molestation' it had nothing to do with any 'Criminal Acts', it was just different things that you know, normal things that you don't like about growing up, or you know we might have had an argument with Malachi, and then we brought up the situation, Jacob kind of fed off of that anger, and he convinced all of us that we should take that anger, and we should go to the Government with a story about his Father. We all went down to Florida, and we had fun, we did our thing, on our way back from Florida, the trip back from Florida, we was driving in Jacob's car again, it was myself, Karima, Nicole, Farah, Naoh, Rasheed, and some other driver I don't remember his name. Jacob brought up the conversation again; how he thinks that we should really go to the Government with a story about his Father. Anything that we didn't like in the Community, we should go because his Father needed to be in Jail, his Father did not do good things, he was not happy with his Father, and he really felt that a case should be brought up against his Father, he really felt that his Father should be put away for Life, that he did not deserve to live!! That conversation subsided and we finally made it back to Georgia, from Florida and Jacob had a conversation with me again, and he told me that there were certain Children that did go to the FBI about different things with myself, and that there was no way I would be able to prove that it didn't happen, that the only way I can make any good of it is to go to the FBI with a story, seek 'Immunity' and just go from there. I still told Jacob that I was not interested in doing that, that there was nothing that I had witnessed or nothing that I had known that was going on umm, but Jacob believed that because the FBI knew who I was, and because they were told things about me that it was best that I go to them, and talk to them and see what's up. At that point I was afraid, I mean nobody really messes with the FBI, so I went to the FBI the following day, with Jacob, they called Jacob at first, I sat in the car, Jacob talked with them, I don't know what the conversation was about, because I was not in the room, and I wasn't told what the conversation was about, but Jacob went up there and he talked to them, and then about an hour later they called me up. I stated my name, I stated who I was, they asked me about different children, they asked me about different, they called out different names like Amalla and Crystal, and I told them I knew those Children, I knew...whatever names they brought out, if I knew the person, I told them if I knew that person, they told me about, I mean they asked me to state, my life and umm, the reasons why I left, and the reason why I was there.

I told them about life in the Community, growing up, why we left, I was questioned about the Money charges, I mean the Money situation, because I deal, I did deal with the Financial situation, I told them how we ran our finances, I ran off, you know different people that I knew that was there, different people that I knew that had left, and why they left.

They asked me about certain Children, they asked me about certain stories that they were told, and I told them that, yeah I went along with the story, I told them that yes, I did do these things, I felt that I had to tell them that yes, because I was told that they already knew, and there was no way for me to deny anything that didn't happen, or anything that did happen, I had to tell them, what I felt that they knew, I felt that, like Jacob told me, they already knew the story, and there was no way that I can, I can say that it didn't happen, I would have to Prosecute myself to make whatever, whatever was said against his Father, make it more real, make it sound more believable, if we all Prosecuted ourselves then what we'd say about Malachi would be believable. That interview ended with them asking me about different people that I knew, that would want to talk, different members, that I knew that would want to assist them in the case. Ummm, the only names that I knew were other members that I knew, that were 'Disgruntled' like Nicole had her own issues with Malachi, Karima had her own issues with Malachi, Sakina also, Amala, Crystal, different people that I knew, that had issues against him, I gave them those names.

So after that, they started calling different people, and everybody kind of got involved, everybody called everybody, and that's how the case kind of got started. The question next would be, why did I go ahead with the story, why did I never take it back, why didn't I ever, you know just tell the truth that time. I felt really pressured to go along with the story, I felt that I was, I had, I had, to go along with the story. We all kind of called each other, and was backing up each others story, if Nicole did an interview with the FBI, then she would call us, and we would, we would you know back up her story, so if Nicole spoke to them, she would call us, or in case they called me, then I can back up whatever Nicole was saying, that's how, that's how we kind of did it, we all just called each other, and said yeah I said this and I said this and that way we can back each other up, to make the story sound real, make sound more believable.

I was afraid that my initial interview that I had given a statement, I was afraid that if I was to take that back, I did not know if I was going to be Prosecuted, its not like I had an Attorney to represent me, I did not have my personal Attorney to tell me, to explain to me what the steps were, what the charges were, what the Immunity really meant, what I believed immunity to mean was that I would be protected, anything that I would state on the witness stand, that could be used against me, anything that I would say, that could be used against me, I would be protected from that, that's what I understood my immunity to mean. It was never explained, in detail what the agreement was about, what the immunity was about, that was the gist of what I understood it was about. Although at the time I went through with the story because I was afraid for my life, afraid that umm, they could take me to Jail, I could be incarcerated, that my Children would be taken away from me. And there was different times during the 2-year process that I spoke to different FBI agents, I spoke to Joan, I spoke to Jalaine, I spoke to Tracey from the Sheriff's department, and there was, on a couple of occasions where they did remind me that "you know Habiba, you can be incriminated for certain things that you're about to say as well, so be reminded of that", umm I felt compelled to just go ahead with the story, I didn't want to change my story at that time, I didn't want to break that agreement, because I did, I was told that by breaking that agreement meant that I would be 'Incarcerated' and I would be 'Prosecuted', because I had given statements already. And like I said I wasn't represented by a personal Attorney, we, we, we had, the Prosecution had an Attorney that represented all of the witnesses, and all of the victims, but I was not represented by a personal Attorney. I didn't really know my rights, I didn't really know what the Laws, I didn't know what I couldn't do, and what I can do, so I felt compelled to just go ahead with the story that everybody else was just telling.

Why I wanna come out with the Truth now, its really, really important for me to come out with the Truth now, because I don't sleep at night knowing that two people are spending their lives in Jail as I speak, because of statements that a bunch of 'Ex' disgruntled members came out with.

The whole trial against Malachi was personal, it was on personal anger reasons, we all had our own issues, why we were angry with him, and Jacob told us that if we can come out with a story, we could eventually file for a class action 'Law Suite', we could all sue him for 'Millions of Dollars' and get money from it, we can even go to making Movies, we can even go to making Books and stuff like that, so everybody fed off of that idea, prior to him telling us about, Jacob I mean, prior to Jacob telling us about ahhm the 'Civil Suit', he showed us 'Video Documentary' on Charles Manson, on the 'The Watergate Jude, umm different Leaders that kind of ran Cults, and Jacob showed us this documentary, he showed it to me, he showed it to Nicole, he basically showed it to everybody that left the Community, the Girls. And he wanted us to look at this documentary and compare it to his Father, the way that we lived, the fact that yes we did live with the Children with the Children, the Parents with the Parents, and the Brothers together, and the Mothers together. He wanted us to compare everything that they've been through with us, so we could start believing, that we could put in our minds that 'No' we didn't live a normal life, 'Yes' we were a Cult. So he showed all of us that Documentary so that we can sort of compare the two, so that before we even start testifying, we could understand that Yes, we were a Cult, you know we, he wanted us, he wanted that to be in our minds so that we could go with that type of mind frame, as opposed to, you know we were normal, we just had our own issues, were Mad, but its all good, No he wanted us to believe that listen this is the documentary on this Cult group, and this is what we lived and he wanted us to compare that so that we could have that type of mind frame, in other words it added on to the anger that Wow, this is how we grew up or this is what it is. Anyways umm, like I was saying, I feel totally guilty for bringing this case against Malachi umm, I don't feel that its right that he is in Jail right now because all of us were angry, and we all got together and agreed to this case, and we went ahead with it, now he's facing life in Jail for it. It's not right; it's not fair, for anybody to be Prosecuted for somebody else's personal reasons, I don't think that he should be incarcerated because of that, umm if we all did have things against him, then that just, that's human nature, but nobody should be sent to Jail because of a bunch of lies, and what was said on that Stand, were a 'Bunch of Lies'. Like I said we all called each other up, we all backed each others story up, we all kind of, ok well you said this to this person, and I said this to that person, ok let, that's fine.

Jacob went to each and every one of us, and tried to make it personal between each and every one of us. With me it was like I was in charge, you had control over a lot of things, and so anybody could say this about you and it would be believable, because She was in charge. There was no denying that I was in charge, I was in charge, umm so I felt, I felt that I had to go along with the story, cus I couldn't prove anything that anybody would say against me I didn't feel that I had, I could prove it, I mean he told me that once they tell FBI something, FBI is looking into you, they start looking into me. There was no way I could prove that what anybody said about me, wasn't that Truth or wasn't a Lie, there was no way, so I felt that, I felt compelled to just go ahead with the story.

As far as Nicole is concerned, Jacob appealed to her because Nicole was in Love with one of the younger Boys, and so Jacob knew that if they found that out about Nicole, Nicole would be so afraid, that she can be Prosecuted, that she, that she would be also compelled to tell a story about his Father because she didn't want to be incriminated for whatever feelings she had, so different people had different reasons. You know Jacob had different, he, he made everything personal between all of us so, so we all had personal reasons for being pressured, or feeling that we had to go through with the story. Like I would say like Nicole Harding, the whole situation with the RICO charges, I know that I previously stated that Malachi York never told us not to structure any Money, and he also never told us not to sign, or not to report, you know when we made over $10,000, he never told us not to ever file that report in court. I was told that Nicole Harding told the FBI's that umm, that he did tell us not to sign the document. I would have known if he would have said that because I was in charge of the Money, I was the person in charge of the financial, because if anything was told about finances it would have definitely came through me, but I do believe that Nicole felt compelled to go ahead with that story because for one, Nicole is the one, Nicole Harding I'm talking about, is the one who did refuse to sign those documents, and she's also the one who always gave the 'Tellers' a problem and a hard time whenever it came to those type of transactions, so I believe that that's the reason Nicole did go ahead and said that, yes he said that. But he's never said that to me, he's never said that to anybody that I've known, and like I said, I was the one in charge of the finances and I would have known everything that he would have said as far as the finances goes.

Back to the reason why I feel, that its important to tell the truth now, like I said, I could have told the truth before, but I didn't, I was afraid, I felt that I was pressured, to just go ahead with story, I was being reminded how I was doing the right thing, this is a good thing that I'm doing, I was doing the right thing, that this is a good thing that I'm doing, I was doing the right thing, and as well I did have to remind myself that I could be incriminated, so I felt that's ok, if you tell me a hundred times that it's the right thing to do, if that what all of the Agents are telling me, and then it is the right thing to do. Umm, I didn't feel that it was the right to do, but I was being told that it was the right thing to do, umm, and I felt really, really pressured. I know you can say that why don't I feel pressured now, its not that I don't feel pressured now, I just feel that the Truth has to come out! There's no way that any person in their right mind can go ahead, and live the rest of their life, knowing that they sent somebody to 'Jail for Life'! On lies, there is just No way. And there's no way that I can live the rest of my life, knowing that Malachi is going to spend the rest of his life in Jail. Knowing that Kathy is in Jail now, because of charges that we brought up against her. Every time I look at my children, I think about her Children, and think about the fact that, her Children doesn't have her, and it's not right. Its, its, it's just not right. I'm also going to talk about, the Money situation, yes I was in charge of the finances, and umm, a lot of the financial decisions that were made were by me at the time that I was in charge, when I wasn't in charge, when it was Kathy that was in charge, the financial decisions were made by her. Malachi did not make financial decisions. We collected the Money, we separated the Money, when I was in charge, I was in charge of where the Money went, how the Money was handled, how it was separated, he never sat us down and told us to avoid the FBI, or avoid the IRS, or avoid, umm, do anything illegal with the Money, as matter of fact he was very, very serious about handling his finances in a legal way. So anything that happened with the finances when I was in charge, it was my decision to decide what happened with the finances, where it went, and how it was handled. And the same goes for anybody else who was in charge, prior to me or after me, that's how it was done. I didn't really understand, the structure charges, and I believed that I expressed that to the Attorney, the U.S. Attorney, and I also expressed that to FBI agent Jalaine, that I didn't really understand the structure charges, and they explained to me that anytime you try to avoid filling that report, then that's a charge, that's a serious charge. And like I stated previously, and I believe that I stated this on my testimony on the stand, that Malachi never told us not to file those reports, he never told us to deny any of the tellers any information, if we did deposit over $10,000, and if we were investigated, he never told us not to follow through with us, he never told not to talk to anyone about it, so that's how I feel about the Money structure charges.

I just want to repeat that, the charges brought up against Malachi were all lies, we did back each others story up. I can't really speak for why other people did it; I know that a lot of them had a lot of their own personal anger issues with Malachi. I want to state that nobody that left the Community, left because they were Molested, that was never a reason why anybody left, that they were Molested, or because he was doing things to them that they did not agree to. Nobody left because he was doing any Criminal acts, nobody had any problem with that, that was never the reason for anyone to leave, Child or Adult, that was never the reason for anybody to leave. Everybody left, because they wanted to leave, because they got fed up, I left because I wanted a 'New Life'; it just wasn't for me anymore. Some people did get kicked out, but it was never because of any Child Molestation issues, nobody left because they felt that they were being Molested. No Child had ever, ever made a statement that "I want to leave because Malachi's Molesting me!!". That never took place, that never happened. Like I said, the charges were all personal charges, all because of Personal reasons, Jacob had at different points in time kept questioning us about, what about this Boy?, what about this Girl? What do you think He's going say? What do you think She's going to say? Did you ever see anything happen with this Girl?, and I would always tell Jake, I've never seen anything happen with this Boy or this Girl. Jacob Forced Us! He really, really wanted us to say "ok this happened with this Boy, this happened with this Girl". Or if you're going to say it then you might as well tell them. So he wanted, he questioned us about different people, and like I said, everybody had their own Personal reasons. Everybody had their reason for feeling that they had to tell the story, for me it was because I was in charge, and I felt pressured, I felt compelled that anything that anybody told that FBI about me it would be so hard for me to try to prove that it was a lie or to prove that it was not the truth, and like I said I was not represented by my own personal Attorney, I didn't really know my rights, I don't understand the Law, I wasn't really told, I would say I was not really informed about everything that was going on. I knew there was charges brought up against Malachi, I knew that we had to testify, I knew what we had to say, that was it, I did not understand that I could just get another Attorney and speak to another Attorney, about not going through there was so many times when I wanted to pull back my statement, umm, when I wanted to just not go through with it, but I didn't have the support, I didn't have the back-up. I didn't feel that I had the Protection, yes I was afraid of going to Jail, I was afraid of having my Children taken away from me, I know that its not right to be afraid for myself, and think that it was right, ok I can protect myself, and he still go to Jail, I know that, that's not right, I know it was a selfish thought, and this is why I'm here now, to tell the Truth, to tell it how it was.

In conclusion, it's really, really time for the Truth to come out! This is going on 2-years, or I think it has been 2-years, so many people have suffered, Malachi is suffering day by day, because of this, and it's really, really not fair. I really, really, believe that somebody had to come out with the Truth, and like I said, everyday I think about him suffering. Everyday I think about how wrong it is, what we've all done, how wrong it is, everyday I think about what happened to the lives of all those Children. So this is why I'm putting my statement on record, because it's the right thing to do. And like I said, I want the Truth to come out. I can't be afraid anymore, I can't feel pressured anymore, I can't say that I can just go on with the rest of my life knowing that I'm hiding the Truth, and holding the Truth. I think it's time to come out, it has to come out, we have to bring out the Truth behind all these Lies that was put out. We have to do the right thing, and I'm here because I want to do the right thing, because I really want to do the right thing.

(Washington, 2004)

Fig.394 Florida Trip: *Nicole "Adah" Lopez &* **(far right),** *Abigail "Habiba" Washington During Trip to South Beach, Florida, in 2001*

Abigail "Habiba" Washington's revelations regarding the source of the conspiracy against Malachi York, were followed by numerous other Prosecution witnesses which included Husna & Hasana Evans, Leah Mabry & Samaya "Jameila" Elis, who all related similar accounts of how Law Enforcement officials and FBI agents forced them to make false testimonies against Malachi York under duress. One of York's former accusers in particular, Samaya Elis, who was one of the Prosecution's 'Key' witnesses, bravely provided a detailed description of the diabolical tactics employed by Federal Investigators to extract false testimonies against Malachi York. Such as repeatedly visiting her at School to illegally threaten her into accusing the Nuwaubian leader of Sexual Molestation, without the knowledge of her Parents or any Legal representative.

In a sworn statement 3 days before Abigail Washington's Recanted Testimony, on Tuesday April 20th Samaya Elis stated the following:

> "My name is Samaya "Jameila" Elis, and today is April 20th, and I'm not under no Drugs, I'm not on Drink, I'm not being forced to say this. It was May 16th, I was at School, on my last period, umm I was called, it was like an hour before it was time to leave School, and I was called to go to the umm 'Counselling' office. And I went to the counselling office, and there was a room, and there was a few people like 30 people inside the room. Umm they wanted to talk to me, and I didn't know what it was about. And I went in the room, they said, they told me, this is between me, umm this is between them and between me, not anybody else. And don't tell my Mother, and anybody else, it just between us. And umm, they was asking me questions about Dr. York, So I'm like no it didn't happen, and one of the umm Females told me, they would have a paper come to me, you know, in regards if I had said anything to help the situation. To tell em you know what happened, you know what they think what happened. And I told em it didn't happen, but they kept forcing me saying that, you know if I don't say this, then they probably put me in Jail, or you know come with a whole bunch of papers and stuff like that.
>
> So they had me in the room for a minute, (a period of time) and I wanted to leave, so I told them what they wanted to hear, and I was very afraid, of the part when the Lady was telling me about how I would go to Jail and stuff. So I told them what they wanted to hear. And after all of that was done, they came again and was telling me how because it was later on, it was getting a little late, and I missed my Bus and how they was going to drop me off but they couldn't do that, and they said that they was going to drop me off somewhere close to me house. I came home, and I told my Mother that they put Fear in me, and that I told them what they wanted to hear, and how I was afraid, and how I just wanted to hurry up and get out of there. And umm the next day I felt bad about it, and I called Miss Franklyn, and I told her how it was a Conspiracy, and none of this happened. And I felt bad, and I felt that he didn't deserve none of this. Dr. Malachi is a Good person, and he didn't do anything you know, nothing happened, or anything like that. And umm he's done well for everybody and umm, and he's a

Good man. So I felt bad, and that's why I called her. And umm, my name is Samaya Elis, and this is April 4th, excuse me April 20th, 2004, and I'm not under no Drugs, and not on Drink, umm this is out of my free will, and I've decided to do this, and that's basically it.

(Ellis, 2004)

Certainly "Habiba" Washington, along with the others who came forward, should be commended for their courage in finally exposing to the world the truth about the conspiracy to destroy the leader of the Nuwaubian movement. However, after examining the details of Ms. Washington's 'Recanted' or retracted testimony, serious questions should be asked about Malachi York's judgement in regards to the leadership selection of his organisation. How was it possible for a man with such wisdom and knowledge to select someone like Ms Washington who is obviously not as intelligent as she had been previously given credit for, to hold such a Powerful position in the organisation?

In her statement, Habiba Washington was clearly hiding details of why she really left the Community, and more shocking of all how she was so easily manipulated and tricked by Jacob York, and the Federal investigators. Either Habiba Washington is very naïve or incredibly stupid to have fallen for such a simple form of psychological manipulation by the authorities. How could she allow herself to be deceived into incriminating herself to the FBI without first seeking expert legal advice, solely on the word of Malachi York's son Jacob, and more importantly, how did Dr. Malachi Z. York allow someone so gullible to be in charge of the financial running of his entire movement? Ms. Washington and the other so-called witnesses, with the exception of the younger accusers like Samaya Elis, have all been proven to be not only remarkably gullible for allowing themselves to be manipulated by Jacob and the authorities, but also extremely deceitful for allowing their petty grievances against Dr York cloud their judgement, and by so doing, not only helped to convict an innocent man to Life Imprisonment, but also assisted the Government in destroying what could have eventually become one of the most powerful and influential independent Black organisations in the World. And by so doing, helped to set back the Struggle for the Liberation of African American's by probably another century. By allowing Stupidity, Naivety, Greed, Personal Grudges & Personal Guilt to get the best of them, Habiba Washington and some of the others made the FBI's job easy, and single-handedly brought untold misery to the lives of countless individuals. There is also a rumour that many of Prosecution witnesses, testified against York to save themselves from being Prosecuted for things, which they had done whilst inside the Community, such as 'Indecent Sexual acts' with minors, which was very often the reason many of them were expelled from the Community in the first place. In her Testimony, Habiba Washington constantly makes references to being **'Incriminated'** for things that the FBI supposedly knew about her. However if she hadn't done anything in the first place, why would she be so worried to the extent of making up false allegations to avoid incriminating herself? Could Jacob York have had some prior knowledge of things Habiba Washington and the others had done, which he used as leverage to encourage them to falsely testify against his Father?

Nevertheless, for a brief period it was hoped that these new revelations by the some of the Main Prosecution witnesses would form the basis of a Re-trial, and more urgently prevent the Government from executing the pending 'Property Forfeiture' orders against the Nuwaubian land. York's followers even made the new evidence available to the mainstream Media, who, not surprisingly, showed little or no interest, cynically refusing to report Abigail Washington's testimony by conveniently dismissing the Recantations as cheap publicity thought-up by the Nuwaubian's to gain their leader's freedom. This is very interesting, and exposes the real agenda of the Media, which is really 'Suppression of Truth'. For example, when Abigail Washington was saying things against York and the organisation, the Media were always willing and available to give her testimony full coverage in the Print & Broadcast media. However when she changed her position in Defence of the Nuwaubian leader, the Media were completely unwilling to listen to, or even report her New Evidence! Fox 24 News channel in particular, made the hilarious claim that they were unable to broadcast Ms. Washington's testimony without first getting permission from Judge Ashley Royal.

Then on Friday 7th May 2004, the Prosecution held their so-called 'Restitution' hearing, which they claimed was intended to obtain compensation for the Defendant's Victims, who had all been initially promised large 'Financial Rewards' following York's conviction. During this Hearing, Judge Royal granted a Motion to award York's victims the sum of almost $600,000 in damages, which was intended to eventually form the basis of the Government's forfeiture of all of Malachi York's assets, which they maintained included the 476 acres of Farmland in Putnam county.

During the 'Restitution Hearing', the Prosecution's former 'Lead Witness' Ms. Abigail Washington again attempted to conduct interviews with several reporters outside the courthouse regarding her new evidence, which could have immediately exonerated Malachi York on the spot. However none of the Journalists present, which included Atlanta-Journal Constitution's Bill Osinski, agreed to conduct any interviews with her, on the grounds that they first needed permission from the trial Judge. Isn't it ironic that as long as Ms. Washington was willing to testify against her fellow Nuwaubian's she was regularly quoted 'Verbatim' on TV & Newspapers by the Media, without the slightest hesitation, however when she finally plucked up the courage to tell the 'Truth' of what really happened, suddenly the so-called mainstream Media were interested.

Despite the Media's reluctance to publicize the New Evidence, the Nuwaubian leadership were working tirelessly behind the scenes to prevent the Government from seizing their property, filing numerous appeals to Judge Royal in an attempt to reverse the Property Forfeiture. In retaliation, the Federal Government employed a number of 'Scare Tactics' which placed greater pressure upon the Prosecution's lead witness Abigail "Habiba" Washington, aimed at forcing her to abandon or withdraw her Recanted statement which was in favour of the Nuwaubian leader. This was done, by first compelling her Lawyer to persuade her to denounce the statements made in her sworn affidavit. When this didn't work, a number of other methods were used which included threatening to imprison her for 'Perjury', and the Removal of her Children, if she didn't revert back to her original testimony. Ms. Washington and a number of other former Prosecution witnesses were even 'Blocked' or prevented from providing evidence for the Defence by Judge Royal on the 7th of May, during the very same 'Restitution' hearing, which refused to admit the new evidence in favour of the Defendant, on the grounds that it was nothing more than **"Hearsay"**.

Throughout the entire episode, one of the only Journalists to query the Prosecution's decision to ignore the new evidence was Athens Banner-Herald reporter Samuel Jackson III, who wrote an article entitled: *"Media, Prosecutors Ignored Evidence Exonerating York"*, dated April 28th, in which he stated:

> Why is there a campaign to suppress the videotaped confession by the prosecution's key witness against Malachi York? Habiba Washington, who testified against Malachi York at trial in Brunswick, has now come forward to tell the truth. She was the witness responsible for the money-structuring counts, which allowed the government to move forward with its case even after the statute of limitations had expired. On Friday, she confirmed what we have been telling the world for the past two years: Malachi York is innocent of all charges. [Ms] **Washington speaks of the entire plot and conspiracy by the F.B.I. and Jacob York to bring Malachi York down. She said she was fearful of her life and of prosecution but now has the courage and will to come forward and tell the truth. As long as she was lying on behalf of the prosecution, she was the star witness. News media quoted the lies and plastered it all over the TV networks. Now that she is telling the truth, it's being suppressed. Why?** Malachi York asked Judge C. Ashley Royal and the prosecution the same question, "Why are you hiding the truth? What are you afraid of? Now that someone is coming forth on my behalf you want to hide it. This is my life!! Why are you afraid of the truth?"
>
> (Jackson, 2004)

However, reporter's willing to report the truth like Samuel Jackson III, few and far-between, and often simply ignored or written off by mainstream reporters as merely being York's supporters. Which is exactly how the Media also portrayed the 8 Police & Fire Department officers who publicly submitted letters of resignation, to Chief Rodney Monroe & Chief J. Harvey

of the Macon Police & Fire Departments, in protest of Malachi York's wrongful conviction. The mass resignations came after several Police officers from Macon County, Ga, obtained a copy of Abigail "Habiba" Washington's Video taped confession outlining Malachi York's innocence.
The 8 officers were:

- **Officer Joseph Hibner**
- **Officer William Walker**
- **Officer Michael Berkley**
- **Officer Leon Adams**
- **Private Randford Ropper**
- **Officer Germal Cedricks**
- **Officer Bobby Dickson**
- **Officer Antioun Dean**

Figs.395 & 396 Mass Resignations: Left- Right: *Officer Joseph Hibner & Group of Eight Emergency Service Workers making Joint Video Statement in 2004*

After viewing Abigail Washington's 'Video-taped' confession the officers immediately contacted Macon's Mayor, Jack Ellis, to present him with the new evidence in the hopes of saving an innocent man from life imprisonment. Being Police officers, they felt bound by duty to publicise this new evidence, which should have been grounds for an immediate Re-trial. Instead what happened following an initial meeting was scheduled to have taken place with Mayor Ellis at City Hall, officers Michael Berkley and Joseph Hibner were later contacted by the Mayor's office and informed that the meeting could no longer take place for undisclosed reasons. After repeated attempts to later contact Mayor Ellis on April 24th officers Michael Berkley and Joseph Hibner along with 6 other colleagues from the Macon Police & Fire Department's, publicly resigned in protest, on the grounds that ***"they could no longer serve a City which condoned the imprisonment of an innocent man"***. In a joint Video-recorded statement, the officers declared the following reasons for their joint resignations:

"...The reason for 'Resignations' is we will not continue to risk our Lives in support of a City, and a Mayor, that turns their back on obvious injustices. A Taped Confession came into our possession, and we tried to bring this 'New Evidence' of Criminal activity to their attention, as it was brought to our attention, in order to help stop an injustice against a 60-year old man, who with this taped confession, will be exonerated of all alleged counts. The City of Macon, and their biased Media affiliates are aiding the Prosecution in hiding the Truth from the Public. Several Key Witnesses have come forth, on behalf of this Man, Malachi York, that can turn this case around. This is just one of the Injustices that we have witnessed in our tenure at the Macon Police Department and the Macon Bibb County Fire Department. And we would be dishonouring our work as Public Servants by continuing in these positions. Thank You".

(Officer Hibner, 2004)

Although there has never been any evidence to suggest that the Officers were members of the Nuwaubian movement, as soon as the story broke, the Media quickly brought the officers credibility into question by dismissing them as simply being 'Low Ranking' officers, who were disgruntled followers of Malachi York, attempting to manipulate public sympathy for their Jailed leader.

On the 20th of May, in retaliation to Habiba Washington's new testimony, US Prosecutor's proceeded to file a Motion regarding a 'Potential Conflict of Interest', against her, during which, Prosecution Attorney, George Christian proposed that Ms. Washington's Attorney, Dwight Johnson be investigated for being affiliated with the Nuwaubian movement, and therefore requested that the court disqualify him from being Ms Washington's Attorney. The Prosecution's decision was prompted by fear, because Habiba Washington was vital to their case, and without whom the Government Prosecutor's knew there was no case against York. Therefore, every available means were now being employed to ensure that Habiba Washington retract her 'New Testimony' which cleared Malachi York of any wrongdoing for both the 'Sexual Child Molestation' and 'Money Structuring / Racketeering' charges. This meant not only discrediting Habiba Washington's Attorney, Dwight Johnson, who assisted her in making the 'Sworn Affidavit', but also threatening Ms. Washington with imprisonment for a plethora of concocted charges related to her original testimony if necessary.

Finally after months of being repeatedly threatened, coerced and blocked from giving evidence in favour of the Defendant, Abigail Washington succumbed to pressure, and reaffirmed her original testimony against Malachi York.

'Land Seizure' & 7-Day Forced Eviction

On Wednesday the 30th of June 2004, a 'Civil Assets Forfeiture' hearing was held in the presence of Judge Royal, to establish whether the Nuwaubian's should retain their 476-acre property. Despite claims by the Nuwaubian legal representatives that the land ceased to belong to the group's leader since 2000, which Anti-Nuwaubian reporter Bill Osinski also confirms in his own book *"Ungodly: A True Story of Unprecedented Evil"*:

> ...York effectively removed himself from the fray. He **legally transferred** the deed to Tama Re to a group of some of his followers. No money changed hands; but now, **York was no longer the titular owner**...
> (Osinski, 2007, p: 198)

Nevertheless the Prosecution insisted that because the land was initially supposedly obtained through some unspecified 'Illegal Means', it was therefore still part of York's property, as leader of the group. Therefore if they could successfully prove this during the hearing, the land would be automatically confiscated by the U.S. Government under the RICO Statute.
As a result of the 'Recanted' New Testimonies by Habiba Washington and the other former Prosecution witnesses, as well as last minute manoeuvres by the Nuwaubian legal team, the forfeiture hearing was postponed for several weeks, pending a reorganization of the Prosecution's witness selection. As customary for the Prosecution, this meant immediately resorting to their old tactics of coercion, applied pressure and threats of imprisonment to persuade any uncooperative witnesses to change their testimonies. Despite the Nuwaubian's best efforts, the situation was looking very bleak, as the Federal Government were clearly determined to execute what appeared to be the final phase of the destruction of Malachi York's Movement, which meant seizing the group's land at any and all costs. Clearly this was the real purpose of the case against York from the outset, which is why the RICO indictment was suddenly included halfway through the Trial, in order to be used as a pretext to eventually confiscate the land, under the so-called 'Civil Assets Forfeiture'. It was feared that with the land still in their possession, the Nuwaubian's could still proceed with their goal of creating a Separate Independent 'Sovereign' Nation/State for African Americans, which had already been ratified a decade earlier by the United Nation's as **UN # 215: Yamasee / Washitaw Nation of Moors**. Therefore this case was not only against the group's founder Malachi York, but rather the entire movement, which is why the Media always dubbed it *"The Nuwaubian Trial"* from the beginning.

Nevertheless on Thursday 15th July, United States District Judge Ashley Royal, granted a Motion permitting Federal officials to immediately confiscate the Nuwaubian's 476 acre property which had almost doubled in value since its original purchase in January 1993, which was for the sum of $975,000. Judge Royal justified his decision to seize the property on the grounds that; *"the land still belonged to the group's founder Malachi York"*, and as such was subject to Government forfeiture, along with a number of other properties scattered throughout Georgia, which would be auctioned off to supposedly cover the costs of 'Restitution' or compensation for Malachi York's victims. Despite ongoing appeals by Attorney Robert Ratliff, the lawyer representing the actual owners of the property, the Judge's ruling was to be final, and would make way for the eventual eviction of the Nuwaubian's from their land. U.S. Attorney Maxwell, who successfully led the Prosecution case against York, naturally expressed his delight at the Judge's decision, but stopped short of confirming to reporters when the actual seizure would take place: *"I don't know when the Government might take possession, it's too early to put a timetable on it."* Attorney Wood also dismissed the claims by York's followers that the land had previously been transferred to their ownership by the group's leader: *"We've said all along that Dwight York has always been in control of these properties...This was just a ploy to create confusion, which has become their usual tactic"*.

Judge Royal's decision to proceed with the land seizure came as a surprise to the Attorney acting for Nuwaubian's, who had expected the Judge to keep his word, following his previous court ruling two weeks earlier, during which he had promised to delay seizing the land until the outcome of York's pending Appeal. Neither were the group's legal representatives provided with an adequate explanation as to why the sudden decision was made. Speaking on the Nuwaubian's behalf, Attorney Ratliff expressed his shock and confusion at Judge Royal's surprise ruling to observers afterwards: ***"I don't understand it, because the U.S. Attorney did agree to delay pending York's Appeal."*** Attorney Ratliff, then added that he intended to pursue every legal option available, to substantiate that the Nuwaubian's had legal ownership of the land. However he ended by stating that if it came to it, the property would be handed over without resistance by his clients. Despite Attorney Ratliff's dismay at Judge Royal's final decision to grant 'Forfeiture' of the land, the pronouncement did not come as a shock to the Nuwaubian's, who were by now well aware of what was bound to transpire once York was convicted. Judge Royal's Judgement was merely one in a long line of actions designed to 'Dismember' the Nuwaubian movement, erasing their presence from Georgia forever.

A fortnight later on the 28th of July, the Nuwaubian administration was served with a notice giving them approximately **'7 Days'** to vacate the property by no later then the 4th of August. Contrary to the misleading Media reports, which claimed that the group were given 30-days to vacate by the court, the Nuwaubian's have Documented evidence which contradicts these reports, and prove that they were only given one week in which to leave the entire property. **(Please refer to Appendix)** For example, in an article entitled: *"Feds to seize properties within 30 days"*, Athens Banner Herald reporter Lee Shearer, purposely deceived the public in order to conceal the truth, regarding the Nuwaubian's sudden eviction:

> "...Federal officials expect to take possession of the properties within **30 days**, said Sue McKinney, a spokesperson for the U.S. Department of Justice's Middle District of Georgia. District Court Judge Ashley Royal cleared the way for the seizure in a July 12 ruling, rejecting the arguments of people who said York had turned over the Athens properties as well as the Cult's Eatonton compound to them..."
>
> (Shearer, 2004)

It was also made clear that any personal belongings left behind would immediately be destroyed by officials from the U.S. Marshals & Justice departments, which included all buildings, monuments and religious structures left on the land. What transpired next would become one of the greatest travesties to befall African Americans in recent history. Reminiscent of the infamous Native American 'Trail of Tears', in 1838, over 50 families, many of which comprised of Young Children and Babies as young as a few months old, were forced by the authorities to transport all their belongings in just one week. The majority of York's followers had come to regard 404 Shadydale Road as their home for over a decade, since leaving their former property in Upstate New York in 1993. Many with nowhere to go, simply took what possessions they could carry, to nearby hotels or to the homes of fellow Nuwaubian's and relatives in the region, or if they were not so lucky, to their Vehicles. As usual the Media tried to quickly suppress the details of the sudden eviction, however outspoken Nuwaubian campaigner Rick Johnson, who was amongst those evicted from their homes, illustrated to 'Black World Today' reporter Herb Boyd, what had actually transpired following Judge Royal's surprise ruling:

> "We had only seven days to leave, and this is contrary to reports that the Judge had given us 30 days. Given the short period of time to prepare, many families are now homeless or forced to live in shelters or with friends and relatives...It's nothing more than a Shakedown...Now, if you look at the land you'll see American flags flying because Sheriff Sills and his deputies have achieved what they have been trying to do for years..."
>
> (Johnson, 2004)

In the days following the court's ruling, the mood amongst the Nuwaubian's became one of not only resignation, but also desperation to get as much done in as little time as possible. Eyewitnesses have described an atmosphere of surreal panic, with no time to really stop and evaluate the situation, but just to remain focused on removing as much belongings as possible before the August 4th deadline. The mammoth task required many of the adults to go without sleep for several days. Just imagine trying to clear the contents of a large house in just one week, let alone enough time to vacate a small village, an area the size of 20 acres of built up land inhabited by over 50 families. This meant arranging 'New' accommodation, Transportation, and Packing the contents of 20 acres of property and belongings. From the accounts of those present, the 20 acres of the property contained many residential buildings, personal belongings as well as the group's Religious monuments and structures, which included:

- Over '30' three Bedroom Houses
- Several Large Temples & 'Pyramid' structures
- A 'Christian' Church, 'Masonic' Lodge & 'Islamic' Mosque
- Buildings containing Irreplaceable 'Religious' Artefacts & Personal Belongings
- Dozens of Statues, Depicting ancient African Gods
- A Replica of the Mahdi's Shrine
- A Replica of King Solomon's Temple
- Dozens of Obelisks, Statues, Arches & Monuments, Depicting Ancient Egyptian Culture
- Numerous Mobile Homes
- Numerous Vehicles, Electrical & Computer Equipment
- A Recording Studio
- Mansion formerly belonging to Malachi York

In spite of the insistence by the authorities of being concerned about the welfare of the children residing on the property, their actions finally proved to the contrary when numerous children were eventually Displaced and made Homeless, in many cases forced to seek shelter with their parents in the back of cars and other vehicles following the sudden eviction. Hundreds of Men, Women & Children were forced off their own property, and kicked out on to the street by the Government to face homelessness, simply because of their Religious beliefs and Colour of their skin. However what is slightly perplexing is why the Nuwaubian's did not mount any kind of final 'Mass' public protest at what was clearly the 'Illegal' seizure of their property. Maybe they had just lost the will fight, or maybe they were understandably frightened at the prospect of a repeat raid by the Government who were clearly determined to obtain their Land at any cost, even if it meant shedding innocent lives in the process.

Following the group's eviction, the United States Attorney General's office indicated that an award for 'Distinguished Services' would be presented to the Team which lead the Investigation and successful Conviction of the Nuwaubian leader, namely; Attorney Richard Moultrie, Attorney Stephanie Thacker, FBI Special Agent's Jalaine Ward & Joan Cronier and last but by no means least: Putnam County Sheriff Howard Richard Sills, for *"their coordinated efforts in securing the Investigation, Prosecution & Conviction of the Nuwaubian leader Malachi York"*. In the wake of the eviction, York's followers later filed a series of unsuccessful appeals to regain the property seized by the Federal Government. Unfortunately all attempts to overturn the court's decision failed. The dye had been cast, with their land gone, Founder & Leader Imprisoned for what would be the rest of his life, it seemed all over for the 'Nuwaubians' who now appeared to exist only in name alone.

Figs.397, 398 & 399 Derelict Property: Top & Bottom:
Destruction of Nuwaubain Property following the Forced Eviction

In the months following their Eviction, the 476-acres of Nuwaubian land quickly fell into disrepair, after first being looted by Sheriff Sills and his cohorts, who were said to have immediately set about removing anything valuable left behind by York's followers during their hasty departure from the property. The property lay idle until May 2005, almost a year after it was seized from its legal owners, the property was hastily auctioned off for an estimated $1.7 Million to Lawson Lawrence, a local property developer who claimed that he planned to re-sell all 476 acres, for a profit within 6 months. In an interview with reporter Tim Sturrock of the Macon Telegraph, Mr Lawrence expressed his desire to quickly remove the Nuwaubian buildings and monuments, along with his eventual plans for the property:

> "It's a really pretty piece of land except of all the stuff that's on it right now…Only 19-acres of the land has any sign that it was used by the Nuwaubian's…I plan to leave the metal buildings in place after tearing off the decoration covering them. The future owner could use the buildings as construction offices. The land could also be used as a hunting lodge, or as farming land, although I might either split up the land before selling it, or just sell it as one piece. I will certainly keep the Mansion formerly belonging to York on the property for now. The demolition could take anywhere up to a month, and cost between 50 to $70,000. I have also donated much of the property left behind, such as; Plates, Pots, & Playground equipment to the local church, although I haven't determined a final price for the property yet, the breath-taking scenery, of rolling pastures and woodland encompassing four lakes would provide a perfect retreat for somebody"
>
> (Lawrence, 2005)

By this time many structures on the land, had already fallen into disrepair, which prompted the 'new owner' to immediately begin demolition of all the religious monuments and dwelling structures. Never one to miss an opportunity to rub their faces in it was Nuwaubian nemesis Sheriff Sills who lead the Demolition team on the morning of Thursday June 9th, in one final act of public humiliation against Malachi York and his followers. Putnam County Sheriff Howard Richard Sills, with 'Cuban Cigar' tightly clenched between his grinning teeth took great satisfaction in Personally tearing down the Nuwaubian's 'Egyptian' Styled' front-gated entrance, which had prevented him from entering on so many occasions. Speaking to reporters outside the property, Sheriff Sills expressed his delight at finally destroying the Nuwaubian structures and buildings, which he simply described as 'Junk':

> "It came down easily, typical Nuwaubian style, 'Stucco and Styrofoam'. It feels good to tear down that 'Son of a Bitch' myself…This gives some finality to it. People need to stay off that property. First it was the property of the United States government, now it belongs to an individual who paid a lot of money for it. If people come on that property they're going to be arrested for it…It will be good to see it go back to what it was before York's habitation…By the middle of next week, there will be nothing but a couple of pyramids…It's nothing but 'Junk', and its been nothing. It like York, was a façade…It is a symbol, to me, of York's despicable, heinous

acts that he perpetrated against those children on that property. This place where so many despicable things happened is gone...I think the young victims, who had so many despicable things done to them on this land, will appreciate Mr Lawrence ridding the land of symbols of that period of their life...It will suit me just fine that any semblance of it at all will be permanently erased from Putnam County."

(Sheriff Sills, 2005)

Fig.400 Final Act of Revenge: Left- Right: *Sheriff Richard Sills Speaking to Reporters outside Nuwaubian Property & Sheriff Sills Triumphantly operating Demolition Equipment to Destroy Nuwaubian Front Entrance*

In the wake of the land's purchase, Federal officials issued a statement that all of the proceeds from the sale of the 404 Shadydale Rd, as well as the other properties belonging to York, estimated at over 3 Million Dollars would be equally distributed amongst the various 'Law Enforcement' agencies involved in the investigation against the Nuwaubian leader. This of-course included Putnam County Sheriff's department, who took full credit for spearheading the initial 'investigation' into York's activities in the county. However this is in direct contradiction to the statement first issued by the Prosecution team at the outset of the trial. Ironically this earlier statement maintained that all proceeds from the sale of the Defendant's Property would compensate the victims, as part of the so-called 'Restitution' for the years of Sexual Abuse committed against them, which to this day, has never been paid to any of them.

Epilogue

After initially being denied a retrial by U.S. District Court Judge Ashley Royal in August 2004, Dr. Malachi York's legal team embarked upon a series of unsuccessful appeal attempts, which culminated in he's conviction finally being upheld by the 11th U.S. Circuit Court of Appeals on October 27th 2005. Recognised as one of the highest stages or levels of appeals within the United States legal system, the 11th U.S. Circuit Court of Appeals, is often the final stage most defendants reach with their appeals for a re-trial. York's legal team lead by Attorney Adrian Patrick appealed on the grounds that the grand jury was tainted by pre-trial publicity and that the Prosecution inappropriately applied Federal Racketeering laws during the appellant's trial. The Defence also argued that Trial Judge Ashley Royal continuously erred when ruling during defence motions, essentially basing Dr. Malachi. Z. York's Appeal upon '10' distinctive points: **(1) The Indictment 'Misjoined' the Sexual Abuse charges with the financial-structuring charges, and the district court erred in refusing to sever those charges; (2) The district court Erred in refusing to dismiss the RICO counts because the United Nuwaubian Nation of Moors is not an "Enterprise" under RICO and because there is insufficient connection between York's alleged acts and the Nuwaubian organization; (3) The district court Erred in refusing to dismiss the Indictment because the Indictment was improperly returned by a grand jury tainted by pre-trial publicity; (4) The district court Erred in allowing the government to call a certain witness in rebuttal, and further Erred by refusing to allow York to call his own rebuttal witness thereafter; (5) There was insufficient evidence to convict York of the charges that he transported minors in interstate commerce with the intent that the minors would engage in unlawful sexual activity, and further, the government did not put forth sufficient evidence to prove that any underlying sexual activity undertaken by York was actually unlawful; (6) The district court Erred in denying York's motion to dismiss two counts of the time Indictment because the minor victim was undisputedly over the age of consent at the time the sexual act took place; (7) The district court Erred in denying York a continuance when York switched lead counsel approximately two weeks before trial; (8) York's sentence violates the Sixth Amendment under <u>United States v. Booker</u>, 542 U.S. _, 125 S. Ct. 738 (2005), because the district court enhanced his sentence based on facts not reflected in the jury's verdict; (9) York's sentence is invalid under <u>Booker</u> because he was sentenced under a mandatory, rather than advisory, guidelines scheme; (10) York's sentence violates <u>the ex post facto</u> clause of the Constitution because York was sentenced under the November 2000 edition of the United States Sentencing Guidelines ("Guidelines") rather than under the November 1993 edition of the Guidelines.**

Outside the Appeals court, York's lead Attorney Adrian Patrick accompanied by New Black Panther Party National Representative Attorney Malik Zulu Shabaaz, along with many of York's supporters, proclaimed to awaiting Journalists: *"We are still affirming that Dr. York is innocent of these charges."*

Figs.401 & 402: Appeal Hearing: Left- Right: *Attorney Adrian Patrick & Attorney Malik Zulu Shabaaz Talking to Reporters outside Appeals Court after submitting oral arguments in September 14th 2005 & York's followers standing in formation outside Court building*

However, unconvinced by the Defence Team's arguments for a re-trial listed above, the 3 panel 11th U.S. Circuit Court of Appeal Judges subsequently unanimously concluded that; ***"After careful review of the voluminous record in this case, as well as the arguments of parties in both their briefs and at oral arguments, that all of York's claims of Error 'Lack[ed] Merit"***, and therefore his 135-year conviction be upheld with immediate effect. Since being incarcerated, Malachi York has received support from an ever-growing number of people, including leading Religious & Political figures in the U.S. In June 2004, after the U.S. Government's raid of the Nuwaubian land, popular Radio talk show host, Scientist & Lecturer, Keidi Obi Awadu, more commonly known as 'The Conscious Rasta', interviewed Nuwaubian campaigner & spokesperson Barnard Foster regarding the group's sudden eviction, and subsequent land seizure during an Online Radio discussion on 'L.I.B. Radio'. The following are comments made by the Conscious Rasta, regarding the issue of Malachi York's innocence and the Federal Government's 'Illegal' seizure of the Nuwaubian property:

> We're talking tonight with Brother Barnard Foster, joining us out of Metropolitan Atlanta to discuss many aspects of this case, that were excluded, or have been excluded from mainstream media, as well as discussing very critically the issue of the Land. This is the People's Land, the People Built it, the People Bought it with their own hand. Now after this Political Convention, what appears by everything that I've seen to be a 'Political Conviction', they have 'Stolen' a Key, Critical piece of Land!!!... Critical Discussion, the Theft of Land, developed for the benefit of African Progress. A Land that connects us with our most 'Ancient Past' definitely connects us with our Future. Our Future here is being infiltrated in the most Violent way, we ask the question, what does this really mean to our Progress as a People?... People don't get the opportunity to hear that there are two sides to these Critical issues. Especially when you're dealing with America and American Corporate controlled media, who we know tell, Vicious, Destructive, Horrifying Lie after Lie after Lie. So that becomes a Critical Mission for we who consider ourselves to be the Black Media, our responsibility is to show the other side of the story, and I think that the more that People hear this particular story of the Persecution slash Prosecution of Dr. Malachi. Z. York, and especially the Theft of the Land. The theft of the Land in itself is Outrageous and Egregious...We're getting a Wonderful response tonight Brother Barnard. I think it's a complement also to yourself, your bringing a very articulate Dialogue to a subject that has been Divisive amongst the Black Community. And I think the main reason, we probably said this earlier, the main reason it has been so Divisive is because we've only been able to hear 'One Loud Voice', and that's the Voice of Beastly Deception, in trying to once again Trounce the aspirations of another African Group, or Leader who steps out on point and says; the People have certain things that they have to fulfil and I can do it so therefore I must!!....
>
> (Conscious Rasta, 2004)

The campaign to secure York's release is being currently spearheaded by Malachi York's daughter Richelle Davis York, who has vigorously and vehemently battled to raise public awareness regarding her father's plight. You may remember that it was Richelle York who first circulated the e-mail to her father's followers drawing attention to he's mistreatment by Prison officials and worsening medical condition not long after his arrest in 2002. Aside from working to raise awareness within the Nuwaubian Community, Ms. York has been able to garner the support of numerous high profile political figures & organisations including; Rev. Jessie Jackson, The Southern Rainbow PUSH Coalition, The Concerned Black Clergy, Rev. Al Sharpton, Sen. Joe Beasley & Rev. Fred Taylor, head of the Southern Christian Leadership Conference (SCLC), who have all pledged their unwavering support for the incarcerated Nuwaubian leader. Through sheer tenacity and steadfastness Ms. York was even able to achieve the seemingly unattainable task of acquiring support from her father's former ideological rival, and arguably the most powerful Black leader in America, Minister Louis Farrakhan. Minister Farrakhan, who had until then remained silent regarding York's predicament, at last added his considerable political weight to the chorus of black leaders in support of the Nuwuabian leaders freedom.

On September 14th whilst on a brief visit to Atlanta, Georgia, Minister Farrakhan made a passionate speech to over 5,000 spectators at the Atlanta Civic Centre regarding the U.S. Government's ongoing effort to prevent the rise of a so-called **'Black Messiah'** by destroying Black leaders throughout history, by drawing the audiences' attention to the current conspiracy against Dr. Malachi. Z. York, stating:

> Whenever a people are oppressed and suppressed and denied basic rights, freedom, justice and equality, which are the essentials of life, they know that the longer that we are deprived, the greater the leader that comes to answer that depravation. So they are watching to see who that leader was… They were looking for the Messiah, just like Pharaoh was looking for the birth of the deliverer and said, "Kill all boy babies" and just like Herod was looking for the Messiah two thousand years ago and killead all boy babies, they are still scanning you and listening to your talk. They heard Malachi York. They heard a Brilliant Black Brother. They saw him building a compound, a small nation here in Georgia. Is he the Messiah? Trumped up charges. Break up his movement. Put the Brother in Jail. Garvey, Malcolm, Martin, the Game is the same. Always watch for the leader who is gaining strength, popularity, power and influence. If you can bring him into court, fine. If you can't, find a way to trump up charges. Find a way to Kill him…
>
> (Farrakhan, 2005)

Fig.403: Historic Meeting: *Minister Farrakhan & Richelle. D. York, With members of both The NOI & Nuwaubian Shriners*

Also working through her Father's office of Liberian Council General & Organisation, The International Ministries & Humanitarian Foundation, established by the Nuwaubian leader prior to his arrest Richelle Davis York has been able to campaign for Malachi York's release through a number of 'International' Diplomatic channels Assisted by Senior Officials within the Liberian Government, such as her father's staunchest supporter, Liberian Councillor and former Presidential candidate Francis Garlawolu. Richelle D. York has also been behind the ongoing appeal to the US State Department to have her father repatriated to his adopted nation of Liberia, since 2004.

Figs.404 & 405 Diplomatic Support: Left- Right:
Richelle York with Liberian Minister Alexander Wallace & Rev. Jessie Jackson

Finally, former student and heir apparent of the late Dr. Khalid Abdul Muhammad, who currently heads the New Black Panther Party & the Southern Muslim Movement, Attorney Malik Zulu Shabaaz, has shown great Solidarity towards the Nuwaubian leader, not only during, but also after the Trial, going on record on numerous occasions to pledge his full unwavering Support for York's innocence despite the tradition of animosity which has existed between the Nation of Islam and the Nuwaubian movement for a number of years.

Figs.406 & 407 Nuwaubian Supporter: Top & Bottom:
*Attorney Shabaaz with Mentor the late Dr. Khalid Muhammad
& Attorney Shabaaz speaking at the Millions More Movement in 2005*

Million Man March *'The Millions More Movement'* rally organised in Washington D.C., by the Nation of Islam, when he proudly proclaimed Dr. Malachi. Z. York's innocence in the presence of over 22, 000 spectators in 2005.

During an interview with Journalist Adeebafolami (AFC) entitled: *"Charges, Conspiracy, COINTELPRO and Malachi York"*, Attorney Shabaaz reaffirmed his belief in Malachi York's innocence, and current predicament as Political Prisoner and victim of a Government conspiracy:

(AFC) - Your response to those who have thrown Dr. York in the trash, saying he's guilty, he got what he deserved, etc. What is the importance of keeping this case in the forefront?

(MZS) - It's important because Malachi York has made great contributions to our people and he has been a dedicated teacher and organizer and helped turn around many lives in his lifetime. I don't believe our enemy has the moral authority to cast judgment, incarcerate and imprison [him]. If [he] is to be judged at all, it can only be by the Black Nation and not by our unrighteous enemy.

We must understand that this case involves conspiracy, the continuation of the Counter Intelligence Program [COINTELPRO] by outside forces manipulating divisions in the Nuwaubian Nation and many of those who testified against York, their credibility is highly questionable. Many were outright coerced and others were part of the system of vindictiveness because of organizational strife.... You can't just look at the surface and say [he] must be guilty until you understand all the circumstances surrounding the case. How the government, FBI and sheriffs in that [Georgia] county were absolutely out to get him, agents were in his organization, some turned on him in his organization. In the beginning, his legal defense was not handled adequately.

The White man is not after York because of some alleged acts of tax evasion and child molestation, they're after him because he has been a consistent organizer and teacher of our people and he has influence.

(AFC) - Once anyone is charged with sexual abuse, it is almost impossible to wipe clean because, even if a person is innocent there will always be a question of doubt to some. Is Dr. York maintaining his innocence on all charges that were brought against him?

(MZS) - Yes. The bottom line is, [he] deserves a new trial and if he gets one the whole world can see and gauge the allegations for themselves. His trial was infected by racism as well as ineffective legal defence, prosecutorial misconduct, coercion. Many of the witnesses who testified at first, have recanted, said they did it out of anger, they were angry at him for some reason.

(AFC) - They were coerced into reversing their position?

(**MZS**) - No, they voluntarily reversed their positions. They participated with the government at an initial level but much of it may have had to do with personal reasons other than what actually happened. Hell knows no fury like a woman scorned - know what I mean?

(adeebafolami.com, 2006)

After carrying out our own extensive examination of most of the available material relating to the case. It is clear that neither the State nor Federal Prosecutors sufficiently satisfied the 'Burden of Proof', such as DNA or other material evidence necessary to secure a (satisfactory) conviction of either the 'Child Molestation' or 'Racketeering' charges against the Nuwaubian leader.

We must therefore conclude that Dr. Malachi. Z. York has been not only wrongfully convicted, but has also been the victim of a well orchestrated conspiracy, involving Law Enforcement agencies, certain aspects of the mainstream Media, as well as the U.S. Judiciary. Rendering his conviction unsafe, and should therefore be overturned, resulting in either an immediate Re-Trial or Acquittal, followed by the complete retrieval of all confiscated properties.

Conclusion

Dr. Malachi. Z. York is currently being held 60 feet underground at U.S. Penitentiary (USP) Federal Administrative Maximum 'Supermax' ADX Prison Facility located in Florence, Colorado, since being transferred there on March 2nd 2006. Often referred to as the *"Alcatraz of the Rockies"*, the maximum security Correction Facility buried deep under the Rocky Mountains is said to be one of the toughest Jails on Earth, containing some of America's most dangerous Prisoners ranging from Terrorists, Multiple Murderers, Serial Killers, Underworld Hit Men, Escapees & Individuals who have either killed Correctional officers or other inmates in the past, and therefore require the tightest security controls. Ironically the High security "Fortress like" facility also contains many of the same Islamic Terrorists York opposed during the early 1990s.

ADX's list of infamous inmates include:

- **Shoe Bomber; Richard Reid**
- **911 Plotter; Zechariahs Moussaoui**
- **Unabomber; Theodore Kaczynski**
- **1st World Trade Centre Bomber; Ramzi Yusef**
- **Terrorist Mastermind; 'Blind Sheikh' Omar Abdel Rahman**
- **1995 Okalahoma Bomb Co-Conspirator; Terry Nicholas**
- **1996 Atlanta Olympics Bomber; Eric Rudolph**
- **Columbian Drug Cartel Assassin; Dandeny Munoz-Mosquera**
- **Larry Hoover; Leader of 'The Black Gangster Disciples Nation'**

Fig.408 World's Most Secure Prison: *Above ground photo of the ADX Supermax Prison*

Fig.409: Dangerous Inmates:
Some of the World's most notorious Criminals being held at 'Supermax' ADX Facility

Since he's conviction in 2004, evidence has slowly emerged of an entire catalogue of Human rights abuses allegedly committed against the Nuwaubian leader, now also known as **Inmate #17911-054**, which make unnerving reading. Denied access to most Visitation, TV, Radio & Phone Call privileges, Malachi York has at times been held under the very 'Highest Security Level', in conditions which are more like that of a 'Political Prisoner' than someone convicted of Child Abuse & Tax Evasion. For example whilst in (USP) Marion, York was allegedly held in what was described as *"One of the Bleakest and Most Austere Prison Regimes on Earth"*, often said to be denied basic necessities such as his Medical Treatment. There have also been disturbing reports emerging that several attempts have already been made upon his very life, after one of his legal representatives Attorney Malik Zulu Shabaaz claimed to have witnessed signs of serious assault and stab wounds on both his shoulders and arms, during a legal visit with the Nuwaubian leader. Except for limited visits from close family members and legal representatives, York is completely isolated from the outside world, held in an 'Isolation Unit' (SHU) on 24-hours a day lock down. Tormented Night and Day, York himself describes being held in complete solitary confinement, in Cold, Unlit, Mildew covered concrete cells, forced to sleep on a concrete slab bed, in a cell occupied by Rats and giant Cockroaches who constantly bite his swollen arms and legs leaving Puss filled sores throughout the night. Forced to often go weeks without being allowed to Wash, Shave or even Brush his Teeth, which in turn has caused his jaw to regularly swell as a result of re-occurring decaying tooth. Refused access to clean water and fresh air, due to unsanitary conditions York's health has been steadily deteriorating to the point where he has already Died on two separate occasions, and had to be resuscitated by Prison Doctors. Battered, exhausted, seriously malnourished, it is now feared that the 62-year old Nuwaubian leader will not survive much longer under such harsh conditions.

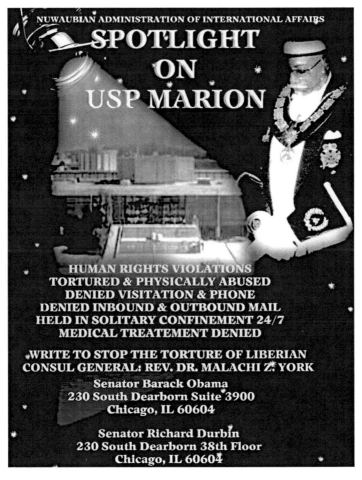

Fig.410 Human Rights Abuses: *Nuwaubian Campaign Poster outlining the extent of Dr. Malachi York's Persecution in Prison*

Ironically the circumstances surrounding York's arrest and treatment in detention have increased the Nuwaubian leader's prominence and support base within the Black Community, which in turn has prompted his followers in the Nuwaubian Nation to change direction from that of a predominately Theological towards a more Political orientated movement.

Future of the Nuwaubian Nation

The diabolical Terrorist attacks of '9/11' provided Right-Wing Christian Conservative elements within the US Power Structure with the perfect pretext or excuse to be less tolerant towards racial & religious group's deemed outside of the mainstream. Naturally this purge would ultimately include progressive Black organisations such as the Nuwaubian's whose Independent 'Black Nationalist' agenda conflicted with the 'Right-Wing Christian 'Neo' Conservative' ethos or agenda. With hysteria and paranoia regarding foreigners at an unprecedented high, the conditions were conducive to launching a new COINTELPRO style Crusade against the current generation of Black consciousness movements. Naturally, it was only a matter of time before York's vision of 'Freedom & Self-Determination' for Blacks in the West, would be deemed as a threat to the White Power Structure elite, which had its own plans for the future of blacks. Therefore this spelt doom for York and his movement, leading to the present 'Nightmarish' reality, which has seen the near destruction of everything it took the Nuwaubian's 30-years to have build in less than 3-years.

Despite damaging information coming to light regarding York's private life following his arrest, including many of the 'Corrupt' inner workings of the organisation, Malachi York's teachings continue to attract ever increasing numbers of followers & initiates which should at least ensure that the Nuwaubian philosophy continues to go from strength to strength for many generations to come. There is even compelling new evidence which suggests that York's intention prior to his arrest in 2002 was to eventually relocate the organisation's entire headquarters to Liberia, West Africa, from which a number of Satellite 'Communities' were to be established throughout the African Continent. This means that in the near future, the group's leadership may one-day carry out York's wishes by moving *en masse* to Africa. Which in turn could lay the foundations for an eventual 'Mass Exodus' or Migration of Western Blacks back to Africa, as Marcus Garvey once predicted in relation to the 'Prophesies' contained within both the books of Genesis & Revelations:

> And He said unto Abram, Know of a surety that thy seed shall be a stranger in a land that is not theirs, and shall serve them; and they shall afflict them four hundred years;
> And also that nation, whom they shall serve, will I judge: **and afterwards shall they come out with great substance. And thou shalt go to thy fathers in peace; thou shalt be buried in good old age...**
> (The Book of Genesis Chapter 15, Verses 13-16)

> And I heard another voice from heaven, saying, Come out of her, my people, that ye be not partakers of her sins, and that ye receive not of her plagues.
> For her sins have reached unto heaven, and God hath remembered her iniquities...
>
> (The Book of Revelation Chapter 18, Verses 4-6)

Which appears to be what the White Power structure fears most, judging by the amount of time and effort it spends discouraging Western Blacks, particularly, African American's from forming any type of 'Independent' movement, which focuses on Africa as a realistic option for future Repatriation:

> Why do they engage in this form of harassment? They engage in such harassment because the American Government wants to turn you against your own kind. In order to keep you from making a 'Mass Exodus', out of this Country, back to your own Country, where you can live amongst your own kind.
> So the American Propaganda is designed to make you think that no matter how much Hell you catch here, you're still better off here in America, than you would be elsewhere. This is their trick. They want you to think you have no place else to go...
>
> (Malcolm X, 1964)

Fig.411 Back to The Mother Land: *Nuwaubian Poster Campaign, Encouraging members to consider a Future in Africa*

Nevertheless, in a series of letters written to his followers, York is said to have expressed a deep desire to return to the 'Mother Land', making repeated requests for his legal team to explore the possibility of his being 'Repatriated' to his adopted Nation of Liberia, West Africa, which has in turn, led to a change in the group's ethos, which has now taken on a more African orientated direction.

Prior to his arrest in 2002, York had already began making links with Liberian Government in his role as Consul General for the West African Nation, adopting the title: **'Bawaba Bassa Africa'**, and laying the foundations in preparation for the eventual repatriation of those within the organisation interested in returning back to Africa.

Following York's arrest, a number of his followers have developed strategies to not only sustain interest in the movement, but to also raise the public's awareness towards their imprisoned leader's plight. Most notable of York's student's to have emerged are a group of 3 individuals referred to as **'The Triad of Neter A'aferti Atum-Re'**, who were being previously groomed by Dr. Malachi. Z. York to propagate the Doctrine before his arrest, and now officially represent the Nuwaubian leader.

Dr. Ahmadou J. Varmah otherwise known as **'Haru-Hotep Tar'** is another high profile students, who has distinguished himself as one of the most outstanding & charismatic young scholars of the Nuwaubian philosophy. Haru-Hotep Tar has authored a series of his own books including: *"Solar Biology or Lunar Astrology"*, and is Co-founder of **'The Journey Home Group'**, which aims to repatriate its followers back to Africa.

Finally, amongst the Nuwaubians most making a difference is; Michael Polight Noak, also known as: **Neb Nawur Re** or 'Brother True Light' who, since the Nuwaubian leader's arrest has not only tirelessly campaigned for Dr. York's release, but also shared the platform with many high profile individuals such as Malik Zulu Shabaaz & Dr. Sebi. He has also been instrumental in helping to spread the Nuwaubian doctrine on the African continent through his charity organisation: **The Golden Ankh, Global Foundation (GAGFINC)**, and is widely regarded as most likely to succeed Dr. Malachi. Z. York as leader of the Nuwaubian movement.

Figs.412 & 413 Possible Successors: Left – Right: *Haru Hotep Tar & Neb Nawur Re*

Since 2004, rumours have also circulated of a number of 'Duplicate' Tama Re-style Nuwaubian Communities, in various locations including the Caribbean island of Barbados. If these reports are factual, then there is the serious possibility that other 'Copy-Cat' Nuwaubian Communities may begin to spring-up in other Islands of the Caribbean, Africa, and even Latin American nation's such as Cuba, Brazil & Venezuela, where York's teachings are known to have a strong following amongst people of African descent. Whether or not any of this transpires is mere speculation. However we can safely say that the imprisonment and deliberate character assassination of Dr. York has by no means brought about the intended demise of the Nuwaubian Movement as anticipated, with increasing numbers of his followers remaining steadfast in their support for their imprisoned leader.

Fig.414 Caribbean Community: *Entrance of Nuwaubian Community on Island of Barbados*

Indeed, since his arrest, Dr. York's Nuwaubian philosophy has continued to attract ever-increasing numbers of new initiates, from many diverse walks of life. Most significant of these recent affiliates, is World famous Honduran Herbalist; Alfred Bowman, more commonly known as **Dr. Sebi**. Widely regarded as having discovered natural cures for a number of incurable diseases including: **Cancer, Sickle Cell Anaemia, Diabetes & HIV/AIDS**, Dr. Sebi's work received worldwide recognition following his landmark victory in the US Supreme Court, after charges were brought against him for:

"practicing medicine without a license, selling products not approved by the FDA (Federal Drug Administration), and claiming to cure AIDS" by United States Attorney General.

Known as the *'The Master Healer'*, Dr. Sebi has treated a wide range of diseases in literally thousands of people throughout Africa, North & South America, Europe as well as his native Caribbean islands, including numerous Political leaders & Media Personalities, such as Basketball legend **Earvin "Magic" Johnson**, who was diagnosed with HIV in 1991, using his own unique form of 'African Herbal Medicine.

As this book went to print, Dr. Sebi who had long been a physician to Dr. Malachi. Z. York, not only declared his support for the imprisoned Nuwaubian leader, but now pledged his full allegiance to Nuwaubian movement in a continued effort to help raise the condition of African people's throughout the Diaspora.

Figs.415 & 416 New Powerful Alliance: Left- Right: *World Famous Herbalist Dr. Sebi & Dr. Malachi. Z. York: Leader of The Nuwaubian Movement*

Following York's conviction in 2004, it was hoped that the 62-year old leader would quickly lose support from the Black Community and be murdered, by fellow inmates in the Prison System. However in 2006, an incident involving Law Enforcement & Correctional officials surfaced, which further demonstrated the far-reaching influence and power of Malachi York's teachings. The controversy was first ignited after several 'High Ranking' Prison officers at ADX Maximum 'Supermax' Correction facility in Colorado, where the Nuwaubian leader is currently being held, were suspended after it was discovered that Wardens at the Prison, were actually active affiliates of the Nuwaubian Movement. An internal investigation alleged that Corrections officers at the facility were loyal to Malachi York after letters written to the 62-year old Nuwaubian Spiritual leader were intercepted by Prison authorities. The enquiry also uncovered that Nuwaubian literature was being circulated to Black inmates at the Maximum Security Prison by officers loyal to York. It appears that York's teachings alarmed the authorities to such an extent that his books have now been completely prohibited, and actually classified as **'Contraband'** material throughout the entire Prison system because of their purportedly overt 'Black Supremacist' content. Former Chief Jailer Brett Hart who first launched the inquiry into Nuwaubian activity at the Prison stated: *They think the White man is 'The Devil',...What gets me the most is how they were passing out information to inmates, convicted felons with no cause in life...The book "Was Adam Black or White?" is also full of racially inflammatory statements...And in the book "Who Rolled The Stone?", Jesus, The Disciples and other key figures in the New Testament are portrayed as being Black...*

Although there has never been any evidence to verify that York's teachings are un-factual, or for that matter, done anything other than promote Peace and Harmonious conduct amongst his followers. Nonetheless after over 35-years as a non-violent organisation, it has been York's uncompromising stance against White Supremacy in America and antagonistic, some would even say 'Audacious' plan to build a separate 'Sovereign African Nation-State' within the U.S., which provided the catalyst for the Federal Government to finally take action. Nevertheless Dr. York's 'Nuwaubu' Philosophy appears to still terrify the White Power Structure to such an extent, that the organisation is now more frequently attacked and falsely labelled 'Black Supremacist' by the mainstream Media. A more recent example of the ongoing clandestine attempts to destroy York's legacy is the damaging new critique by Anti-Nuwaubian reporter Bill Osinski of the Atlanta Journal-Constitution, entitled: ***"Ungodly: A True Story of Unprecedented Evil"*** released in May 2007.

Often acting as the 'un-official' mouthpiece for the Prosecution leading up to and during the trial, Bill Osinski has been identified amongst a handful of 'Racially' biased reporter's directly involved in what is clearly a conspiracy to write damaging and completely 'Un-factual' material for the purpose of undermining the Credibility of York and the Nuwaubian movement.

In a pathetic attempt to gain literary notoriety, second-rate, 'small town' Journalist & amateur screen writer, Bill Osinski, recently released a hastily produced, 272 page Joke entitled: ***"Ungodly"*** which contains so many distorted facts and contradictions, that it is difficult to keep up with, and reads even worst than many of his past articles. In this poorly researched, bile filled Diatribe, Osinski changes the names of York's supposed victims (including many of the facts) with such frequency that the book should accurately be regarded as a substandard Novel, complete with Scary image of an unidentified Black child, crying on its front cover. As one of the lead reporters investigating the case, Osinski has played a central role in the conspiracy to destroy Dr. Malachi. Z. York, and has spoken and appeared at numerous engagements, as well as TV & Radio stations, around the U.S., including **The Montel Williams show** which aired on CBS on September 2007 to peddle the lies in his book.

Osinski's book, like the actual case is disappointingly thin on facts, and entirely based upon the testimonies of ex-Nuwaubian's. In the book, Osinski to great lengths to portray the Nuwaubian's as a Dangerous Cult, even making the baseless assumption that York was complicit in the 1979 murder of Community activist Horace Green, which Green's own Wife & Daughter have refuted this claim on numerous occasions. Black Supremacist though they might be in their ideology, York's movement has no history of any kind violence against either its own members or White's for that matter. York's 'Peaceful' strategy, (which Osinski acknowledges on page 128 of his book) was to use the Pen against his opponents rather than the Sword. In the early part of the book, Osinski attempts to use Green's murder, as justification for portraying the group as Violent, when in fact the opposite was true, with several Nuwaubian's being the victims of violent attacks, including York's own son Yadullah Muhammad, Murdered by his father's opponents in 1998, a fact Osinski conveniently fails to make mention of. Meanwhile, some readers may also be left feeling slightly uncomfortable with many of the books graphically detailed references to York's unsubstantiated Sex with underage children, which may in fact be some type of coded references to Osinski's own 'Innermost' dark fantasies of Paedophilia.

Osinski also hilariously attempts to portray Sheriff Sills as a benign 'Heroic' public servant, only concerned with doing his job, so often hindered by bureaucratic officials, whose sole concern was with maintaining political correctness in the Racist Deep South. And not the 'Rabid' Corrupt Racist that Sills actually is, who has so often been overheard refereeing to the Blacks in Putnam County as *"His Niggers"*.

Then in what are clearly attempts to mislead the reader, and at the same time cover his own countless lies and contradictions, Osinski really goes out on a limb by trying to obscure Jacob York's (whom he refers to as Malik for some unknown reason) involvement in the case. For example; in one of his own previous articles dated July 7th 2002, Osinski stated that: *York's son said, he learned York was continuing to have sex with underage members of the community.* ***Some of the children were ones he remembered from when he was growing up in Ansaru Allah…His home soon became a sort of halfway house for people leaving the Nuwaubian community.*** However on page 257 of his book, Osinski contradicts his previous article by claiming that Jacob **Never** knew his father's victims: *Leah Mabry, one of York's daughters, testified that Malik (Jacob) had a "vendetta" against York. She stated that Malik had tried to recruit her into his conspiracy, but she offered no insight into how Malik had orchestrated the testimony of so many witnesses,* ***most of whom he'd never met****…*

Fig.417 **Anti-Nuwaubian:** *Bill Osinski Speaking on The Montel Williams show in 2007*

Figs.418 & 419 **Untruthful: Left- Right:**
Reporter Bill Osinski & Cover of his book: "Ungodly"

Finally, absolutely no mention is made in Bill Osinski's book of former 'Key' Prosecution witness Abigail "Habiba" Washington's highly publicised 'Recanted' Video taped confession recorded April 23rd 2004, which he probably assisted in blocking from public scrutiny, which however is now available to view on You-Tube.

Instead of facts, the majority of the book is concerned with what amount to cheap personal attacks against the Nuwaubian movement and its leader. Nevertheless undeterred by this kind of negative racially-biased representation by the Media, most of York's real followers have displayed unwavering support for their imprisoned leader staging a series of 'Peaceful' Public Protests & Demonstrations such as the 'Walk For Freedom': *"Walkathon"* & The 'Free York' Campaign since 2006. Also hosting a number of online Campaigns such as the recently launched WNUB TV station, and the number of other web pages devoted to raising public awareness of Malachi York's plight, which include:

www.publicoutcry.com
www.hesinnocent.com
www.gagfinc.com
www.lightandwater.com
www.nationofnuwaubu.org
www.malachiyorkisinnocent.com
www.wu-nuwaubu.com

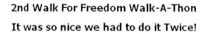

Figs.420 & 421 Solid Support: Left- Right:
Posters from Nuwaubian Campaigns to Free Dr. Malachi. Z. York

Figs.422, 423 & 424 Solid Support: Top, Left- Right
Members of the Nuwaubian Movement during Various York Freedom Relies

In spite of the efforts by some outstanding individuals within the movement, such as Oba Muhammad, **Waikia, Richelle & Hagar York**, Deputy Grand Master of the Grand North Lodge; **Michael "Truelight" Noakh**: The Golden Ankh, Global Foundation (GAGFINC) & **Daddy Kuwsh**, along with a handful of others to secure their leader's release. Sadly, it has been the **Isolationist**-'Cult' mentality of negative elements within the movement, whose continuous 'Factional Infighting', has not only prevented the Nuwaubian's themselves from fully galvanising support from the wider 'Mainstream' public towards Dr. Malachi York's unjust imprisonment. But also severely hindered the work of Dr. York's Non-Nuwaubian supporters, like **Attorney Malik Zulu Shabaaz**, who is currently spearheading the legal effort to exonerate the imprisoned Nuwaubian leader, and has often been obstructed by what he has described as: "difficulties in navigating the maze of the Nuwaubian Nation"…as a result of the **"friction and division in the [Movement]"**.

Meanwhile, despite the favourable position this publication has taken towards the Nuwaubian leader's plight, it too, has also been routinely hindered by what can only be described as Jealous Hypocrites within the organisation, (some even claiming to be York's children) who have for various reasons, chosen to boycott and obstruct the efforts made by the authors of this book to raise greater public awareness of the Nuwaubian leader's case, appearing to prefer for Dr. York to instead remain behind bars to maintain their own Selfish & Power hungry agendas. Unfortunately, if this attitude persists, it may ultimately cause the Nuwaubian's to miss what might very well be their last opportunity to secure York's release before its too late.

Nevertheless, in conclusion, the 'Nuwaubian Dream' of what Bill Osinski describes as **'A Black Utopia'** is nothing less than a complete Nightmare for the White Establishment, which desperately so needs Blacks to remain in their current position as 'Modern Slaves', to ensure the future Prosperity & Survival of the Western World. With a worldwide following, at one stage estimated to have been in the Millions, York was the first leader since the Hon. Marcus Garvey endowed with the ability & charisma to build a truly Global Black movement, through his teachings.

Being himself an African raised within The United States, York was in a unique position, which provided him with extraordinary insight into the mental condition of blacks throughout the Diaspora. If nothing else, York should certainly be remembered as one of the Greatest Black leaders of the 20th century who refused to back down or compromise his beliefs in the face of considerable odds for the liberation of his people. After 30-years, Dr. York's movement clearly outgrew the American political/social landscape, and it was his preoccupation with 'Playing God' to his followers within the US which eventually brought about his ruin, and in many ways caused him to squander what he could have easily built into a truly Global movement. It can also be said that too greater an emphasis was placed on acquiring information without discipline for his followers, which also helped to foster an arrogant 'Know it all' street corner intellectual attitude amongst the Nuwaubian's, which has also succeeded in alienating the movement from the wider Black Community.

Yet, the miracle of Dr. Malachi. Z. York's teachings lay in its ability to offer hope to many, along with a feeling they were part of something much greater than themselves, which would one day change the world for the better. Like nothing before it, Nuwaubu has touched the lives of so many individuals that Dr. York's legacy will ultimately survive through his many Books and Lectures, which have still remained bestsellers, even in the Islamic World where he was so reviled, which will therefore enable the movement to grow and diversify well into the future.

Dr. York's teachings may yet prove to be the Catalyst, which sets in motion a new awakening amongst African's throughout the Diaspora, to begin a new chapter in their 400-year Mental & Physical Bondage.

Rather than destroy the Movement, York's imprisonment appears to have Strengthened the Nuwaubian resolve to strive even harder to reach their goal of Self Determination & True Emancipation through the principles of:

Truth, Justice, Peace, Freedom, Love, Joy, Unity & Success by:
"Holding Onto The Rope As One Community, And Never Be Divided!"

Bibliography

Books, Journals, Periodicals, LP's, Videos & Audio Material

A Noble Lineage

The New Encyclopaedia Britannica: *The Mahdi, Muhammad Ahmed,* 15th Edition, University of Chicago Press, 1990.

Nhial Bol. The Final Call Newspaper: Al-Bashir Wins National Elections in Sudan, *1996*

Bilial Phillips. *The Ansar Cult, 1989.*

As Sayyid Isa Al Haadi Al Mahdi. *The Ansaar Cult in America Rebuttal to the Slanderers,* 1989.

Professor Mattias Gardell. *In The Name of Elijah Muhammad, Louis Farrakhan and The Nation of Islam,* 1996.

Robin Dam. The Guardian Magazine: *Freedom at a Price,* 1998.

Dr. Malachi. Z. York. *Nuwaubu & Amunnubi Rooakhptah: Fact or Fiction?,* 1993.

J. M. Roberts. *History of the World,* 1992.

York's Past & Early Influences

As Sayyid Isa Al Haadi Al Mahdi. *The Ansaar Cult in America: Rebuttal to the Slanderers,* 1989.

Dr. Malachi. Z. York. *Does Dr. Malachi. Z. York Try To Hide That He Was Imaam Issa?,* 1996.

As Sayyid Isa Al Haadi Al Mahdi. *The The Book of The Five Percenters,* 1989.

As Sayyid Isa Al Haadi Al Mahdi. *Wolves in Sheep's Clothing,* 1992.

Al Hajj Malik El Shabazz (Malcolm X). Letter To The Honourable Elijah Muhammad, 1964.

Amunnubi Rooakhptah (Malachi York). *The Degree of Muhammad-Ism,* 2002.

Professor Mattias Gardell. *In The Name of Elijah Muhammad, Louis Farrakhan and The Nation of Islam,* 1996.

Alex Haley. *The Autobiography of Malcolm X,* 1965

The Ansaarullah Community

Professor Vibert. L. White. *Inside The Nation of Islam, A Historical and Personal Testimony by a Black Muslim,* 2001.

The New Encyclopaedia Britannica: *Ansaar,* 15th Edition, University of Chicago Press, 1990.

The Holy Qur'an: *The Repentance, Chapter 9,* M. H. Shakir Translation, Tahrike Tarsile, Qur'an Inc, New York.

Rabboni Y'Shua Bar El Haady. *Why Did We Use Islam,* 1994.

Jane I. Smith. *Islam in America,* 1999.

Jimmy Breslin. Newsweek magazine, *Combating Crime By Force – Of Will,* 1989.

Daniel Pipes & Khalid Duran. *Muslims in the West: Can Conflict Be Averted?,* 1993.

Minister Akbar Muhammad. *Part II of Saviour's Day Speech,* 1993.

Memorie Knox. The Final Call newspaper, *The Un-winnable War: Analysts chart new course for Black community in America's anti-drug efforts,* 2001.

Professor Mattias Gardell. *In The Name of Elijah Muhammad, Louis Farrakhan and The Nation of Islam,* 1996.

As Sayyid Isa Al Haadi Al Mahdi. *The Ansaar Cult in America: Rebuttal to the Slanderers,* 1989.

Rob Peecher. The Macon Telegraph, *Cult Leader Ignores his own Rules,* 2002.

Bilial Phillips. *The Ansar Cult,* 1989.

Con Coughlin. *Saddam: The Secret Life,* 2002.

As Sayyid Isa Al Haadi Al Mahdi. *The The Book of The Five Percenters,* 1989.

Adib Rashad (James Miller). *Elijah Muhammad & The Ideological Foundation of The Nation of Islam,* 1994.

Dr. Malachi. Z. York. *The Truth: The New Covenant,* 1994.

Elijah Muhammad. *Message to The Blackman,* 1965.

Jesus Muhammad-Ali. *The Evolution of the Nation of Islam,* 2002.

Eric. C. Lincoln. *The Black Muslims in America,* 1961.

Minister Louise Farrakhan. *The End of Allah's Mercy & Grace,* 2003.

Minister Louise Farrakhan. *Birth of a Nation,* 2006.

Attorney Jeff Hass. *The FBI's War on Black America,* 1990.

Tyrone Powers. *Eyes To My Soul: The Rise or Decline of a Black FBI Agent,* 1996.

As Sayyid Isa Al Haadi Al Mahdi. *As Sayyid Al Imaam Isa Al Haadi Al Mahdi Explains The Secret Meaning of Qur'aan To The A'Immah of The Ansaaru Allah Edition,* 1985.

Sunni Terrorist Aggression vs. Ansaar Afro-Centrism

Daniel Pipes & Khalid Duran. *Muslims in the West: Can Conflict Be Averted?,* 1993.

J. M. Roberts. *History of the World,* 1992.
'Al Jahiz' Abu Uthman Amr Ibn Bahr Al-Kinani Al-Fugaimi Al Basri. *The Book of Glory of the Blacks over the Whites,* Edited by William Preston 1981.

The New Encyclopaedia Britannica: *Al Hadi ibn Abd ar-Rahman,* 15th Edition, University of Chicago Press, 1990.

The Holy Qur'an: *The Repentance, Chapter 9,* M. H. Shakir Translation, Tahrike Tarsile, Qur'an Inc, New York.

Dr. Malachi. Z. York. *Does Dr. Malachi. Z. York Try To Hide That He Was Imaam Issa?,* 1996.

The Holy Bible: *The Book of Matthew, Chapter 15,* King James Version, Collins' Clear-Type Press.

Bilial Phillips. *The Ansar Cult, 1989.*

As Sayyid Isa Al Haadi Al Mahdi. *The Ansaar Cult in America: Rebuttal to the Slanderers,* 1989.

The Macon Telegraph, *Cult Leader Ignores his own Rules,* 2002.

As Sayyid Isa Al Haadi Al Mahdi. *Who Killed This Believer? Imaam Rashad Khalifah, Ph.D Martyred 1935 A.D.-1990 A.D. The Righteous Do Not Really Die,* 1990.

Daniel Pipes. *The Hidden Hand: Middle East Fears of Conspiracy,* 1999.

As Sayyid Isa Al Haadi Al Mahdi. *The Murderers,* 1990.

Professor Aminah Beverly McCloud. *African American Islam,* 1995.

Christianity & Euro Supremacy Unmasked

J. M. Roberts. *History of the World,* 1992.

Professor Marimba Ani. *Yurugu: An African-Centred Critique of European Culture Thought and Behaviour,* 1994.

As Sayyid Isa Al Haadi Al Mahdi. *Diynu Allah? Diynul Islaam?,* 1992.

The Collins English Dictionary: *'Heathen',* Edited by Alexander H. Irvine, Great Britain, 1972.

Charles. W. Jones. *Knickerbocker Santa Claus. The New-York Historical Society Quarterly, Vol. XXXVII # 4,* 1954.

Gerard & Patricia Del Re. *The Christmas Almanack,* 2004.

Helene Adeline Guerber. *Myths of Northern Lands,* 1895.

The Holy Bible: *The Book Jeremiah, Chapter 10, Verses 1-5,* King James Version, Collins' Clear-Type Press.

Rev. Albert B. Cleage Jr. *The Black Messiah,* 1968.

Dr. Malachi. Z. York. *The Holy Tablets,* 1995.

Dr. Malachi. Z. York. *The Year 2000 A.D. AND what To Expect,* 1996.

Dr. Malachi. Z. York. *Introduction to: El's Holy Torah,* 1997.

The Holy Bible: *The Book of Psalms, Chapter 46,* King James Version, Collins' Clear-Type Press.

Donna Kossy. *Kooks: A Guide to the Outer Limits of Human Belief,* 1989.

The Holy Bible: *The Book of 2 Timothy, Chapter 1,* King James Version, Collins' Clear-Type Press.

The Holy Bible: *The Book of Matthew, Chapter 10,* King James Version, Collins' Clear-Type Press.

Dr. Malachi. Z. York. *666 Leviathan, The Beast: As The Anti-Christ,* 2001.

J. M. Roberts. *History of the World,* 1992.

Piers Paul Read. *Christ's Apostle or Maker of Myth?,* 1977.

The New Encyclopaedia Britannica: *'St Paul'*, 15th Edition, University of Chicago Press, 1990.

Dr. Malachi. Z. York. *Does Dr. Malachi. Z. York Try To Hide That He Was Imaam Issa?*, 1996.

Dr. Malachi. Z. York. *Are There Black Devils?*, 1997.

As Sayyid Isa Al Haadi Al Mahdi. *Sex Life of a Muslim*, 1989.

Kathleen Malone O'Connor. *Black Zion: African American Religious Encounters with Judaism*, 2000.

As Sayyid Isa Al Haadi Al Mahdi. *The Paleman*, 1990.

The Gales Encyclopaedia of Medicine: *Leprosy*, 1999.

The Gales Encyclopaedia of Medicine: *MICROBACTERIUM LEPRAE*, 1999.

Dr. J. H. Hertz, C. H. *The Pentateuch, and Haftorahs*, 1960.

The Gales Encyclopaedia of Medicine: *Vitiligo*, 1999.

Robert Conner. The Independent Newspaper: *Scientists Unravel DNA of 38,000-Year-Old Neanderthal*, 2006.
As Sayyid Isa Al Haadi Al Mahdi. *Wolves in Sheep's Clothing*, 1992.

Steve Jones. *In the Blood: God, Genes & Destiny*, 1996.

Rob Peecher. The Macon Telegraph, *Cult Leader Ignores his own Rules*, 2002.

Anonymous Author, Guardian Newspaper, *Goodbye Albino gorilla dies*, 2003.

Dr. Malachi. Z. York. *Let's set the Record Straight*, 1996.

David Icke. *Children of The Matrix*, 2001.
Anthony T. Browder. *Nile Valley Contributions to Civilization*, 1992.

As Sayyid Isa Al Haadi Al Mahdi. *The Science of Healing*, 1985.

David Icke. *The Biggest Secret*, 2001.

Bobby Hemmit. *An Occult History of Melanin*, 2005.

Steve Connor. The Independent Newspaper: *Gene Testing Breakthrough Offers Fresh Hope to Thousand, IVF: The Next Generation*, 2006.

FBI Cointelpro: *Aims & Objectives*.

John Judge. *Who Controls America*, 1990.

Christopher Hitchens. *The Trial of Henry Kissinger*, 2001.

John Pilger. *Heroes*, 1986.

Dr. Malachi. Z. York. *The Man From Planet Rizq*, 1998.

Dr. Len Horowitz. *Emerging Viruses: AIDS & Ebola-Nature, Accident or Intentional?*, 2001.

Dr. Malachi. Z. York. *Shamballah and Aghaarta, Cities Within The Earth*, 1998.

The Nubian Nation

As Sayyid Isa Al Haadi Al Mahdi. *Wolves in Sheep's Clothing*, 1992.

Bilial Phillips. *The Ansar Cult*, 1989.

The New Nation Newspaper: *NATION OF ISLAM COMES INTO LINE, Farrakhan ready to court mainstream Muslim world*, 1999.

Professor Vibert. L. White. *Inside The Nation of Islam, A Historical and Personal Testimony by a Black Muslim*, 2001.

Dr. Malachi. Z. York. *The Year 2000 A.D. And What To Expect*, 1996.

Dr. York, his Music, and The Hip Hop Generation

Vibe Magazine. *Hip Hop Divas*, 2000.

Dr. Malachi. Z. York. *Does Dr. Malachi. Z. York Try To Hide That He Was Imaam Issa?*, 1996.

Dr. Malachi. Z. York. *Let's Talk: Dr. York: The Man Behind The Empire*, 1988.

Rabboni Y'Shua Bar El Haady. *Special Edition The Truth Bulletin: Who Do People Say I Am?* 1992.

Jeff Chang, *Can't Stop, Won't Stop*, 2005.

Source Magazine. 2003.

Ice T. *Original Gangster*, 1991.

Ice T. *Home Invasion*, 1993.

Source Magazine. 1997.

MC Tragedy-Khadafi. *Capone-N-Noriega: The War Report*. 1997.

Ethan Brown. *Fat Cat, 50 Cent, and the Rise of The Hip Hop Hustler*, 2005.

Professor Aminah Beverly McCloud. *African American Islam*, 1995.

Brand Nubian. *All For One*, 1989.

As Sayyid Isa Al Haadi Al Mahdi. *The The Book of The Five Percenters*, 1989.

Keidi Obi Awadu. *Rap, Hip Hop & the New World Order*, 1997.

The Encyclopaedia Britannica: *Slang*, University of Chicago Press, 1989.

Rabboni Y'Shua Bar El Haady. *The Nebuchadnezzer Era: The Dangers of Slang*, Edition No.18, 1993.

Professor John McWhorter. *Losing The Race: Self-Sabotage in Black America*, 2001.

Dr. Malachi. Z. York. *Let's set the Record Straight*, 1997.

Professor Felicia M. Miyakawa. *Five Percenter Rap: God's Music, Message, and Black Muslim Mission*, 2005.

Professor Mattias Gardell. *In The Name of Elijah Muhammad, Louis Farrakhan and The Nation of Islam*, 1996.

Dr. Malachi. Z. York. *Dr. York, Are You A Muslim?"*, Factology vs Theology # 6, 1997.

Professor Vibert. L. White. *Inside The Nation of Islam, A Historical and Personal Testimony by a Black Muslim*, 2001.

William Shaw. *Westsiders: Stories of The Boys In The Hood*, 2000.

The Nubian Hebrew Mission

Dr. Malachi. Z. York. *Does Dr. Malachi. Z. York Try To Hide That He Was Imaam Issa?*, 1996.

Rabboni Y'Shua Bar El Haady. *Nubian Bulletin*, Edition No.2: *What Color Are You?* 1992.

The Holy Bible: *The Book of Acts Chapter 13*, King James Version, Collins' Clear-Type Press.

Stephen W. Angell. *Black Zion: African American Religious Encounters with Judaism*, 2004.

The Holy Bible: *The of Genesis Chapter 15*, King James Version, Collins' Clear-Type Press.

Keidi Obi Awadu. *The Conscious Rasta Report: Rap, Hip Hop & The New World Order*, 1997.

Dr. Malachi. Z. York. *360 Questions to ask A Hebrew Israelite*, 1995.

James Landing. *Black Judaism: The Story of an American Movement*, 2002.

As Sayyid Isa Al Haadi Al Mahdi. *The Book of Revelation*, Chapter 13, 1991.

Dr. Malachi. Z. York. *Let's Set The Record Straight*, 1997.

The Holy Bible: *The Book of Genesis, Chapter 4*, King James Version, Collins' Clear-Type Press.

H.T.M. & Black Indigenous 'Native Americans'

Rabboni Y'Shua Bar El Haady. *History of the Black Indians*, 1992.

The Holy Bible: *The Book of Judges VI*, King James Version, Collins' Clear-Type Press.

Dr. Malachi. Z. York. *The Holy Tablets*, 1995.

The New Encyclopaedia Britannica: *Continental Drift*, 15th Edition, University of Chicago Press, 1990.

The Collins English Dictionary: *'Hypothesis'*, Edited by Alexander H. Irvine, Great Britain, 1972.

Sarah Toyne. The Times Newspaper: *Aborigines were first Americans*, 1999.

Ralph Ellis. *Thoth: Architect of the Universe*, 1997.

Graham Hancock. *Finger Prints of The Gods: A Quest for the Beginning and the End*, 1995.

Michael A.Cremo & Richard L.Thompson. *Forbidden Archaeology: The Hidden History of the Human Race*, 1993.

Dr. Malachi. Z. York. *Does Dr. Malachi. Z. York Try To Hide That He Was Imaam Issa?*, 1996.

The New Encyclopaedia Britannica: *Yamasee war*, 15th Edition, University of Chicago Press, 1990.
Kevin Chappell. Ebony Magazine: *Black Indians Hit Jackpot In Casino Bonanza: Pequot descendants flock to Connecticut to cash in on gambling craze*, 1995.

Sheridan Murphy. *Thousands denounce ongoing genocide in American Indian Movement encampment*, 1999.

Steve Walker. *ONEIDA NATION LAND CLAIM SHAKES UPSTATE NEW YORK: THE BIG PAYBACK*, 1999.

Muhammad Shabazz. *Black Indians hold Pow Wow in Oklahoma*, 2003.

The Rastafarian's Addressed

Rabboni Y'Shua Bar El Haady. *The Real Messiah*, 1993.

Dr. Malachi. Z. York. *Is Haile Selassie The Christ*, 1994.

Spiritual Masters & Extraterrestrial Entities

The Holy Koran: IFTA, *Koran Commentary*, The Presidency of Islamic Research.

Professor Marimba Ani. *Yurugu: An African-Centred Critique of European Culture Thought and Behaviour*, 1994.

Henry Corbin. *Creative Imagination in the Sufism of Ibn 'Arabi*, 1990.

Patrick Franke. *Encountering Khidr*, 2000.

Bilial Phillips. *The Ansar Cult, 1989.*

As Sayyid Isa Al Haadi Al Mahdi. *The Man of Miracles in This Day and Time*, 1983.

The Holy Koran: *Surah Al Baqarah Chapter of the Cow*, The Presidency of Islamic Research.

Dr. Malachi. Z. York. *Fake Gods False Christs*, 1994.

Benjamin Crème. *Maitreya's Mission"*, Vol.1, 1986.

As Sayyid Isa Al Haadi Al Mahdi. *The Science of Healing*, 1983.

Zecheria Sitchin. *The Twelfth Planet*, 1976.

Kiki King. The Mail on Sunday, *Scientists discover a whole new world*, 2005.

David Icke. *The Biggest Secret*, 1999.

Dr. Malachi. Z. York. *Are There (UFOs) Extraterrestrials In Your Midst?*, 1994.

Dr. Malachi. Z. York. *Are The Holy Tablets*, 1995.

David Hatcher Childress. *The Fantastic Inventions of Nikola Tesla*, 1993.

Michael A. Cremo and Richard L. Thompson. *Forbidden Archaeology: The Hidden History of the Human Race*, 1993.
Allah Jihad. *The Immortal Birth of Allah: Rise of the Five Percenters*, 2004.

Rabboni Y'Shua Bar El Haady. *Why did we use Islam*, 1994.

Brenda Denzler. *The Lure of the Edge: Scientific Passions, Religious Beliefs, and the Pursuit of UFOs*, 2001.

Dr. Malachi. Z. York. *Are Theology vs. Factology: Leave My Stuff Alone*, 1998.

Dr. Malachi. Z. York. *Does Dr. Malachi. Z. York Try To Hide That He Was Imaam Issa?*, 1996.

Rabboni Y'Shua Bar El Haady. *The Truth Bulletin: Prophecy Fulfilled*, 1993.

John Judge. *The Black Hole in Guyana: The Untold Story of the Jonestown Massacre*, 1993.

The Holy Bible: *The Book of Genesis, Chapter 22*, King James Version, Collins' Clear-Type Press.

As Sayyid Isa Al Haadi Al Mahdi. *The Book of Revelation*, Chapter 13, 1991.

Jim Keith. *Secret & Suppressed*, 1993.

David Icke. *Children of The Matrix*, 2001.

Rabboni Y'Shua Bar El Haady. *Why did we use Islam*, 1994.

The Holy Koran: *Surah Al Baqarah Chapter Maryam*, The Presidency of Islamic Research.

The Hypocrisy of David Icke

David Icke. *The Robots' Rebellion*, 1994.

David Icke. *The Biggest Secret*, 1999.

The Cold Reality of 'Right Knowledge'

Dr. Malachi. Z. York. *Does Dr. Malachi. Z. York Try To Hide That He Was Imaam Issa?*, 1996.

Andrew Robinson. *Lost Languages: The Enigma of the World's Undecipherable Scripts*, 2002.

The Holy Bible: *Book of Genesis Chapter 12, Verses 6 - 9*, King James Version, Collins' Clear-Type Press.

Dr. Malachi. Z. York. *First Language*, 1993.

The Holy Bible: *Book of Genesis Chapter 10, Verses 6 - 10*, King James Version, Collins' Clear-Type Press.

Zecharia Sitchin. *The 12th Planet*, 1976.

Rabboni Y'Shua Bar El Haady. *Elohim: The New Covenant*, 1993.

Dr. Malachi. Z. York. *Egypt of The West Saviour's Day*, 1998.

Bilial Phillips. *The Ansar Cult, 1989.*

As Sayyid Isa Al Haadi Al Mahdi. *The Ansaar Cult in America Rebuttal to the Slanderers*, 1998.

Zechariah Sitchin. *The Twelfth Planet*, 1991.

Bobby Hemmit. *Melanin Conference*, 2001.

Dr. Malachi. Z. York. *Mechanics of The Mind*, 1995.

Jainacharya Vijay Laxmansurishverji Maharaj. *Atmatatva Vichar or Philosophy of The Soul*, 1986.

Sacred Orders & Mysteries Revealed

As Sayyid Isa Al Haadi Al Mahdi. *Secret Societies Unmasked*, 1990.

Dr. Malachi. Z. York. *Are Caucasians Edomites?*, 1995.

Dr. Malachi. Z. York. *The Year 2000 A.D. And What To Expect*, 1996.

The Holy Bible: *Book of 2nd Samuel, Chapter 5,* King James Version, Collins' Clear-Type Press.

The Holy Bible: *Book of 1st Chronicles, Chapter 14,* King James Version, Collins' Clear-Type Press.

Louis M. Epstein. *Sex Laws and Customs in Judaism,* 1991.

Henry L. Feingold. *Zion in America: The Jewish Experience from Colonial Times to Present,* 1991.

Harold Sharfman in *Documentary History of Jews in the United States,* 1991.

Professor Tony Martin. *The Philosophy & Opinion of Marcus Garvey,* 1986.

Laurie Gunst. *Born Fi' Dead,* 1995.

Allah Jihad. *The Immortal Birth of Allah: Rise of the Five Percenters,* 2004.

Dr. Malachi. Z. York. *The Grand Mufti: The Only True Shriners,* 2001.

Dr. Malachi. Z. York. *Ahli'l Bait,* 2001.

Skippy Davis. The Macon Telegraph: *Nuwaubians to buy Shrine Temple in Macon,* 2001.

Stephen Knight. *The Brotherhood,* 1983.

New York to Georgia: The Great Nubian Exodus

Bill Osinski. The Atlanta Journal-Constitution: *Cult Leader ignored his own rules,* 2002.

Terry Dickson. *Nuwaubian leader guilty,* 2004.

Emory Lavender. The Countryman: *Malachi York,* 1993.

Adam Heimlich. New York Press: *Black Egypt,* 2000.

Rob Peecher. The Macon Telegraph: *Special report,* 2000.

Dr. Malachi. Z. York. *Saviours Day Speech,* 1997.

Sheriff Richard Sills. Fox Channel 5 News, 1998.
Dr. Malachi. Z. York. *Holy Tabernacle: Family Guide,* 1993.

President Bill Clinton. *National American Indian Heritage Speech,* 1999.

Matt Labash. The Washington Post: *The Second Time as Farce: Not that the first time was serious,* 2005.

United Nuwaubian Nation of Moors: *Torn From the Land,* 2002.

Rob Peecher. Eatonton Messenger: 2003.

Staff Writer. The Macon Messenger: *A John Gotti Hiding Behind a Badge,* 2003.

Staff Writer. The Macon Messenger: *Putnam County Sheriff Howard Richard Sills plans to reattack Nuwaubians land,* 2003.

Dr. Malachi. Z. York-El. *Let's Set The Record Straight: No More God Games,* 1999.

Rod A. Janzen. *The Rise and Fall of Synanon: A California Utopia,* 2001.

State Senator Floyd Griffin. Union Recorder: *Griffin Concerned About 'Overreaction' to Nuwaubians,* 1998.

Minister Francis Garlawolu. *World Conference on Racism*, 2001.

Rev. Alfred. C. Sharpton. *Speech Condemning Racial Profiling, on Tama Re,* 1999.

Rev. Jessie Jackson. *Nuwaubians are Living the American Dream,* 2001.

Rob Peecher. The Macon Messenger: *Snipes' Company may buy property: Actor's Amen-Ra films is interested in Putnam land adjacent to Nuwaubians,* 2000.

Patricia Shipp. *Enquirer: Wesley Snipes: I'm not a Nuwaubian,* 2000.

Lisa. M. Lohr. *Parade Honors Black History,* 2001.

Vicky Eckenrode. *Nuwaubians' notoriety in Georgia growing,* 2001.

Jim Thompson. *Nuwaubian leader assists with canned food drive,* 2001.

Anonymous Author. *'Special Alert' to all Nuwaubians living in the State of Georgia,* 2003.

Southern Dream turns to Nightmare: The fall of Malachi York

Bill Osinski. Atlanta Journal-Constitution: *Nuwaubian Leader York Pleads Not Guilty to Sex Charges,* 2002.

Attorney Dawn Baskin. Covington News: *Newton May Host Nuwaubian Trial,* 2002.

William Daniel. *Criminal Trial Law Practice,*1989.

KUBARK. *'Declassified', Counterintelligence Interrogation,* 1963.

Oliver Burkeman. Reuters*: Chicago Police Torture Black Suspects,* 2006.

As Sayyid Isa Al Haadi Al Mahdi. *The Ansaar Cult in America: Rebuttal to the Slanderers,* 1989.

Joanna Soto Carabello. Athens Banner-Herald: *Crazy or not, York is a Criminal in need of Punishing,* 2003.

Wayne Crenshaw. The Macon Telegraph: *Woman testifies she groomed younger victims for York,* 2004.

Rolling Stone Magazine. *Cam'ron's Ad Is Pulled: Cam'ron's album advertisement violated NBA trademark and was removed,* 1999.

Beth Landman Keil & Deborah Mitchell. *NBA Says Rapper's Got No Game,* 1999.

WMZ, Eye Witness News. *Nuwaubians Charged in Multi-Million Scheme,* 2003.

Bill Osinski. The Atlanta Journal-Constitution: *Cult leader ignored his own rules,* 2002.

Rob Peacher. *York's accusers describe years of sexual abuse,* 2003.

Bilial Phillips. *The Ansar Cult,* 1989.

Bill Osinski. *Ungodly: A True Story of Unprecedented Evil,* 2007

Bill Torpy. The Atlanta Journal-Constitution: *Sect leader guilty of molestation,* 2004.

Lee Shearer. The Athens Banner Herald: *Feds to seize properties within 30 days,* 2004.

The Holy Bible: *Book of Genesis Chapter 15, Verses 13-16,* King James Version, Collins' Clear-Type Press.

The Holy Bible: *Book of Revelation Chapter 18, Verses 4-6,* King James Version, Collins' Clear-Type Press.

Webliography

A Noble Lineage

1. Staff Writer. BBC News Online: *"The Saviour of Sudan"*
Available at: http://www.bbconline.com

2. Staff Writer. *"Public Outcry"*
Available at: http://www.heisinnocent.com/news2.html

3. Carolyne White-Feather. *"Carolyne's Genealogy Helper"*
Available at: http://www.angelfire.com/tx/carolynegenealogy/

York's Past & Early Influences

1. Robert Stacey McCain. Washington Times: *Nuwaubian Nightmare,*
Available at: http://www.findarticles.com/p/articles/mi_go1637/is_200206/ai_n6999165

2. Muhammed Abdullah Ahari. *Islam in America: Origins & Later Development, The Islamic Community In The United States: Historical Development,*
Available at: http://www.sunnah.org/history/islamamr.htm

The Ansaarullah Community

1. Abdul Haadi Umar. *"Truth Has Come And Falsehood Is Destroyed!"*
Available at: http://www.siddeeq.homestaed.com/Falsehood-ns4.html

2. Amiyr Abu Hamin. *"Leader Malachi York of Nuwaubians, GUILTY on All Counts of Uppityness!"*
Available at: http://www.onepeoples.com

3. Anonymous Author. *"The African Islamic Mission".*
Available at: http://www.inetmgrs.com/onepeoples/african_islamic_mission_1390_be.htm

4. Joan Oleck. *"A Cyber-Community Grows in Brooklyn".*
Available at: http://www.thecybercamp.com/kibibi_oyo_editor_in_chief.htm

5. Anonymous Author *"The Prophet of Bushwick"* ,
Available at: http://www.sacredandprofane.org/archives/2003/05/,

6. Anonymous Author. *"Black males lock on jail time threatens us all".*
Available at: http://www.ajc.com/opinion/content/opinion/tucker/2003/042003.html

Sunni Terrorist Aggression vs. Ansaar Afro-Centrism

1. Runoko Rashidi. *"THE GLOBAL AFRICAN PRESENCE"*
Available at: http://www.cwo.com/~lucumi/runoko.html

2. Anonymous Author. *"Al-Jahiz Brought The World Truth About Race"*
Available at: http://onepeoples.com/current/al-jahiz.html

3. Bilial Philips. *"The Ansar Cult In America".*
Available at: http://www,Bilialphilips.com/books/ansar01f.htm

4. Anonymous Author. *"Suffer The Little Children Part 4: Nuwaubian Power & Control Curtailed".*
Available at: http://www.ccgm.org.au/Articles/ARTICLE-0045.htm

5.Yvonne Yazbeck-Haddad & John L. Esposito. *"The Dynamics of Islamic Identity in North America: Immigration-Convert Relations: An African-American Complaint".*
Available at: http://arabworld.nitle.org/texts.php?module_id=9&reading_id=71&sequence=8

6. Daniel Pipes & Khalid Duran. *"Muslims in the West: Can Conflict Be Averted?".*
Available at: http://www.danielpipes.org/article/232

7. Amiyr Abu Hamin. *"Leader Malachi York of Nuwaubians, GUILTY on All Counts of Uppityness!"*
Available at: http://www.onepeoples.com

8. Mikail Juma Tariq, *"ISLAM A Brief Introduction to the Muslim Faith".*
Available at: http://www.geocities.com/mikailtariq

Christianity & Euro supremacy Unmasked

1. E. Lee Sullivan. *"Are African Americans The Descendants Of Christ?"*
Available at: http://www.afromerica.com/columns/lsullivan/notherzone/descendantsofchrist.php

2. Adam Edgerly and Carl Ellis. *"Emergence of Islam in the African-American Community"*
Available at: http://www.answering-islam.org/ReachOut/emergence.html

The Nubian Nation

1. Amiyr Abu Hamin. *"Leader Malachi York of Nuwaubians, GUILTY on All Counts of Uppityness!"*
Available at: http://www.onepeoples.com

2. `Hisham Aidi. *"Jihadis in the Hood: Race, Urban Islam and the War on Terror",* Available at: http://www.merip.org/mer/mer224/224_aidi.html

Dr. York, his Music, and The Hip Hop Generation

1. Laonja Muhammad. *"Has Hip Hop Lost it's Righteous Spirit".*
Available at: http://p076.ezboard.com/fpoliticalpalacefrm17.showMessage?topicID=352.topic

2. Dr. York. *"Soul walking".*
Available at: http://www.soulwalking.co.uk/Dr%20York.html

3. Afrika Bambaataa. *"Return to planet Rock (The Second Coming)".*
Available at: http://caction.users.netlink.co.uk/bambaataa/1989a.htm

4. Davey D. *"Zulu Nation: From Gang to Glory".*
Available at: http://www.daveyd.com/zulunationhistory.html

5. James McNally. *"Confessions Of A Mask".*
Available at: http://www.stonestrow.com/madvillain/hhc-feature.html

6. C. Finan. *"Business vs. Friendship: Jaz-O speaks on his legendary history in hip-hop and his relationship with his protégé Jay-Z".* Available at: http://www.maintainmag.com/apr02/jazo.html

7. MTV. *"404 Soldierz March Out New Album".*
Available at: http://www.mtv.com/news/articles

8. MTV. *"THE HITS KEEP COMING",*
Available at: http://www.mtv.com/news/bands/404_soldierz.jhtml

9. Othello 'Isaiah' York. *"True Vision Entertainment Inc",*
Available at: http://truevisionent.com/main/oyorkbio.html

10. Kedar Massenburg. *"Best Music of 1997",*
Available at: http://www.time.com/time/archive/preview/0,10987,1101971229-137111,00.html

11. Michael Muhammad Knight. *"The Nation of Gods and Earths"*,
Available at: http://www.muslimwakeup.com/main/archives/2005/01/remembering_the_1.php

12. Adam Edgerly & Carl Ellis. *"Emergence of Islam in the African-American Community"*
Available at: http://www.answering-islam.org/ReachOut/emergence.html

13. Beloved Allah. *"The Bomb: The Greatest Story Never Told"*,
Available at: http://trueschool.com/lok/thebomb.html

14. Five Percent Nation. *"Dr Pork"*,.
Available at: http://www.libtv.com/7MAC/catalog/

15. Keidi Obi Awadu. *'The Conscious Rasta': "Rap, Hip Hop & the New World Order"*.
Available at: http://www.auser.org/knowledge/drpork.htm

16. Nin Shajiyah El. *"Shaky Sources"*,
Available at: http://www.factology.com/guest_commentary.htm

17. Attorney Malik Zulu Shabazz. *"New Black Panther Party Report into the Death of Dr Khallid Abdul Muhammad"*,
Available at: http://afgen.com/khallid.html

18. Adam Heimlich. *"Black Egypt"*,
Available at: http://www.nypress.com

19. The Lost Children of Babylon. *"Right Rhyming"*,
Available at: http://www.citypaper.net.articles/020801/mus.lost.shtml

20. Michael A. Ralph, Jr. *"What's Beef: One Rap Feud as Meta for Competing Post-Industrial Ideologies: Words, Beats & Life Journal "*,
Available at: http://www.wblinc.org/journal/issue1/beef.html

The Nubian Hebrew Mission

1. Muhammad Abdul Ahari. *"Islam in America: Origins & Later Developments"*,
Available at: http://sunnah.org/islamamr.htm

2. Bill Osinski. *"Cult Leader ignored his own rules"*,
Available at: http://www.atlanta_Journal-Constitution.com

3. ADL. *"Leader of Anti-Government Sect Arrested on Sex Charges"*,
Available at: http://www.adl.org/learn/news/Malachi_arrested.asp

4. UNNM. *"Defamed By the Anti-Defamation League"*,
Available at: http://www.unnm.com

H.T.M. & Black Indigenous 'Native Americans'

1. Zacharia Sitchin. The Case of The Missing Elephant,
Available at: http://www.sitchin.com/elephant.htm

2. Zacharia Sitchin. The Olmec Enigma: Astronaut Corroborates Sitchin,
Available at: http://www.sitchin.com/astronaut.htm

3. Dr. Malachi. Z. York-El. The Legacy of The Black Thunderbird, Available at:
http://www.officialnaia.org/Office%20of%20The%20Consul%20General/LEGACY%20OF%20THE%20BLACK%20THUNDERBIRD.htm

4. Paul Barton. Black Civilizations of Ancient America (MUU-LAN), Mexico (XI), Available at:
http://www.geocities.com/maatguidesme2u/daughters_of_ruth_moabite/washitaw.htm

5. Robert Strongrivers. Lost Feather,
Available at: http://members.tripod.com/pointingbird/lostfeatherintl/id66.htm

6. Robert B. Betts. *In Search of Ben York,* Available at:
http://www.nps.gov/archive/jeff/LewisClark2/CorpsOfDiscovery/TheOthers/Civilians/York.htm

7. Staff Writer. What Does UN# 215/1993 Mean?
Available at: http://www.unnm.com

8. Staff Writer. United Nuwaubian Nation of Moors Press Release,
Available at: http://www.unnm.com

9. Hakim Bey. *The Biography of Noble Drew Ali: The Exhumation of a Nation,*
Available at: http:// www.mu-atlantis.com

The Rastafarian's Addressed

1. Crispin Sartwell. *"A Brief History of Rastafarianism",*
Available at: http://www.crispinsartwell.com/rasta.htm

2. Anonymous Author, *"Rastafari Speaks",*
Available at: http://www.triniview.com.cgi-bin/rasta/webbbs_config.pl/

Spiritual Masters & Extraterrestrial Entities

1. Keir Robyn. *"Home About Us: Sudan",*
Available at: http://keir-robyn.com/pictures/cairo/sudan/pictures.htm

2. Sathya Sai Baba. *"International Sai Organisation",*
Available at: http://www.sathyasai.org/

3. Amiyr Abu Hamin. *"Leader Malachi York of Nuwaubians, GUILTY on All Counts of Uppityness!",*
Available at: http://www.onepeoples.com

4. Anonymous Author, *"So Sick Knowledge",*
Available at: http://www.sosickrecords.com.

5. John Judge. *"Jonestown Massacre",*
Available at: http://www.ratical.org/ratville/JFK/JohnJudge/Jonestown.html

6. Peter Farley. *"Who Stole Our History",*
Available at: http://www.4truthseekers.com/treeoflife/

7. Mary Rodwell. *"The Star Children",*
Available at: http://www.thelosthaven.co.uk/StarKids.htm

The Hypocrisy of David Icke

1. Anonymous Author, *"The History of the White Race",*
Available at: http://www.stormfront.org/hist_wht.htm

2. Encyclopaedia, *"Hyksos Dynasty",*
Available at: http://lexicorient.com/e.o/hyksos.htm

The Cold Reality of 'Right Knowledge'

1. Wikipedia. *"Nuwaubianism",*
Available at: http://en.wikipedia.org/wiki/Nuwaubianism

2. Jim Marrs. *"Religious rift brews in rural Georgia",*

Available at: http://www.cnn.com/US/9906/29/nuwaubians/

3. Professor Bruce Foremen. *"T.S. Eliot on the Necessity of Christian Culture"*,
Available at: http://www.frc.org/get.cfm?i=WT01A1

4. Amiyr Abu Hamin. *"Leader Malachi York of Nuwaubians, GUILTY on All Counts of Uppityness!"*,
Available at: http://www.onepeoples.com

5. Bobby Hemmit. *"An Occult History of Melanin"*,
Available at: http://www.tehutionline.com/ newpage31.htm

6. Adam Heimlich. *"Black Egypt"*,
Available at: http://www.nypress.com

7. Anonymous Author, *"The meaning of Nuwaubu"*,
Available at: http://www.think-aboutit.com/Spiritual/right_knowledge.htm

Sacred Orders & Mysteries Revealed

1. Lafeare Ward. *"Masonry the root of all wickedness"*,
Available at: http://www.daghettotymz.com/rkyvz/articles/masonry/masonry1/masonrypt1.html

2. Jehvon I. Buckner. *"Boule 3 dying wit secrets"*,
Available at: http://www.daghettotymz.com/rkyvz/articles.boule'series

3. MWPHGL. *"Dr. Charles. H. Wesley, Masonic Research Society"*,
Available at: http://princehall.info/014twr.html

4. Ezekiel. M. Bey. *"Ezekiel. M. Bey & Dr. Malachi. Z. York Debate"*,
Available at: http://www.freemasonry.org/phylaxis/directory.htm

5. News 4 Jaxs. *"Charges Considered against Nuwaubians in Christmas Parade"*,
Available at: http:www.news4jax.com/news/2690659/detail.html

New York to Georgia: The Great Nubian Exodus

1. Staff Writer. *"Why did Malachi Move to Eatonton?!!!!"*,
Available at: http://www.unnm.com

2. Staff Writer. *"THE FATHER, MALACHI YORK IS ACCUSED OF THE SON, JACOB YORK'S CRIMES"*,
Available at: http://www.unnm.com

3. A. A. News. *"Agents Sweep Religious Cult Compound, Charge Founder With Child Abuse"*,
Available at: http://wwwfreethoughtfirefighters.org/agents_sweep_religious_cult_comp.htm

4. Mara Shalhoup. Atlanta News: *"Nabbing the man from outer space"*,
Available at: http://atlanta.creativeloafing.com

5. Online Athens *"Innocent, pleads sect leader York"*,
Available at: http://www.onlineathens.com

6. Roy L. Parish. The Black World Today: *"Nation Under Distress"*,
Available at: http://athena.tbwt.com

7. Rob Peecher. Macon Telegraph: *"Opinions Mixed on York's arrest"*,
Available at: http://www.macon.com/mld/macon/

8. Robert Stacy McCain. The Washington Times: *Nuwaubian nightmare*,
Available at: http://washingtontimes.com

9. Elijah Muhammad. *"Muslim Programme"*,
Available at: http://www.noi.org

10. Matt Labash. *"The Second Time as Farce: Not that the first time was serious"*,
Available-at:
http://www.weeklystandard.com/Content/Protected/Articles/000/000/006/248lcgie.asp?pg=2

11. Staff Writer. *"Innocent pleads sect leader York"*,
Available at: http://www.onlineathens.com

12. Staff Writer. *"Wesley Snipes denied building permits"*,
Available at: http://www.onlineathens.com

13. Staff Writer. *"Nuwaubian leader assists with canned food drive"*,
Available at: http://www.onlineathens.com

Southern Dream turns to Nightmare:
The fall of Malachi York

1. Staff Writer. *"Fell In The System, Trap of Immunity!!!"*,
Available at: http://www.unnm.com

2. Reporter: Stephen Gurr. Augusta Chronicle: *"Man sues sect leader, alleging child abuse"*,
Available at: http://www.rickross.com/reference/nuwaubians/nuwaubians41.html

3. Rob Peecher. Macon Telegraph: *"York's accusers describe years of sexual abuse"*,
Available at: http://www.rickross.com/reference/nuwaubians/nuwaubians46.html

4. Debbie Rhyne. Macon Telegraph: *"York admits federal child-sex charge"*,
Available at: http://www.macon.com/mld/macon/5017973.htm

5. Staff Writer. *"Culture of Harassment Victimizes Nuwaubians"*,
Available at: http:// www.atlanta_Journal-Constitution.com

6. Staff Writer. *"Maku is a Secured Party"*,
Available at: http://www.unnm.com

7. Malik Zulu Shabazz. Final Call Newspapaer: *"Interview with Malik Zulu Shabazz"*,
Available at: http://www.noi.org

8. Staff Writer. *"UNNM: Medical Records Don't Lie"*,
Available at: http://www.unnm.com

9. Staff Writer. *"UNNM: Judge Helps Prosecution Buy Time"*,
Available at: http://www.unnm.com

10. Staff Writer. *"UNNM: Does Common Law Still Exist?"*,
Available at: http://www.unnm.com

11. Staff Writer. *"There Is Only ONE Tama-Re "AL TAMAHA!!!"*,
Available at: http://www.unnm.com

12. Adeebafolami. *"Charges, Conspiracy, COINTELPRO and Malachi York: A conversation with Malik Zulu Shabazz"*,
Available at: http://adeebafolami.com

13. Keidi Obi Awadu. *"Concious Rasta, Discusses the Theft of Nuwaubian Land, with Bernard Foster"*,
Available at: http://www.libradio.com

Nuwaubian Related Web-Pages

www.officialnaia.org/
www.hesinnocent.com/
www.agodwithin.com/
www.geocities.com/Area51/Corridor/4978/
www.al-raatib999.org/
www.phpbbcity.com/forum/index.php?mforum=peaceinthelamb
www.nuwaubians.org/
www.malachiyorkisinnocent.com/
http://getfrombehindthe9ball.com/
www.nuwaupik.com/
www.houseofnubian.com/
www.wnubradio.com/
www.spreadfacts.co.uk/
www.factology.com/
http://elharu9.proboards17.com/index.cgi
www.zulunation.com/
www.nationofnuwaubu.org
www.nuwaubian-hotep.net/
www.mytruehair.com/
www.ahsheetc.com/
www.teltruvision.com/
www.chatwiththegods.com/
www.ummijarrett.com/
http://apublicoutcry.com/
www.oesworldwide.com/
www.thelightandwater.com/
www.hierographxdesign.com/
www.nubianpride.nl/
www.nubianlove.biz/
www.truthsnevertold.com/
www.ntelek.nuwopsoldiers.com/
www.alchemyoflife.org/
http://holytablets.org/
http://nuworldorder.com/index.php
http://aeoeonline.com/shop/
http://vids.myspace.com/index.cfm?fuseaction=vids.individual&videoid=730066040
http://vids.myspace.com/index.cfm?fuseaction=vids.individual&videoID=751674962
www.supremegrandlodge.com/index.php
http://outformation.co.uk/
www.blackconsciousness.com/sshop/esoteric.html
www.geocities.com/ourstoryposter/
www.nubianheritage.co.uk
www.gagfinc.com
www.gopetition.com/petitions/support-for-maku-chief-black-eagle-dr-malachi-z-york-el.html
http://nuwopsoldiers.com/
http://www.dryork.nuwopsoldiers.com/truth.html
http://www.free-dr-york.com/iamnotapedophile.html
www.wu-nuwaubu.com

To Support the Freedom for Dr. Malachi. Z. York Campaign
Please Log onto: http://www.hesinnocent.com

To Support the Freedom for Mumia Abu-Jamal Campaign
Please Log onto: http://www.freemumia.com